THE PLAINS INDIANS

THE PLAINS INDIANS

A CULTURAL AND HISTORICAL VIEW OF THE NORTH AMERICAN
PLAINS TRIBES OF THE PRE-RESERVATION PERIOD

COLIN F. TAYLOR Ph.D

a Salamander book
Published by Salamander Books Limited
LONDON

A SALAMANDER BOOK

Distributed by Random House Value
Publishing, Inc.
40 Engelhard Avenue,
Avenel, New Jersey 07001

A CIP catalog record for this book is
available from the Library of Congress.

Printed in Spain

ISBN 0-517-14250-3

CREDITS

Editor: Richard Collins
Designer: Mark Holt
Color photography: Don Eiler, Richmond,
Virginia (© Salamander Books Ltd)
Maps and artwork: Janos Marffy
(© Salamander Books Ltd)
Filmset: SX Composing Ltd, England
Color reproduction: Scantrans, Singapore

front endpaper: *Five Crow chiefs*
page ii: *Old Crow and his wife*
pages iv, v: *Little Raven's sons*
back endpaper: *Sioux women and children*

CONTENTS

FROM
WHENCE
WE CAME

CHAPTER I

Below: 'A herd of bison crossing the Missouri River.' Painting by William Jacob Hays, probably based on sketches made on a trip in 1860. This panoramic view gives a feel for the extent of the Great Plains environment and one of its most important water courses. The buffalo roamed in their millions and were surprisingly sure-footed when traversing the steep trails from the high bluffs down to the water.

Land of Sun, Wind and Grass

The Great Plains, the heartland of North America, are some 2500 miles long (4000km) and nearly 600 miles (950km) at the widest point. Their western boundary is formed by the Rocky Mountains although some areas of the foothills extend to the Continental Divide. To the north, flatlands extend almost to the Arctic Circle but just beyond mid-Saskatchewan, Alberta and Manitoba in Canada there are extensive boreal pine forests. The eastern boundary is formed by the Missouri–Mississippi rivers where there is extensive prairie terrain, characterized by

rolling hills and wooded areas. The southern boundary follows the Rio Grande but not so far as the Gulf of Mexico. In all, the Plains are approximately 1000 miles (1600km) inland from the Atlantic, 750 miles (1200km) from the Pacific and some 300 miles (470km) from the Gulf of Mexico.

The Great Plains feature at least two out of the three following geographic characteristics: they are extensively flat and wide; they have limited rainfall which is generally insufficient for farming normally associated with humid climates; and they are devoid of trees and forests. Only on the central or high plains of this vast area do all three characteristics come together; here the land is flat, treeless, the climate semi-arid.[1]

The Prairie Plains of the East

To the east of the high plains, the Plains environment is defined by the timber line which includes a now humid but generally treeless level land referred to as the prairie plains or simply the prairies. To the west of the high plains, the surface is no longer level but two of the characteristics mentioned above remain – semi-aridity and absence of trees. While the region is dry it is not exclusively so for within this region there are beautiful valleys and wooded islands, and rivers and streams which offer sanctuary to both animals and human beings.

The western and eastern forests join in Canada, forming a continuous sub-Arctic of mainly pine forest which extends from the Pacific to the Atlantic, while to the south the forests unite in Mexico; the massive land area between – the Great Plains – has been described as 'a barrier between the species of the two regions even more effectively than a body of water of the same extent' (Webb,1931:28).

Within this region there were three main types of grass, corresponding to the amount of rainfall in the areas, all of which thrived in conditions ranging from extreme drought or rainfall to fires which could destroy trees. Typical of the prairie plains

Below: *A buffalo herd between the Yellowstone and Big Missouri, circa 1880. By this time the vast herds were heavily depleted as the hide hunters took their toll. In the 1870s United States surveying parties reported that there were some two thousand hunters on the Plains killing these animals solely for their hides, and by the mid-1880s the buffalo was facing extinction.*

Above: *A buffalo pound – an ancient technique of trapping buffalo – by Paul Kane. Kane accompanied Indians, almost certainly Cree, on a buffalo hunt near Fort Carlton (in present-day Saskatchewan) in September 1846 and made detailed sketches on which this painting is obviously based. Note the men rising behind the posts and waving buffalo robes to frighten the animals.*

in the eastern part of the region were the tall grasses such as blue-stem bunch grass, slender wheat grass and needle grass, while the short or Plains grasses – such as galleta, mesquite and buffalo grass – characterized the high plains region. To the west were found sagebrush, creosote bush and southern-desert shrub. The short buffalo grass of the high plains grew quickly with the spring rains, lying dormant during the summer; cured by the hot sun, it provided nutritious winter forage for the many animals which thrived in the region.

Buffalo, Pronghorn and Elk

The most important of the Plains animals was the buffalo, the true name of which is bison (*Bison americanus*) which roamed in vast herds. Originally, its range was not confined to the Plains, and English settlers record seeing buffalo as far east as the Potomac River in 1612. Father Hennepin observed them near the Great Lakes in 1679 and buffalo were found in Virginia and North Carolina by the Colonel William Byrd survey party in 1729; by 1850, however, they were virtually extinct east of the ninety-fifth meridian. But the real home of the buffalo was the Great Plains. Here they appeared in such vast numbers as to make a marked impression on the lifestyle of the human inhabitants. The naturalist W. T. Hornaday observed: 'Of all the quadrupeds that have lived upon the earth, probably no other species has ever marshaled such innumerable hosts as those of the American bison. It would have been as easy to count or estimate the number of leaves in a forest as to calculate the number

of buffaloes living at any given time during the history of the species previous to 1870' (Hornaday,1887, part II:373).

The same authority has estimated that the herds could total up to 12,000,000: others refer to herds covering some fifty square miles. Thus, under the natural conditions which prevailed on the Plains, there was an almost inexhaustible supply of meat unrivaled anywhere else in the world.

Another important Plains animal was the pronghorn or American antelope (*Antilicapra americana*), which was also found in vast numbers across the Plains. A smaller and less conspicuous animal, it did not impress observers in the same way as the massive, dark buffalo. However, the pronghorn has been described as the purest type of Plains animal indigenous only to the plains of North America. Unrelated to the antelope family of Asia and Europe, it is something between the deer and the goat – it shed its horns like deer but its horns were hollow like those of goats or cattle. It had the curiosity of goats but the timidity of deer. It avoided canyons and woods, living almost exclusively on the Plains, from Mexico to Saskatchewan and from the Rocky Mountains to the Missouri. Early white hunters found the pronghorn to be a curious animal which was attracted to unusual objects and seldom associated a particular sound with danger; hence it could be attracted to a scene by gunfire, with the predictably fatal results. Early Plains human inhabitants, however, found them difficult to approach and the bow or spear was virtually useless against pronghorns; thus they could only be captured by being driven into the winged enclosures where they were trapped in large numbers.[2]

In addition to these two main meat-producing animals, the Plains country abounded with other wild life. The wapiti, or elk, roamed in large herds in mountainous meadowlands. Although related to the European red deer, elk were generally bigger, standing at about 5 feet (1.5m) at the shoulder. Less common

Right: *Archeological evidence suggests that man has long lived in the Plains region. Some of the earliest evidence is in the form of beautifully chipped flint lance and arrow points dating back at least 10,000 years. Later, possibly due to influences from the east, nomadic hunters used the atlatl, bone knives and awls. Then at about the time the Athapascans moved down from the north, earth lodges were being built on the Missouri River and the historic Plains culture slowly emerged. By the early nineteenth century Siouan, Algonquian and Caddoan speaking people largely occupied the Plains region. Here they used the horse and bow, and the eastern groups on the Missouri made good quality pottery.*

PALEO-INDIANS 10,000BC

| Clovis | Folsom | Sandia | Scottsbluff |

Nomadic hunters. Ancient bison and mammoth. Spear throwers (atlatl) not in use. Gathered wild plants. Brush shelters. Possibly ancestors of Shoshones on the High Plains.

ARCHAIC PERIOD 6000–0BC

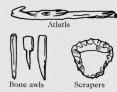

Atlatls

| Bone knives | Bone awls | Scrapers |

Nomadic hunter-gatherers. Antelope, deer, buffalo. Wider variety of wild seeds, berries, roots. Transitional period to post-glacial environment. Thrust from Mississippian and Ohio cultures in the east.

PLAINS–WOODLAND PERIOD 500BC–AD1000

Grooved mauls Shell ornaments

Pottery Shell buttons and beads

Hunter-gatherers. Pottery and established village sites suggest more sedentary life-style. Horticulture (?). Shell ornaments – trade connections?

TRANSITIONAL PERIOD 900–1500 PLAINS–WOODLAND TO PLAINS CULTURE

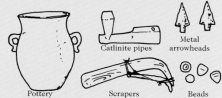

Arrow smoothers

Pipes

| Pottery | Bone fish hooks | Flint knives |

Hunter-horticulturalists. Maize. Large earth lodges now used on eastern Plains. Athapascans move from Mackenzie Basin through Plains region. Padouca nation begins to dominate the Plains.

HISTORIC PLAINS INDIAN CULTURE BEGINS 1500–1800

Catlinite pipes

Metal arrowheads

| Pottery | Scrapers | Beads |

Plains Apaches imitate Spaniards – rawhide armor for men and horses. Siouan and Algonquian groups move out onto Plains.

was the moose, predominantly associated with the more northern edge of the Great Plains, and generally of a solitary disposition. It has the heaviest antlers of the whole deer family and legs which are so long that it often has to kneel down to graze. Additionally, there were the white- and black-tailed deer and the mule deer, found during the winter in small herds but more solitary in spring and summer; neither was exclusive to the Plains.

Plains animals exhibited definite common characteristics. All, except the wolf and coyote, were grass-eaters and two species, the jack rabbit and antelope, were noted for their speed in open country. All could survive without a regular supply of water, indeed, the jack rabbit and prairie dog need none. All these creatures were extremely cautious and had enormous vitality and in this respect the pronghorn was supreme. One nineteenth-century observer of the Plains region recorded that nothing but the breaking of the backbone or a shot in the brain would bring one down and 'any one of these animals is liable to run for a quarter of a mile, though his heart be split as with a knife' (Dodge,1877:112).

Before Christ: Shoshones on the Northern Plains

Recent archeological discoveries indicate that man has lived on the Plains for more than 10,000 years. Called Paleo-Indians, these inhabitants hunted bison and mammoths using spears with heads of beautifully chipped flint, classified as Clovis or Folsom points (see left).

Approximately 6000 years ago, the Great Plains seem to have experienced a much hotter and drier climate and most of the animals and hunters retreated to the mountain valleys to the north and west. There were obviously, however, forays to the Plains region and particularly toward the end of the dry period there was increased occupation of the Plains region. There is considerable evidence that at about the time of Christ there was a thrust from the Mississippian and Ohio cultures in the east. This evidence is in the form of burial mounds, semi-permanent villages and various types of pottery; from the Missouri to the Rocky Mountains there is archeological evidence too which shows that peoples from the east introduced a *Woodland type* culture to the Great Plains. However, by 1500, many of the settlements had been abandoned, probably due to further climatic change and pressure from powerful enemies.

Possibly some of these aggressors were related to the Shoshone who, one authority suggests, occupied 'the high western Plains long before the birth of Christ' (Hultkrantz,1968:59). Certainly there is considerable evidence which suggests that it was the Shoshone who lived on the fringes of the western Plains during the eighteenth century and then expanded to a vast domain with the acquisition of the horse, c. 1700, and then, just as suddenly, there was an abrupt contraction two generations later, c. 1760, due to lack of firearms, to smallpox and immense pressure of the tribes from the east.

CEREMONIAL STYLE OF ROCK ART AD 1000–1700

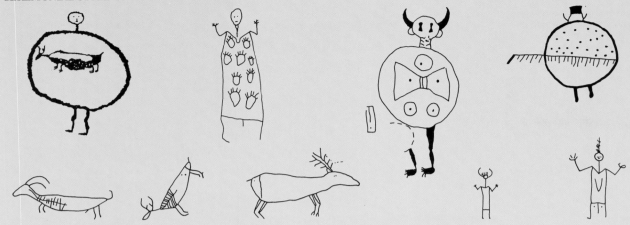

Shield-bearing pedestrian warriors and V-neck human figures. Symbolic animals. Highly symbolic art. Primarily individualistic and ceremonial in nature

TRANSITION FROM CEREMONIAL STYLE TO EARLY BIOGRAPHIC STYLE OF ROCK ART, CIRCA 1730

Scenes of warfare and interaction between individuals. Horse armor, clubs, guns and spears

BIOGRAPHIC STYLE OF ROCK ART, CIRCA 1830–50

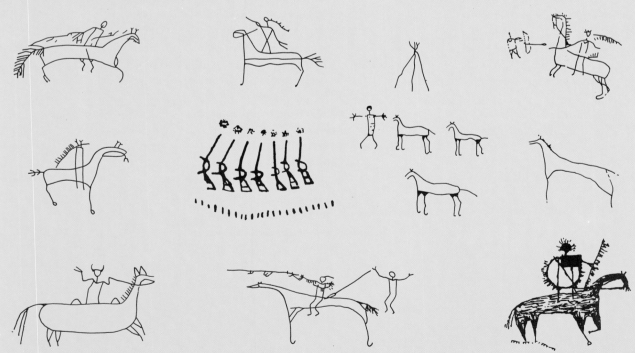

The emphasis on action scenes with horses and guns. 'Storylines' which enable a basic understanding of events depicted)

Above: *An unusual headdress made of swan skin with buffalo horns attached. This is obviously an accouterment which was highly symbolic to its Assiniboin owner who lost it in battle to a Crow chief, Bear-in-Water, some time prior to 1888.*

Left: *Petroglyphs and pictographs on rocks and walls of caves are scattered across the Plains. Such images give useful insights into the ceremonial of the pedestrian nomads who lived there. Prior to circa 1730 the scenes depict largely pedestrian nomads with an emphasis on the ritualistic. Then, with the introduction of the horse and gun, the scenes tend to put emphasis on intertribal warfare. Invaluable details of weapons, headgear, painted shields, horse armor and costume are often in evidence.*

Rock Art: Documents by the People

Some of the most interesting evidence for the sudden cultural shift on the Plains comes from the studies of petroglyphs and pictographs on rock faces, which are to be found throughout the Plains region; those in Montana and Wyoming and in the Canadian province of Alberta[3] have received particular attention, yielding considerable information about the changes which were occurring on the central and northern Plains in the early 1700s.

Two main types of rock art have been identified – Ceremonial and Biographic – the latter developing from the former. The ceremonial type gives considerable important information on various items of material culture used by the early pedestrian nomads such as the type of weapons, decorated shields, headgear and other ceremonial regalia; it also shows that there was a spiritual relationship between the artist and animal spirits. In about 1730 there was a marked change from animal pictures to scenes of warfare and the large shields traditionally carried by pedestrian nomads were replaced by small shields and now carried by horseback warriors, while the pedestrians are increasingly shown carrying guns.[4] Fortunately, there is a first-hand account of these turbulent changes which were occurring at this time and which are so graphically illustrated in the rock art images (see left for development of Ceremonial style through transition to Biographic style).

This account comes from a Cree warrior called *Saukamappee* who, as a young man, joined the Piegan and warred against the Snake (Shoshone) Indians who then occupied the Plains bordered by the north and south branches of the Saskatchewan River of present-day Alberta and Saskatchewan. Referring to a battle which took place in the early 1700s near the Eagle Hills in present-day Saskatchewan, and which he witnessed as a boy of sixteen, he tells of mounted Shoshone warriors bearing down on the horseless Piegan and despatching them with stone-headed war clubs. A decade or so later, the Piegan – now allied with the Assiniboin who had acquired guns from eastern traders – again confronted the Shoshone. Although still pedestrians, the Piegan–Assiniboin gun-carrying alliance had the upper hand; in that encounter many Shoshone warriors were killed and, as Saukamappee observed, there was 'consternation and dismay' among the gunless Shoshone (Thompson, Tyrrell ed.,1916:332).

Unable to acquire the gun from their traditional trading posts in New Mexico due to a strict Spanish policy, the Shoshone were progressively driven in retreat to the Plateau region, a process which was accelerated as the frontier tribes, such as the Piegan and Assiniboin, moved from the east and began to acquire guns and horses. By the 1780s, Blackfeet, Cree and Assiniboin, powerful Algonquian and Siouan tribes, dominated the northern Plains.

Horsemen Extraordinary: Comanches on the Southern Plains

Shoshoneans never completely left the Plains, but several groups who were known historically as Comanches (from the Ute word *Cumanche*, meaning 'enemies') left the main body of Shoshone, joined up with some of the Ute bands and moved south from their traditional homeland – in what is now Wyoming – in search of game, ponies and new territory. Here, they encountered the so-called Padouca Indians, a chain of Apachean groups – Kiowa-Apache, Jumaro and Lipan – who had long occupied the region

These Padouca were part of the two-pronged migration from the far north which occurred in about 1200 when powerful groups of Athapascans left their homelands in the Mackenzie region in Canada, and started their long trek southward. One group advanced through the Great Plains, the other through the Plateau country west of the Rockies, and finally settled around the Rio Grande where they displaced the ancient Pueblo settlements. This group called their new home *Tinetxah* and the world now knows the occupants as Navajos.

The other group, the Padoucas, who were made up of various tribes of the Apaches, were met by Coronado's expedition in 1541–2. Coronado's journals state that the Padoucas spent their winters on the eastern borders of the Plains in what is now southeastern Kansas but that they also visited, traded and wintered among the Pueblo tribes in the Rio Grande region. As the ethnologist Hyde suggested, these Apaches were thus 'in control of the southern plains across their entire width, and from northern Texas up to the Arkansas River or beyond' (Hyde,1959:7). Indeed, since the Apache tribes were probably

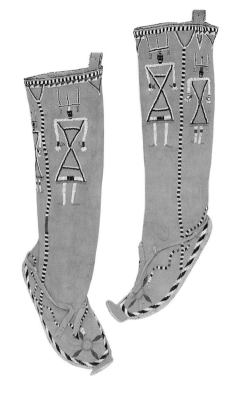

Above: *Apache moccasins. These date from circa 1880 but their basic structure, with protective heavy rawhide soles and disc toe, is typical of early Plains Apacheans.*

Below: *Kiowa woman's saddle. Its frame is wooden, covered with rawhide and embellished with brass studs; the girth, however, is of commercial leather.*

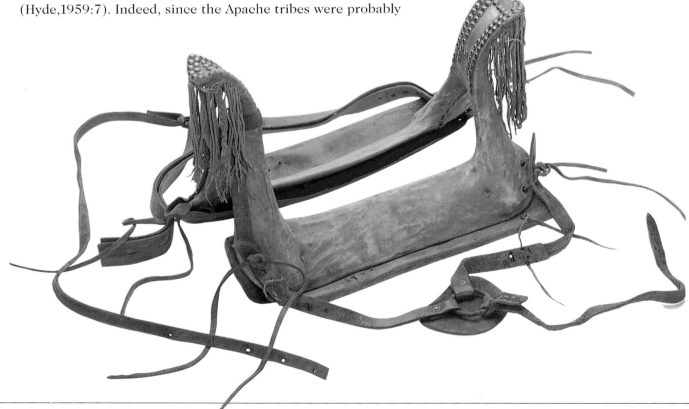

14

Above: *A Kiowa painting on buckskin depicting a Sun-dance scene, collected by James Mooney in 1891. Generally celebrated annually in the middle of June each year, part of the initial ceremonial involved the procession of the women to cut down the tree which would be used as the center pole of the medicine lodge. This scene seems to make reference to that episode by use of realistic images in exquisite colors. Traditionally, the Kiowa Sun-dance did not involve self-torture, which was a marked feature of adjacent tribes, and even the accidental shedding of blood might cause the dance to be abandoned. An important central figure in the Kiowa Sun-dance was the tai-me; some 2ft (0.6m) in length, it represented a human figure with a stalk of tobacco for a headdress. It was said to have originated anciently among the Crow, being obtained through an Arapaho who married a Kiowa woman.*

still (1540 or so) migrating southward from the great hive of Athapascan peoples in the Mackenzie Basin, it is suggested that Apache groups, in 1540 or thereabouts, held much of the Plains region from Wyoming to Texas.[5]

The lifestyle of these Apachean groups was entirely different from that of the earlier big game hunters of the Paleo-Indian period[6] who lived in permanent villages edging the Plains. Instead, the Apache were pedestrian nomads who transported their possessions on pack dogs and lived in tents of skins covering a conically shaped pole structure, the forerunner of the tipi (see Chapter 2). The Apache greatly impressed the Spaniards – Coronado in 1541, Záldivar in 1598, and Oñate in 1601 – who repeatedly referred to this lifestyle; typical was the comment 'They travel the plains with the cows (buffalo) living in tents "like Arabs"' (Bolton ed.,1916:257).

Such a lifestyle, characterized especially by nomadism, big game hunting, the use of (possibly bone) bows, sewn skin tents and transportation by pack dogs, is suggestive of a much older way of life such as exhibited in the reindeer and the caribou cultures of Siberia, northern Europe and northern North America.[7] Thus, it is probable, as some scholars have suggested, that the nomadic hunting ways of the Apache groups, which eventually evolved into the horse and buffalo economy of later Plains tribes, was 'actually derived from an Old World economy and imported by these Apacheans' (Gunnerson and Bouc, 1984:56).

By the first quarter of the eighteenth century, however, virtually all the Padoucas had been forced off the plains of Texas by the Comanche who, unlike their Shoshone cousins to the north, had acquired guns from their allies the French.[8] Thus by 1750 the Comanches, probably because of Kiowa pressure from the north, were to be found southwest of the Arkansas River and this became their traditional territory until the Reservation period. Of considerable interest, even after the final separation of the Shoshone and Comanche, they kept close contacts and 'whole groups migrated back and forth' (Hultkrantz, 1968:62).

Likewise, the Kiowa, a group without any agricultural tradition whatsoever, moved from what is now western Montana, crossed the Yellowstone, and finally settled in the Black Hills, perhaps in about 1700. They formed a close friendship with the Crow to the north from whom they obtained their *tai-me*, or 'Sun-dance medicine'; together they attempted to stem the advance of the Sioux and Cheyenne.[9]

By 1805, Lewis and Clark found the Cheyenne in possession of the Black Hills and at war with the Sioux. The Kiowa had been forced further south where they encountered the Comanche; this resulted in more warfare and the Comanche crossed the Arkansas. By 1790, however, they had made a treaty with the Kiowa through the good offices and great bravery of *Guikate*, or Wolf Lying Down, who visited the Comanche in about 1790 and negotiated peace. Since that time, as one authority has pointed out, the Comanche and Kiowa, together with the Kiowa-Apache,

Above: A Kiowa hair ornament embellished with twenty-three silver conches attached to a buckskin base. Such ornaments were widely distributed across the Plains and were particularly popular with the Kiowa, being referred to as early as 1832 in their Winter Counts. The metal was purchased in sheets from the traders and then cut and hammered into shape. The end (right) is a tuft of colored horsehair.

Below: Kiowa artifacts, mostly dating from about 1870 onwards. The several model shields shown at the top were collected by James Mooney in the 1890s as part of a project dealing with Kiowa heraldry, Mooney obtaining information on the meaning of the painted designs directly from their owners. The beaded shirt (lower left) was formerly the property of Little Bluff, a famous Kiowa chief. It is of Crow style and was probably obtained as a gift or in trade from these close Kiowa allies.

Above: *Little Spaniard, painting by George Catlin, 1834. This warrior was half Spanish, half Comanche and his deeds of valor had led to his renown in the tribe.*

Below: *She who bathes her knees, Cheyenne, portrait by George Catlin, 1832. The wife of the chief Wolf on the Hill, she wears a deerskin dress, the tail at the neck.*

have consistently lived in close proximity and acted together on all important occasions even though there were great differences in language, temperament, and ceremony[10] (Mooney, 1898:163).

A unique documentation of Kiowa history and culture which recorded all these events is embedded in three pictographic calendars which were collected by James Mooney in 1892. They relate tribal history by use of two pictographs of some memorable event of each year, one in the winter, the other in summer and begin in the winter of 1832.[11]

The close friendship between the Crow and Kiowa continued after the Kiowa had moved south to the Arkansas and they combined with the Crow in a common cause against the Cheyenne and Lakota who were coming in from the east. In addition to the Sun-dance *tai-me* medicine which the Kiowa obtained from the Crow, they also acquired from them a sacred arrow lance which was hereditary in the *Tän-gŭădal* family,[12] and considered powerful war medicine, only two lances of this type being found in the tribe. For many years — and well into the Reservation period — Kiowa parents visited the Crow and left their young children with them for up to three years so that they learned the customs and language of the Crow and hence maintained the friendships forged many years before when the Kiowa were in the north. In the 1890s, there were still several elders among the Kiowa with an extensive knowledge of the Crow language; the Crow in turn referred to the Kiowa as their relatives.[13]

Migration of the *Tsistsistas*: Cheyenne Move to the Plains

Among the most notable of Plains Indians are the Cheyenne, the *Tsistsistas* (meaning 'The People'), as they call themselves. Before the end of the seventeenth century, the Cheyenne lived just south of Lake Superior in present-day Wisconsin; then, probably as war intensified with the introduction of firearms, they migrated west. Although the picture is not completely clear, it seems probable that the Cheyenne occupied several villages on the Red River, Sheyenne River (in North Dakota) and probably the Missouri River, where they became closely associated with the Mandan, Hidatsa and Arikara. Reporting in 1799 on his conversations with a Chippewa chief, David Thompson describes the destruction of one of the main Cheyenne earth lodge villages (c. 1780) on the Sheyenne River by a war party of about one hundred and fifty men; they burned the village to the ground and killed most of the inhabitants, although it seems that many of the men were out hunting for horses. This was a time of great dynamism when some of the tribe was partly

sedentary, others migratory, some actually established at one place and others moving about, wandering across the Plains in pursuit of buffalo. The attack undoubtedly speeded up the process of nomadism and by 1795, when the fur trader Trudeau was engaged in trade with them, they were fully developed equestrian nomads.[14] Trudeau observed, 'Now that the Cheyennes have ceased to till the ground, they roam over the prairies west of the Missouri on this side of the Black Hills, from which they come regularly at the beginning of August to visit their old and faithful allies, the Ricaras' (Trudeau,1914:472).

In the spring of 1795, Trudeau summoned the important men of the Cheyenne villages in an attempt to place the Cheyenne–European trade on an organized basis. At the Arikara villages, he pointed out that the Cheyenne and other western tribes would be able to obtain guns, powder and other European goods in exchange for their horses to the Arikara and their furs with the white men (ibid.:467). Thus, the horse and gun, essential components of the Plains Indian culture, were met at the Upper Missouri villages of the Arikara, Hidatsa and Mandan.

Mississippian Influences on the Central and Northern Plains: 500 Years of Mandan Cultural History

Of all the Missouri River tribes it was perhaps the Mandan who had the most influence in the cultural exchanges and trade to the north and west. The Mandan were a Siouan-speaking group who, at the time of their earliest contact with Europeans, lived in villages of circular earth lodges which were situated on the banks of the Missouri River in what is now North Dakota.

They called themselves *Numangkake* ('men'), often identifying their descent by adding the name of their village. The his-

Above: *The Mandan village of* Mih-Tutta-Hang-Kusch, *by Karl Bodmer, 1833. The principal village of the tribe, it had some sixty-five earth lodges surrounded by a wooden defensive palisade.*

Below: *Six exploit sticks and a wooden knife which belonged to the Mandan chief* Mató-tópe, *or Four Bears. The sticks commemorate his six musket wounds, the knife a battle with a Cheyenne chief.*

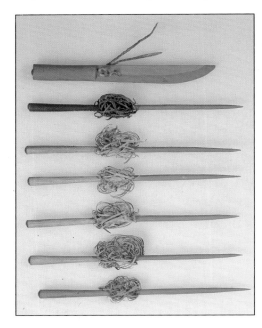

Below: *Exploit robe which also belonged to the Mandan chief* Mató-tópe, *or Four Bears, which was collected by Prince Maximilian in 1834. The pictographic style developed by Mató-tópe is outstanding in its realism and detail for this period. The battle with the Cheyenne chief (see the knife opposite) is shown lower right. The robe is decorated along its center with a band and discs of porcupine quillwork and scalp-lock fringes embellish the front edge of the hide. Other exploits which were recorded direct from Mató-tópe by the artist George Catlin refer to clashes with Arikara, Assiniboin and Sioux; they total twelve battles in which Mató-tópe took fourteen scalps.*

toric Mandan culture was probably developed in about 1500 and their villages became important centers for trade to the pedestrian and later equestrian nomads of the Plains to the north and west. At this time their subsistence was about equally based on horticulture and hunting and a culture, rich in ceremonialism much of which pivoted around the so-called medicine bundle complex, was rapidly expanding. In particular they developed the *O-kee-pa*, one of the most important and lengthy ceremonials of any Plains tribe. The *O-kee-pa* dramatized the creation of the earth and all living things and told of the struggles that the Mandan experienced during their cultural history.

Archeological research suggests that during the period 1100–1400 the earliest manifestations of Mandan culture began to emerge. Their villages, which were to be found on terraces strung along the Missouri River for a distance of some 500 miles in present-day North and South Dakota, generally consisted of small, isolated and probably largely unfortified settlements of between fifteen and forty households. Here were built large rectangular-shaped earth lodges often some 50 feet (15m) long and 28 feet (8.5m) wide. These had a central ridge pole which

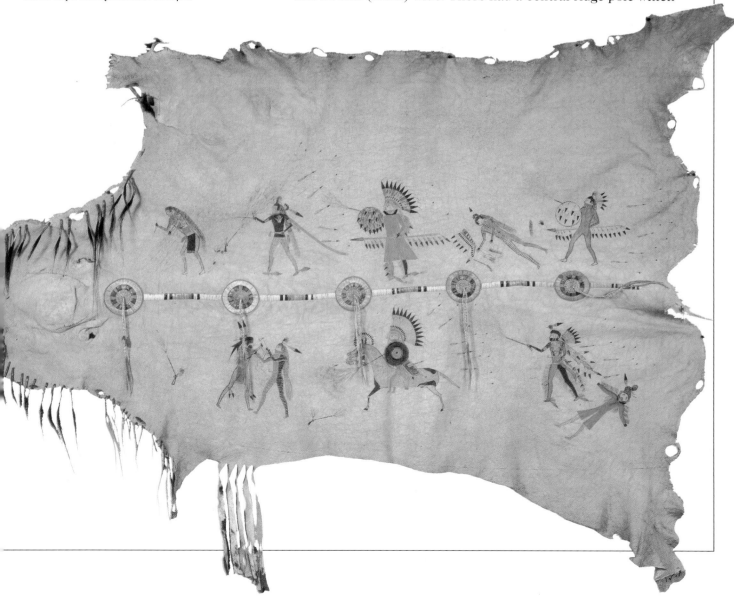

was supported by two entrance posts together with a large center and end post. The side walls were at least 5 feet high (1.5m) and the floor was set into a pit with the entrance projecting into the floor area as an earthen ramp. There was a primary fireplace between the entrance and center post, the roof was covered with consecutive layers of wooden slats, grass and earth. By 1500, the historic Mandan culture had just about fully emerged. The known villages were now relatively compact and fortified with about one hundred rectangular earth lodges and a total population of nearly one thousand. By this time, each village had a central open plaza some 164 feet (50m) in diameter which allows us to speculate as to the tribal organization, since the transition from small unfortified, relatively isolated villages of some thirty lodges to much larger, high population density villages, would suggest the development of a complex clan and society system with the elaboration of such ceremonials as the O-kee-pa – all of which would have acted as crucial integrative elements in the tribal organization.

The fortification of these villages suggests that there was considerable aggression by outside groups and it is reasonable to suppose that this show of force was matched by an increase in group solidarity.[15] Generally, one edge of the village was flanked by the Missouri River while the other three sides were fortified by upright posts, bastions at the corners (and at intervals between) and a deep ditch running in front of the palisade. Some of the lodges were now circular, approaching those associated with the historic period and, as the tribe progressively migrated north, the circular earth lodge was adopted more and more, since it was more suited to the extremes of cold and heat so characteristic of the Middle Missouri region.

In October 1738, the French fur trader Pierre La Verendrye visited the Mandan and observed that they kept the 'streets and

Above: *Assiniboin chiefs at Rocky Mountain House, painting by Paul Kane in 1848. At the left is* Mah-Min, *or The Feather, a head chief, and at the right is* Wah-he-joe-tass-e-neen, *or The Half White Man, described as a second chief. Rocky Mountain House, in present-day western Alberta, was established by the North West Company as early as 1799 for trade with the Cree and Assiniboin. Both men wear buckskin shirts decorated with colored cloth, beads and quills.*

Right: *Mandan snow-shoe, one of a pair collected by Prince Maximilian in 1834. In comparison to the snow-shoes made in the Subarctic, these are somewhat diminutive and the webbing, instead of the usual rawhide strip, is of buckskin over a wooden frame. While snow-shoes were recorded for the Plains region, few appear to have been collected, so this pair is of particular interest because it gives details of construction techniques and style.*

Above: Sha-ko-ka, *or Mint, a twelve-year-old Mandan girl, portrait by George Catlin in 1832. Her white-streaked hair was an albinism found among some Mandan families; men hid it but women were proud of it.*

open spaces very clean'; he also gave an account of the village fortifications and described circular earth lodges. The Mandan, La Verendrye found, were already operating a flourishing trade center and were in possession of metal weapons and utensils which they obtained from Assiniboin and Cree, who acted as middlemen between the European traders to the north and east[16] (La Verendrye, Burpee ed.,1927). These villages appear to have been very crowded, one white observer describing them as follows: 'These houses were thickly studded together to economize the space within the stockade, so that in passing through the village you walk along semicircular footpaths which turn at a few paces both to the right and left. There is not only no street, but it is impossible to see in any direction except for short distances' (Morgan, White ed.,1959).

As a symbol of village unity, there stood at the center of the village plaza a sacred cedar pole. This cedar, uncarved and decorated only with sacred red paint, was surrounded by a palisade of cottonwood planks. The post was said to represent the body of Lone Man, a mythological figure important in the O-kee-pa ceremonial. The surrounding palisade symbolized the wall which Lone Man was said to have erected to protect the people from the flood, one of the many references to the deluge myths widely distributed in North America. In 1781, the Mandan and Hidatsa were devastated by smallpox which struck the central and northern Plains; now, greatly reduced in numbers, they moved farther north settling in two villages, *Mih-Tutta-Hang-Kusch* and *Ruptare*, four miles below the mouth of the Knife River and on opposite sides of the Missouri.

It was here in 1804 that Lewis and Clark, leading their Corps

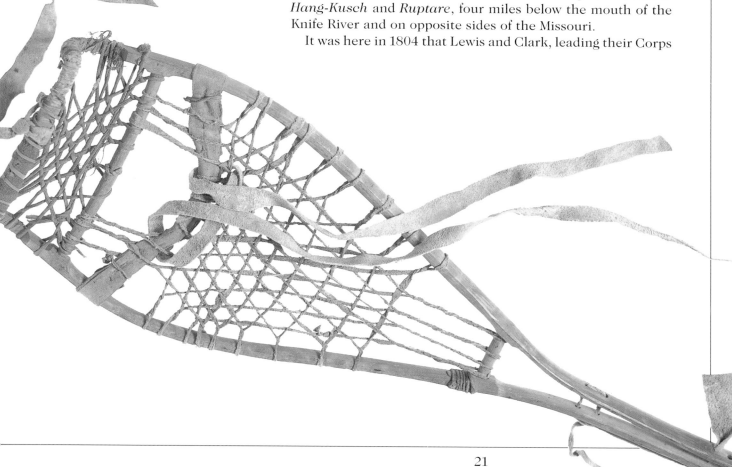

of Discovery after the Louisiana Purchase, first met the Mandan and wintered with them, building a rude fort adjacent to the villages. They found the Mandan a friendly and accommodating people who supplied the exploring party with corn and furnished information on the resources of the region and the Indian tribes to the west, with whom they carried on an extensive trade. For more than a generation – until the second devastating smallpox epidemic of 1837 all but destroyed the tribe – the Mandan villages remained important trade and cultural centers, mainly to the central Plains and Plateau (via the Crow) but also to the southern Plains via the Cheyenne and northern Plains via the Assiniboin and Cree.

Horticulturists and Buffalo Hunters: the Complexity of Hidatsa and Crow Migrations

Strongly associated with the semi-sedentary Hidatsa were the nomadic Crow who acted as an important link between the Middle Missouri village tribes and the Plateau tribes, such as the Shoshone and Nez Perce. The Crow can be split into two main divisions – River and Mountain Crow – whose early history can be reconstructed from archeological and early narratives, together with the fascinating oral history of the tribe itself.

Perhaps the earliest reference to the tribal designation 'Crow' comes in a statement made by the trader James Knight in 1716, when he recorded that so-called 'Mountain Indians' had visited the Hudson Bay Company's trading post at York Factory (on the shores of southwest Hudson Bay), bringing with them 'Crow Slaves' (Ray,1974:57). The next reference comes from the trader Jean Baptiste Trudeau who, while among the Arikara in 1795, reported that 'a war party of the Ricaras arrived on the fifth of June with the scalp of a man of the Crow Nation a people who live near the Rocky Mountains' (Trudeau,1914:22). The reference is almost certainly to the so-called Mountain Crow who undoubtedly occupied the central Plains as semi-sedentary hunters well before the arrival of the horse,[17] and

Above: A Crow lance case collected by Capt. Charles E. Bendire, circa 1880. Made of incised buffalo hide its triangular front is beaded in Crow period style.

Below: A Crow war whistle collected in the early 1840s by Count d'Otrante. It was reported to have been made from the bone of a swan's wing rather than an eagle's.

Above: *The Crow chief He who ties his hair before, portrait by George Catlin, 1832. The Crow were noted for their long hair which sometimes reached to the ground.*

Right: *A suggested pattern of the Hidatsan migration which perhaps commenced in the east as early as the middle of the sixteenth century. This led to the peopling of the Plains by the River and Mountain Crow in the seventeenth and eighteenth centuries. The map is based on archeological data, the maps and writings of early travelers and the oral testimony of Hidatsa Indians who related traditions to the anthropologist Alfred Bowers in the 1930s.*

who followed a different cultural history to the River Crow who occupied the Plains much later; both tribes, however, derived from the Hidatsa.

The Hidatsa clearly recognized three independent but closely related village groups. Of these, the Hidatsa proper – called by Lewis and Clark the 'Minnetarees of the Willows' – were the largest. This group had arrived from the northeast 'in late pre-historic times' (Bowers,:15) and learned how to cultivate corn from the Mandan and then established themselves on the Missouri near the mouth of the Knife River. This group referred to itself as the *Mirokac*, now identified as the, then, combined Hidatsa–River Crow; prior to 1782, oral traditions indicate that they actually comprised 'both an agricultural and nomadic population' (ibid. 1965:18). The ratio of nomads to agriculturalists varied from season to season and archeological evidence suggests that the numerous bands which comprised this group gradually moved apart as some became farmers and others nomadic hunters. Thus, by the late eighteenth century, the River Crow had split from the Hidatsa to become equestrian nomadic hunters whose domain became the Powder River country of present-day eastern Montana.

On the south bank of the Knife River lived the Minnetaree; Lewis and Clark named them *Metaharta* in order to distinguish them from the Minnetarees of the Willows but the other Hidatsan groups called them *Awatixa*; all archeological evidence suggests that they were among the first of the Hidatsan groups to move to the Missouri probably arriving as early as 1550, and that they were heavily influenced by the Mandan with whom they formed close ties.[18] Part of the original group soon separated by mutual consent while living on the Missouri between the mouths of the Knife and Heart rivers and one group, the Mountain Crow, wandered out on to the Plains. This complex migration pattern is shown in in the map (below).

Of very considerable interest – because it indicated how oral

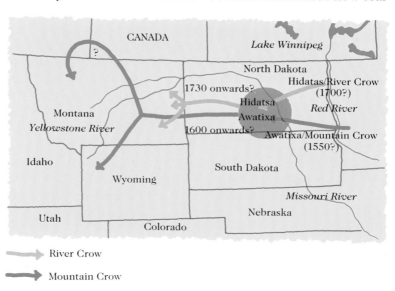

history was retained by the Plains tribes – is that all these ancient traditions were apparently kept well alive by successive generations who could point out to anthropologists and archeologists not only the ancient village sites, but also even earlier eastern sites occupied by the various Hidatsan groups.

Because of these divisions at different times and by different groups, the major contact at the Middle Missouri villages was predominantly with the River Crow. Not only were their associations more recent and stronger but additionally they were considerably closer to these villages than the Mountain Crow and hence acted as middlemen between their western and eastern relatives and friends. A complex trade pattern was thus developed across the Plains, the River Crow trading east, the Mountain Crow west, both coming together at a central rendezvous point on the headwaters of the Bighorn River. Although mutually benefiting from their different trade transactions, the Mountain Crow always remained the wealthiest in terms of horses.[19]

Move of the Serpents: the Migration of the Teton Sioux to the Western Plains

One of the earliest recorded meetings between the Siouans and whites comes from the Jesuit Relation of 1640, where positive documentation is made of the Winnebago, Assiniboin and Dakota; just eighteen years later, the same missionaries had recorded the existence of a number of Dakota villages in the vicinity of Green Bay in present-day Wisconsin and also farther in the forested regions of southern Minnesota. These people were referred to by the Chippewa as *Nadowe-is-iw*, signifying 'adder' or 'snake'. This Chippewa word was later corrupted by the French to *Nadowessioux*, which in turn was abbreviated to 'Sioux' by the English traders. The Sioux, however, referred to themselves as 'the *Otchenti Chakowin* or Seven Council Fires' (Hyde,1937:3). These Sioux, who had inhabited the woodlands for many generations, at this time lived in birch bark covered houses, used the canoe and dog for transportation and were divided into many groups, in perhaps up to thirty villages.

When the chronicler Hennepin traveled to the region in 1680, he recorded that in the neighborhood of Mille Lac (in present-day central Minnesota), and on the other various lakes and rivers in the region, lived 'the Issati, Nadouessans, Tinthonha (which means 'prairie men'), Ouadebathon River People, Chongaskethon Dog or Wolf tribe . . . and other tribes, all which we comprise under the name Nadonessiou' (Hennepin, in Hodge ed.,1965:377). Here, Hennepin distinguished the Issati (probably Mdewakanton) from the Tinthonha (Teton), Ouadebathon (Wahpeton), Chongaskethon (Sisseton) and Nadouessans (probably Wahpekute); significantly, he places the Tinthonha or *Gens des Prairies* well to the west on the Upper Mississippi and closest to the Great Plains. These people had obviously long ago established a reputation as great warriors, hunters and trend-setters for, as the English officer Lieutenant

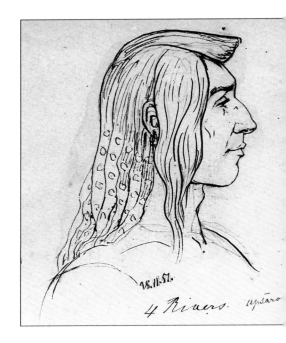

Above: *Four Rivers, a Crow chief, sketched by the Swiss artist Rudolph Kurz at Fort Union, Upper Missouri, in November 1851. Kurz described Four Rivers as a very powerful man 'both in regards to physique and in relationships' (Hewitt ed., 1937: 243). Note the hair-style bunched and spotted with white clay at intervals and trailing down the back. While not exclusive to the Crow, it was much favored by them and was often used to artificially lengthen the hair.*

Below: *A shield cover, probably Crow and dating from about 1840, formerly in the old War Department Collection. Protective bear power seems to be evoked by the painted symbols, the dominant red paw warding off enemy fire and protecting other bears represented by the smaller paws below. Ambitious Plains warriors, many of whom recognized the strength and courage of the grizzly, sought to acquire some of its power for themselves in dreams and visions of the bear.*

Gorrell observed in the mid-1700s, they were 'certainly the greatest nation of Indians ever yet found. Not above 2,000 of them were ever armed with fire-arms, the rest depending entirely on bows and arrows and darts, which they use with more skill than any other Indian nation in North America. They can shoot the wildest and largest beasts in the woods at 70 or 100 yds. distance. They are remarkable for their dancing; the other nations take the fashion from them' (Gorrell, *Wisconsin Historical Society Collection*: 1, 36, 1855, ibid.).

Lieutenant Gorrell further observed that the Sioux were always at war with the Chippewa to the east. Although considered great warriors, the Chippewa had a decided advantage

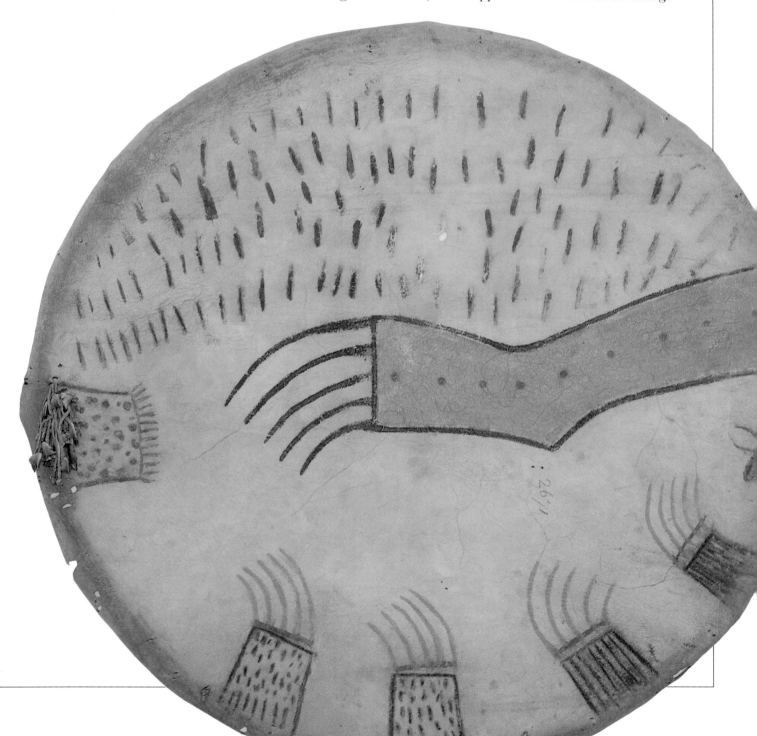

over the Sioux because, through their long-standing friendship with the French, they were very well armed with guns and the persistent Chippewa attacks gradually forced the Sioux bands westward. By the early 1700s, the most western of the Sioux bands, the Assiniboin – who split off from the Yanktonai and strengthened their bonds with the Cree – were west of Lake Winnipeg and were rapidly adapting to the Plains environment.[20] This Assiniboin–Cree alliance was beneficial to both sides; the Cree were the principal suppliers of guns while the Assiniboin had horses which they obtained from the Mandan villages to the south and west – two essentials for an effective Plains lifestyle[21] (Sharrock,1976:109).

The first Teton bands of Sioux made their appearance on the Middle Missouri about 1750; these were the Oglala and Brulé. In their slow drift westwards, they finally reached the James River where they probably encountered the Arikara who themselves had been displaced from the Lower Missouri due to pressures from the Omaha and Iowa in the south. The Sioux bands – referred to by themselves as *tiyospaye* and led then by chiefs called *itancan* (Bray,1982:2) – were, as one historian put it, 'no conquerors, but poor people afoot in the vast plains, [who] first came to the Missouri in a hard season, to beg at the Arikara towns' (Hyde,1937:15). Times changed rapidly, however; the Sioux had never really been a suppressed people but for a while they were humble beggars, then 'they returned on another day to waylay the Arikaras and kill them, and from the very first they must have proved bad neighbors' (ibid.:16).

The Gun and Horse Frontier

'English and French traders approaching the Great Plains from the north and east had no horses to trade, but they were not restrained from bartering firearms to the natives. Consequently, horses were diffused northward from the southwest, while guns and ammunition were diffused southward and westward from the French and English of Canada. At the horticultural villages on the Upper Missouri the expanding frontier of the horse met the expanding frontier of the gun' (Ewers,1968:23–4).

Thus, to make him efficient as a warrior, the Plains Indian required both the deadly firepower of the gun and the increased mobility offered by the horse; a tribe possessing only one of these essentials was at a decided disadvantage to a tribe which had both. As one ethnologist has put it: 'Consequently, there was a lively demand for guns on the part of the mounted tribes living south and west of the Missouri, and no less of a demand for horses by those tribes of the Great Plains north and east of that great river' (ibid.:24). Responding to this demand, the strategically located Mandan, Hidatsa and Arikara on the Missouri took an active and early part as middlemen in this trade. At this time, a good horse was as valuable as a gun and perhaps one hundred rounds of ammunition.

Left: *An Assiniboin man painted by Karl Bodmer at Fort Union on the Upper Missouri in the summer of 1833. Unnamed, he wears a superb hide shirt with the decoration of a large quilled disc dominating his chest. The flintlock gun was a coveted trade item.*

Below: *'Catching wild horses', painting by Paul Kane. The artist makes reference to roaming bands of horses in the vicinity of present-day Edmonton – Blackfeet, Cree and Assiniboin territory – in the winter of 1847.*

Thus, when the horse and gun frontier met at the Missouri villages, there was a rapid magnification of the Plains culture; pedestrian bow-carrying nomads who used the dog for transportation were now transformed into equestrian gun-carrying and aggressive warriors. By the time Lewis and Clark traveled in 1804–6, the historic Plains culture was in full flower[22] and for the next three quarters of a century these warriors would be a dominant force from the Saskatchewan River to the Rio Grande and from the Missouri to the foothills of the Rockies.

Coming from such diverse regions, six different linguistic families (or stocks) were represented in the Plains region – Algonquian, Athapaskan, Caddoan, Kiowan, Siouan, and Uto-Aztecan. This distribution is shown in the table (below), together with an indication of the approximate population of each tribe.

TABLE I.1: THE TRIBES OF THE PRAIRIE AND HIGH PLAINS, CIRCA 1850

HIGH PLAINS TRIBES

ASSINIBOIN A tribe of Siouan linguistic stock whose name is derived from a Chippewa term signifying 'one who cooks by the use of stones'. Hence the tribe was sometimes referred to as 'Stonies'. According to tradition the tribe separated from the Yanktonai when they were in the vicinity of the Lake of the Woods and Lake Nipigon and just prior to contact with the whites. They moved west to the vicinity of the Assiniboin and Saskatchewan rivers and allied themselves with the Cree. Mooney estimated the population in 1780 as 10,000. Today the Assiniboin are settled on several reservations in the United States and Canada, mainly at Fort Belknap and Fort Peck in Montana and Morley (this group refers to itself as 'Stoney'), Alberta. The total population in 1970 was about 6000.

Blackfeet A tribe of Algonquian linguistic stock, the name derives from *Siksika*, signifying 'black feet', probably referring to the ancient use of black buckskin for their moccasins. There are three divisions of the tribe: the *Siksika* or Blackfeet proper; the Kainah or Bloods, both of whom live in southwestern Alberta; and the Piegan, who live in northwestern Montana. According to tradition the Blackfeet moved to their present territory from the northeast, their movement probably accelerated by the acquisition of horses. The estimated population in 1780 was 15,000. In 1970 the total population was 18,000, of which approx. 6000 were in Canada.

SARCEE A small Athapaskan speaking tribe who moved to the northern Plains in the late 18th century, where they allied themselves with the Blackfeet for protection against their enemies the Assiniboin and Cree. In the late 17th century their population was estimated at 700. They now reside on a reservation in Alberta, where their population in 1970 was numbered at 467.

PLAINS OJIBWA A tribe of Algonquian linguistic stock who split off from the Chippewa and moved westward toward the end of the 18th century, occupying southern Manitoba, northern North Dakota and southeastern Saskatchewan. The estimated total number of Chippewa in 1650 was 35,000, some 3000 more than the estimated number of Plains Ojibwa at present residing on several reservations in North Dakota, Montana and Manitoba, although this includes a large number of individuals of mixed descent.

GROS VENTRE A tribe of Algonquian linguistic stock who split off from the Arapaho in their migrations from the northeast in the 18th century. For a long time they maintained an alliance with the Blackfeet. In the early 19th century they roamed the region between the Saskatchewan River in Canada and the Milk River in Montana. In 1780 their population was estimated at 3000. Today they reside on the Fort Belknap Reservation in Montana, where their population (1985) was given as 1900.

CROW A tribe of Siouan linguistic stock, closely related to the Hidatsa from whom they separated several hundred years ago to roam the region of the Yellowstone and Missouri rivers. The tribe was split into two main groups – the River and Mountain Crow – the latter moving south and west into Wyoming. Mooney estimated the population (in 1780) as 4000 but this is probably too low (see Chapter 1). They now reside on a reservation in southern Montana where their population (1980) was given as 6000.

SIOUX A collective term referring to seven closely related tribes who belonged to the Siouan linguistic stock. These seven were the Mdewakanton, Wahpeton, Wahpekute, Sisseton, Yankton, Yanktonai and Teton. The first four constitute the Santee or Eastern division and were generally referred to as 'Dakota'; the Yankton and Yanktonai the middle division, or 'Nakota'; while the Teton, the largest of all these tribes, were referred to as the 'Lakota' or Western Sioux. All these groups are now referred to

as High Plains tribes. Their population (in 1780) was estimated at 25,000, in 1937 33,625 and in 1970 – including both United States and Canada – over 50,000. The main reservation areas are in North and South Dakota.

ARAPAHO A tribe of Algonquian linguistic stock who migrated from the northeast, probably originally located near the headwaters of the Mississippi. By the first quarter of the 19th century they were split into two main divisions – the Northern and Southern Arapaho – occupying eastern Wyoming and Colorado. Their population was estimated at 3000 in 1780, virtually the same as that returned in 1970. Today they reside on the Wind River Reservation in Wyoming (Northern branch) and Oklahoma (Southern branch).

CHEYENNE A tribe of Algonquian linguistic stock whose name derives from a Dakota term meaning 'people of an alien speech'. Prior to 1700 the Cheyenne lived in what is now Minnesota. They moved west after their main village was destroyed by the gun-armed Chippewa in about 1790. The tribe split into two groups in the 1830s, the separation being recognized by the 1851 Fort Laramie Treaty. An associated tribe were the Sutaio, who merged with the Cheyenne and lost their own identity by the middle of the 19th century. In 1780 their population was estimated at 3500. Today the Northern Cheyenne have a small reservation in Montana and the Southern in Oklahoma. Total population in 1970 was estimated at just under 7000.

COMANCHE A tribe belonging to the Shoshonean linguistic family, which is a branch of the Uto-Aztecan. The Comanche split from the Shoshone in the latter half of the 17th century and as early as 1719 were recorded as being in the vicinity of present-day southwestern Kansas, which they fiercely defended against the Spaniards and Americans. The Comanche were split into several sub-tribes, the best known being the Kwahadi or Antelope band to which the famous leader Quanah Parker belonged. Their population in the late 17th century was estimated at 7000, in 1970 it was somewhat over 4000. Their reservation is in Oklahoma near the North Fork of the Red River and Washita River.

KIOWA A tribe belonging to the Tanoan linguistic stock most closely related to the Northern Pueblos such as San Ildefonso and Santa Clara with whom they carried on an extensive trade. According to tradition at one time they lived at the head of the Missouri River but moved to the vicinity of the Black Hills from which they were driven out by the Lakota in the 18th century, finally settling on the Arkansas where they made peace with the Comanche. Their population (in 1780) was estimated at 2000 and in 1970 approx. double that number, They were assigned a reservation in southwestern Oklahoma (1868) along with the Comanche and Kiowa-Apache where they reside today.

KIOWA-APACHE A small Athapaskan speaking tribe long associated with the Kiowa with whom they occupied a definite place in the camp circle. They have been described as a remarkable example of a tribe incorporated into the social organization of another tribe of entirely alien speech and origin, being associated with the Kiowa from the earliest traditional period. Their population was estimated in 1780 as 300, in 1981 at a little over 800. In 1868 they were placed on a reservation (along with the Kiowa and Comanche) in southwestern Oklahoma.

LIPAN APACHE An Athapaskan speaking tribe who formed close political relations with the Jicarilla Apache and ranged from the Rio Grande in New Mexico and western Texas. In the late 17th century their population was estimated at 500. By 1980, however, the tribe had virtually lost its identity although a few were said to be living with the Kiowa-Apache in Oklahoma.

TONKAWA A group of small tribes who lived in central Texas constituting a distinct linguistic family but with associations with Coahuiltecan and possibly Karankawan and Tunican groups. The name probably derived from the Waco word 'Tonkaweya', meaning 'they all stay together'. Their population in 1780 was estimated at about 1600 but smallpox and massacres by Delaware and Shawnee Indians in the second half of the 19th century dramatically reduced their numbers. In 1937 the population was said to be 51, mostly living in Kay County, Oklahoma.

PRAIRIE TRIBES

HIDATSA A Missouri River tribe belonging to the Siouan linguistic stock, their closest relatives within it being the Crow. They lived in several earth lodge villages at various points on the Missouri between the Heart and Little Missouri rivers in North Dakota. Traditionally the Hidatsa formerly lived by a lake in the northeast, some groups moving to the Missouri River region in the mid-16th century where they joined the Mandan. Their population in 1780 has been estimated at 2500 but in 1837 their numbers were reduced to just a few hundred when smallpox struck the tribe. The survivors consolidated into one tribe and moved to Fort Berthold in North Dakota. Their population was given as some 1700 people in 1970 but this includes people of mixed parentage.

MANDAN A tribe belonging to the Siouan linguistic stock who lived in earth lodge villages on the Missouri River just south of the Hidatsa. They have distinct traditions of an eastern origin and may have migrated from the region of the Ohio. In 1750 there were nine villages but by 1804 these had been reduced to two. In 1837, they, as with other Missouri River tribes, were struck down by smallpox and their numbers were reduced to little over 100. Their population was estimated in 1780 at 3600. In 1845 the Mandan accompanied the Hidatsa to the Fort Berthold region. Today they have largely merged with the Hidatsa although there are still identifiable Mandan segments on the reservation in North Dakota.

ARIKARA A Missouri River tribe of the Caddoan linguistic stock who lived just south of the Mandan. Their closest relatives were the Pawnee to the south from whom they separated probably about the middle of the 18th century. In 1862, much weakened by smallpox epidemics and wars with the Lakota, they moved to the Fort Berthold region. The Fort Berthold Reservation was created in 1880 and the Arikara, Hidatsa and Mandan have resided there ever since.

OMAHA A tribe of that section of the Siouan linguistic stock referred to as Dhegiha and which includes the Ponca, Kansa, Osage and Quapaw. According to tradition the Omaha and others belonging to the same linguistic group formerly lived on the Ohio and Wabash rivers. In 1854 they sold much of their land but retained a portion of it as a reservation in Thurston County, Nebraska. In 1882, through the work and support of Alice Fletcher who for years took a great interest in the tribe, they were granted lands in severalty and prospective citizenship. Their population was estimated at 2800 in 1780; today is estimated at 2000. However, statistics are difficult since many no longer live on the reservation.

PONCA This tribe speaks virtually the same language as the Omaha and formed with them, the Kansa, Osage and Quapaw, the Dhegiha group of the Siouan linguistic stock. The tribe was forced to move to Indian Territory (Oklahoma) in 1877 although a few under Standing Bear returned to their old homeland in Nebraska, where they were allowed to remain. The probable size of the tribe in 1780 has been estimated at 800. In 1937 the United States Indian Office gave 825 in Oklahoma and 397 in Nebraska. It was reported that there were some 1200 Ponca in Oklahoma in 1970 but those in Nebraska had widely dispersed, making an estimate impossible.

IOWA A tribe of the Siouan linguistic stock belonging to the section referred to as Chiwere, which includes the Oto and Missouria, their traditional territory being within the boundaries of the state of Iowa. It has been estimated that their population in 1780 was about 1200. In 1923 the United States Indian Office Report gave 338 on the Great Nemaha Reservation in Eastern Kansas and 82 in Oklahoma. Today there is so much intermarriage with other tribes and whites that accurate estimates of population are virtually impossible.

OTO(E) and MISSOURIA These two tribes have long been associated with and belonged, together with the Iowa, to the Chiwere group of the Siouan linguistic family. Tradition relates that tribes together with the Iowa and Winnebago were anciently one people. The total population of both tribes has been estimated for 1780 as just under 2000. Descendants now live in the vicinity of Red Rock, Oklahoma, and are designated as the 'Otoe-Missouri tribe of Oklahoma'.

KANSA A tribe of the Siouan linguistic stock belonging to the section called Dhegiha. They were also referred to as Kaw. According to tradition they, together with others of the same linguistic group (see above) originally lived on the Ohio River. Later they occupied several villages in succession along the Kansas River. In 1873 they moved to a reservation in Oklahoma adjacent to the Osage. Their population was estimated at 3000 in 1780; today it is about 600. Their present reservation is in Kay County, Oklahoma.

OSAGE The largest and most important tribe of the Dhegiha Siouan linguistic stock. The tribe was traditionally split into two groups, the Great and Little Osage, residing in the region of present-day central Missouri. During the 19th century they were continually at war with several High Plains tribes, particularly the Kiowa and Comanche in whose territory they hunted buffalo. Their population in 1780 has been estimated at 6200, in 1937 it was some 3600. Today the population is widely dispersed although a proportion still live on the Osage reservation in Oklahoma.

QUAPAW A Siouan speaking tribe of the Dhegiha division who originally lived near the mouth of the Arkansas River, although prior to about 1670 they lived on the Ohio River, above its junction with the Wabash. Their population in 1650 was estimated at 2500 but this had fallen to 222 by 1930. Most now live in Ottawa County, Oklahoma, where their population in 1970 was given as some 750.

PAWNEE An important tribe of the Caddoan linguistic stock and related to the Arikara and Wichita. Their name is said to be derived from the native word *pariki*, 'a horn', referring to the peculiar way of dressing the scalp-lock. Traditionally they lived in the region of the Platte and Republican rivers in Nebraska and constituted four groups – Grand Pawnee, Republican Pawnee, Tapage Pawnee and Skidi Pawnee. Their population in 1780 was estimated at 10,000 but a cholera epidemic in 1849 reduced their numbers to 4500. In 1970 they numbered just under 2000, most of whom live in Pawnee County, Oklahoma.

WICHITA The principal tribe of the Caddoan linguistic family who lived on the Canadian River in present-day Oklahoma, an area which the Spanish explorer Coronado described as the province of Quivira when he visited the Wichita in 1541. They continued to live in southwestern Oklahoma until the Civil War, when they moved to Kansas. Their population in 1780 was estimated at 3200. They were allocated a reservation in Caddo County, Oklahoma, in 1867 where most still remain, their population in 1970 being just under 500.

KITSAI A Caddoan tribe whose language was midway between Wichita and Pawnee. Their population was estimated to be 500 in 1690 but a census of 1910 returned a total population of 10, descendants of whom now live in Caddo County, Oklahoma. (The above data and statistics are based on Swanton (1952) and Johnson (1994).)

TABLE I.2: CROW POPULATION CIRCA 1800–1870

Date	Population	Source
1803–4	1000 lodges	Tabeau's narrative
1804	Crows – 'Raven Nation' 350 lodges	Lewis and Clark
1805	300 lodges	Larocque
1810	1000 lodges	Bradley
1825	950 lodges	Curtis
1832	800 lodges	Catlin
1833	800 lodges	Denig
1833 (June)	400 lodges	Maximilian
1850 (circa)	460 lodges	Denig
1850 (July)	400 lodges	Culbertson
1856	450 lodges	Vaughan
1862	350 lodges	Morgan
1871	460 lodges	Pease

Left: Tabulation showing Crow population from the early nineteenth century (from Tabeau's narrative) to 1871.

Table I.1 is a simplification of a very complex picture, particularly in the case of population statistics. For example, if we take the case of the Crow, the historical record varies widely with regard to their numbers; thus Table I.2 shows an apparent large variation in population in less than a decade (1803–10) ranging from 1000 lodges in 1803, 350 in 1804, 300 in 1805 and then, apparently, back to 1000 lodges in 1810!

A major difficulty actually arises from the true identification of the various tribal groups by early observers. In the map below the original of which was drawn under the direction of William Clark in 1805, the 'Paunch' Indians and 'Raven' Indians are considered quite separate tribes; in reality, they were actually Hidatsan who became known to history as the Mountain and

Below: Redrawn extract from an early map originally drawn under the direction of William Clark in 1805. Here, Clark shows the Al-la-ka-we-ah, or Paunch Indians, on the Yellowstone and the Kee-hat-sa, or Raven Indians, to their north. This is almost certainly a reference to groups who were later identified as Mountain and River Crow.

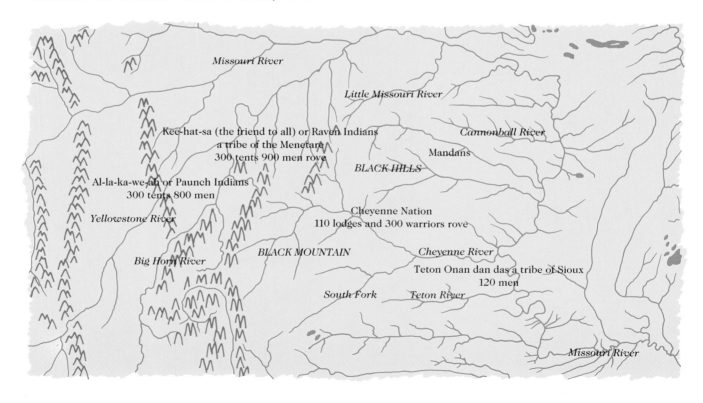

River Crow respectively; so if we add the Paunch numbers (three hundred lodges) to those of the Raven, then up to about 1833 only Larocque stands out as a particularly low estimate. Dramatic changes in population occurred, particularly after two devastating smallpox epidemics in 1780 and 1837, when some tribes – such as the Mandan – were virtually exterminated; within two months, their population dropped from eighteen hundred to less than one hundred and thirty.[23]

FOOTNOTES: CHAPTER ONE

1 See Webb,1931:3-9.

2 Grinnell (1923:vol.I:278-9) gives a particularly good account of hunting antelope by the Cheyenne, who said that there were many antelope pits in existence when they first came to the Plains region. The Cheyenne did not know who had built these pits but they repaired and used them frequently.

3 The largest petroglyph site on the northern Plains, and referred to as 'The writing on stone' site, is located in the Milk River Valley of southern Alberta. More than seven hundred images executed over an extended period have been identified (Keyser,1977:19-22).

4 See Keyser (1987) and Conner and Conner (1971) for more details of this cultural shift and the attempts at the development of a lexicon to interpret more fully the content of these petroglyphs.

5 The dominance of the southern Plains by Apachean groups is discussed in detail by Hyde (1959:4-51). In particular, see his interesting map relating to the Athapascan movements from c. 1500 onwards (p.33). See also Gunnerson (1956) and latterly Gunnerson and Bouc (1984) who support Hyde's thesis.

6 A convenient designation 'Paleo-Indian' refers to the early big game hunters who hunted mammoth and later buffalo on the Great Plains, perhaps as long as 10,000 years ago. A very good discussion relating to prehistoric man on the Great Plains is in Chapter III of Wedel (1961). Wedel was for many years curator of the Division of Archeology of the United States National Museum, Smithsonian Institution, Washington, and had a special interest in the prehistory and human ecology of the North American Great Plains.

7 In support of a Siberian-Northern Europe link, it should be noted that the Athapascans were probably the most numerous migrants to North America and that their language is the only one of the American Indian tongues related to one in the Old World, Sino-Tibetan (see Gunnerson and Bouc (1984:56).

8 At about the same time as the Comanche were pressing on the Padouca from the north, the Caddoan-speaking Pawnee to the east, now also armed with metal weapons and some guns obtained from the French traders, were forcing the Apache from the Plains in present-day Nebraska.

9 The Pawnee themselves were being forced from their traditional homes in the area of present-day Minnesota by well-armed Chippewa from the east.

10 The former hostile relationship between Comanche and Kiowa is reflected in the name used by the Kiowa for them, Gyäiko, or 'Enemies'.

11 As J. C. Ewers has pointed out, three or four generations of Kiowa Indians have relied upon this work for an account of the history of their tribe (Ewers ed.,1979:xii).

12 This medicine lance, or zebat, was shaped and adorned like an arrow; one version of this lance had a detachable wooden point which was inserted on ceremonial occasions but a steel blade was used in battle.

13 It is probably for this reason that the ethnographical collections made from the Kiowa tribe and now residing in museums not infrequently contain objects which are obviously of Crow manufacture. See, for example, Sturtevant and Taylor, Collins ed.,1991:74, which displays a fine beaded Crow shirt, and this volume, page 16.

14 The historic Cheyenne actually consisted of two groups, the Cheyenne proper and the Suhtai, the latter being said to speak a dialect of the Cheyenne language. For many years after crossing the Missouri River, the Suhtai lived in close association with the Cheyenne but were considered quite separate even up to 1832. The Suhtai were gradually absorbed by the Cheyenne but a large number of old-time beliefs and customs were handed down, including the Issïwun – the sacred hat of the Cheyenne – which was believed to have been brought to the Suhtai by their culture hero. (For a detailed discussion of early Cheyenne/Suhtai history, see Grinnell (1923,vol.I:1-46) and Powell (1969:18-41).

Today (1994), the Cheyenne are split into two groups one, the Northern Cheyenne, are on a reservation in Montana while the Southern Cheyenne are settled in Oklahoma.

15 Howard's work (1962) on the Huff site, an important Mandan village dating from about 1500 and situated about eighteen miles southeast of the city of Mandan in North Dakota, suggests that part of the fortification consisted of a sort of cheval-de-frise of sharpened stakes slanting outward.

16 Other influences, however, were imported from the southeast and are of a less tangible nature; the complex societies which developed in the Mississippi Valley and which put great emphasis on the cosmic war which was perceived to take place between Underwater and Sky powers had reverberations as far as the northern Plains, transmitted by the Assiniboin of southern Manitoba. (see Brasser,1987:100-102 for an interesting discussion of this influence.)

17 The Hagan Site near Glendive, Montana, and others at Piney Creek and Big Goose Creek in Wyoming as well as the so-called Cluny Site on the Bow River in southern Alberta, provide archeological data which suggests a sixteenth-century arrival of a ceramic-bearing cultural group who used earth lodges, indicating cultural roots in the Middle Missouri region (see particularly Mulloy,1942:99-102, and Forbis,1977:6-10).

18 It has been pointed out, and as was discussed earlier in this chapter, that the Mandan reflect many Middle Mississippi cultural traits, while the Awatixa showed stronger Woodland influences (see Bowers, 1965:15-22).

19 The relative abundant wealth in horses of the Mountain Crow was commented on by their agent who, in January 1874, reported that the Mountain Crow had between seven and eight thousand horses while the River Crow were 'comparatively poor in horses having twelve to fifteen hundred' (Letters sent Fort Ellis, National Archives).

20 These were the Plains Cree who spoke an Algonquian dialect, deriving their biological and cultural heritage from the Woodland Cree who originally inhabited the Eastern Subarctic Woodland area to the west and south of Hudson Bay. With the westward movement of the Chippewa which led to both economic and population pressures, some of the Cree migrated from the Woodlands 'westward onto the prairies and plains and began to adopt a Plains lifeway' (Sharrock,1976:99).

21 As has been mentioned earlier, horses spread from the Spanish settlements in the Southwest (New Mexico and Texas). However, pedestrian Plains people quickly adopted the new animal for use in hunting buffalo, moving camp and in intertribal warfare. There was, however, a Spanish law – first introduced in 1501 – prohibiting the sale of firearms to Indians and this was, on the whole, strictly observed by the southwestern Spanish colonies. On the other hand, the French and English traders who traveled to the Great Plains region from the east and north, were not forbidden to trade in guns – but they did not have horses.

22 The La Verendrye Journals, covering the period 1735-43, clearly indicate that there were no horses east and north of the Missouri River at that time. One of La Verendrye's sons brought two of the animals from the vicinity of the Black Hills in 1741, traveled via the Mandan villages and to the Canadian trading posts to the northeast. This event seems to have marked the beginning of the trade in horses from the nomadic tribes southwest of the Missouri, through the Mandan, to tribes east and north of them. (See Ewers,1955:5 and Jablow,1950:9.)

23 Smallpox, however, was not the only white disease which devastated some groups: cholera, whooping cough and influenza took their toll, the effects of which are reflected in Table I.1, particularly from 1833 onward. See Denig,1953:57, for a discussion relating to the factors which reduced the Crow population in the middle of the nineteenth century.

SOCIAL
AND CEREMONIAL
ORGANIZATION

—— CHAPTER II ——

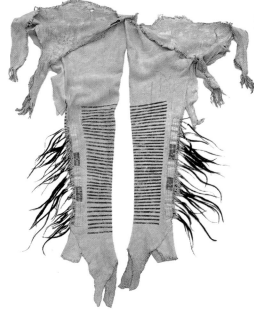

Above: *Quilled and hair-fringed leggings dating from prior to 1850. Regalia of this type distinguished the wearer, proclaiming his achievements and tribal standing.*

Left: *A fine beaded and hair-fringed shirt, collected from the Omaha by La Flesche in 1898. The designs refer to images seen by the wearer in his vision.*

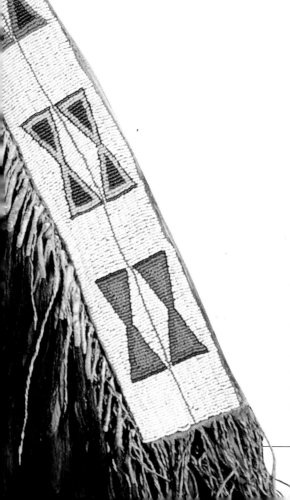

The Plains Tribes and Democracy

'Is the democratic element strongly implanted? Very. The whole is a pure democracy . . .' (Denig,1930:445)[1]

As Denig has made clear, Plains society was highly democratic and there were no hereditary classes as such. Nevertheless, in common with the rest of mankind, the offspring of more distinguished families obviously had considerable advantages although orphans or captives were not excluded in the quest for distinction and, often by seeking supernatural favor or by deep involvement in tribal ceremonialism, some of these individuals gained high status. For example, among the Mandan, if a young man consulted his elders on important matters he was considered wise and the older people would say, 'He will become eminent because he endeavors to regulate his behavior along the line laid down by the sacred things long ago' (Bowers, 1950:341).[2]

While great dependence on the buffalo characterized the Plains Indian lifestyle, the *social* organization of the semi-sedentary Prairie tribes differed considerably from that of the nomadic tribes of the high plains, and even within these two broad distinctions there was considerable variation. Typical, however, in the case of the village tribes, were settlements which consisted of tightly grouped clusters of earth lodges often within a palisade surrounded by a dry moat. While each village was considered a permanent and separate economic, politically independent social unit, the villages were not entirely independent. In the case of the Mandan, for example, a cedar pole which stood in the center of the village was considered to be a symbol of tribal unity; however, the so-called turtle drums ceremonially used in the *O-kee-pa* and which were considered to be the most sacred objects of the tribe were actually held by the Nuptadi Mandan and the other villages were obliged to borrow them for any ceremonial purpose. In this respect it can be said that the Mandan 'considered the turtle drums a symbol of tribal unity' (ibid.:36).

Thus, the collective villages – and this extends to the Pawnee, Omaha, Hidatsa, Arikara and other semi-sedentary tribes of the Upper Missouri – were considered a 'tribe' since they not only had common ceremonial and social organizations with clans extending through all the villages, but the entire tribal population was generally viewed as 'relatives' and was treated as such. The complexity of tribal kinship varied considerably. Thus, in the case of the Chaui Pawnee, the tribe, in the sense of a politically autonomous unit, coincided with the residents of a *single* village, while in the case of the related Skidi Pawnee who, like the Mandan at one period early in their history occupied some thirteen villages, there was only a loose unity. Indeed, the chiefs could not prevent inter-village disputes any more than they could prevent the removal of 'part of a village to form a separate village' (Wood,1967:13).

In contrast to the earth lodge village people, the purely nomadic groups tended only to come together as a tribe during the spring and summer for the great ceremonials of the Sundance, tribal buffalo hunts and for the annual reorganization of the military societies. During the winter, they were split up into smaller units so that the essential resources – wood, and feed for horses – were not exhausted in one particular area. It is said that in the early nineteenth century the Cheyenne decided to stay together during the winter season; within a few weeks, wood, forage, even the bark of trees was exhausted, and all nearly died as a consequence. Thus economic factors dictated lifestyle and the complex *tribal* activities and ceremonials only took place in the spring and summer months.

The components of a typical large camp of the nomadic tribes, such as would have come together at this time and perhaps numbered some one hundred to two hundred tipis, was enumerated by the fur trader Denig for the Assiniboin:

Above: *Mandan Buffalo Society leader, painted by Karl Bodmer on the Upper Missouri in 1834. Of the six age-graded societies among the Mandan, that of the Buffalo Bull's was the most prestigious. This man wears the distinguishing buffalo head mask of the society but the wolf tails at his heels probably refer to more personal feats of arms.*

1. Leading chief
2. Other chiefs
3. Chief of the soldiers
4. Cook of the soldiers' lodge
5. Soldiers
6. Elderly men
7. Haranguer
8. Master of the Park
9. Warriors and hunters
10. Partisans[3]
11. Doctors and conjurors
12. Very old men
13. Young women
14. Old women
15. Middle-aged women
16. Boys and girls
17. Very small children
(Hewitt ed. 1930: 441.)

Right: *Péhriska-Rúhpa, or Two Ravens, a Minnetaree leader. Portrait by Karl Bodmer at Fort Clark, 1834. Péhriska-Rúhpa, who was a close friend of the Mandan chief Mató-tópe, wears a superb quilled shirt and carries an elaborately decorated buffalo robe, while his necklace is of grizzly bear claws. Such valuable regalia identified men of distinction and high standing.*

Plains Indian Military and Social Societies

Denig's mention of the 'soldiers' lodge' among the Assiniboin is obviously a reference to one of many societies or fraternities of a ceremonial or military character which were a feature of the Plains Indians' social organization. The fundamentals of such societies almost certainly developed among the Missouri River tribes, where – in particular but not exclusively – women's societies were also found. Several of these societies were age-graded, children being encouraged to join and, on advice from their parents, purchased additional rights and associated society regalia from older members. Thus they progressed as they qualified by age.

It has been reported that the Hidatsa – and this probably extends at least to the linguistically related Mandan – placed great importance on relative age in determining behavior between individuals and that there was a recognizable tendency to arrange the entire male and female population into a series of groupings which were based on age. Thus, the age-graded military societies were but a reflection of a particular tribal ethos, elements of which extended to the nomadic Blackfeet, Arapaho and Gros Ventre, who also had a definite system of age societies. The functions of such societies were extensive, while at the personal level it gave the individual a club where he might

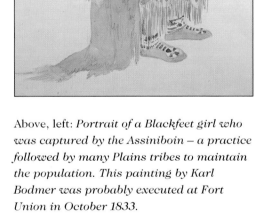

socialize with his fellows. There was also the possibility of more important public duties such as organizing the tribe when traveling or in the ceremonials and, perhaps most importantly, policing the buffalo hunts.

This type of government extended throughout the Plains. It developed into a camp organization which had, as its main goal, the supervision and conservation and control of the tribe when pursuing buffalo; it even extended to the Missouri River tribes who normally lived in earth lodges and cultivated corn. Thus, when they left their villages to hunt buffalo, the soldier-band police took control, the tipi was used and a camp circle formed – adopting all those traits so typical of their purely nomadic cousins, underlining the fact that the Plains Indian lifeway pivoted firmly on economic factors to which the buffalo was of paramount importance.

While the Assiniboin, Lakota, Cheyenne, Pawnee, Arikara and Crow did not emphasize age-grading, the functions of their societies were similar. Typical of such societies were the Lumpwoods and Foxes of the Crow who always attempted to strike the first blow against the enemy; the leaders who carried specially shaped staffs were expected to dismount in the face of the enemy, plant their emblems of office in the ground and make a stand even if all the other members were fleeing. This

Above, left: Portrait of a Blackfeet girl who was captured by the Assiniboin – a practice followed by many Plains tribes to maintain the population. This painting by Karl Bodmer was probably executed at Fort Union in October 1833.

Above: A young Piegan woman, portrait by Karl Bodmer at Fort McKenzie on the Upper Missouri in August 1833. She wears a typical Blackfeet style skin dress and leggings and moccasins embellished with blue and white trade beads.

Right: A blue and red cloth banner which went over the head and hung down the back of the wearer. Almost 7½ft (2.3m) in length, it is decorated with fine porcupine quilled rosettes, rawhide bands wrapped with quills and embellished with turkey feather tips. Mandan or Minnetaree in origin, it was collected by Friedrich Köhler prior to 1846.

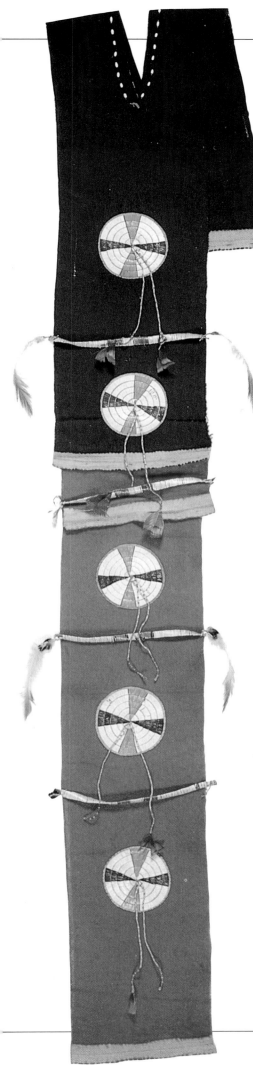

'no retreat' ethos extended to several other Plains tribes and not only individuals but several members of the society might be expected to make a stand. Thus, the *Kangi'yuha*, or Crow Owners of the Lakota, when attacking an enemy, were required to thrust their lances into the ground 'and not leave the spot unless released by some of their party pulling up the lances'[4] (Wissler, 1912:24).

The *women's* societies among the Hidatsa and Mandan were age-graded although younger women were sometimes co-opted by some societies as singers or pipe carriers. Generally, the societies for younger women were concerned almost exclusively with war, thus members of the Skunk and Enemy societies danced for and received presents from the men who returned from a successful war expedition and they played an important part in victory parades. The Goose Society, whose members were usually between the ages of thirty and forty on the other hand, was associated with agriculture and was concerned with rites for ensuring good crops.[5] The most important meetings of the Goose Society were held in the spring when the first water birds arrived from the south and a feast was prepared and prayers offered for good crops. It heralded the first arrival of the water birds who, it was believed, brought the corn spirits back with them and proclaimed the end of winter. When droughts threatened, appeals were made to the sacred corn bundle owners and members of the Goose Society would perform rituals which, if the drought were prolonged, involved extending invitations to those who had rain ceremonial rights. It is said that on one occasion in the 1860s the rainmaker rituals failed even though several rainmakers were consulted. Help was sought from Broken Ax, a Mandan, who was noted for his numerous performances of the *O-kee-pa*; Broken Ax was successful and the rains came, 'penetrating the soil to the depth of a hand's width' (Bowers, 1965:203).

The place of not only mythology but the more practical side of agriculture in the life of the village tribes was emphasized further by the ceremonial offerings of the Goose Society during the fall migration of the water birds. It was believed that, as they traveled south, the geese and other water birds 'took the spirits of the corn and other garden crops with them to the Old-Woman-Who-Never-Dies who spent the winter months in a large earth lodge on an island near the mouth of the Mississippi River' (ibid.:204).

The important role of the buffalo in the life of the tribe was not forgotten, ceremonials for its return to the villages during the winter being performed by the highest of the organized age-grade women's societies, namely the White Buffalo Cow Society. Of Mandan origin and illustrated by Karl Bodmer in 1834, the women wore headdresses of the albino buffalo in a hussar fashion and surmounted by feathers; they danced in imitation of buffalo walking through snow, raising each foot alternately higher than the other and waddling from side to side.

The Political Organization of the Teton Sioux (Lakota)

The political and social organization of the nomadic tribes was, in earlier years, an evolving and dynamic process as they adapted from sedentarianism to nomadism. Typical is that of the Teton divisions of the Sioux.

Teton derives from the Sioux word *Tintatonwan*, or 'prairie village', and when they encountered Lewis and Clark in 1804 they were divided into four separate tribes on both sides of the Missouri (see below). To the south were the 'Tetons of the Burnt Woods', or Brulés, who occupied the territory between the mouths of the Bad and White rivers; north of the Brulé were the 'Tetons Okandandas', or Oglalas. Then there were the 'Tetons Minnekineazzo', the Miniconjou, and finally there were the 'Tetons Saone' who lived between the mouth of Beaver Creek and the Grand River in present-day southern North Dakota (this latter tribe's hunting grounds were, at this time, predominantly east of the Missouri).[6]

In turn, each of these four tribes was sub-divided into a number of smaller units called *tiyospaye*, or 'bands', which, in order to survive, were the actual working units of the Teton Sioux for most of the year. By about 1830 the Saone had split further to give seven divisions of the Plains Sioux which established the general pattern of organization well into the Reservation

Below: *The Teton Sioux world, 1804–25. This map shows the approximate location of the various Teton groups after they had migrated from the east and crossed the James River, retreating from the Chippewa who had been supplied with guns by the French. In 1804–5 Lewis and Clark traveled through this region and encountered most of these groups, although several were further east at that time. As they migrated west the Tetons met the sedentary tribes of the Missouri region from whom certain social and ceremonial practices may have been adopted. Note the various white trading posts established even as early as the 1820s. (Based on Bray, 1982.)*

—— *Sioux territory in 1804.*

—— *Boundaries of Sioux tribal sub-divisions*

⛺ *Sites of Sioux camps*

◗ *Earth lodge villages of farming tribes*

■ *Trading posts*

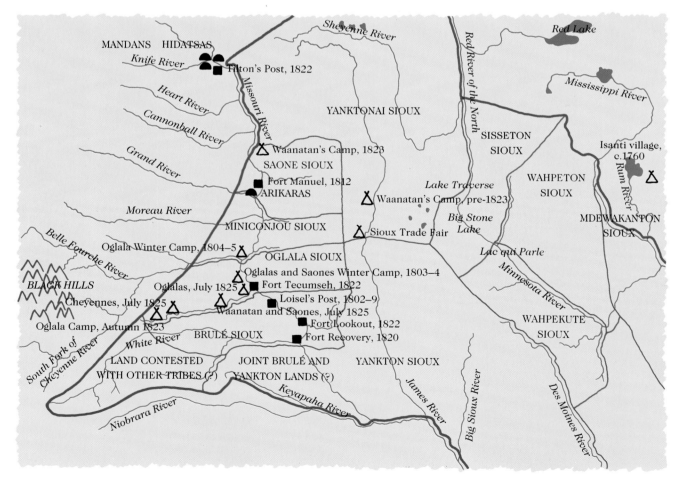

period. The complexity of the structure of the Sioux nation is illustrated in the map on page 38, being based in part on observations made by a traveler through their territory in 1850 (Culbertson, McDermott ed., 1952:135–6).

The individual bands were led by chiefs called *itancan* who, in the summer, came together to form a tribal council. One chief, usually of the most populous or influential band, was recognized as the tribal head-chief, eligible to speak first in council and to represent the tribe at inter-tribal convocations. The larger bands, led by ambitious chiefs, invariably had designs on the tribal leadership, while smaller camps tended to make political alliances with one or other of the bigger bands which might then absorb them. Strong chiefs would attract to their bands groups from other *tiyospaye* but upon their decline they would be abandoned again. So chiefs' fortunes fluctuated and the rivalry which existed between chiefs and bands sometimes led to quarrels which tended to undermine the unity of the tribe. Nevertheless, there were forces which at various times did unify the different bands into a tribal whole.[7] In the case of the Oglala, for example (and this is typical of many nomadic Plains tribes), the tribe's political life commenced at the beginning of the summer when the various bands came together in one encampment. Here, the tipis were erected in a

Above: Shonka, *or Dog, chief of the Bad Arrow Points Band of the Teton Sioux. Painted by George Catlin on the Upper Missouri in 1832, Shonka was described by Catlin as an ill-natured and surly man.*

Below: *A fine quilled and beaded bag of soft buckskin, probably Sioux, dating from the last quarter of the nineteenth century and used by the nomadic tribes for keeping and transporting clothing.*

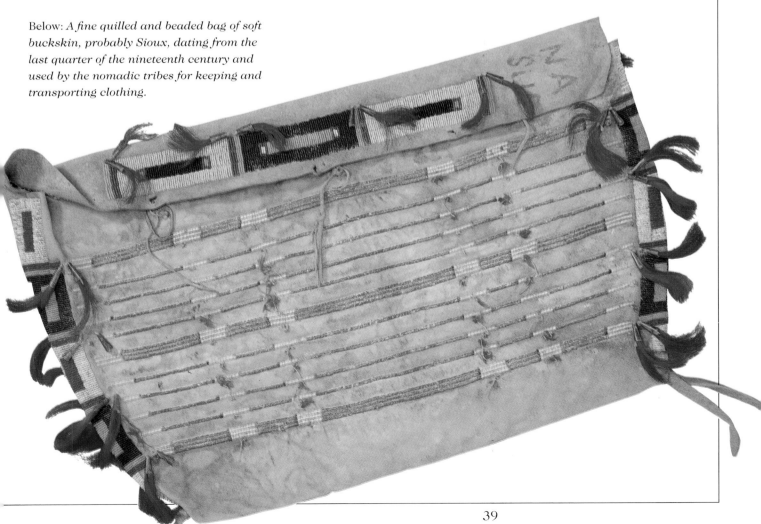

great circle – the *cangleshka wakan*, or 'Sacred Hoop' – with an opening, the *tiyopa*, 'door', facing east. At the center of the great circle stood the council lodge, a meeting-place for chiefs and head-warriors. Each of the bands was assigned a particular place in the circle, the most honored being that opposite the entrance which corresponded to the seating within the tipi (*catku*, 'seat of honor'). This was generally occupied by the band led by the tribal head-chief, while the band considered that year to be made up of the bravest warriors was assigned a position at the entrance, fit to protect the *cangleshka wakan* from enemies.

The political strength of the tribe derived from a group of band chiefs referred to as the *Naca Ominicia*, or 'Chiefs Society'.[8] The qualifications for membership of the society were varied and extensive; as one authority observed, 'A Naca might be a former headman of one of the bands, a leading shaman of proven integrity and magnetism, or a hunter or warrior whose outstanding career had brought him renown. Then, of course, the elders, recognized for their qualities of bravery and fortitude, wisdom and generosity, were also members of the group' (Hassrick,1964:25). In turn, the Chiefs Society appointed from among its members several of the most outstanding leaders to act as spokesmen, who activated the policies of the larger council. These were referred to as *Wicasa Itancan*, 'Chief Man', being generally regarded as the real government of the tribe.

This pattern was replicated in the other Sioux divisions but there were variations in the number of Chief Men; among the Oglala it was seven, while among the Brulé it was ten. One of the most important duties of the Chief Men in all the divisions was the appointment of the *Wakincuzas*, or 'Pipe Owners', their badge of office being a specially designed and embellished long pouch or bag with flaps at the extremities together with a long-stemmed pipe; these were presented at the time of appointment.

Generally four in number, the pipe owners' responsibilities were extensive. They assigned the various bands their locations within the camp circle; organized the periodic moves necessitated by the demands of a large camp for fresh pasture and clean water; decided on the times for the buffalo hunts and chose the head-soldiers, the *akicita itancan*, who arranged policing of the camp and were in charge of the buffalo hunt. One very important ordained responsibility was in the 'Making of Brothers' or 'Peace Ceremony'[9] (ibid.:27).

Of equal importance, perhaps more so among the southern branch of the Oglala, were the *Ongloge Un*, or 'shirt wearers', four councillors who, upon investment of office, were given 'a special form of hair-fringed shirt' (Wissler,1912:7). These shirts were spoken of as being 'owned by the tribe' and such regalia was exclusive to these men. During his investiture, the recipient was lectured as to his responsibilities of office: 'Though you now wear the shirt, be a big-hearted man . . . This shirt here

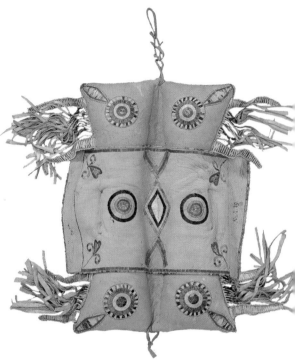

Above: *A beautifully quilled man's pad saddle collected by L.A. Schoch prior to 1837, and now in Bern. Although labeled as Sioux this may well be from the Red River region and of Metis manufacture, such goods being produced for intertribal trade. This complex trade pattern across the Plains and beyond led to a wide distribution of items from their original source, causing difficulties with tribal identification.*

Above: *The intense ceremonialism which characterized Plains Indian society is nowhere better illustrated than in this depiction of the Medicine Pipe-stem dance of the Blackfeet produced by Paul Kane, artist of the Canadian scene, in 1846. The pipe-stems, elaborately embellished with eagle feathers, ermine and porcupine quills, were said to have been copied from one that was given to the tribe as a token of friendship by the thunder powers.*

means that you have been chosen as a big-heart; you are always to help your friends. These rules are hard to comply with, but we have given you this shirt' (ibid.:40). There was apparently some degree of inheritance in the office of shirt wearer since a devoted father 'endeavored to bestow this high honor upon his son' (Hassrick,1964:27). Sons of obscure parents were not, however, excluded if they displayed outstanding leadership qualities. Crazy Horse, for example, whose father was a comparatively obscure shaman, was elected to the office of shirt wearer well before his thirtieth birthday. The main distinguishing feature of all these shirts was the hair-lock fringe on the sleeves; these fringes were said to represent the people of the tribe for whom the shirt wearers were responsible 'for they were the owners of the tribe' (ibid.:26).

Thus, under the supervision of the *Wakincuzas/Ongloge Un*, the head-soldiers and their chosen *akicita* 'soldiers' patroled the camp circle with authority to intervene in any internal disputes and, as necessary, resolve them with summary justice. Likewise when hunting they policed the hunters, ensuring that no over-eager group made a premature foray among the buffalo and so dispersed them. Here too they were 'entrusted with punitive powers against serious offenders, who might expect their property destroyed, their lodges torn up, their horses killed, and a sound whipping for themselves into the bargain' (Bray, Taylor ed.,1982:21).

While the above discussion relates specifically to the Teton Sioux, studies of other tribes indicate that with some local variations (see below) the general pattern extended to both the nomadic and semi-sedentary groups, particularly when the latter were on tribal buffalo hunts into the Plains grasslands; it was an ordered scheme evolved and developed by the nomadic tribes and because of its practical value in the Plains environment was largely adopted by others, both village or Plateau, when they used tipis.

Ceremonial Organization of the Cheyenne: the Assembly and Formation of the Cheyenne Sun-dance Camp Circle

The anthropologist George Dorsey, who spent many years studying the Cheyenne, reported on the organization of their camp circle when the various bands came together for the annual Sun-dance at the turn of the nineteenth century. As with the Sioux, a warrior society was used in the organization and the entrance to the camp circle pointed east; however, there was no 'chief', his place being taken by the one who had vowed to organize and perform the dance, designated as the Pledger and called the 'Lodge-maker'. His second in rank was his wife, while the Chief Priest of the ceremony, referred to as the one who 'Shows How', was selected by members of the Lodge-maker's own society. Qualification for this honor was that he must previously have been a Pledger of the ceremony and able to fast four days, the duration of the Sun-dance.

Dorsey observed that the first to arrive was a band consisting mainly of Dog-men, warriors who pitched their tipis on the right bank of the river which had been selected as the site of the ceremonial and when other bands arrived they simply erected their tipis nearby. The situation changed, however, on the arrival of the Pledger and his band, who by use of members of his own warrior society, began to organize the camp circle. First, their own tipis were laid out in the proper place in the circle and after the 'Warrior's tipi' had been selected, the rest of the bands took their designated positions. A good deal of time was taken up by the formation of the camp circle and several more bands would arrive over the following two days, at the end of which the camp circle would have been more than a mile in diameter, with an open space or entrance on the eastern side probably a quarter of a mile wide. The Cheyenne observed strict rules and symbolism in the formation of the camp circle, Dorsey reporting that it was always to be located on the south bank of a river, that it was symbolic of the 'circle of stars overhead, which is often called the camp-circle', and further it was likened to a big tipi with its entrance facing east, and bearing the same name as the door of the tipi (Dorsey,1905:62).[10]

Above: *A fine Crow or Hidatsa crupper collected by Friedrich Köhler prior to 1846. Made of heavy rawhide and soft bucksin, it is elaborately decorated with red trade cloth and blue and white pony beads. As the Plains tribes adapted to equestrian nomadism they adopted styles of horsegear much of which had been introduced in the southwest by the Spaniards. The end product, however, was generally distinctively Indian.*

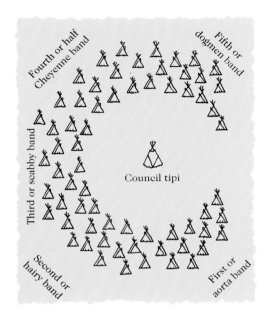

Above: *The Cheyenne camp circle (after George A. Dorsey). The entrance was always to the east and each division occupied a distinct position; facing the entrance were the Suta-yo, among the most ancient and honored of Cheyenne bands.*

Below: *The figures given here are only approximate and varied considerably with time. Not shown is the distinction between the River and Mountain Crow, the latter having a horse: person ratio of 4:1.*

The camp circle conformed to the various divisions among the Cheyenne and, as with the Sioux, honored positions were at and facing the entrance (see left).

Trade Patterns and the Horse in Plains Indian Life

The occupation of Plains men contrasted markedly with that of the women although there were some notable exceptions, such as the role of the *Berdêches*,[11] or the occasional woman who took on a warrior's role.[12]

Of prime importance was the man's obligation as a provider, protector and hunter, much, particularly in the case of the purely nomadic tribes, depending on the wealth in horses. While horses were obtained by raiding enemies' camps, or by barter, access was via one of the extensive trade routes which extended from the James River in present-day South Dakota, to the Plateau and on to the Northwest Coast (see the map on page 45).

The horse-to-person ratio varied considerably from tribe to tribe. (Table II.1 gives an indication of the distribution across the Plains and Plateau during the nineteenth century.) As can be seen for the semi-sedentary tribes such as the Mandan, Hidatsa, Arikara and Omaha[13] it was probably less than 0.4:1 in contrast to the horse-rich Kiowa and Comanche with more than 3:1 while for the Blackfeet and Crow it varied between 1:1 and 2:1.[14] Note the estimate for the Flathead, Nez Perce and Pend d'Oreilles (Plateau) in 1857 – an astounding ratio of 10:1.

A complex trade pattern extended across the Plains giving access to the horse-rich Plateau tribes; this lively trade was observed at the Hidatsa villages on the Missouri by the fur trader Charles Mackenzie. Here, in the spring of 1805, he witnessed the spectacular arrival – in all their finery – of 'three

	Tribe	Date	Lodges	Population	Horses	Horse: lodge ratio	Horse: person ratio
Northern Plains	Piegan	1860	460	3700	3980	8.6	1.1
	Blood	1860	150	1200	1200	8.0	1.0
	North Blackfeet	1860	300	2400	2400	8.0	1.0
Central Plains	Oglala/Brulé	1871	600(e)	5000	2000	3.3	0.4
	Hunkpapa/Miniconjou	1878	360(e)	2900	3500	9.7	1.2
	Cheyenne (Black Kettle's camp)	1868	51	400(e)	700	13.7	0.6
	Crow	1871	460	4000(e)	9500	8.7	2.4
	Omaha	1871	120(e)	984	650	5.4	0.7
	Hidatsa	1833	170(e)	1500	300	1.8	0.2
	Arikara	1871	180(e)	1650	350	1.9	0.2
Southern Plains	Comanche	1869	300(e)	2538	7614	25	3.0
	Pawnee	1871	260(e)	2364	1050	4	0.4
	Apache (at Fort Sill)	1871	42(e)	378	1250	30	3.3
Plateau	Umatilla/Walla/Cayuse	1871	106(e)	850	10,000	94	11.8
	Nez Perce	1871	310(e)	2807	9000	29	3.2
	Northern Shoshone	1872–6	170(e)	1500	3000	17.6	2.0

TABLE II.1: DISTRIBUTION OF HORSES ACROSS PLAINS AND PLATEAU, SECOND HALF OF THE NINETEENTH CENTURY

Estimated (e) figures using 8–9 per lodge. (Based on Ewers, 1955; and Taylor, 1981.)

TABLE II.2: HORSE VALUES

Tribe	Date	Item	Number of horses
Mandan	1830	Eagle feathered headdress	1–2
Assiniboin	1850	Quilled shirt and leggings trimmed with hair	1
Assiniboin	1850	War-eagle feather cap	2
Assiniboin	1850	Beaded scarlet blanket	1
Assiniboin	1850	Quilled shirt and leggings trimmed with ermine skins	2
Upper Missouri tribes	1850	Fifteen eagle feathers	1
Crow	1850	Ten weasel skins	1
Crow	1850	One hundred elk teeth	1
Crow	1850	Woman's dress of bighorn decorated with 300 elk teeth	3 (approx.)
Crow	1850	Carved pipe bowl	1 packhorse
Kiowa	1870	Muzzle loading gun	1
Blackfeet	1870	Medicine pipes	9+
Blackfeet	1880	Catlinite carved blackened pipe bowl with ash stem	1

Horse Values: In the middle of the nineteenth century one buffalo robe was valued at about $3. A horse at 10 robes each or $30. Values, however, varied with time. In the 1870s, for example, the Blackfeet valued a horse at 8 robes. (The above table is based on Denning, 1930; Kurz, 1937; and Ewers, 1955.)

hundred tents of Crow Indians' who were on a trading expedition to the Hidatsa. After smoking the pipe of friendship, the Hidatsa laid before the Crow presents 'consisting of two hundred guns, with one hundred rounds of ammunition for each, a hundred bushels of Indian corn . . . kettles, axes . . . etc'. In return, the Crow gave 'two hundred and fifty horses, large parcels of buffaloes, robes, leather leggins, shirts, &c.'. Mackenzie then explained that the 'Mandane villages exchanged similar civilities with the same tribe' (Mackenzie, in Masson,- 1889:346). In addition to this 'trading on the pipe', there was, of course, individual trading, much of which was conducted by the women in a country-fair type atmosphere.

Above: *While horse values varied considerably, the number of horses owned was a good index to the quality of lifestyle of a Plains family.*

Below: *A Crow woman's saddle and stirrups collected by Hoffman at the Crow Agency, Montana, in the 1890s. These distinctive saddles, with the high pommel and cantle decorated with flaps of red cloth and beads, were part of the ceremonial regalia of the wives of notable men.*

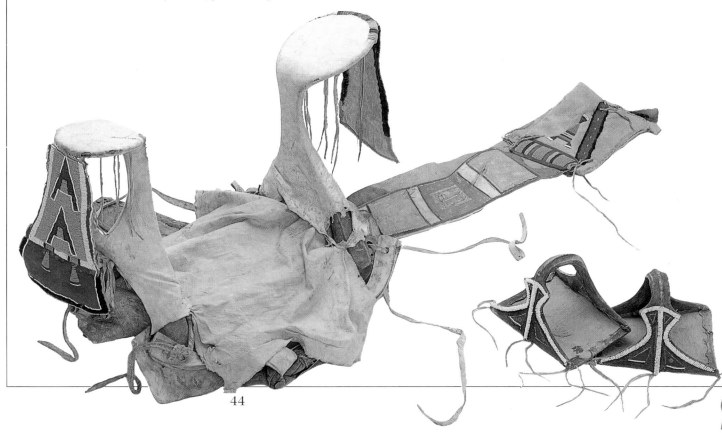

Below: *Intertribal trade networks across the Great Plains and beyond. Many of these routes were established hundreds of years before the arrival of the white man. Greatly prized trade goods, such as shells, turquoise and obsidian, were transported hundreds, sometimes thousands, of miles from their origins. On the central and northern Plains a major focus was at the earth lodge villages on the Missouri River; here, the semi-sedentary Mandan, Hidatsa and Arikara all acted as intermediaries between the horticulturalists to the east and the nomadic hunters to the west. (Redrawn map after Swagerty, 1988.)*

- Primary or major trade centers
- Significant permanent secondary centers
- Other permanent secondary centers
- Significant intermediary secondary centers
- Tertiary centers

Similar trade patterns were associated with the Cheyenne who traveled from the southwest up to the Arikara just south of the Mandan (Jablow,1950:49). This trade for horses from the western tribes for European goods from sources to the east was fiercely contested. Thus, at one time the Cheyenne attempted to forge links with the Hidatsa but the strong family ties which existed between the Crow and Hidatsa made this virtually impossible and they had to content themselves with the Arikara trade[15] (Taylor,1981:17).

The goods moved rapidly from east to west; thus when the Crow returned to the Yellowstone region they were in turn visited by the Shoshone and the more western bands of the Crow (the Mountain Crow). The European goods which they had obtained at the Missouri villages were then exchanged for horses, mules, bridles and blankets, the latter two being of Spanish or southwestern origin. The western tribes were clearly in almost constant contact with the Plateau tribes such as the Nez Perce, Coeur d'Alêne, Cayuse and, to the south, the Bannock and Ute. The Plateau people were particularly rich in horses and also had contacts with the Spanish settlements to the south. This complex trade pattern is summarized in the map (below).[16] (Table II.2 indicates horse values.)

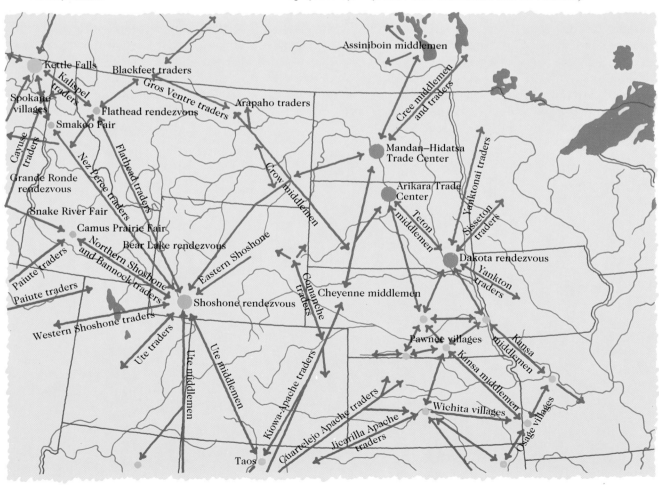

The Development of the Tipi

The mobility of the nomadic tribes not only depended upon a good supply of horses but also on an easily transportable dwelling – the tipi. How the tipi developed is not clear but recent researches suggest that it is a modification of the circumboreal council lodge (the 'wigwam') and had its origin in the northeastern boreal forests (Brasser,1982:309).[17]

An early style of tipi was recorded in use near the Texas Panhandle as early as 1541, when Coronado met nomadic pedestrian Indians who lived in dwellings made of poles covered with dressed buffalo skins which they dismantled and transported using large dogs. In 1599, Don Juan de Onate described a camp of about fifty skin tents in present-day northern Oklahoma and made an apparent reference to smoke ears, the most distinctive feature of the tipi (Wedel, 1959:59; and Brasser, 1982:309,312).

By 1820, the dwelling had evolved to provide a comfortable and well-ventilated abode, its shape a tilted cone, the back being steeper than the front to brace it against the prevailing west winds. The entrance, generally an oval opening with a flap, always faced east toward the rising sun. The cover was semicircular and, typically, in the mid-nineteenth century, comprised twelve or more cow buffalo hides, trimmed and sewn together with sinew and pulled around the frame like a mantle. The straight edges of the cover met at the front and were laced together with wooden pins; pegs, stones, or sod held down the lower edge. Stones were not transported when a camp moved on, hence the presence of so-called tipi rings still to be seen on remoter parts of the Plains.

Above: *Kiowa-Apache tipis on the southern Plains, circa 1870. The earliest descriptions of the true tipi come from the chroniclers of Coronado's expedition who traveled through the southern Plains region in the sixteenth century. Such tipis were smaller than those shown here, since transportation was by means of dogs.*

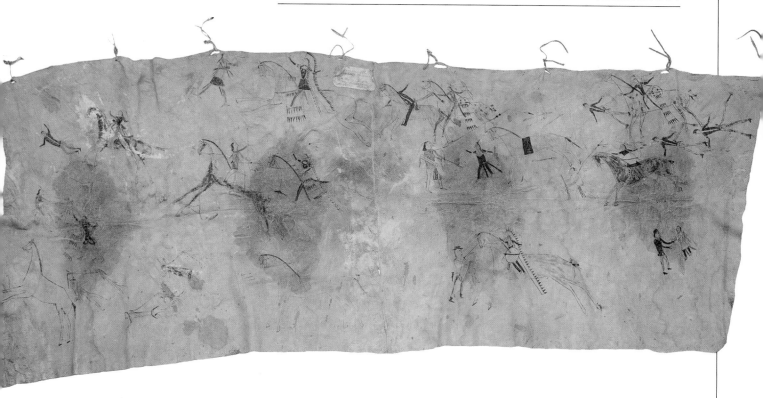

Above: A Cheyenne – or possibly Sioux – tipi liner embellished with the owner's war exploits. Liners were tied to the inside of the tipi poles, extending 5–6ft (1.5–2m) above the ground, protecting the interior and reducing draughts. During winter the space between the tipi cover and liner could be stuffed with grass insulation.

Left: A Cheyenne hide tipi camp, circa 1870. Such dwellings were ideally suited to the Plains environment; they could easily withstand the high winds which often swept across the Plains, and during the summer they were cool and in winter warm – even with the smallest of fires burning at their center.

Long poles of pine or cedar, eighteen to twenty altogether, provided the framework, three or four of them being used in the foundation and tied about 5ft (1.5m) from the top, the lower ends being spread out. Other poles were stacked into the crotches. The cover was then folded on to the last framework pole and securely tied about 5ft from the top. This 'lifting pole' was set in place at the rear (west), then the cover pulled around the conical framework to overlap at the center on the east side, where it was laced together with wooden pins passing horizontally through holes. Finally, wooden pegs were passed through holes or buckskin loops near the lower edge of the cover.

A mid-nineteenth-century buffalo hide tipi weighed from '90 to 105 pounds' (Ewers,1955:133) and when pitched it was about 19–21ft (6–6.5m) in diameter and accommodated some eight to ten people of the same family. It required the combined effort of two women to lift the cover on to a horse or travois for transportation; the poles were divided into equal bundles and tied to the sides of pack-horses by use of hide ropes which passed through holes burned near the upper ends of the poles. The total load of a Blackfeet buffalo hide lodge has been estimated at '560–585 pounds' (254–265kg) and 'it required three horses to transport' it (ibid.:134).

The hide tipi seldom lasted more than two years. It was considered the property of women and when a tipi had to be renewed, several women worked together in cutting and sewing the dressed hides. A number were painted (typically 20 per cent) with war exploits or references to sacred powers (see Chapter III).

The interior of the tipi was always furnished with an inner lining – frequently painted with war or other exploits – which

47

extended 5–6½ft (1.5–2m) from the ground and was tied to the poles which gave protection from drafts and raindrops. Tipi furnishings consisted primarily of willow backrests supported on tripods which could be used as beds when further supported and covered with buffalo robes. At the center was a small fireplace for cooking and heating.

The use of a three- or four-pole foundation gave a distinctive appearance to the protruding poles. Those with three poles spread out 'like a fan' while the four pole base tended to 'group the poles on the sides and looks somewhat square at the top' (Laubin,1957:121–2). The latter was mainly used on the northwestern Plains close to the mountains where the winds were not as strong but there were notable exceptions; for example, the Comanche were four-pole people surrounded by tribes such as the Kiowa, Apache and Southern Cheyenne, who used three poles. Smaller versions of these tipis were used for hunting trips, particularly by the semi-sedentary tribes who traditionally lived in the earth lodge.

The Travois

Tipi covers were transported on a pack-horse or a travois which consisted of two long poles whose front tips converged to be attached to the horse's shoulders while the butt-ends dragged along the ground. Approximately midway was a frame either of an oval, netted style or of ladder form, on to which the load was tied. Considerable effort was required to move a set of some

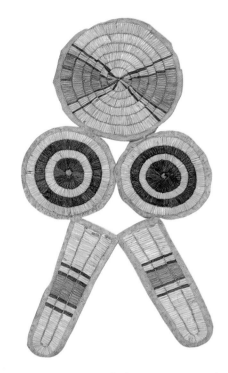

Above: *Arapaho quilled ornaments used on the back rest of the tipi owner. Such ornaments were almost certainly symbolic of the buffalo's brain, eyes and ears.*

Below: *Band of Teton Sioux (Lakota) moving camp. Painting by George Catlin, 1837–9. It shows the use of both horse and dog travois, as well as excessive loading.*

nineteen poles, each of which was 18–20ft (5.5–6m) long and weighed about 20lb (9kg). As Ewers points out, 'The dragging ends of the poles provided considerable friction in travelling over rough country, limiting the number of poles each horse could transport to 5 or 6 each side, or a total of 10 or 12. Consequently it required two horses to transport the poles of the average lodge' (Ewers,1955:133).

The travois was originally used with dogs by the pedestrian nomads and the dog travois continued in use among the semi-sedentary tribes to help women carry firewood, it being estimated that fifteen or twenty dogs could transport enough wood to last a family a month. While men might take travois dogs on hunting or war parties, it was the women who raised and trained them and used them the most, the dogs being selected for their gentleness (Gilman and Schneider,1987:54–5).

The Earth Lodge

As has already been mentioned, those tribes who lived a semi-sedentary life on the Missouri River, such as the Mandan, Hidatsa and Arikara on the Middle Missouri and the Omaha, Pawnee, Ponca, Kansa and Oto to their south, used a dome shaped structure called an earth lodge. Such dwellings were predated by long rectangular structures which, probably because of climatic changes or the progressive moves north (Stewart,1974:292), evolved into the circular type earth lodge 'about AD 1600' (Wood, 1967:160). During the historic period –

Above: *A Cheyenne dog travois. The addition of a cage arrangement, as shown here made of willow saplings, was to carry puppies or protect small children.*

Below: *A Cheyenne horse travois. These were generally owned and made by women, and were constructed entirely of wood which was lashed together with rawhide.*

from about 1797 onward – the ceremonial lodge associated with the *O-kee-pa* ritual of the Mandan had a flat front reminiscent of the earlier archaic style (ibid.:166). Although there were some variations, the general form of the earth lodge may best be illustrated by the Hidatsa type.

To begin with, ten to fifteen stout posts were set in the ground; these were about 5¾ft (1.8m) high and spaced some 10ft (3m) apart in a circle, so defining the floor area of the lodge. Solid beams were laid on the tops of these posts extending from one upright to the next. In the center of this circle four massive posts were set in the ground each rising to a height of 11–16ft (3.4–5m) and in a square of approximately 16ft (5m), their tops then connected with four heavy beams laid horizontally. Long, slender poles were then laid from the external beams to the heavier four central beams, each at an angle of about 30° to the horizontal. This framework was covered with successive layers of willow branches, grass thatching, shingles of sod and then earth. A number of saplings were laid horizontally to cover in the space between the four central beams, a hole being left for the combined chimney and skylight, this frame also being covered with willow, grass, sod and earth.

The covered entrance passage was built in a similar way with cross pieces for the roof and posts for the sides and extended some 6½–11ft (2–3.4m) from the door which was a rectangular

Above, left: *A Pawnee earth lodge. In the period 1500–1700 the lodge evolved from a rectangular to a circular shape, possibly in response to climatic changes and to give more compact village sites. Internal variations of style did exist: the Pawnee floor was 3ft (1m) below ground level.*

Above: *A George Catlin painting (1832) of an episode in the O-kee-pa ceremonial being performed within the Medicine Lodge of the Mandan. The lodge stood adjacent to the central village plaza and incorporated some features of the ancient rectangular style, such as the flattened front.*

Left: *Two typical Plains Indian musical instruments. Far left, a rattle of deer dew-claws and cone jingles, possibly Oto-Missouria and collected by Friedrich Köhler prior to 1846. Left, a wooden flute 21in (50cm) in length, which was collected in 1834 from the Mandan by Maximilian, Prince of Wied.*

piece of buffalo rawhide stretched on a willow frame, hung at each end and arranged to swing inward. It could be firmly secured at night by a piece of wood wedged between the door posts and two stout posts on the inside.

The fireplace was a circular depression at the center of the lodge about 1ft (33cm) deep and 3¼–4¼ft (1–1.3m) square, with a surround of flat rocks. Wilson describes the use of the *frame* of an old bull boat turned upside down over the smoke hole, stating 'its chief use seems to have been to keep puppies from falling through the smoke hole' (Wilson,1934:368). More importantly, however, was that during a storm a bull boat was commonly dragged to the roof, overturned and propped up on its own paddle to keep out the rain. With careful adjustment, the draft offered ventilation to keep the interior clear of smoke. When the government furnished plank doors to the Hidatsa during the Reservation period (about 1880), the lodges were found to be much smokier. It was thus obvious that the age-old technology of a skin door allowed a much freer circulation of air.

There were some variations on this basic design. For example, while the Hidatsa skillfully fitted all the posts, beams and rafters with careful joinery, the Omaha tied all the wooden parts of the structure with cords. The Pawnee excavated the floor so that the lodge was semi-subterranean, the difference in

level thus affording an earthen ledge which encircled the entire lodge. The Hidatsa and Mandan seldom did this, having instead wooden branches and backrests to seat the occupants, although sometimes they did dig down 1ft (33cm) or so to find earth compact enough to form a firm floor. The number of central posts varied among the Pawnee, while the Omaha – a short distance northeast of them – used from four to eight posts. Structure and orientation embodied much symbolism, particularly for the ceremonial earth lodges of most of the Missouri River tribes.

The Hidatsa reckoned the earth lodge to last between seven and ten years, its durability depending on the care taken in its construction. The most vulnerable parts were the posts which tended to rot at the base, making it necessary for the lodges to be dismantled. This was a joint effort by both men and women and, while much of the material could be reused, particularly the four central posts, most families preferred to use fresh earth for the outer covering. Hidatsa lodges still standing in 1912 measured between 11¾ and 14ft (3.65–4.35m) in height and from 45¾ to 54½ft (14–16.65m) in (outer) diameter, typical for most earth lodges on the Missouri.

*

Left: *The interior of a Mandan earth lodge –*
a painting by Karl Bodmer at the village of
Mih-Tutta-Hang-Kusch (1833–4). The lodge
belonged to Dipäuch, *a much respected*
elder of the tribe who acted as a valuable
informant on Mandan customs and
ceremonial.

Below: *A rattle made of rawhide and*
collected from the Assiniboin by Armand
Fouche d'Otrante at Fort McKenzie on the
Upper Missouri in the early 1840s. It is
decorated with otter and white fox fur and
was hung from the belt when not in use.

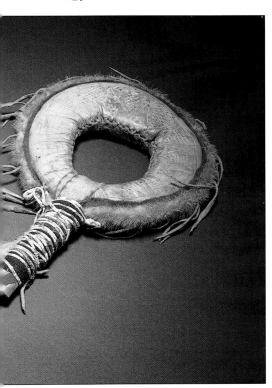

'These were our old houses,' Buffalo Bird Woman reminisced in 1908; 'When we used them we were healthy and there were many children and old people'.[18]

The Coming of the White Man: Trading Expeditions to the Plains

Perhaps the first white men met by Plains Indians were members of the Pierre La Verendrye fur trade expedition who visited the Mandan earth lodge villages on the Missouri River in 1738.[19] At that time, these villages were thriving trading centers to the nomadic western tribes and would remain more or less so for nearly a century until the smallpox epidemic of 1837 virtually exterminated the Mandan as a tribe. These earth lodge villages were a major destination for white trading parties who traveled up the Missouri from St Louis or southward from the trading posts in present-day Manitoba and Ontario in Canada. In 1727 La Verendrye had been given authority to establish a string of small forts stretching west from Lake Superior to challenge the English fur traders centered at Hudson Bay and also act as bases for further exploration of western North America (Smith, Wood ed.,1980:2–7).

These early fur traders quickly recognized the well-organized trade patterns established by the Plains tribes. The main focal points of this trade system were the earth lodge villages of the Arikara near the mouth of the Grand River and also those of the Mandan and Hidatsa on the Knife River in present-day North and South Dakota respectively. This very favorable geographic location 'as well as resource and craft specialization enabled these tribes to assume the position of middlemen linking riverine horticulturalists with upland hunters' (Swagerty, Washburn ed.,1988:353).

Initially, the white traders, mainly concerned with obtaining furs, acquired what they could from the inhabitants and visitors to the Missouri; the end-products, however, were not altogether to the liking of European tastes. Typical is the remark by Charles Mackenzie who observed at a Hidatsa village in 1805, 'I traded a few things with the *Corbeaux* [but] their beaver skins were badly dressed and split upon the back, in place of on the belly, a proof that they were not much acquainted with the importance of that favorite article of commerce' (Mackenzie, in Masson,1889:346). It was obvious that the source was not to be a dependable one, the Plains pattern of trade goods placing far more emphasis on other commodities. The Plains tribes clearly needed to be *taught* what was required if the European fur trade was to succeed. First, the white traders sought to create a demand, for what were initially *luxury* goods, from a Stone Age economy; as Tabeau observed at the time (1804): 'It is evident that with the bow and arrow the Savages of the Upper Missouri can easily do without our trade, which becomes necessary to them only after it has created the needs ... it is not to be doubted that custom, intercourse, the spirit of imitation, rivalry, the idea of luxury will give birth among the Savages to new needs; and the necessity of enjoying will produce the activity required to procure the means for them' (Tabeau, Abel ed.,1939:72, 166).

Even as Lewis and Clark descended the Missouri in 1806 from their fact-finding expedition after the Louisiana Purchase of 1803, they encountered nearly a dozen separate parties of American traders intent on setting up trade with not only the Pawnee and Arikara but also with the nomadic Sioux. This was a time when large numbers of hunters, whites, Hawaiians, blacks, Iroquois, Shawnee and Delaware Indians competed with one another, as well as with the resident hunters, to gain a share in the lucrative fur trade.[20] Clearly, the fur trade had come to stay and over the next thirty years the importance of the Upper Missouri village tribes, as primary or major trade centers, progressively declined, as trading posts and later forts, independent of the villages, were established not only on the Middle and Upper Missouri but across the American Plains.

The Impact of European Diseases

Disruption of trade was not the only evil brought in by the white foreigners and the result was 'near-catastrophic' (Swagerty, Washburn ed.,1988:360). Waves of epidemic disease – small-pox, cholera, bubonic plague, influenza, measles and whooping cough – passed through the tribes; having little resistance, thousands died. As early as 1780, at least one-third of the residents of the northern Plains – Blackfeet, Cree and Assiniboin – died of smallpox and, in 1798, streptococcal infections attacked the Sioux and later the Assiniboin and Cree. In 1806, influenza struck the Blackfeet and Mandan and a dozen or so years later an estimated four thousand Comanche died from smallpox while an outbreak in 1837 all but destroyed the greatest trading cultures of the Missouri; 'seven-eighths of the Mandan and over one-half of the Arikara were gone' (ibid.).

Forts Across the Plains

There was, nevertheless, continued stimulation of the fur trade both by government and private sources and by the 1830s a string of forts (several preceded by smaller trading posts) had been built along the Missouri River: Fort Pierre (1832) in present-day South Dakota; Fort Clark (1831) and Fort Union (1829) near the confluence of the Yellowstone and Missouri and in present-day North Dakota; further west was Fort McKenzie (1832) and Fort Assiniboine (1834) up near the headwaters of the Missouri; while to the south was Fort Cass (1833) on the Yellowstone in present-day Montana and Fort Laramie (1834) near the Platte River in present-day Wyoming; in Colorado was Bent's Fort (1833) on the Arkansas River which became the principal trading post for the southern Plains tribes. One very tangible spin-off from these early contacts was the wealth of valuable ethnographical data which was accumulated, not only

Above: Cunnawa-bum, *or One that looks at the stars, a Cree half-breed girl painted by Paul Kane who visited Fort Edmonton on the North Saskatchewan River in December 1847. She wears a typical early style dress.*

Above: *François Lucie, a Cree half-breed guide, based on sketches made by Kane at Fort Edmonton in 1847.*

Right: *Fort Pierre, Dakota Territory, circa 1855, from a watercolor by F. Behran. Many fur trading posts were built along the Missouri River from 1820 to 1850.*

Above: Tatsicki-Stomick, *or Middle Bull, a Piegan chief painted by Karl Bodmer at Fort McKenzie in August 1833. His face is covered with a special paint which was part of the attire of Medicine-Pipe owners.*

by educated fur traders such as Larocque, Mackenzie and Menard (and later Edwin Denig and William Bent among others) but also by such explorers as Meriwether Lewis and William Clark; Zebulon Pike; Thomas Freeman; and later in the 1830s by artists and scientists such as George Catlin, Maximilian and Karl Bodmer, all of whom have left a priceless record of Plains Indian life at this time.

The Impact of the Fur Trade on the Canadian Plains Indians

In Canada, the exploitation was less catastrophic, mainly due to the ordered and structured approach to the fur trade by the Hudson's Bay Company which was founded on 2 May 1670 and was given a Royal Charter by King Charles II. Representatives of the Company were among the first white men that the northern Plains Indians had seen, although initially the contacts were indirect, the Blackfeet, for example, acquiring their first trade goods – which included guns – from the Cree prior to 1730.

Later, in 1754, the Company sent Anthony Henday [21] on a fact-finding expedition to the northern Plains, traveling from York Factory on the western shores of Hudson Bay and in company with Cree canoe-men, somewhat north of present-day Calgary, Alberta. Here, he entered a great encampment of Archithinue Indians (almost certainly Atsina or Gros Ventre of the prairie) and through an interpreter explained his mission,

suggesting to their chief that he send his men to York Factory to trade. The journey to York Factory was something over a thousand miles and even the possibility of obtaining much coveted guns and ammunition was not sufficient enticement, the insistent reply being that they 'rode horses rather than paddled canoes, and lived off buffalo' (Williams,1983:15). Henday was also aware of a conflict of interests with his Cree companions who, like the Mandan and Hidatsa to the south, acted as middlemen between the Archithinue and other tribes, carrying their beaver and wolf skins to York Factory; as Henday observed 'if the Archithinues and Aseenepoets could be brought down to trade, the others [Cree] then would be obliged to trap their own furs, which at present two thirds of them does not' (ibid.).

With a fleet of some sixty canoes laden with furs, Henday returned to York Factory but not before observing, and subsequently reporting on, the complex network of trade throughout the Canadian Plains, the extensive French interests there and the reluctance of the interior tribes to travel to the Hudson Bay to trade. Within the next few years, however, the situation was to change markedly. By 1760, with the conquest of Canada, the French domination of the fur trade was destroyed; the French were forced to abandon the western fur posts, and the rich Plains country from the Red River in the east to the Rocky Mountains in the west was open to unopposed development. One Duncan M'Gillivray of the North West Company whose headquarters were in Montreal[22], however, echoed the sentiments expressed by Tabeau for the more southern groups, observing in 1794, 'The inhabitants of the Plains are so advantageously situated that they could live very happily independent of our assistance. They are surrounded with innumerable herds of various kinds of animals, whose flesh affords them excellent nourishment and whose skins defend them from the inclemency of the weather, and they have invented so many means for the destruction of animals that they stand in no need of ammunition to provide a sufficiency for their purposes. It is then our luxuries that attract them to the fort and make us so necessary to their happiness' (M'Gillivray,1929:47).

Thus, almost overnight, guns, ammunition, knives, axes and hatchets, metal spear and arrow heads, iron and brass kettles, metal traps, steels for firemaking, buttons, bells, beads, shells from far off exotic places, thread, steel needles and awls, cloth, blankets and even (ironically) tobacco, carrots and pipes became available to the Plains tribes. Within a few years they were transformed from a Stone to an Iron Age culture.

Indentured Servants

There was, however, another side to the coin. As the competition in the fur trade intensified and the number of trading posts on the northern Plains increased, the Cree and Assiniboin shifted from hunting mainly for survival to hunting for the fur companies, killing far more animals than were required for

Left: Wah-nis-stow, *or The White Buffalo, a principal chief of the 'Sarsi' sketched by Paul Kane east of Fort Pitt in June 1848. The Sarcee were a small Athapascan tribe who originally occupied territory in the Peace River area. They early affiliated themselves with the Blackfeet.*

Below: *A superb Blackfeet ceremonial shirt acquired in 1837 by L.A. Schoch and now in Bern. The shoulder and arm bands are in blue and white pony beads while the chest and back are decorated with large porcupine quill discs. Human hair fringes embellish the sleeves and neck flap.*

their own purposes. These tribes 'were slowly transformed into indentured servants who, in hard times, became highly dependent upon their employer for survival' (Newman,1989:88). The Blackfeet, on the other hand, refusing to trap beaver and thus become subservient to the whites, were put under increasing pressure by the now well-armed Cree who, adept at trapping beaver, ventured into Blackfeet territory and changed the balance of power in the area. Further, as beaver stocks were depleted, the Cree ventured to the Rockies, forming alliances with the Kalispel, Flathead and Kutenai in the bid to satisfy demands. Now gun-armed Plateau tribes pressed the Blackfeet from the west and, responding to a need to obtain more guns, the Blackfeet began supplying pemmican, dried meat and berries, backfat and horses to transport supplies to the outlying trading posts. Thus, the Blackfeet were *forced* into a position of

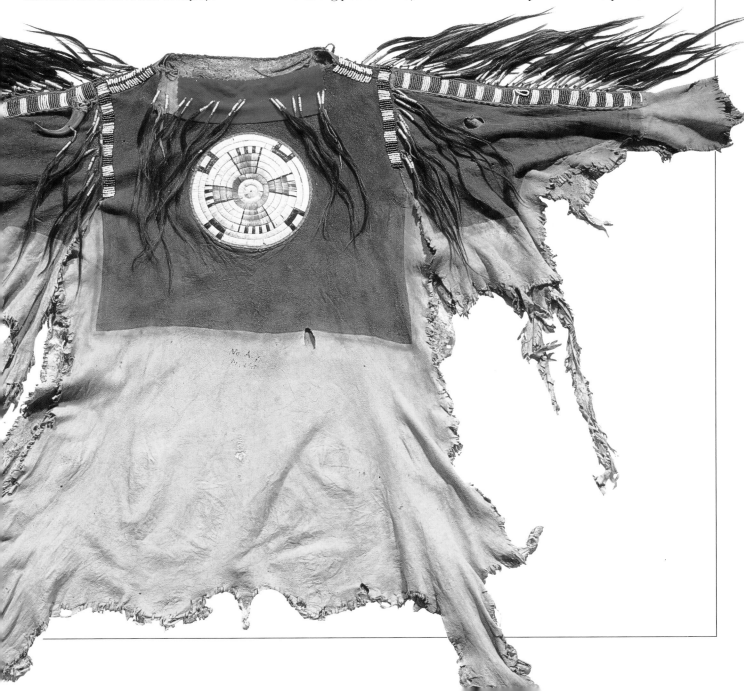

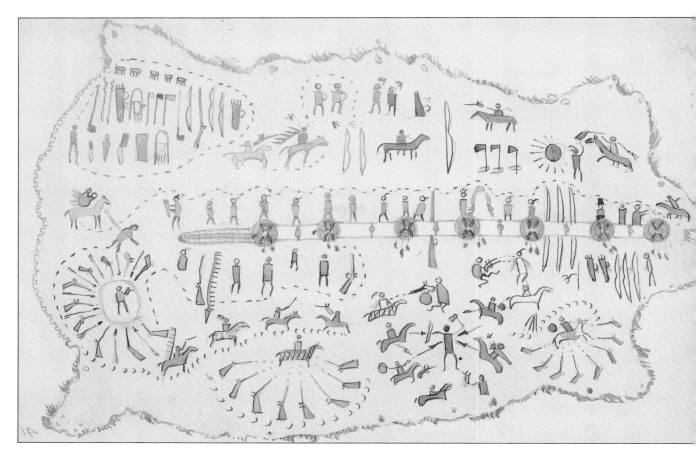

dependence for they needed white trade goods – particularly guns – in order to maintain their dominance on the northern Plains.

Although by the 1850s the demand for beaver pelts had dramatically decreased due to the increased popularity of the silk top hat over the beaver hat in the east and in Europe, the Hudson's Bay Company (now merged with its only real competitor, the North West Company) continued in the Canadian fur trade, exerting – by the readily available trade goods and the imposed economical pattern – a marked influence on Plains Indian culture. These northern Plains tribes, subjected as they were to a highly centralized and efficient organization in the form of the Hudson's Bay Company were, albeit at a distance, being subjected to a process of colonization by a long established and smoothly running British Empire, the philosophy of which has been well expressed by one observer:

'Inspired though they may have been by prudence and self-interest, rather than by enlightened motives of native welfare, their dealings with the Indians were marked by a sense of trusteeship and strict integrity'[23] (Stanley,1936:197).

Above: *A buffalo robe which depicts the exploits of Sa-co, or Sinew Piece, a Blood chief. This was copied by Paul Kane, probably at the time he met a group of Blackfeet and their allies, including Wahnis-stow, near Fort Pitt in 1848. Across the robe is a band of quillwork, broken at intervals by seven discs. The various episodes are rendered in typical Blackfeet style; in particular the objects shown at top left – bows, guns, quivers and scalps – obviously make reference to the coups credited to Sa-co. In contrast to pictographic work by tribes further south, such as the Lakota and Mandan, figures tend to be rendered in a somewhat static form, the recording of war episodes rather than the production of visually pleasing artwork being the main objective. The predominance of guns shows strong contacts with white traders.*

FOOTNOTES: CHAPTER TWO

1   This was in reply to an 1851 circular from Henry R. Schoolcraft of the Office of Indian Affairs, Washington, D.C. Edwin Denig was, for many years, Superintendent of the American Fur Company, Fort Union, near the mouth of the Yellowstone River in present-day North Dakota, and a recognized authority on the Indian tribes of the Missouri River region.

2   One of the most famous of Lakota leaders, *Tatan'ka-iyo'take*, better known as Sitting Bull, was particularly renowned for his spiritual leadership and grasp of ceremonial intricacies: for example, the finer details of the ritual significance of left-handedness and colors (see Mary Collins in Dorsey,1894:531-2), clearly marked him as an individual of unusual perception and discernment among his peers, while his leadership in performing the Sun-dance just prior to the Custer battle (Diessner,1993:71-2) underlined his high status among the Lakota, who continued to maintain a fierce independence of white domination.

3   Denig employs the word 'partisan' in the sense of 'a leader of a war party', Denig,1930:441.

4   (a) The *Kangi'yuha*, or 'Crow Owners', was a society which was widespread among the Plains tribes, the crow and raven being closely associated with success in war. (See Densmore,1918:318, and Fletcher and La Flesche,1911:441.); (b) Of considerable interest is that most of these societies, as with the sacred ceremonies, had origins embedded in tribal mythology; when no myth was associated or the symbolism incongruous, it was generally the case that the society in question was a recent borrowing from some alien group.

5   In the summer of 1805, Charles Mackenzie observed, 'I must not forget to mention that there was a fine harvest at the Missurie [sic] this season. I never witnessed anything equal in richness to the appearance of the fields. The stalks of the Indian corn were generally eight feet high, the leaves of the kidney beans were entirely covered with blossoms, promising [sic] abundance; the pumpkins were already gathered, cut into slices and dried in the sun ready for use' (Mackenzie, in Masson,1889:351). See also Chapter III which considers the produce and preparation of these foods in more detail).

6   In the 1750s the Chippewa destroyed the ancient Mdewakanton Sioux village of *Isanti* which was located on the shores of present-day *Mille Lacs* of Central Minnesota. The survivors eventually crossed the Mississippi and established a new village on the bank of the Minnesota River some twelve miles above its mouth, which they named *Tintatonwan* in recognition that it was in land formerly occupied by the Teton Sioux who at this time were drifting west to the Missouri River region (see Hodge,1910:Part 2:755, and also Meyer,1967:13-14).

7   Speaking of the Assiniboin, for example, Edwin Denig said that the bands were usually distinct and camped in 'different sections of country'; however, he observed that 'they mingle for a short time when circumstances require it, such as scarcity of buffalo . . . or on an approach of a numerous enemy' (Denig, Hewitt ed.,1930:431).

8   These also had several satirical nicknames: *Tezi Tanka* 'Big Bellies'; *Hanskaska* 'Tall Ones'; *Tatanka Wapahaun* 'Wearers of the Buffalo Bull Headdress'; *Pehin Ptecela* 'Short Hairs'. Tradition has it that the Chiefs Society was founded by an Oglala called Paints-his-ear-white (see Wissler,1912(b):37).

9   The pipes and associated distinctive bags are illustrated in Mallery,1886:74. See also Blish,1967:83.

10   In the case of the Pawnee, every person in the village was under the tutelage of a given star, thus all the people in the village were considered as kindred but their specific cosmic derivation gave them different social ranking according to their star affiliations. Some were thus born as chiefs, 'some as braves, and some as commoners; their social functions in the community were thus relatively preordained' (Weltfish,1977:19).

11   Denig makes reference to the *Berdêches*, or hermaphrodites, among the Crow, noting that 'Most civilized communities recognize but two genders, the masculine and feminine. But strange to say, these people have a neuter . . . he is not to be distinguished in any way from the women, 'tho is seldom much respected by either sex' (Denig, Ewers ed.,1953:58). A similar sentiment was expressed by Maximilian: 'They have many bardaches [sic], or hermaphrodites, among them, and exceed all other tribes in unnatural practices (Maximilian, 1906,Vol.22:354). The Laubins also reported on the Lakota *winkta* – men who had dreamed of being women and 'henceforth dressed and behaved as women'; they were highly respected and often had important roles in ceremonies. A *winkta* that they had met at Fort Yates was considered 'one of the best bead and craft workers on the reservation' (Laubin,1977:365-7).

12   There are several instances of women attaining high warrior-like status among the Plains tribes. Perhaps the best known was Running Eagle, a noted Piegan woman, whose exploits were the basis of James Willard Schultz's *Running Eagle, the Warrior Girl* (1919). Additionally, Edwin Denig has reported in detail on the exploits of Woman Chief, a Crow woman as well as a brief reference to an Assiniboin woman who also attempted to take on a warrior role (Denig, Ewers ed.,1953:68).

13   Although noted horsetraders, the Mandan obviously kept few of the horses which passed through their hands for their own use.

14   These figures are mainly based on Ewers (1955), Table 2. There is, however, some danger in generalizing from statistical tabulations. Thus, for example, recent researches suggest that in the 1870s the Mountain Crow had a horse to person ratio of about 4:1 while that of the River Crow was, at best, 1:1 (see Taylor,1981:13 and 29).

15   This trade was only part of an extensive and incredible network west of the Missouri–Mississippi where surplus subsistence economies in the form of garden crops from the Plains and Southwest and fish products from the Plateau and Northwest Coast, European trade goods, meat, deer hides, mountain sheep bows, buffalo robes, buckskin clothing, quillwork and featherwork, shells and flint were made available to distant tribes.

16   It is probably more correct to say that most of the 'horses' used by the historic Plains tribes would be classified as 'ponies', being described as some '14 hands high' and 'fine tractible animals, . . . lively and clean made' and 'of different colors' (see Hendry, Burpee ed.,1907:338 and Cocking, Burpee, ed.,1908:106). They weighed 'about 700 pounds' and were 'close to being a type' (Ewers,1955:33), and although descended from the Barb horses of Spain and North Africa – being introduced to North America by the Spanish in 1519 – inbreeding and change in climate resulted in a smaller animal. The Appaloosa which was bred by the Nez Perce and Cayuse, was a heavier animal. A few were traded to the Plains tribes such as the Crow and Blackfeet and were worth two or three ponies, as were mules which came from the Spanish settlements in the south, although it is recorded that the Sioux stole them from the U.S. army (see Ewers,1955:55 and 342).

17   (a) No known illustrations of tipis for this period exist. However, they must have closely resembled that reproduced by Isham in 1743 in his 'Observations on Hudsons [sic] Bay'; the dwelling has all the characteristics of a Plains tipi, including a pole to adjust the smoke flap. It differed in one respect, the covering being of deer or moose hide instead of buffalo (see Williams,1983:18); (b) The earliest published illustration of a Plains tipi was based on a field sketch by Titian Peale who accompanied the Long expedition in 1819-20. It was published in James (1823). Jonathan Carver made a sketch of a Naadowessie 'tent' which he observed in 1766 but this was not published until much later (see Carver,Parker, ed.,1976:97); (c) A small tipi cover, probably of buffalo hide, was collected by Kohler in 1840. It undoubtedly resembles the style transported by dogs in pre-horse days. This exceptional piece, possibly for housing a medicine pipe and hence of ancient style, is now in the excellent collection at the Museum für Volkerkunde, Berlin

18   *Diary*, Vol. 6, Wilson Papers, Minnesota Historical Society, 1908. See Gilman and Schneider,1987:121.

19   Some of the earliest examples of headdress were brought back from these Mandan villages by La Verendrye and other French explorers and are now in the Musée de l'Homme in Paris, in particular specimen number 78.82.156 (see Taylor,1962:8).

20   For a broad discussion of Plains Indian trading, see Swagerty (1988:360-74).

21   Henday had been preceded by Henry Kelsey, who carried out a series of explorations to the Plains as early as 1690. However, as Williams has observed, there was little interest by the Hudson's Bay Company in his activities and it was 'as if the expansionist ideas suggested by the great charter had disappeared . . . ' (Williams,1983:8).

22   The Hudson's Bay Company, which is the oldest chartered trading company in the world, combined with the North West Company in 1821. The Company's trading activities then gradually spread across the whole of Canada.

23   This contrasted markedly with attitudes in the United States, where not only had relationships with the Blackfeet started off on a bad footing when Meriwether Lewis killed two Piegan in 1806, but the policy of the American Fur Company of sending white trappers into Indian country, rather than depending on Blackfeet hunters, infuriated the tribes and led to continued conflict. As Lewis observed, 'the American fur trade reflected the rugged individualism and lack of organization of the newly developing capitalist economy of which it was a part' (Lewis,1942:27).

RELIGION
AND CEREMONIAL

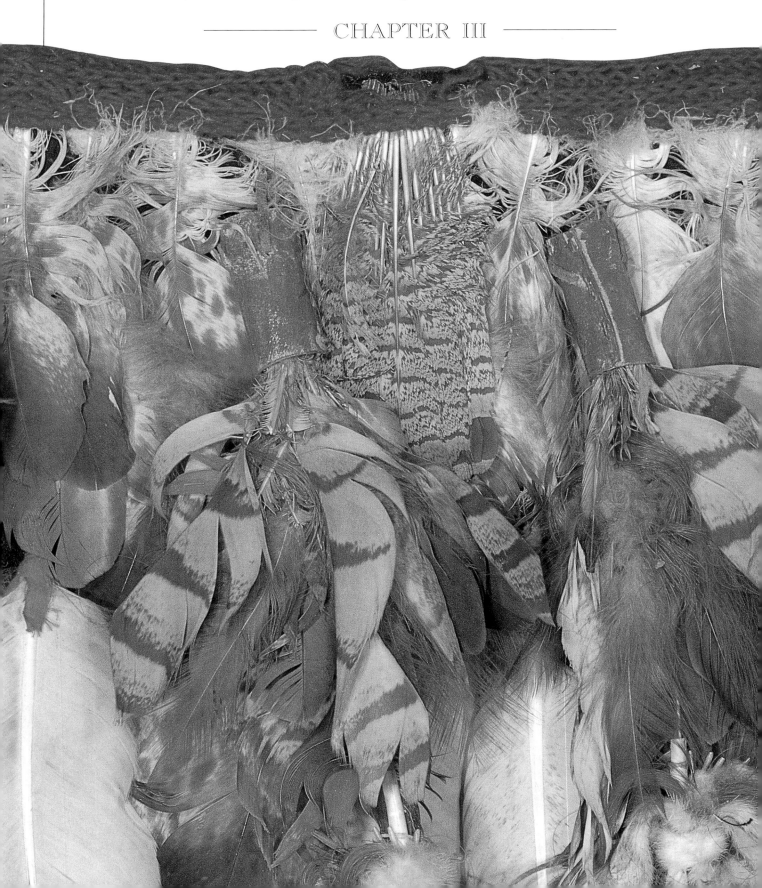

Below: *Close-up of a Blackfeet dance bustle showing hawk and owl feathers. Such costume used many animal parts in fantastical combinations to great effect in dance and ceremonial.*

'All animals of the Plains at one time heard and knew him, and all birds of the air heard and knew him. All things that he had made understood him, when he spoke to them – the birds, the animals and the people' (Blackfeet tradition of harmony among all living things and the creator. Grinnell, 1893:137)

Plains Indian Religion – the Oneness of All Things

A powerful element of incomprehensibility characterized the Plains Indians' stance toward their universe, one in which they stood in fear, awe and veneration. It was an holistic philosophy which recognized man as part of nature and not outside it. As the Lakota holy man, Black Elk, observed, their belief was 'This truth of the oneness of all things' (Brown ed., 1971:95).

To the Lakota, anything strange and mysterious was described as *wakan*, or having the attributes of *Wakan-Tanka*, the greatest of the sacred ones. *Wakan-Tanka* had parallels in other groups – *Wakonda* for such tribes as the Omaha, Ponca and Osage; *Tirawahat* of the Pawnee; *puha* of the Comanche and for the Blackfeet, *Natojewa*, or 'sun power' – the greatest of the powers of the universe. Such concepts are the essence of Plains Indian religion, an acute awareness of some all-pervading force – the power or moving force of the universe – that emanates from unknown sources and to which a special name was given. In turn this became an attribute which was applicable to its various manifestations which could become a source of power and status to those who dared to use it, often at the expense of great personal sacrifice.

As with the Blackfeet, the commonest understanding among the Lakota was to identify *Wakan-Tanka* with the sun; however, according to one respected student of their culture, the shamans viewed the powers in a far more complex way which was not fully understood by the people at large, a situation not far removed from that in Christian and other world religions. There was, for example, the use of ancient or esoteric language – a 'sacred language' – and an attempt at systematic and all-inclusive classification of the distribution and function of power in the Lakota universe. Thus, the shamans classified the good *Wakan-Tanka* into a system known as the *Tobtob Kin*, or 'four times four' (see page 62), which embraced all the physical and spiritual aspects of the world and which linked up the various *wakan* beings by means of human kinship terms: the buffalo were considered to be the brothers of the Lakota, invoking all the moral obligations of mutual respect and support which this relationship demanded in Lakota society (see Walker, 1917:78–88; DeMallie and Lavenda, 1977: 154).

This unity of the *Tobtob Kin* – the 'four times four' – has only been identified for the Lakota thanks to the dedication and deep interest of a Dr J R Walker who lived and worked at Pine Ridge from 1895 to 1915;[1] nevertheless, there are strong parallels elsewhere as DeMallie and Lavenda (1977) have observed. The similarities between the concept of power for the Omaha

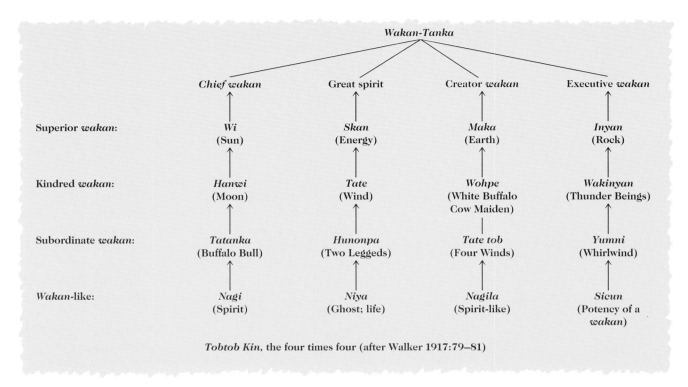

Tobtob Kin, the four times four (after Walker 1917:79–81)

	Chief *wakan*	Great spirit	Creator *wakan*	Executive *wakan*
			Wakan-Tanka	
Superior *wakan*:	Wi (Sun)	Skan (Energy)	Maka (Earth)	Inyan (Rock)
Kindred *wakan*:	Hanwi (Moon)	Tate (Wind)	Wohpe (White Buffalo Cow Maiden)	Wakinyan (Thunder Beings)
Subordinate *wakan*:	Tatanka (Buffalo Bull)	Hunonpa (Two Leggeds)	Tate tob (Four Winds)	Yumni (Whirlwind)
Wakan-like:	Nagi (Spirit)	Niya (Ghost; life)	Nagila (Spirit-like)	Sicun (Potency of a wakan)

and Lakota are 'striking' and the linguistically related Winnebago (a non-Plains tribe) used the spirits as a loci of power 'and form a classification of the world' (ibid.:161, 163), sentiments which can certainly be identified in the religious concepts of such widely separated groups as the Blackfeet and Pawnee, dictating ritual and ceremonial, while the emphasis on both the Sun and buffalo stood high in the hierarchy of powers.

The Sacred Beliefs of the Blackfeet

To the Blackfeet, *Napi*, or 'Old Man', was considered to be the creator and, under numerous other names, Old Man was known to the Cree and other Algonquian-speaking people. The Blackfeet said that *Napi* could never die and that long ago he disappeared in the mountains but that one day he would return. In the 1890s, one close observer of the Blackfeet reported that many of the old people were convinced that some day *Napi* would come back to bring with him the buffalo which they believed the white men had hidden. Some also said that *Napi* and the Sun were actually one and that '*Natos* is only another name for *Napi*'; certainly, every good thing – success in the chase and war, health, a long life, and happiness – came by special favor of the Sun. But at times Sun, in the form of *Napi*, became a great trickster who used his supernatural powers for both good and ill with a curious mixture of completely opposite attributes, all powerful but also at times impotent; full of all wisdom, yet at times so helpless that he has to seek aid from the animals. Sometimes he sympathizes with the people, and at others, 'out of pure spitefulness, he plays them malicious tricks that are worthy of a demon. He is a combination of strength,

Above: *A detailed analysis of the religious concepts of the Lakota (DeMallie and Lavenda,1977) has identified four of the most important* wakan *beings who were considered to be older than all the others – the sun, energy, earth and rock. From these four superior* wakan *came four others, each pair being aspects of the same power; for example, the wind derives from energy and the moon from the sun. The successive pairing, as shown here, gives rise to a total of sixteen classes – the* Tobtob Kin.

Right: *Lakota style Sun-dance stick collected by Rudolph Kurz, 1848–52. Those who took part in the Sun-dance wore small decorated sticks of this type in their hair and during the course of the ceremonial they were not allowed to touch the body by hand; such sticks were used for that purpose. The stick is embellished along most of its length with flattened porcupine quills, feather tips are attached to skin thongs which are bound at intervals with porcupine quills.*

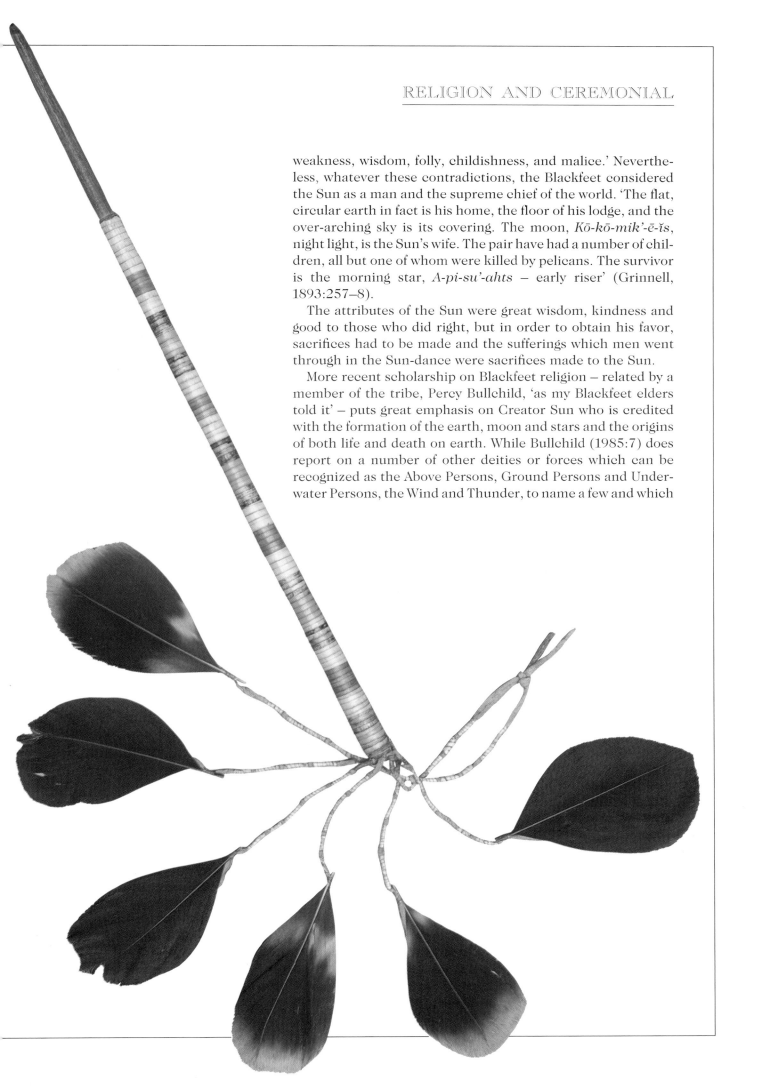

weakness, wisdom, folly, childishness, and malice.' Nevertheless, whatever these contradictions, the Blackfeet considered the Sun as a man and the supreme chief of the world. 'The flat, circular earth in fact is his home, the floor of his lodge, and the over-arching sky is its covering. The moon, *Kō-kō-mik'-ē-ĭs*, night light, is the Sun's wife. The pair have had a number of children, all but one of whom were killed by pelicans. The survivor is the morning star, *A-pi-su'-ahts* – early riser' (Grinnell, 1893:257–8).

The attributes of the Sun were great wisdom, kindness and good to those who did right, but in order to obtain his favor, sacrifices had to be made and the sufferings which men went through in the Sun-dance were sacrifices made to the Sun.

More recent scholarship on Blackfeet religion – related by a member of the tribe, Percy Bullchild, 'as my Blackfeet elders told it' – puts great emphasis on Creator Sun who is credited with the formation of the earth, moon and stars and the origins of both life and death on earth. While Bullchild (1985:7) does report on a number of other deities or forces which can be recognized as the Above Persons, Ground Persons and Under-water Persons, the Wind and Thunder, to name a few and which were recorded by earlier observers (Grinnell, 1893:259; Wissler, 1912(b):71–90), there is a definite insistence on the Sun's primacy, before all other forces and spirits.[2] This is consistent with sentiments which initiated the Blackfeet Sun-dance and the associated prescribed rites which needed to be carried out by its most important functionary – the holy woman – prior to its performance. The woman seeks help by a vow, often made at a time when a member of her family is dangerously ill; in prayer, she appeals to the Sun that health may be restored. Unless, however, she had been truthful, industrious and, above all, loyal to her marriage vows, her appeal would go unanswered by this mightiest of powers, and if she were to proceed with the Sun-dance – or even to take a secondary part in it – 'the wrath of the sun would be invoked' (Wissler, 1918:232).

Pawnee Religious Beliefs

The religious beliefs of the Pawnee contrast somewhat with those of the Blackfeet who put emphasis on sun power, in that *Tirawahat* was considered the first god and the first cause of all. It was *Tirawahat* who both created and governed the universe through the commands executed by all the lesser gods.[3] As with the Siouan *Wakan-Tanka*, *Tirawahat* was considered as an all-powerful force or spirit and not identified with any natural phenomenon or object. However, Skidi Pawnee informants did suggest that *Tirawahat* and the clear blue sky were synonymous and that blue was generally considered to be his color, sentiments similar to those expressed by Lakota shamans who stated that *Skan*, or *To*, the energy or moving force of the universe, was the 'immaterial blue of the sky which symbolizes the presence of the Great Spirit' (Walker, 1917:81).

The wife of *Tirawahat* was the Vault of Heaven but it was actually through *Cu:piritta:ka*, 'female white star' or the Evening Star in the west, that *Tirawahat* linked with the world below.[4] Evening Star was conceived as a beautiful woman, a Goddess of Night and Germination in whose garden corn and buffalo were constantly being renewed. The four assistants of Evening Star were the Wind, Cloud, Lightning and Thunder, through whom were transmitted her mandates.

The first god placed in the heavens by *Tirawahat* was Morning Star *Opirikata*, of the eastern sky, considered a god of light, fire and war and a warrior who drove all other stars before him across the sky. He was considered the most powerful of the stars and it was believed that Skidi Pawnee warriors obtained their powers from him.[5] It was the union between Morning Star and Evening Star, from which sprang the girl who was the first human being to be placed on earth. Pawnee mythology relates that, as Morning Star rose, he sent a beam into the entry of the earth lodge – which was oriented east – symbolically lighting the fire in an act of cosmic procreation and it was to Morning Star that the Skidi band of the Pawnee offered a human sacrifice.

Above: *Esteemed Son, a* Kitkehahki, *or Republican Pawnee, in buffalo robe with wolfskin turban. The Pawnee were of Caddoan linguistic stock and long resided in the valley of the Platte River (in present-day Nebraska). They referred to themselves as* Chahiksichahiks, *or 'men of men'. Their religious beliefs were complex with* Tirawahat *considered as the power of the universe comparable to the Lakota concept of* Wakan-Tanka.

Right: *Little Raven, a Skidi or Wolf Pawnee. While many of the religious ceremonies of the Pawnee were connected with the cosmic forces and heavenly bodies, the Skidi Pawnee put particular emphasis on the Morning Star and on occasions, as part of a series of ceremonies relative to the bringing of life and its increase, they practiced human sacrifice.*

Next in rank came the gods of the four world quarters who stood in the northeast, southeast, southwest and northwest and supported the heavens. To these gods, *Tirawahat* gave the task of dividing up the earth into the four divisions. Below them were three gods of the north, 'the North Star, who presided over the council of the stars, and who gave the ceremony for the creation of chiefs to men; the North Wind, who sent men the buffalo, and Hikus, who gave the breath of life' (Linton, 1922(b):6). Unlike the lore of the Sioux and Blackfeet, the Sun and Moon were ranked relatively low but they were credited with the union from which sprang the second being on earth, who, mating with the offspring of the Evening and Morning Stars, produced the human race.

Thus, in Pawnee religion, the greater part of the important heavenly gods were firmly identified with the stars, and the

sacred medicine bundles (in which powers of the heavens were believed to be centered), associated with each village, were said to have been given by one of these heavenly beings. Therefore, when the villages of each band assembled for ceremonials, they arranged themselves according to the place of their stars in the sky and nothing on earth could move without evoking the power of the heavens. Further, no practical task – the breaking of the ground, planting of the seeds, indeed the whole of the Spring Awakening after the first thunder – could be undertaken unless the appropriate ceremony preceded it.[6]

'They sang this song above, they have spoken.
They have put new life into the earth.
Paruxti speaks through the clouds,
And the power has entered Mother Earth.
The earth has received the powers from above.'

(First song in Pawnee Thunder ceremony (ibid.:10).

The Morning Star Ceremony of the Skidi Pawnee – Captive Girl Sacrifice

While human sacrifices were very rare in North America, it was common among the Aztecs of Mexico[7] and also occurred among the Natchez in the southeast; only the Skidi Pawnee practiced it on the Great Plains, and it appears even there that it was carried out somewhat unwillingly and that the officiating priests 'always found it a sore trial' (Linton, 1922(a):22). The practice was embedded in the mythology associated with the great trials of Morning Star in fathering the human race and the belief that for this he demanded human sacrifice in the form of a young girl, although a male might be selected on some occasions. In this respect, then, the whole performance was considered a religious duty.

This appeasement of Morning Star was not an annual one, taking place every three to five years, but it was an essential ceremonial to ensure the renewal of life on earth and the prevention of its destruction by the fire of the sun; also, according to one observer, it was considered 'a period of ceremonial sexual license to promote fertility' (Weltfish, 1977:114).

It was necessary for both astronomical and religious elements to be correct for the initiation of events leading up to the ceremonial sacrifice. These could occur through a vision or dream in which the Morning Star demanded it, or perhaps on a supposed sign from the heavens in the form of an unusual aura or bright appearance of the Star itself. As soon as possible after one of these events, the keeper of the Morning Star Bundle was contacted and, on approval, a warrior's costume and other sacred objects were removed from the Bundle. These were to be worn by the leader of the expedition to capture the girl, many warriors usually volunteering to join since its objective was thought to ensure success.

Left: The winds of change . . . 'Pawnee watching a wagon train', painting by Alfred Jacob Miller, circa 1837. In 1838, the estimated number of Pawnee was about 10,000 but the opening of a principal emigrant trail directly through their country in the 1840s introduced European diseases and alcohol, leaving them less able to defend themselves against enemy tribes. By 1849, cholera and war with other tribes had reduced their numbers to less than 5000. By 1879 the entire tribe numbered only 1440. This continued influx of whites, which included Presbyterian and Methodist missionaries, progressively weakened the organization of the tribe and, in common with the Reservation life of most Plain tribes, led to the gradual abandonment of ancient customs, particularly those associated with ceremonial and religion.

The capturing war party

The war party now set out to the country of the enemy, the leader carrying the sacred objects from the Morning Star Bundle and part of any game killed on the way was offered to the Morning Star, reinforcing the purpose of the expedition. On location of the enemy scouts, a special ceremonial was enacted, a circle being cleared, a central fireplace excavated and the contents of the sacred pack laid out. Smoke from the fire was viewed as an offering to the sky gods and songs referred to the union of the Morning and Evening Stars from which the first human – a girl – was born. The leader then addressed the assembled party: 'Warriors, young men, we are now sitting in a place dedicated to the Morning Star. We are about to sing the song that the Morning Star himself sang when he was in search of a woman, who put obstacles in his way. I want you all to dance with all your might and to be brave. Whoever shall be so lucky as to catch the girl must call her Opirikuts as he touches her. Others must move away and not touch her. The life of anyone who touches her afterward will be in danger. Everyone must now dance toward the center. Let the fire be like the enemy' (Linton, 1922(a):26).

The enemy camp was then surrounded; even here a cosmic order was observed, the leader to the east and another to the southeast.[8] This latter warrior was instructed to give the cry of a wolf as the Morning Star rose above the horizon; this was the signal for the attack, being reminded not to kill unless necessary but to find a suitable young captive and to pronounce her *Opirikuts*, 'holy', for the Morning Star.[9] Generally, little attempt was made at pursuit by the enemy tribe as there was 'a feeling that this was a kind of cosmic destiny' (Weltfish, 1977:109), although retribution could (and often did) come later in the form of a war party against the entire Pawnee tribe.

The captured girl was now placed on a pony behind her captor and the party made for home but all the time she was strictly under the care of both the leader and the man who had made the wolf cry; having been pronounced sacred, it was said that anyone touching her would die of infection. At the Pawnee village she was treated well and made as comfortable and happy as possible and placed in the care of one who represented the Wolf Star, wolf in Pawnee mythology being blamed for bringing death into the world. This transfer sealed the captive's fate of a sacrificial death, although it might be months before the time was considered right by the Morning Star priest. In this case, every effort was made to conceal the ordained ritual from the girl and she was further feted. Her body was rubbed with a mixture of red ochre and buffalo fat and she was regaled in the ceremonial costume from and associated with the Morning Star Bundle which included a fine buffalo robe; her hair was decorated with a soft downy feather and she was given – for her exclusive use at meal times – a wooden bowl and spoon from the Morning Star Bundle.

Right: *Brave Chief, a Skidi Pawnee, painting by George Catlin, 1832. The hairstyle of this man shows the unusual way that this tribe dressed the scalp-lock which was referred to as* pariki, *or 'a horn', and was said to be the origin of the name Pawnee. The painted hands indicate hand-to-hand combat in which Brave Chief was victorious.*

Captive ceremonial

In all subsequent ceremony – which could last for months – the participants sat within the captor's lodge in proper cosmic positions. It is possible that a chart recording many star features may have been used in this context, since it is known that a chart of the heavens was used in some Pawnee ceremonials[10] (see drawing of the star chart, below).

At the commencement of the time for the sacrifice, the chief of the village had his earth lodge cleared of all furniture and the participants were summoned to the ceremony. These included not only the girl but also her captor, who was dressed in another costume associated with the Morning Star Bundle. This consisted of leggings and moccasins made from black buckskin and a fan-shaped headdress of twelve eagle feathers attached so as to stand upright over the head, almost certainly being a personification of the Morning Star deity, for it is said that this is how he appeared in visions or dreams.

The entire ceremonial was replete in symbolic statements which included references to earth and animal as well as sky

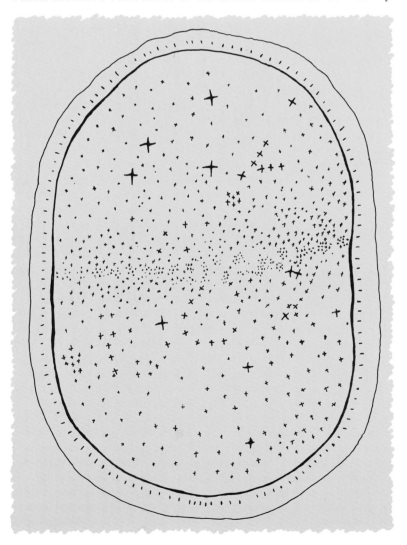

Left: The Skidi Pawnee Chart of the Heavens. This was painted on a finely tanned thin piece of buckskin of oval shape measuring approximately 22 × 14in (56 × 38cm). On it references are made to such astronomical features as the Morning Star (top center), the Pleiades (cluster, upper right), and the Milky Way (across center), which divides the chart in half. The sacred medicine bundles of the Pawnee contained many representations of things which were essential to the traditional way of life and this star chart is in that category. Thus, it was probably never intended to be used as a star map but rather to incorporate powers of the stars and bring these powers to the people when it was opened. The chart underlines the great emphasis which the Pawnee put on astronomical phenomena in their religious and ceremonial practices. (Drawing based on original star chart.)

Below: *Morning Star ceremony of the Pawnee from an engraving after Seth Eastman. This illustrates an episode near the climax of a complex ceremonial where two men bearing firebrands lightly touch the arms and loins of the captive girl, probably symbolically to overcome obstacles in the path of Morning Star. Although lacking details (see page 72, caption), this is one of the few extant illustrations of the Morning Star ceremony and is probably based on eyewitness accounts. The girl who was sacrificed seems to have been conceived of as a personification of the Evening Star surrounded by her powers and when she was overcome, symbolically the life of the earth was considered to be renewed, ensuring universal fertility.*

powers. Thus, four long poles some 12 feet (approximately 4m) in length were located by the priests and brought into the chief's lodge. These were then placed with their ends in the fire, forming a cross with the ends pointing in the semi-cardinal directions and resembling a four pointed star, the fire glowing at the center. The poles were of elm which represented the bear and the northeast; box elder, the mountain lion and the southwest; cottonwood, the wildcat and the northwest; and willow, the wolf and southeast. These represented the four star beasts who in Pawnee mythology opposed the Morning Star as he sought union with the Evening Star. These poles were long enough to last the four days of this part of the ceremony and as they were gradually consumed they were pushed into the fire but kept the shape of the cross as they were consumed; symbolically then, the opposing star beasts were progressively destroyed. During the entire four day period and also for three days after the actual sacrifice, the ordinary social rules of conduct were ignored, the priests announcing to the gathering that if any man desired a particular woman and approached her, she

was expected to go with him so that the tribe might increase.

The captured girl was, however, treated with great respect and given every consideration and told that the performance was in her honor, everything being done to allay her fears and to protect her from the real truth of things to come.

Weakening of the cosmic protective powers

As the wood was consumed, so symbolically were the protective powers of the animals gradually reduced and the captive became increasingly vulnerable so that, at the beginning of the fourth day, a sacrificial scaffold was constructed, one or two miles east of the village. As with the wooden cross poles, so too with the scaffold – elm and cottonwood for the uprights, willow and box elder for the cross pieces. Symbolically, the animals' powers were retained on earth but now the upright posts were to hold up the sky.

The girl was now dressed in a black robe and moccasins, her body painted black on one side, red on the other, signifying night and the Evening Star and day, the time of the Morning Star. Her head was embellished with eagle feathers and a hawk skin signifying the messenger bird of the Morning Star. Songs relating to the origin of the Morning Star and its emergence from a meteor were sung during this part of the ritual.

Procession to the scaffold

The procession to the scaffold commenced before dawn of the next day, the rate at which it moved depending on the attitude of the girl, everything being done to conceal the truth from her and force of any kind was to be avoided unless absolutely neces-

Below: *Diorama of the Morning Star Sacrifice, Field Museum, Chicago. Here, the captive girl has been tied to the scaffold with two men coming forward with firebrands. They are dressed as priests with owl skins hung from their necks representing the messengers of the Morning Star. Another man concealed in the small ravine waits with his bow and sacred arrow to perform the final act of sacrifice. There was a great deal of opposition to this brutal ritual and it had virtually ceased by the 1830s.*

sary. The timing was such that the procession reached the scaffold a few minutes before the Morning Star rose in the sky. The girl was then persuaded to climb the scaffold where her hands and legs were tied with thongs made from the skins of the sacred animals. She faced east.

'Wirihu.kit.rik[i]
Now she is standing upon it.
Wirihu.kitawa.wi
Now she is arranged upon it.
Wirihu.kitawicpa
Now she has completed (her) climbing up.'

(Extract from the Sixteenth Song in the Pawnee Morning Star Ceremony. Murie, Parks ed., 1981, Part 1:133)

As the Morning Star appeared, two men, previously hidden, approached the girl bearing firebrands and lightly touched her on her loins and arms.[11] Now a third man approached the girl (probably the visionary warrior who had originally initiated the ceremony). He carried a bow and arrow from the sacred Skull Bundle, the arrow being specially made for the sacrifice; coming close he fired the arrow through her heart. A fourth man came forward carrying a club from the Bundle and struck the maiden on the head. It was believed that the dead girl's soul went straight to *Tirawahat* who, in turn, directed her to the Morning Star from whom she received a clothing of glowing flint and was placed in the great vault of the heavens where the people for whom she had given her life could always see her. Her body too, placed face downward, was said to enrich the earth. Now there was general rejoicing in the village, crops and game would now be abundant and warriors successful in war but, as one scholar has observed, more than ever 'the people had been reminded, in a way they could not possibly forget, of their celestial origin. Again they had been taught of the struggles of the great male star in subduing the female white star in order that life might come to earth. They had acknowledged their celestial parentage and returned one of their own kind as they believed they had been commanded to do. Now everything would be well with them, as they had gained favor in their father's sight' (Chamberlain, 1982:66).

The role of *Petalesharro*
The Skidi Pawnee were virtually unique among the Plains tribes in the human sacrifice to the Morning Star.[12] Evidence suggests (Wissler and Spinden, 1916) that there were strong similarities between the Pawnee sacrifice and that of the Aztec, who also used scaffolds, and a Mexican origin has indeed been suggested. Further, similarities between the Aztec and Pawnee ceremonials have also been more recently documented (Chamberlain, 1982:68), such as the use of sacred bundles which bore the

Above: Petalesharro, *or Man Chief, Skidi Pawnee, after a portrait by Charles Bird King, 1821. In 1816, the Skidi Pawnee captured an Ietan girl with the intention of sacrificing her to the Morning Star. This sacrifice was strongly opposed by Knife Chief whose son,* Petalesharro, *subsequently rescued the girl near the climax of the ceremonial.*

names of the gods who were thought to have given them to the tribes together with the associated songs. In addition, there was emphasis in both ceremonials on four directions together with a central focus, although the Pawnee differed from the Aztec in that they used semi-cardinal directions; further, color and animal symbolism and four gods occurred in both the Aztec and Pawnee ceremonials.

As early as 1811[13] it is clear that, even among the Pawnee themselves, this ritual of human sacrifice was a controversial issue but it was clearly a custom imposed on the people by inherited religious practices which few would dare violate. Dramatic opposition to its performance, however, came in the spring of 1817, when Man Chief, or *Petalesharro*, supported his father, Knife Chief, in an attempt to prevent the sacrifice of an Ietan – probably Comanche – girl captive. Knife Chief had addressed the people in an effort to get them to abandon the custom but his arguments were ignored and on the appointed day the girl was led to the scaffold. Just as the fatal arrow was to be fired, *Petalesharro* intervened, putting himself between the girl and the gathered crowd. Although only in his early twenties, *Petalesharro* was a highly respected warrior and the crowd held back, stunned by his bravery, since Pawnee belief was that a violation of the ceremonial would bring certain death to those that opposed it; *Petalesharro* was thus seen as forfeiting his life for the Ietan captive. He took the girl down from the scaffold, gave her a horse and told her to rejoin her people, which she subsequently succeeded in doing.

When Man Chief visited Washington in the fall of 1821, the story of his brave deed had already been published and he was much feted, although he confessed that at the time of carrying out the rescue he had not 'known it was brave' (Weltfish, 1977:116). *Petalesharro* was presented with a large silver medal engraved with 'To the Bravest of the Brave', returning home showered with gifts from admirers (see right).

Although no further sacrifices appeared to have taken place during his lifetime, *Petalesharro*'s brave stand was not entirely successful. The Pawnee were increasingly subjected to factors now mostly out of their control, and in 1825 a treaty with whites reduced their land. Additionally, astronomical observations in the next two years – the red star (Mars) in the morning sky dimming as it moved toward the west and then a particularly brilliant Morning Star (Venus) increasing in intensity – were read as signs by the frustrated Pawnee that a sacrifice was demanded by their gods. In May 1833, despite the efforts of the Pawnee agent John Dougherty at Bellevue and the opposition of chiefs, Big Axe and Black Chief, a Cheyenne woman was sacrificed at the behest of fanatical priests, who said that if the sacrifices were abandoned the crops would fail and the tribe would be destroyed. Again in April 1838, a Lakota (Oglala) girl of about fifteen was sacrificed to the Morning Star; this was the last recorded case of a dreadful ritual.

Above: Petalesharro, *Pawnee, photograph by Antonio Zeno Shindler, Washington, D.C., 1858. This man has often been confused with the Skidi hero but the latter died before 1833. This Petalesharro was probably a Chaui, or Grand Pawnee.*

Below: *Silver medal given to the Skidi warrior Petalesharro by the girls at a select female seminary in Washington in recognition of his bravery in rescuing an Ietan girl from sacrifice in the Morning Star ceremonial. Here the 'Bravest of the brave' hastens away the female captive.*

Above: *Skidi Pawnee earth lodge village on the Loup Fork of the Platte River, Nebraska, photograph by W. H. Jackson, 1868–9. This village was built about 1830 and it is probable that* Petalesharro *died here shortly after (Hyde, 1974:162).*

Below: *Obverse of the* Petalesharro *medal showing the empty scaffold from which the Skidi hero rescued the Ietan girl in 1817. The medal was found in 1883 near Fullerton on the Loup Fork of the Platte River at the original location of the Pawnee village.*

From that time on, the fortunes of the Pawnee progressively worsened. By 1849 their population had dropped from an estimated 10,000 in 1838 to 4500; cholera, smallpox and other diseases, as well as attacks by the numerically more powerful Sioux, continued to deplete their numbers and by the early 1900s fewer than 650 Pawnee were left. And what of *Petalesharro*? All evidence suggests that this tall, handsome man, regarded by all in his day 'as the bravest warrior in the tribe' (Hyde, 1974:160) died unusually young – in his mid-thirties – at the Skidi village on the Loup Fork, in present-day Nebraska where he was buried. *Petalesharro* was not allowed to rest, however; in 1883, his grave was desecrated and his coveted medal taken from his remains. Could it be that Morning Star was wreaking revenge?

The Vision Quest

An important stage in the life of a Plains youth was marked by the seeking of a supernatural helper where a strong relationship was forged with some divine power or element. Retreating to some secluded place, the young vision quester passed through this experience on his own; little food was eaten and it was during a sleep or trance and in a highly intensified state that, if the gods were with him, he would see the special medicine through which he would receive supernatural aid. Frequently, the vision was accompanied by a call or song which could be used to summon aid in time of need. Such quests could last up to four days and nights but might be shorter; it all depended upon the suppliant's ability to cope with the demanding ordeal.

One of the few pictorial recordings of a vision was produced by the *Okicize-tawa*, or His Battle, a Lakota (Hunkpapa)[14]

Left: *The vision of* Okicize-tawa, *or His Battle, sketched circa 1880 and collected at Fort Yates, Standing Rock Indian Reservation, by the artist DeCost Smith. Here, the various supernaturals show their support of His Battle, all being joined by lines which converge to his sacred pipe. His Battle shows the dragon-fly and swallow emerging from a mirror which were often given mystical properties in Plains Indian symbolism.*

warrior who in his later years became a much respected healer. Here (see above) at the center of the drawing is His Battle holding a pipe which will henceforth be sacred; by him are the Pipestone and Cedar Spirits. *Wakinyan*, the Thunder God, has emerged from the clouds, who on flashing the mirrors on his wings has brought forth the Swallow and Dragon-fly. The power of the Thunder God appears to have been enhanced by the addition of horns – suggestive of buffalo spirits – but His Battle gave no explanation of this. He did, however, refer to Coyote emerging from the cloud and from other regions came two Hawks and a Fox . . . the lines linking these various supernatural creatures to the central figure conveying that they all smoked the pipe with him and took him under their protection. As messengers from *Wakan-Tanka* they would help him,[15] not only in his role as a warrior but later as a *pejuta wicasa*, 'medicine man', one who cured his patients mainly by the use of herbs.

A Crow vision quest

While His Battle's spirit helpers made him successful as a warrior and healer, the vision quest of Plenty Coups foretold his future role as an outstanding chief of the Crow. At the age of nine, after the death of a beloved brother at the hands of Lakota enemies, Plenty Coups sought supernatural power to revenge his loss, the first of several vision quests he would undertake throughout his long and successful life. His experiences tell us much of the psychology and practicalities of the vision quest: 'Nobody saw me leave the village. I slipped away and climbed The-buffalo's-heart, where I fasted two more days and nights, without success . . . The fourth night, while I was asleep, a voice said to me, "You did not go to the right mountain, Plentycoups".[16] *I knew then that I should sometime succeed in dreaming*' (Linderman, 1930:35) (author's italics).

Plenty Coups subsequently climbed to the top of the south Twin Butte in the Little Rockies (in northern Montana, close to the Canadian border), having first taken a sweat bath. There he made a bed of sweet-sage and ground cedar and, determined that 'no smell of man' should be on his body, he burnt a root of *e-say*[17] mixed with sweet-sage and stood in the smoke rubbing his body with sage. Exhausted by the climb and heat, he laid

Above: *Crow delegation to Washington in 1880. Standing are (left to right), A.M. Quivly (interpreter), Two Belly, Agent Augustus R. Keller, and interpreter Tom Stewart; seated are Old Crow, Medicine Crow, Long Elk, Plenty Coups and Pretty Eagle. Most, if not all, of these men would have undertaken a vision quest receiving signs from a higher power which would guide and protect them throughout their life. Thus, in one such quest, Plenty Coups was told that he possessed the power to become a great man – but success would only come to him by his own efforts.*

down in the fasting bed – which like all such structures was oriented east–west so as to face the rising sun. He woke in the middle of the night and looking up at the clear sky he saw that The-seven-stars (the Big Dipper) had now turned around The-star-that-does-not-move (North Star): 'The night was west-ward. Morning was not far away, and wolves were howling on the plains far below me' (ibid.:35–6).

Suddenly, a voice called his name. 'My name was spoken! The voice came from behind me, back of my head. My heart leaped like a deer struck by an arrow. 'Yes,' I answered, without mov-ing. "They want you, Plenty-coups. I have been sent to fetch you," said the voice yet behind me, back of my head' (ibid.:36).

In his dream, Plenty Coups traveled to a sacred lodge with its entrance facing east. There he met an assembly of ancient war-riors each distinguished by many coups, signified by the breath and first feathers of the golden eagle displayed before them.[18] Some Plenty Coups seemed to have recognized as the great forces of nature – the Winds, Storms, Thunder, Moon and Stars 'all powerful, and each of them braver and much stronger than men'. Then the person at the head of the lodge on the north side, handed him 'several beautiful first-feathers of a war-eagle' (ibid.:38–40). This person he recognized as Chief of the Little People, who in Crow mythology were beings, although of small physical size, said to possess great physical strength and super-natural power.[19] The Dwarf-chief, before the assembled all powerful Persons of the sacred lodge, now counted coups in

Left: *Plenty Coups, Crow chief, photographed in Washington, D.C., 1880, was one of the most famous Crow chiefs (1848–1932). At an early age he received revelations during a vision quest – where he met the great forces of nature and beings powerful in Crow mythology – and it was revealed that he would become a chief. In subsequent years he gained a large following and became the last traditional chief of the Crow. Honored by whites and Indians alike, he was chosen to represent all American Indians at the unveiling of the tomb of the unknown soldier of World War I at Arlington Cemetery, Virginia, in November 1921.*

Plenty Coups' name: ' "He will be a Chief," said the Dwarf-chief. "I can give him nothing. He already possesses the power to become great if he will use it. Let him cultivate his senses, let him use the powers which *Ah-badt-dadt-deah* has given him, and he will go far . . ." ' (ibid.:42).

Plenty Coups learned and understood that whatever he accomplished it had to be by his own efforts and he recognized that he could be successful if he used the powers that *Ah-badt-dadt-deah* had given him. 'I *had* a will and I would use it, make it work for me, as the Dwarf-chief had advised. I became very happy, lying there looking up into the sky. My heart began to sing like a bird, and I went back to the village, needing no man to tell me the meaning of my dream. I took a sweat-bath and rested in my father's lodge. I *knew* myself now' (ibid.:44).[20]

Interpreting the vision obligations
While Plenty Coups claimed that he needed no man to interpret the meaning of his powerful dream, lesser individuals worked under the direction of a shaman, who among the Lakota was referred to as a *wicasa wakan*, 'holy' or 'mystery man'. Thus, when a Lakota youth underwent the *hanbleceya* (crying for a dream or vision), his subsequent dream symbols were interpreted by one fully informed and conversant with the tribe's religion, although there is some evidence to suggest that there was a degree of specialization and another might be summoned if the true meaning could not be established by one shaman alone (Walker, DeMallie and Jahner eds, 1980:18).

The visionary was then instructed to go out and collect certain objects which were referred to in the dream and from these a *wasicun*, or personal medicine bundle, was constructed by the shaman who infused it with *wakan*, power.[21] These bundles differed considerably both in content and function from the tribally owned or used bundles such as the Lakota Calf Pipe Bundle, Blackfeet Beaver and Pipe Bundles, Mandan Lone Man Bundle and Pawnee Star Bundles. The *wasicun* gave protection in battle or special skills in hunting or healing, perhaps even in love. In contrast, tribal bundles were almost exclusively employed in the major tribal ceremonies, many of them being associated with buffalo-calling rituals or for ensuring bountiful crops and thus protecting the people at large from hunger and strife.[22]

The vision quest of the Plains Indian has been subjected to psychological analysis by several scholars (Benedict, 1924; Lowie, 1935; Devereux, 1969; Powers, 1986; DeMallie and Parks eds, 1987) and their conclusions leave little doubt that the great majority of the visionaries firmly believed in the truth and reality of their experiences.

There were few who did not covet a personal revelation of some kind but not all were successful and attempts at deception brought only failure. However, for these not all was lost for transfer of power by a successful visionary or medicine bundle owner to another less fortunate was a custom widely practiced on the Plains.

The Shaman

The holy man or woman played an important role in Plains Indian society. Such individuals were almost entirely self-selected, since the most important visions which elevated their position above those of others occurred without any conscious preparation, as in the cases of His Battle and Plenty Coups already related. In the same category were such individuals as Sitting Bull (Vestal, 1957), Crazy Horse (Sandoz, 1961) and Black Elk (Neihardt, 1932) and more recently the Comanche holy woman Sanapia (1895–1969), who acquired supernatural power from a *medicine eagle* representing in her remarkable success in healing ancient Comanche ways but who was still practicing in the mid-1950s.[23] While eagle power was evoked, Sanapia utilized more than fifteen different herbs to treat cataracts, insect bites, tuberculosis and even epilepsy (Jones, 1972:47–64).

It is notable that the most important visions frequently occurred when individuals had an illness or were under some other physical or mental stress. Thus, just prior (mid-June 1876) to the Custer Battle, Sitting Bull had a great vision wherein he, just as did Plenty Coups (pp.76–9) heard a voice from above saying, '*I give you these because they have no ears*'. When he looked up he saw white soldiers falling into camp, they were upside down, interpreted by the Lakota that the soldiers would be killed (Vestal, 1957:150; Diessner, 1993:71).[24]

Both Black Elk and Sitting Bull seemed at an early age to have an awareness of their destiny as spiritual leaders; before his Great Vision at the age of nine, Black Elk remembers a voice calling him from the clouds: 'Behold, a sacred voice is calling you; All over the sky a sacred voice is calling' (Neihardt, 1932:19).

In his vision, Black Elk stood central to a myriad of visual symbols – animals, plants and *wakan* beings – describing himself as surrounded by 'nations' of animals approaching him from all over the earth as the *wakan* powers were transmitted to him and which charted the rest of his life as a holy man. Such roles did not, however, come easily. As Lakota informants recorded, it required great 'effort and study' (Densmore, 1918:85) to interpret their meaning; success in such endeavors was the mark of the outstanding shaman who, by contemplation, systematized and brought order to a confusion of visual and auditory symbolic images. In Black Elk's case, he was subsequently able to meet both his own and his people's spiritual needs. As a human receptacle of the recognized *wakan* powers of the Lakota universe, it gave him an understanding of the meaning of life and his message, since first reported more than sixty years ago, has been enthusiastically received by successive generations of readers.

Right: Tatan'ka iyo' take, *or Sitting Bull (1834–90) by D. F. Barry circa 1885. Sitting Bull stood high among his own people being respected for his generosity, quiet disposition, keen discernment and adherence to Indian ideals. At an early age he became aware of his destiny as a spiritual leader or holy man and later, in the performance of the Sun-dance just prior to the Custer Battle, he had a vision of soldiers falling from the skies upside down and thus predicted the successful outcome of the engagement. He was politically active in the late 1880s opposing the sale of tribal lands. In 1890, he gave support to the Ghost-dance movement and for this an attempt was made to arrest him in his camp on the Grand River (December 1890). In the ensuing battle, Sitting Bull was killed.*

Sacred language of the shamans

It has been recorded (ibid.:85, 120; Powers, 1986:3, 10) that, as with the Mandan, a particular body of speech and song was utilized by shamans in order that persons intimate with the supernatural beings could communicate with the supernatural powers that held sway in the Lakota cosmos or among themselves when discussing Lakota philosophy, without being understood by the common people. Only shamans could supervise many rituals and, since the 'Sacred language' was unintelligible to the majority, it served to increase the status of the *wicasa wakan*.

The full meaning of the Lakota shaman's sentiments could only be gained from the context in which the word was used and, to one unfamiliar with the complexities of a particular ritual, it would not be understood. Thus, a song commonly used by the Lakota *wicasa wakan* as a prayer for the sick contains the phrase *cante matokecaca*, literally translated as 'with a heart that is different'; however, in the 'sacred language' of the shaman, such familiar words take on a mystical meaning and carry the idea of the fierceness of a bear, while the term *wahu nonpa*, literally 'two-legged object', refers to a human being. Further, as one keen observer has reported 'in the mind of the Sioux the meaning of the word *wakan* contains more of mystery and a greater element of the supernatural than we are accustomed to associate with the words "sacred" or "holy", though these are used as its English equivalent' (Densmore, 1918:120–21).

Medicine bundles

In addition to the personal medicine bundles often made up after a vision quest and advice from those considered specialists in the religious ethos of the tribe (referred to earlier), many tribes had larger and more pretentious bundles containing a variety of objects considered sacred because of their powers as pronounced by the supernatural beings. Some were huge, such as the Beaver and Pipe Bundles (see right) of the Blackfeet; others, such as the Sacred Tribal Flat Pipe of the Arapaho, were kept in a special tipi and suspended so that they never touched the ground. The Pawnee had their Star Bundles made up, it was said, according to instructions received through visions from particular stars and several contained fossils or pyrites believed to be fragments of meteorites – visiting stars with messages from the heavens (Chamberlain, 1982:144, 152). Additionally, there were the four Medicine Arrows of the Cheyenne and the *Issiwun*, or 'Sacred Buffalo Hat' of the *Suhtai*; the *Tai-me*, or 'Sun-dance medicine', of the Kiowa (which they obtained from the Crow in the 1760s); the Buffalo Calf Pipe of the Lakota; and the *O-kee-pa* drums of the Mandan, to name but a few of the most famous. Keepers of such bundles directed, or were involved in, many of the major ceremonials, such as the Sun-dance and *O-kee-pa*. Such individuals were held in very

high esteem and were generally viewed with awe by the people at large.

Medicine pipe bundles

Among the most ancient of medicine bundles are those associated with pipes which almost certainly have their origins in the early calumet ceremonials described in the 1500s and 1600s for the eastern tribes in North America (Paper, 1988:18–21). The Blackfeet, just as their immediate neighbors such as the Cree and Assiniboin, claimed that the original pipe was revealed to them by the Thunder and while Wissler found at least seventeen pipe bundles among the various groups, most he felt had a common origin (Wissler, 1912(a):136). Often referred to as the Thunder Pipe Bundle, the outer wrappings were composed of the skins of a black bear and elk. A broad band of elk hide held the bundle together since traditionally it consisted of two separate parts (see left). The main or primary bundle always contained a decorated pipe stem, a headband of white buffalo skin and an eagle's feather for tying on a pipe owner's head. The contents of the secondary bundle might vary but generally consisted of a smaller pipe-stem and the skins of the owl, loon, swan, crane, musk rat, otter and fawn. In addition, there was a rattle, whistle and occasionally the skin of a prairie dog. Tobacco was put on the bird skins, the rattle was kept in a sheath of prairie dog skin and the whole wrapped in pieces of brightly colored calico.

When not in use, the bundle was always hung so that the mouthpiece of the pipe-stem pointed north and as a guide the ends of the sheath holding the stem were tied with different colored cords. The bowls for such pipes, generally made of black steatite and of the 'Modified Micmac' style (West, 1934 vol.1:315), were not kept in the bundle, the medicine stem seldom being smoked.[25] However, pipe bowl and stem (see left) were united when the bundle was opened at the Sun-dance ceremonial and brought into the sacred enclosure; at that time, custom dictated that the pipe should be lighted 'with flint and steel by a person who has captured a medicine-pipe from the enemy' (Wissler, 1912(a):137).

A square-shaped bag or parfleche (rawhide) embellished with painted geometric designs and heavily fringed with buckskin along its sides was associated with the bundle; in this were kept paints, sweetgrass and other scented materials, beads, a necklace for the wife of the owner, a wooden bowl, whip and a rope.

Owners of a Pipe Bundle were referred to as *ninampskan kweniman*, or 'medicine pipe men'. The owner received great social, religious and sometimes political recognition and his wife was also afforded considerable honor, being given a seat in a host's tipi not lower than that of the head wife. Loud or boisterous behavior was forbidden in their presence. In daily life, however, the owner was obliged to observe many burdensome rules: never to point at a person with any digit but the thumb;

Above: *Blackfeet medicine pipe. Among the important medicines of the Blackfeet were the sacred pipe bundles which were said to be a gift of the thunder. Ceremonials associated with pipe bundles were often for the benefit of the people.*

Above: *The medicine pipe bundle. Blackfeet. Possession of such bundles gave the owner* natosini, *or 'medicine power'. As can be seen here, the contents were made up into two bundles the smaller of which could be carried on the warpath.*

Left: *Medicine bag. Blackfeet(?). This unusual early piece was collected by Maximilian, Prince of Wied, in 1832–4. It is made of a complete albino badger skin with an opening slit on the underside of the neck. The use of the entire skin to make this bag reflects a widespread belief on the Plains – and beyond – that symbolically the powers of the animal would be retained. It measures about 32in (83cm).*

never to appropriate any object which he might find or ask for any loaned objects to be returned; always to handle the pipe in a certain manner; and when camp was on the move, paint his horse a certain way. During the day the bundle was to be kept hung outside on a tripod, while each morning his wife was to make a smudge and throughout the day shift the position of the bundle in a sunwise sequence, always ensuring that the mouth-piece of the stem pointed toward the north, never touching the ground.

It was also obligatory for the owner to open the Pipe Bundle at the return of the thunder in the spring. The pipe was carried out of the tipi and prayers made to the Thunder-powers with the mouthpiece held up toward the sky; tobacco was then taken out of the bundle and distributed to the people who had gathered, its possession and smoking being believed to bring the all-pervading good will of the thunder. Prayers for plenty of all things – meat, vegetables, berries, children, long life and success in undertakings – were given and there was a specific request for protection against lightning.[26] Also, when someone in distress had vowed to the sun to dance with the pipe-stem and requested use of the pipe, the owner was obliged again to open the bundle. Clearly, ownership of such bundles, with its many obligations, was a costly affair. Thus, only individuals with the necessary resources, confidence and standing in the tribe, were prepared to take on such onerous commitments and it was not unusual for many to avoid any involvement with it.[27]

Honoring Buffalo Powers

When the enormous economic importance of the buffalo to Plains tribes is considered, it is not at all surprising that the animal figured prominently in religious ceremonials and rituals throughout the Plains region and beyond.[28] Thus men who had received buffalo power in their vision quests often formed a select group of Buffalo doctors and such individuals were considered to be specialists in setting broken bones or treating wounds, while in warrior fraternities the dress and dance were indicative that the warriors considered themselves to have the fortitude and strength of the buffalo and, like the old bulls, the wisdom to guide and protect. This sentiment was emphasized by those tribes who had age-graded warrior societies, when the Bull Society was invariably near the top, composed of older, semi-retired men (Lowie, 1916:893, 906).

Other dances, such as those associated with the Mandan *O-kee-pa* and Hidatsa Red Stick ceremony, were performed to honor the 'Buffalo tribe'[29] – giving thanks for the provision of food and to 'call' the buffalo to the vicinity of the village; such ceremonies often introduced an element of sexual licence. Thus, in the Red Stick ceremony, the sexual act constituted a transfer of supernatural powers from the older buffalo impersonator to a 'son' through the 'son's' wife who, prior to the sex act, was a 'daughter-in-law' to the buffalo impersonator. It

Above: *Participant in the bull-dance associated with the O-kee-pa ceremonial of the Mandan. Painting by George Catlin based on sketches made at the Mandan village near Fort Clark in July 1832. The bull-dance was part of the buffalo-calling ceremonials where the participants imitated the motions of the buffalo. Of the eight principal dancers, two, designated as the leaders, wore as shown here a complete buffalo head mask with the horns still attached. Such buffalo-calling rituals were widespread on the Plains and were of ancient origin.*

Above: *The Alo'wanpi, or Hunka, ceremony of the Oglala (1907). The central idea of this ceremony, which traditionally extended over several days, was the great affection of a father for his child and the desire that only good should come to it. It is replete in buffalo power symbolism. Thus, the ceremonial was carried out in accordance with the instructions given by the White Buffalo Maiden, an important mythological figure. Crucial to the proceedings, as shown here, was the use of a painted buffalo skull lying on a bed of sage through which the child would be blessed.*

was considered that through the medium of the sex act 'the older men's supernatural powers to call the buffaloes were transmitted to the younger generation' (Bowers, 1965:455).[30]

Buffalo symbolism played a prominent part in the Sun-dance which was performed by all the Plains tribes in one form or another (see below) and was also present in the various versions of the Calumet ceremonies of such tribes as the Omaha and Ponca (*Wawan* ceremony), Lakota (*Hunka* ceremony) and Pawnee (*Hako* ceremony). Additionally, there were many ceremonies invoking or dedicated to the buffalo among these and other tribes which often involved the impersonation of the animals where certain individuals wore headdresses of the buffalo scalp and horns and danced imitating the bison bull, such as in the Arikara Buffalo Society dances.

The Arikara Buffalo Society

The Arikara Buffalo Society affords a good insight into the buffalo ceremonialism of the Plains tribes, all of which was highly complex and composite and generally embedded in mythological origin tales and religion. Thus, in the Buffalo Society or 'clan' of the Arikara there was a combination of buffalo-calling, thanksgiving rites and curing ceremonials and the Medicine Bundle which was used by the Society contained objects each of which could be categorized in terms of their function and symbolism in traditional Arikara religion.

The customary position in the Arikara Medicine Lodge of the bundles and Buffalo Society members was at the southwest, corresponding to a grouping of powers or elements dedicated by the Arikara to the guardian spirit of the buffalo, each of the semi-cardinal points – as with the Pawnee – being consecrated to one of four guardians. The contents of the Buffalo Society Bundle consisted not only of various holy objects which would

Below: Arikara Buffalo Society members about to enter the Medicine Lodge. E. S. Curtis photograph, 1908. This Society combined buffalo-calling and thanksgiving rituals with curing functions. Such activities were generally limited to the select Buffalo Society although there were variations across the Plains. The emphasis on honoring the 'Buffalo people' and giving thanks to the species for providing food was, however, widespread as was the idea of 'calling' the animal to the area by the performance of the buffalo-dance and the use of the buffalo headdress.

be used in the complex ceremonial, but also the regalia which would be worn by the various participants. The origin of the bundle was explained in terms of several tribal myths (Howard, 1974:243) of which 'Why the Buffalo No Longer Eat People' is a good representative. In this myth, a young Arikara warrior finds that the Buffalo people, who look like humans but have horns and a tail, are systematically hunting and killing humans. These ancestors of the Arikara are trying to come to the surface from a subterranean world but their attempts are continually foiled and their numbers depleted. The young warrior, following the advice of a supernatural buffalo cow, fabricates a number of bows and arrows and arms the humans, who now get the better of the Buffalo people; as they flee, these anthropomorphic creatures tuck pieces of human flesh beneath their arms, changing into buffalo, the human flesh becoming part of the buffalo.[31] The hero and his supernatural helper now claim the bundle formerly used by the Buffalo people when they had hunted humans; the couple marry, their descendants forming part of the Arikara tribe to whom the Buffalo woman teaches the songs and ceremony which go with the bundle. Of considerable interest is that musical rasps made of human arm bones were part of the ritual equipment which was supposedly used by the Buffalo people in the mythical period.

The ceremony was both an annual and lengthy affair beginning in late spring at the time of the ripening of squashes and continuing intermittently, until fall. Members, dressed and painted as prescribed by the myths, danced around a cedar post and stone which was in front of the Medicine Lodge. The cedar represented a mythical grandmother, the stone a mythical grandfather, to whom they appealed for success in the hunt and in war and protection from diseases. An important part of the ceremonial was a demonstration of magical feats for which the Arikara were famous; thus the trader, Pierre A. Tabeau who witnessed the ceremonial in the early 1800s, reported:

'I saw a man, named *Scarinau*, absolutely naked, his hands empty, the lodge well lighted, show to me, nearby, a leather garter and, after having rolled it in his hands, throw it on the ground, changed into a living adder . . . He repeated the same trick ten times without giving the least hint as to the means that he employed . . . Another shoots a gun through the body of his companion who falls down upon his back, dead. The blood gushes forth from two openings, showing that the bullet has gone through the body; but, after a great many grimaces and lamentations, he also is mysteriously healed' (Tabeau, Abel ed., 1939:188–9).

Tabeau also described a man being struck by a tomahawk while other men had knives thrust through the hand, arms and thighs or arrows thrust into their bodies, none apparently with any ill effect. It was all part of demonstrating the supposed

ability of the buffalo powers as inherited by the Society members, to treat wounds and cure illness and, while most obviously recognized it as clever trickery, Tabeau was moved to conclude that what he had observed was 'most striking and could scarcely be better done' (ibid.:189).

Two buffalo headdresses with horns and feather and grass ornaments attached within an Arikara Bundle described by the anthropologist James Howard (1974:261–2) constituted major elements of the bundle. They were worn by two Buffalo priests 'who were painted and mimed the actions of the great beasts', the object being 'to call the bison by means of sympathetic magic'[32] (ibid.:262)

Such performances combined characteristic ritual ideas of the Plains people, the Medicine Lodge, the bundle with its thought evoking contents, song, dances, prayers and sacred objects on display, face painting and regalia, which all initiated animal and higher powers. As with the *O-kee-pa* and Sundance, there was a strong notion that many blessings could be forthcoming through the innumerable powers evoked. Nevertheless, since Plains ethos stressed military prowess, ample opportunity was always given to warriors to recount their deeds of valor – their coups – before appreciative audiences, even though once removed from the avowed purpose of all such tribal ceremonies – the people's welfare.

Below: *Blackfeet horned headdress, circa 1870. Horned headdresses took on a variety of forms as shown with this fine specimen where the horns have been made from rawhide attached to a cap of red cloth which is decorated with strips of ermine, colored feathers, brass studs and beads. Such regalia distinguished individuals as having a particular status – as with the leaders in the O-kee-pa bull-dance and Arikara Buffalo Society and possibly in this case they herald in the Brave Dogs Society. Widespread, however, was the recognition that the wearing of a horned headdress and the accompanying dances were a reference to the fortitude and strength of the buffalo bulls.*

FOOTNOTES: CHAPTER THREE

1 There is evidence to suggest that some ceremonial regalia, such as the so-called famous 'Red Cloud shirt' now in the collection of the Plains Indian Museum in Cody, Wyoming, seems to have incorporated several features of the *Tobtob Kin* in both the beadwork and fringe embellishments (see Chapter VII). Dr J R Walker was a physician at Pine Ridge from 1896 to 1914 and collected material relating to almost every facet of the early Lakota way of life (see Walker, DeMallie and Jahner eds, 1980).

2 More recently, another member of the tribe, Allan Wolf Leg, has suggested parallels between Christianity and Blackfeet religion, nature itself being considered to be the true counterpart of Jesus Christ (Abley, 1987:460). See also Harrod (1987:41-5, 69-82) for a further analysis of Blackfeet religious concepts.

3 It was reported by Alice Fletcher that when old Pawnee religious leaders referred to *Tirawahat*, he was spoken of in a whisper and called by a *sacred name* which was not then known by the common people (Fletcher, 1903:10).

4 The term 'Evening Star' may owe more to white convention than Pawnee concepts and possibly, as Von Del Chamberlain has observed, may impose conceptual limitations which were not actually in Skidi thought. It is clear that the Pawnee considered the home of this star to be in the western sky and that they were also aware that this bright star spent part of its time in the morning sky. It was, however, most frequently seen with the moon in the western evening sky and has been identified as the planet Venus (see Chamberlain, 1982:52-3).

5 After detailed analysis, the astronomer Von Del Chamberlain of the Smithsonian Institution, Washington, D.C, concluded that Mars was the 'most likely candidate for the main Morning Star' (ibid.:89).

6 The position of the stars was also an important guide to the time when ceremonies should commence. The earth lodge acted as a type of astronomical observatory, the priests viewing through both the smoke hole and the east-oriented entrance way (see Weltfish, 1977:78-87).

7 The most detailed comparisons between the custom in Mexico and among the Pawnee are by Wissler and Spinden (1916) who suggest that the transfer was from the Aztec between 1506 and 1519.

8 Pawnee directional symbols not only put emphasis on the conventional cardinal points but also on the intercardinal directions – northeast, southeast, southwest and northwest. The meaning of these directions as 'entrance corridors in the sky' has been discussed by Dorsey (1904:14-20).

9 The word *Opirikuts* was both a dedication and a curse. The moment it was pronounced, the girl was sacred to the Morning Star and she was destined for sacrifice (Linton, 1922(a):28).

10 A star chart used in the Pawnee Great Cleansing Ceremony – 'a summary of all the Pawnee religious beliefs and practices' (Weltfish, 1977:151) – is now in the Field Museum of Natural History, Chicago (specimen number 71898).

11 One account of this part of the ceremony suggests that the firebrands represented the moccasins of the Morning Star.

12 Hyde (1974:161) records that the Arikara formerly also had this custom but abandoned it before 1833. The Arikara were associated with the Skidi Pawnee from whom they separated prior to 1770.

13 In 1811, the Skidi Pawnee leader, *Ritsirisaru*, Knife Chief, told William Clark, then Superintendent of Indian Affairs in St Louis, that he was opposed to the holding of the sacrifice; he knew that it was regarded with abhorrence by the whites but when he talked to 'the warriors of the tribe . . . [they] were hostile and defiant' (Weltfish, 1977:115).

14 His Battle was also known as Jaw (*Cehupa*). The artist DeCost Smith met him at Standing Rock in 1884 (Smith, 1943:125-7). The ethnologist Frances Densmore met His Battle in 1913 when he was sixty-three years old. She reproduced a number of his drawings (Densmore, 1918:Plates 60 and 62).

15 These pictographic images are well within the range of protective symbols used by the Lakota and similar renderings are to be found on Ghost-dance garments (see Wissler, 1907).

16 Among the best-known fasting areas in Crow country are the so-called Castle Rocks on the northeast edge of the Pryor Mountains. As Conner has reported, ascent and descent of these cliffs 'are not for the fainthearted . . . It is no wonder the spirits are generous with fasters here' (Connor, 1982:100). The author's visit to this area in the summer of 1993 was rewarded with never-to-be-forgotten views of the spectacular Crow domain.

17 This is probably *Pursh* (alum root – *Heuchera hispida*) which gives a sweet aroma when burned.

18 (a) The breath feathers grew under the tail feathers of the eagle and could be up to 11in (30cm) long. Fluttering of objects was believed to indicate communication with the higher powers (see Fletcher, 1887(a):283); (b) This is almost certainly a reference to the feathers from the immature golden eagle which are characteristically white with dark brown tips. After the age of four years the feathers begin to mottle and eventually become completely brown.

19 Arrow Rock in the Pryor Gap, Montana, was said by the Crow to have been the original home of the Little People. Tribal historian, Joe Medicine Crow, described the garments and hairstyle of these Little People to the author at Lodge Grass, Montana, in July 1993.

20 Plenty Coups (*Aleek-chea-ahoosh*), meaning 'Many Achievements') went on to become a renowned chief of the Crow and was subsequently greatly honored by whites as well as his own people. At the unveiling of the memorial to the unknown American dead of the First World War, he was chosen to represent all American Indians and laid a Crow eagle feathered headdress on the casket of the unknown soldier. That headdress can now be seen in the Amphitheater at Arlington Cemetery.

21 Curtis (1908:62) reports that the power transmitted was referred to as *wowasake*, 'strength'.

22 One of the most comprehensive discussions of the Plains medicine bundle is by Ewers (Wildschut, Ewers ed.,1960:147-73). More recently, Harrod has drawn attention to the bundles as being complex symbolic realities which are associated with various dimensions of 'transcendent meaning' (Harrod, 1987:68).

23 It is of interest to note that the Lakota used the term 'medicine man' (*pejuta wicasa*) to describe the individual who cured patients by means of sacred herbs.

   Raymond DeMallie was of the opinion that any nineteenth-century Lakota warrior who had vision experiences and *wakan* powers 'was by this very fact a 'medicine man', a *wicasa wakan*, but he felt that the degree to which one was so recognized 'related to the type of power one had – whether it extended to the areas of healing or foretelling the future' (R. DeMallie to C. F. Taylor, 11 March 1988).

24 A glimpse of Sitting Bull's spirituality and its associated obligations is given by the missionary Mary Collins, who visited Sitting Bull only one month before this unusual spiritual leader of the Lakota was killed (15 December 1890). The missionary refers to going to 'the sacred tent' and talking to Sitting Bull. She reported that his 'Hands and wrists were painted yellow and green; face painted red, green, and white . . . As I started toward him he said, "Winona, approach me on the left side and shake my left hand with your left hand" emphasizing that left-handedness was more often than not adopted in ritual (in Dorsey, 1894:531-2).

25 The Blackfeet pipe bowl underlines an influence from the Woodlands in pipe/calumet symbolism. The Blackfeet style differs mainly from the true Micmac in that it lacks a perforation 'that the true Micmac has at the back of the bowl' (West, 1934:315).

26 Lightning strikes are common on the treeless Plains and much Plains symbolism and mythology refers to lightning powers. A zigzag line *forked at the ends* appears on a shirt which is said to have belonged to Crazy Horse (Museum of the American Indian, New York. Specimen number 16/1351): the Lakota interpreted this as the wearer having direct contact with *Wakinyan*, the 'thunder being'.

27 Walter McClintock describes the unwillingness of Big Spring, a prominent Blackfeet warrior, sleeping away from camp because he was unwilling to stand the expense and trouble of keeping a Medicine Pipe: 'If they catch a man unawares and offer the Pipe to him, he dare not refuse, lest sickness or even death come to him, or to some member of his family' (McClintock, 1968:252).

28 As Howard (1974) has observed, Buffalo dances were widespread in eastern North America and the mid-west, reminding us that the range of the bison in early days (see Chapter I) was not limited to the prairie and high plains. Buffalo dances were also to be found among the Pueblo tribes and certain Plateau groups.

29 In the myth relating to the gift of the White Buffalo Calf Pipe to the Lakota, there is a strong reference to the 'Buffalo tribe' and the symbolism associated with buffalo powers (Densmore, 1918:64).

30 The Bulls Warrior Society of the Arikara was probably a late borrowing from the Hidatsa and Mandan (Lowie, 1916:893).

31 It is said that for this reason the Arikara used to discard the meat from beneath the buffalo's shoulder (Howard, 1974:244).

32 When Howard examined two Buffalo Society headdresses of the Arikara in 1973, he was led to observe 'their great curving black horns and shaggy wool, surmounted by the holy 'breath' feathers and other ornaments, presented an awesome appearance. We can imagine their effect in their true cultural setting, as the garb of priests intent upon bring food to the people' (ibid.:262).

WOMEN
AND CHILDREN
IN PLAINS SOCIETY

'Their shrill, metallic-voiced songs of encouragement urge on the departing war-party to greater exertions, to braver deeds, and the same shrill voices give them praise and welcome on their return . . . In this and many other ways they shape and control the public feeling and opinion of the camp, and this is the greatest force which controls the destiny of all Indian tribes' (Clark, 1885:408).

Napi's Distinction between Man and Woman

In 1846, the missionary Pierre De Smet recorded one of many mythological explanations the Plains tribes gave when illustrating the distinction between men and women. Speaking of the Blackfeet, he reported that one myth related that men and women emerged from two different lakes and for some time lived separately. The men, however, were poor and naked since they did not know how to tan hides, while the women also suffered because they had no skill in hunting. Thus, Old Man (or *Napi* – see Chapter III), a Blackfeet culture hero, brought the two sexes together: the union proved to be so beneficial to both that it was decided to make it permanent. 'It was agreed that the men should become the protectors of the women, and provide all necessaries for their support: whilst all other family cares would devolve upon the women.' Even though arranged by *Napi*, Blackfeet women bitterly complained to De Smet 'of the

Left: *A Southern Arapaho boy's shirt, circa 1890. This is of buckskin with extensive fringing so characteristic of southern Plains costume. The large neck flap is beaded along its edges to which is attached a sacred medicine pendant. Although not identified as such, it is possible that this garment was associated with the Ghost-dance movement.*

Right: *Powder Face, wife and son. Southern Arapaho, circa 1880. Family ties were generally very strong in Plains society and parents were entirely devoted to their children, bestowing upon them the fullest expressions of affection and care. Some say that this strong relationship brought out the finest traits of Indian character.*

astonishing folly of their mothers in accepting such a proposition declaring, if the compact were yet to be made, they would arrange it in a very different manner'! (De Smet, Chittenden and Richardson eds, 1905:244).

The major role of Plains women, as with most other cultures throughout the world, was one of maintaining the established household, bearing children and preparing the food. In the horticultural societies they also tended the fields, planting and harvesting the crops, while, in the case of the nomadic buffalo-hunting western tribes, they helped butcher the animal, brought the meat into camp and subsequently prepared the meat and hides for future use. Woman's control of food production and other economic factors which included the right to distribute it obviously gave them considerable status. This was further recognized by their often deep involvement in tribal ceremonials such as the Sun-dance, their weight of opinion relating to the warpath (Stands in Timber and Liberty, 1967:63; Clark, 1885:408) and in some cases their attendance in council, although, as one anthropologist has observed, they could 'hardly be said to be politically dominant' (Weltfish, 1977:27).

Traditional Values

The importance of women in the domestic sphere, however, was predominant and it was a position strongly supported by traditional values. Typical Plains female virtues given by the Arapaho for a girl of marriageable age were 'modesty, attentive-

Above: Tow-ee-ka-wet, *a Cree woman, portrait by George Catlin. The words 'motherhood' and 'woman' were used interchangeably by the Cree.*

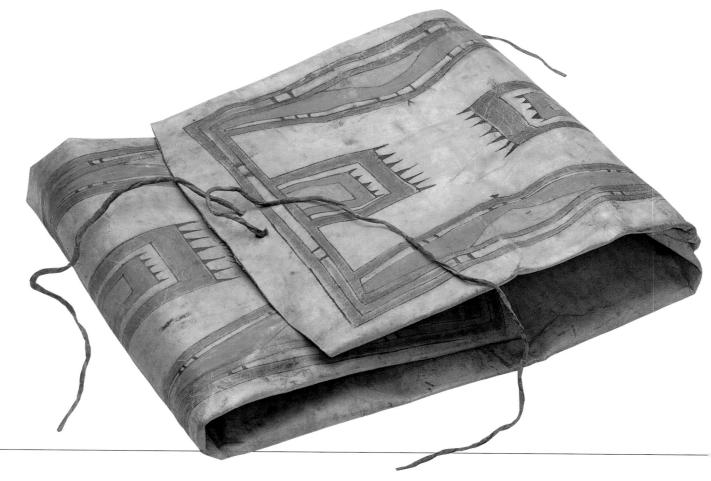

Above: *Arapaho (top) and Cheyenne (above) fully beaded moccasins, dating from circa 1890. Craft traditions were passed on by grandmother and mother. One of the most important tasks to be acquired by a girl was the production of moccasins which required considerable skill to cut both uppers and sole to the correct size and then sew with sinew.*

Left: *A Cheyenne parfleche, circa 1870. An important activity of the Plains craftswoman was the production of parfleches. Generally, the complete rawhide was stretched out and the geometrical designs painted on the surface, after which the hide was cut to the correct shape for the finished parfleche. The painting on Cheyenne parfleches was particularly distinctive, of which this one is a good example.*

ness to duty, diligence, and knowledge of a woman's work' (Hilger, 1952:198), while those for the Lakota, which were the symbolic four in number, were bravery, generosity, truthfulness and childbearing[1] (Hassrick, 1964:39). This last virtue was particularly emphasized by the Cree, who used the words 'motherhood' and 'woman' interchangeably and excluded women – as did most Plains tribes – from certain roles, such as shamanism, until they had passed through menopause, underlining another important facet in the life of a Plains Indian woman; as they grew older they gained far more control over their lives – and they did not necessarily require the support of a male to achieve this (Kehoe, 1973:267).

These values, and others such as premarital chastity, were emphasized to girls from early childhood;[2] as they grew into their teens they increasingly lost their freedom, being chaperoned by relatives particularly older brothers. Among the Lakota such chaperons were referred to as *hakatakus*, 'who served as guardians, watching and protecting her from the advances of other men' (Hassrick, 1964:113).

Girls were deeply influenced by both mother and grandmother and they were taught the crafts of hide-working – production of both rawhide, and the all-important parfleches which carried food and clothing, and soft-tanned skins for tipi making and clothes – as well as the skills of the decorative arts, such as quilling and beading, all so important. As one Cheyenne lady recalled, 'My mother taught me everything connected with the tipi, such as cooking and tanning hides for different purposes. The first pair of moccasins I made were for my father. "You are very good in making moccasins", he said with a smile, "they are very nice". This encouraged me greatly. My mother would show me how to twist the sinews, and how to cut the soles and uppers of the moccasins for different sizes. I became very competent in this work at an early age. I used to make moccasins for other children, beaded as well as plain ones. I was always well rewarded for my work by the parents of the children' (Michelson, 1932:2).

While girls were expected to have little contact with young men, the opposite was not true; young men were both encouraged and advised by relatives in their choice of a future wife. An Arapaho youth was thus advised by his mother, 'when you want a woman look for a good young girl. Select one that is good herself and has good parents.' The mother further said that girls who were especially liked were those who 'didn't look all around but kept their eyes cast down, and girls who always minded their own business' (Hilger, 1952:198).

Generally, marriage arrangements were made between the husband-to-be and one of the bride's male kinsmen and sometimes this came as a surprise to the potential bride. A Cheyenne girl related her experience on returning home one day after visiting a friend: 'there were a number of old men in my father's tipi: I also noticed much fresh meat. I asked my mother what it was all about, and what those old men were here for. She said, "My daughter, these men are here to deliver a message, asking the consent of your father that you marry a male of their family. And I want to tell you that your father has consented. However he will speak to you later". My father said to me, "My daughter, these men have come here to ask my consent to your marriage. Five horses and other things will be sent over in the morning. I have consented. *Now I myself want to hear what you think*" (author's emphasis) (Michelson, 1932:5–6). Family harmony was important and, to avoid trouble, if the girl refused that generally ended the matter. Agreement brought an exchange of gifts between the two parties; the narrative continues, 'My people saddled one of the horses on which I rode over to my future husband's people, leading the four other horses. My future husband's women folk met me near their camps and I dismounted. They carried me on the blanket the rest of the way, and let me down at the entrance of my future husband's tipi . . . In the meantime my mother and aunt had prepared a large feast . . . [a] cryer called in a loud voice inviting all my husband's relatives, naming my husband as the host . . . they told jokes, and some related their war exploits; still others narrated funny things that had happened to them in the earlier days'.

It was usual for the bride's family to provide a tipi and most of the furniture such as back rests, beds, cooking and eating utensils; many of these were also given by relatives of both families. Women were generally considered to be the owners of the tipi and held considerable sway in the way it was managed. They also owned the goods which were brought with them at marriage as well as the horses for their own or children's use and,

Below: Arapaho Sun-dance, 1893. Although much of the ceremonial was dominated by men, women played several key roles. For example, one important activity concerned the episode involving the ceremonial digging stick, where the wife of one of the principal priests both provided the stick and addressed a lengthy prayer to the higher powers. Shown here is the Offerings Lodge with the central pole and its bundle of willow and cottonwood at the top representing the Thunderbird's nest. Women around the Lodge wearing colorful shawls or blankets will sing and encourage the dancers within.

Above: *Two Lakota children photographed circa 1890. Children were considered both a gift and blessing from the higher powers; they tended to be unaggressive and non-confrontational toward each other. Fighting was almost unknown.*

while men traditionally generated wealth from horse raids and the hunt, the economic value of women was increasingly recognized as the impact of both the horse and fur trade became apparent.[3] The astute trader Edwin Denig recognized this when he observed in the 1850s, 'when buffalo are plenty, anyone can kill. The raw hide of the animal has no value. It is the labor of putting in in the form of a robe or skin fit for sale or use that makes its worth.[4] *Women therefore are the greatest wealth an Indian possesses next to his horses [and] often they are of primary consideration*' (author's emphasis) (Denig, Hewitt ed., 1930:506). Neither was this dependence on women confined to the buffalo hunting tribes. Thus tribes on the Missouri River such as the Mandan, Hidatsa, Arikara, Pawnee and Omaha, who depended for a good part of their subsistence on horticulture, traded immense numbers of goods to both the nomadic tribes and the fur companies. In this, the women were active participants in the intertribal trade networks, not only in producing the subsistence goods but also in controlling the distribution of surplus, both within and beyond the tribe. This role flexibility was an important component of Plains Indian social organization. As Weist has observed, 'in few other non-Western societies were some women able to participate so readily in those male activities that led to high prestige. Likewise, men could take on the roles of women' (Weist, 1980:262).

While, as has been mentioned earlier, the typical Plains woman was seldom involved in the political sphere to any great extent, her contribution in the *religious* sphere was considerable.[5] In addition to the women's societies which performed various ceremonials, particularly those associated with food production, bountiful harvests and buffalo-calling, there were symbolic links between women and buffalo, chastity and ritual, fertility and intertribal warfare. Indeed, as has been observed for the Blackfeet, 'Women were perceived as having within them the power of life and thus power over the continuity of existence' (Hanks and Richardson, 1945:20).

Women also assisted their husbands in the handling and care of his medicine bundles[6] and a number performed key roles in the Cheyenne, Arapaho, Crow, Cree and Gros Ventre Sundances. In the case of the Blackfeet, their involvement was extended still further in that a virtuous woman was the key ceremonialist, her husband assuming a supportive role (Wissler, 1918:229). Such ceremonials evoked much social responsibility and high-standing and confidence was pivotal to its success and the honor of the woman's family could be badly damaged if things were perceived to go wrong. Thus, when the center pole of the medicine lodge was raised into position, it was essential that it stood upright in the hole dug to receive it and 'the medicine women stood by, praying that this pole raising might be accomplished successfully. Should the pole fail to stand upright, people would surely accuse her of being less virtuous than she proclaimed to be'[7] (Ewers, 1958:180).

The Gift of a Child

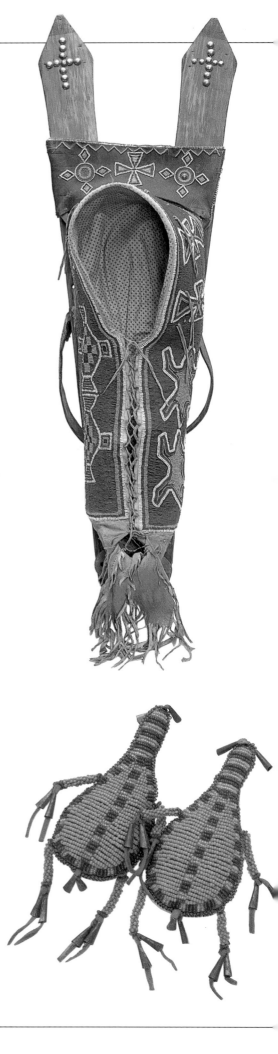

'It is strictly believed and understood by the Sioux that a child is the greatest gift from Wakan tanka, *in response to many devout prayers sacrifices, and promises'* (Robert Higheagle. Densmore, 1918:70).

From the moment of conception, most Plains tribes considered the fetus human and if born prematurely it was always given burial 'like an adult' (Hilger, 1952:5).

Plains children were treated with great tenderness and often nursed for several years; further pregnancies were spaced by couples keeping apart after the child was born, the husband then having relations with his other wives. One much respected Gros Ventre informant, Coming Daylight, told the ethnologist Regina Flannery that in the buffalo days, 'most women had only two or three children, – at most five, – and that some had none at all' (Flannery, 1953:128). Although a man might have several wives, it was the custom for each wife to have one or two children only; no one of them would have a great many even though one of them might be his favorite. The usual period of childbearing was eighteen to thirty-five, menopause usually occurring at forty, perhaps earlier and, as with all human beings, a family brought many obligations and sorrows – the gift from *Wakan-Tanka* was very vulnerable in the hazardous Plains environment. As Edwin Denig observed of the northern Plains tribes in the mid-nineteenth century, 'not more than two out of five children live until youth is passed' (Denig, Hewitt ed., 1930:513).

In the reported cases for the Arapaho – and this is also typical of many other Plains tribes – babies were generally born in the home tipi but the medicine bundles were always removed before birth. If inadvertently left in the tipi, 'they had to be removed within a day after the birth and purified by being fumigated' (Hilger, 1952:15). A woman knelt when giving birth, bracing herself by holding on to a horizontal rod above her head, with both hands; she was assisted by her mother and at least one older woman who was considered a professional midwife. Immediately after the delivery, one of the women attendants cut the umbilical cord and its end was tightly bound with sinew. Parts were kept and placed in a special amulet which often had a particular shape, depending upon the sex of the child; among the Blackfeet, for example, it had the shape of a lizard for boy and a frog for a girl.

The amulets – which were regarded as longevity charms – were generally attached to the infant's cradle; they were often beautifully quilled or beaded, perhaps by a proud grandmother, and became treasured heirlooms. If sold (and many were to souvenir-hunting whites in the Reservation period when the people reached a low ebb), the amulet cord was always removed, carefully buried and the buckskin container resewn.[8] (An example of such an amulet – Crow in this case and of late date – is shown right.)

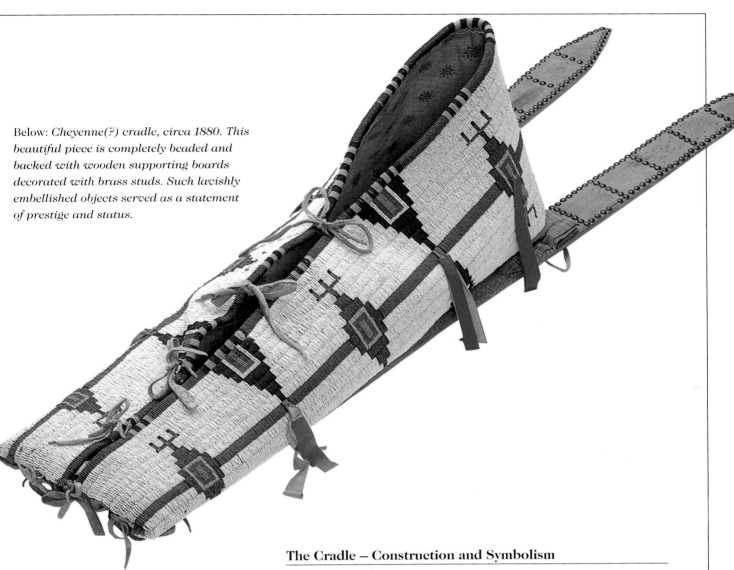

Below: *Cheyenne(?) cradle, circa 1880. This beautiful piece is completely beaded and backed with wooden supporting boards decorated with brass studs. Such lavishly embellished objects served as a statement of prestige and status.*

Above, left: *A Kiowa cradle dating from circa 1880. Here the carrying bag is tied or lashed to a lattice of flat boards, the whole surface of the bag being decorated with beadwork. Although structurally there were similarities for several central and southern Plains tribes, there was a marked difference in both colors and patterns in the beadwork and some definitive area styles are identifiable.*

Left: *A double umbilical cord amulet collected from the Crow and probably dating from circa 1890. Collection data suggest that these were for twins; such amulets were not infrequently tied to the child's cradle.*

The Cradle – Construction and Symbolism

Cradles varied considerably in both the method of construction and form. On the northern Plains and among the Crow as well as with some adjoining tribes on the Plateau, such as the Nez Perce and Flathead, the cradle consisted of a long, elliptical shaped board much broader at the top than at the bottom, the whole covered with buckskin and often heavily beaded; the lower half was made into a bag, laced at the front, into which the child was placed.

From at least the mid-nineteenth century, Lakota, Cheyenne, Comanche and Kiowa used two styles of baby carrier. One had a long straight-sided bag embellished with quill or beadwork attached to a pair of narrow wooden slats which projected above the baby's head and which were painted at the ends. The slats were held apart by cross-pieces, the whole frame having the appearance of an inverted 'A'. The other type was a triangular shaped hood of buckskin, quilled or beaded, to which was attached a large rectangular piece of skin. This folded around the baby and was tied at the front with thongs; when the lower corners of the hood were tied, it produced a head covering rather like a sun-bonnet.[9]

Cradle making was considered a ceremonial act and the beautiful embellishments of quillwork and beadwork, unessential to the practical function of carrying the child, acted as symbols of prestige. Among the Lakota, for example, they 'were status symbols, designators or rank, indicators of status, reinforcers or enhancers of status and reflections of a family's prestige' (Lessard, 1990:49).

Among the Arapaho – who had a distinctive form of cradle which was elaborately embellished with highly symbolic quillwork – the pieces were prepared separately and then attached to the cover, a large quilled disc being sewn directly to the hood, while a band and pendants were sewn around the opening for the child's head. Quilled wrapped rawhide or heavy buckskin strips about 1mm wide were attached to the edge of the opening and hung down each side of the cradle. Arapaho informants said that these should 'number at least 90; more than 90, however, even 100, were quite desirable as it was said that the bars indicated the number of years the maker hoped the child would live. The disc over the head was said to symbolize the sun, and the crown of the child's head, hence its intelligence. The red and yellow sections of the disc meeting at right angles formed a cross which was said to symbolize either the Morning Star or a woman. The white sections represented the four corners of the earth; the yellow, the light of the sun; the red, its heat; and the black, night. Four pendants were said, among other things, to represent the four periods of life while the long strips around the lower part of the cradle symbolized the child's ribs and the long pendant with bells, its energy and movement.[10] (Report by George Dorsey on the symbolism of an Arapaho cradle. See Hilger, 1952:33.)

Below: A Crow cradle, circa 1890. This example shows the elaborate decoration which went into the embellishment of cradles, particularly in the Reservation period. The flat board which forms the base of the cradle tapers toward the bottom. It is covered with buckskin with a bag at the front which will secure the child who is held in place by three pairs of broad straps. Such articles exemplify the finest of Crow beadwork.

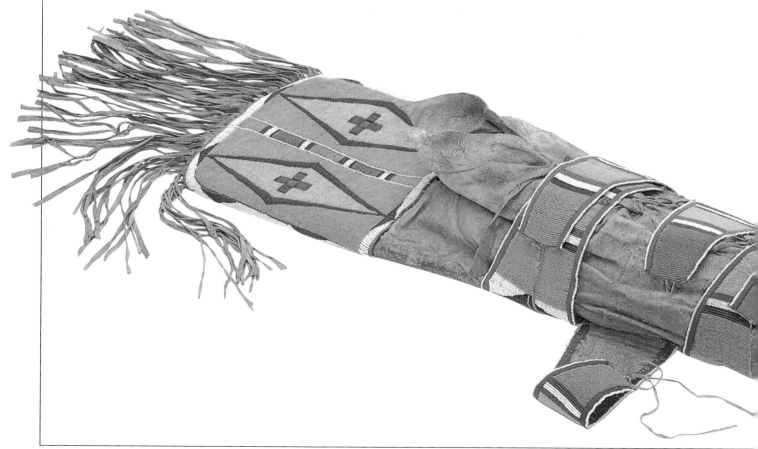

Right: *Blackfeet woman with cradle, circa 1900. Of interest here is that this woman, dressed in a typical Blackfeet style dress decorated with pony beads, is carrying a superbly embellished Lakota cradle. There was a great deal of intertribal trade and gift-giving during the Reservation period which probably explains the use of this alien piece by a Blackfeet woman.*

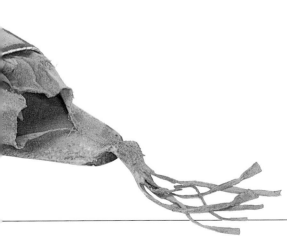

Also replete in symbolism was the Pawnee cradle board re-flecting much of the star lore and religion of the tribe (see Chapter III). The cradle was made of a long flat cottonwood board slightly wider at the top than at the bottom. A traditional embellishment was a carved and painted symbol of the Morning Star often combined with a symbol of the sun or lightning. The covering was of the spotted skin of a wild cat – an emblem of the starry sky – while above the board, over the head of the child, was a hoop which symbolized a rainbow. The Pawnee explained the origin of both the cradle and its designs in lengthy ancient myths, most of which centered around the Morning Star. Curtis reports, for example, that one myth tells how the Morning Star won the cradle board which hung with many others upon posts within a lodge in the heavens. All the cradles were embellished with emblematic designs; the one acquired by Morning Star was subsequently copied and has been used by the Pawnee ever since, who thus claim that the designs came from the stars and that 'the design tells that the child is under the protection of the morning star and is watched over by the Powers of the West, because of the rainbow' (Curtis, 1907:101–3).[11]

Lullabies

As in cultures throughout the world, the Plains Indian child was soothed with lullabies. One Arapaho explained that they were sung to lull babies to sleep, to entertain them, to quieten crying ones, and 'for no reason except that I'm holding my grandchild and like to sing to it'! (Hilger, 1952:38).

In the long winter nights, the mother or grandmother often sang the child to sleep and, in addition to lullabies, women might sing the songs of traditional dances such as those of the social dances. Sick Arapaho children had songs relating to the Sun-dance sung to them.[12] Games were also played with children where songs were sung; thus the Mandan and Hidatsa had a buffalo calf song in which the situation was made as exciting and amusing as possible, a play-fine being imposed on any child who laughed. The nonsense references in wavering intonation, to beaver teeth, worn out feet, wriggling bags, belly buttons, crabs and confused fat buffalo calves – all designed to amuse and bring laughter – tell much of the Plains Indians' sense of humor. The following is perhaps typical:

wedo'likadepe'na	lay a big, fat
hu'hamak ni'kasi	young buffalo calf
dě'ptaśedo'sedo	with a soft belly-button
ma'na	walking
wo'daśkiśki	crumbling sticks
do'ki	crab shells
wena'lipapa	have a dance
ista'	he
ka'daliunk'tka	knocked his eye out

(Densmore, 1923:172)

Sick Children

While it was customary on the Plains to give to a child the name of a person who had grown old and enjoyed good health, the belief being that such names assured those blessings, more practical steps were to take preventive measures to restore the health of a child. Thus, children were given a potion of peppermint plant but vapor-bathing, inhalations and fumigations were common and herbal concoctions were available from certain medicine men or women who had knowledge of the remedial use of roots, herbs and barks. While male physicians could be both herbalists and shamans, healing and religion often being inseparable in the practice of a medicine man, it was more rarely the case with women. Most women were herbalists.

When making curative fumes, Arapaho doctors placed cedar twigs or roots on hot coals and wafted the fumes over all parts of the child's body. Often he carried the fumes in the hollow of his hands joined in a bowl shape and held them so that the child would inhale the fumes. If the medicines were ineffective, the

Above: *A young Crow girl, circa 1880. This girl is wearing an elaborate dress embellished with elk teeth and unusually beaded leggings. The dentalium shell ear pendants are obviously attached through pierced ears. Among Plains tribes, the ceremonial piercing of the child's ears for the insertion of ornament was not infrequently made an occasion of public celebration.*

powers present at such religious ceremonials as the Sun-dance were sought. Perpetuating an age-old tradition, and typical of such practices, was the action of the several mothers and grandmothers of sick and crippled children at the close of the Northern Arapaho Sun-dance in the summer of 1940. Each dancer had his hands on the head of the sick child, 'raised his eyes heavenward and prayed for the recovery of the child' (Hilger, 1952:57). Likewise, the Lakota parents of a sick child vowed that if the child should live until the next Sun-dance its ears would be pierced, it being considered somewhat related in status to the men whose flesh was cut and lacerated in the Sun-dance. Gifts and feasts were expected, however, and it was generally impossible for poorer members of the tribe to meet the requirements.[13]

The Origin of Names

Every Plains Indian child was given a name either at birth or soon after, but it was unusual for the child to retain that name throughout life. During adolescence or as adults, both women and men either personally changed their name or may have had a new one forced on them. Plains Indian names usually originated from the observed characteristics or a particular person, in an activity associated with warfare or some unusual experience. The childhood name of Sitting Bull, for example, was *Hunkeshne*, which means 'Slow' or 'Thoughtful One', and was based on the observed fact that, even as an infant, when a piece of food or other object was put into his hand 'he did not immediately stick it into his mouth, like other children, but held it in his hand, turning it over and looking at it, until he had made up his mind' (Vestal, 1957:3). In later years when he struck his first enemy, his father gave him the name, *Tatanka Iyotake*, 'Sitting Bull', recognizing that his brave fighting qualities and heedless courage were like those of the buffalo bull held in such high esteem by the Lakota (ibid.: 13 and 19).

Once a name was established it was usually retained by relatives, particularly so if the person who bore the name grew old in good health and had the esteem of the tribe. Typical was the sentiment of the Gros Ventre who said it was believed that a person who had lived to a great age had been privileged by the Supreme Being and it was thought well to name the child after him or her (Flannery, 1953:196).

An Arapaho informant, Sage, related how his childhood name 'Mysterious-Magpie', which was given to him by his uncle, came about. While on the warpath, he noticed that a magpie always flew ahead of them. When the party reached a certain place, some of the warriors wanted to turn south. ' "Let's go in the direction of the magpie," said the others, "there must be something in this." Some went south; the others followed the magpie . . . Those that followed the magpie were the victorious ones; those that went south were defeated . . . When I came into the world, he said, "Here's Mysterious-Magpie"' (Hilger, 1952:58).

Below: *Plain Feather Woman, Crow, circa 1890. This unusual name suggests some passing incident or the commemoration of some event. Generally, a girl received different successive names at puberty, childbirth and in old age; many such names were hereditary and often bestowed by the grandparents, perhaps to the exclusion of the parents. Translations were, however, sometimes grossly misleading, thus the name of the famous Lakota chief, 'Young-man-afraid-of-his-horses' really signifies 'Young-man-whose-very-horses-are-feared'.*

Most of Sage's aunts, brothers, and cousins were named by his mother's grandfather, basing the names which he gave them on his war experiences, such as Striking-at-Night, Man-Going-Ahead, Striking-First and Travelling-Behind, all referring to his brave deeds and coups.

If parents decided to have a child named at a feast, they often invited several esteemed elderly men and women to their tipi, one of these persons having been asked to name the child. The group sat in a circle within the tipi, the namer sitting to the left of the door. The mother then handed the child to the namer while the father asked the group to pray for the child so that 'it would grow up to be a good person. The namer then called the child by the name he was giving it, held it in his arms, prayed for it, sometimes breathed on it and stroked it, and then passed it to the person at his left. The child was thus passed clockwise around the circle, each person holding it, praying for it, pronouncing its name, and possibly breathing on it and stroking it. The person at the right of the door, the last one to hold the child, handed it to its mother' (Hilger, 1952:62).

Buffalo Bird, a Hidatsa woman who was born about 1850, looked back on her childhood as the 'happiest time' of her life. She explained that for playgrounds in good weather, the children had the level spaces between the earth lodges or the ground under the corn stages, while if it rained there was the big roomy floor of the earth lodge. The children saw the year around with a variety of games. In winter sledding was a very popular sport. The simplest form of sled was a folded rawhide curved up at the front but several tribes, such as the Mandan and Hidatsa, made their sleds from buffalo ribs; typically, five to eight of the ribs were connected at one end with a wooden slat and buckskin strip while the top ends were held together with thongs passed through holes bored in the bone. A hide strap was tied at the front for pulling the sled along.

In March and April the boys located a level area where the snow had melted to play the hoop game where one team threw wooden hoops laced with a rawhide net into the air and the other side attempted to catch them on sticks. When the ice broke on the Missouri, the hoops were thrown into the water: 'We boys were taught, and we really believed it, that these hoops became dead buffaloes after they passed out of sight around the next point of land . . . Many dead buffaloes came floating down the Missouri in the springtime and their flesh was much valued' (Wilson, 1913:33, in Gilman and Schneider, 1987:27).

A popular sport played by girls (as well as women) was the stick and ball game where two teams attempted to get the ball through each other's goals. The sticks were generally made of curved willow and curved at one end, while the ball was of several pieces of buckskin and decorated with quill or bead-work.[14] Larger buckskin balls were actually popular toys for girls; a skilled game involved bouncing the ball on the toe, competing for the most bounces. The ball game became more

Above: *Playing with plum stones. Sioux. Engraving after a pencil sketch by Seth Eastman, circa 1845. Both games of chance and dexterity were highly popular with Plains tribes and a type of dice game was widely played. Here, the plum stones, probably seven or so, would be variously marked for scoring. A spider might count four, a lizard three and a turtle, six. The highest score after an agreed number of throws designated the winner, although there were considerable variations on the basic game.*

Right: *Crow girl with doll and cradle and, far right, a Lakota doll. Girls were their mother's companions and the games which they played often related to their role in adult life. They were particularly fond of puppies which the girls frequently dressed and carried on their backs like babies in imitation of their mothers. This girl holds a miniature cradle in typical Crow style; the head of the doll inside can just be seen.*

complex for older girls and women, who let the ball fall 'alternately on their foot and knee, again throwing it up and catching it, and thus keeping it in motion for a length of time without letting it fall to the ground' (Maximilian, Thwaites ed., 1906, vol. XXIII:299).

Throughout the year, boys and girls tended to play separately, learning their roles in life. As Buffalo Bird Woman's[15] mother told her, 'If you play with girls you will grow up to be a woman' (Wilson, 1913:17 in Gilman and Schneider, 1987:29). Girls played with dolls which were made of rushes or buckskin, the latter often beautifully beaded, imitating typical tribal styles of dress.

Many toys and activities reflected the life of grown-ups, reinforcing the mature role to be followed in life: girls erected miniature tipis, carried their dolls in cradles and played with model travois; boys fought play-battles. Wolf Chief, the Hidatsa, remembered learning the rudiments of warfare, observing 'If the two sides were brave the fight might be long. We thus learned to handle a bow & [how to] stick to the side of our ponies. If the pony was sweaty it wasn't such a task as it might seem. This was of value later for it help[ed] us learn to avoid arrows in real warfare' (Wilson, 1907:80 in ibid.:28).

Teaching Children to Ride

Children of the purely nomadic tribes were obviously accustomed to horses from infancy and became skilled riders at an early age. Early white observers of Plains Indians marveled at their skill on horseback. Typical was the comment by the explorer Victor Tixier who wrote of Osage boys who he saw in the summer of 1840 that they 'were riding alone bareback, and managed their horses with skill', although they 'could not have been more than five or six years old' (Tixier, McDermott ed., 1940:167).

Blackfeet informants told the ethnologist J. C. Ewers that their children usually learned to ride in their fifth year, riding lessons being given by fathers and mothers. Initially, the horse was led at a slow walk but, as the child gained in experience and confidence, the horse was led at a swifter pace. A widely used technique for younger children was to tie the child in the saddle when the camp was on the move, the horse being led by an adult. It could, however, be a dangerous way of teaching a child, it being reported that in the 1860s a fatal accident occurred when a Piegan father was leading his little son tied in the saddle when the horse bolted; the saddle slipped and the little boy was

Above: *Girls playing with toy tipis, Sioux, circa 1890. As with all children throughout the world, girls enjoyed 'playing house'. Here, they are seen playing with miniature tipis – the conically shaped portable dwelling which was so important to the Plains Indian nomadic way of life. Although a pastime, the handling of these models enabled a girl to become familiar with its structure, erection and adjustment of the smoke flaps.*

kicked to death. From then on the Piegan relied upon the child keeping its balance on a high pommel and cantle saddle (generally considered a woman's saddle) without being tied in. Certainly, by the age of six or seven, most Plains boys and girls were good riders; however, because the horse was relatively big for these youngsters, it is reported that they sometimes tied a short rawhide rope to the horse's mane. This was employed as a handhold 'as an aid in climbing onto [the] horse's back' (Ewers, 1955:67).

Even today among, for example, the Crow in Montana, youngsters from this traditionally horse-rich tribe are to be seen in parades (such as at Crow Fair), riding not now the relatively small Indian pony but the big 'American horse' with astonishing skill and expertise.

Keeping the Spirit – Insights into the Ethos of a People

Plains Indians valued life highly and, as has been discussed, prayed for long lives, children often being named after an

Below: *Crow girls on horseback, circa 1904. The high pommel and cantle saddle so typical of the Crow are used on the horses by both these girls as well as beautifully decorated cruppers, horse collars and headstalls. Accustomed to the saddle from an early age, Crow youngsters became highly proficient riders. Here they are obviously dressed ready for a parade so popular with the Crow at this time, where the finest of regalia would be worn and proudly displayed.*

esteemed aged person, in the hope that the child would receive a similar blessing from the higher powers.

The Lakota had a custom of 'keeping the spirit' of a lost one, prolonging the period of mourning perhaps for several months or a year and then 'letting it go' by means of certain ceremonials. The spirit of a child was 'kept' more often than that of an adult; typical of such ceremonials was one explained by the Lakota informant, Bear Face, whose son died at the age of fifteen. This ritual tells us so much regarding the holistic ethos of a typical Plains tribe – the preciousness of children, the virtues of generosity and kindness, community spirit, hospitality, care of the underprivileged, esteem and mutual respect – that it is worth recording in detail.

Having decided to keep the boy's spirit, Bear Face then announced that fact to the tribe: a lock of the boy's hair was cut off by a man 'whose record was without blemish'.[16] The hair was now wrapped in red cloth, and taking the bundle in his arms as if it were the body of the child, the spirit-keeper rode around the camp lamenting the child's passing. Thus, the keeper announced that he had taken upon himself all the responsibilities of the subsequent rituals associated with the Ceremony of Spirit-keeping. A specially decorated cover was now purchased and the boy's hair-lock was wrapped in this together with sweetgrass and shed buffalo hair, all in accordance with the instructions said to have been received from the White Buffalo Maiden, a powerful supernatural being who figures prominently in Lakota mythology.[17] The bundle was then attached to a long straight pole – generally pine – and erected outside the door of the spirit-keeper's tipi where it was to remain for four days.[18] During this period a special wrapping was made for it. This con-

Above: *A wrap for a spirit bundle and braid of sweetgrass. Lakota, early 1800s. The original owner indicated that this was of great age and used in the ceremonials relating to the 'keeping the spirits' of both her mother and grandfather. It is embellished with porcupine quills.*

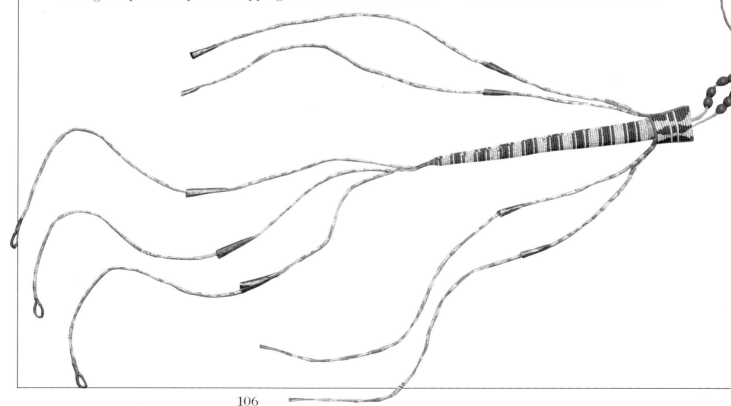

Above: *The spirit post, Lakota, circa 1900. The spirit post was generally made of cottonwood and carved in the spirit lodge after suitable purification ceremonials had been completed. At the right is the dressed spirit post, the costume being decorated with elk teeth and a woven beadwork belt.*

Left: *Awl case, central Plains, circa 1850. Collected by Rudolph Kurz, it was one of the several gifts which were donated during the spirit keeping ceremonial. Awls such as this were an essential component in any Plains woman's sewing kit and much time was expended on their decoration. The case here is embellished with beads and pendant from the top and bottom are long skin thongs which are wrapped at intervals with porcupine quills with metal cones part way down the length and at the ends.*

sisted of a large heavy piece of buckskin embellished with parallel lines of quillwork and edged with beads. During the four day period, feasts were given to others who had previously performed the spirit-keeping ceremonial. At the end of the allotted period, the bundle was removed and placed in its elaborately decorated wrapping together with articles which were intended as gifts to all those who took part in the ceremony. This larger bundle was now supported on a tripod of stakes a short distance from the door of the spirit-keeper's tipi – now designated a *wanagi* tipi, or spirit lodge. Gifts were now collected – tobacco, knives, awls, needles and pipes – for the man who would be in charge of the final part of the ceremonial.

A small circular area inside the tipi and toward the back was now 'mellowed'; that is the earth was cleared of all vegetation, the soil dug to the depth of the index finger and then broken by hand so that it had a fine sand-like texture.[19] Two wooden implements, one pointed, the other broad at the end, together with a buffalo chip, were now placed at the center, and these were to be used whenever sweetgrass was burned in the subsequent rituals. Throughout the whole period, the spirit-keeper and his wife wore no ornaments and their manner was always quiet and reverent 'as though the body of the relative whom they mourned was in the lodge' (Densmore, 1918:80). The spirit bundle and its supporting tripod were brought in every night, the bundle being set in the place of honor – at the back of the tipi, opposite the door – where it was treated with the utmost respect, no one passing between it and the fire. Bear Face acquired the robe of a white buffalo which was spread in the place of honor; a most desired article, it signified that all the objects associated with the ceremonial had been purified and that the spirit was being kept pure. The robe could only be moved by a specially designated person, such as a recognized ceremonialist or a child who had been through the *Alowanpi*.[20]

At the expiration of the time for keeping the spirit – perhaps several months or even a year – the *Waki cagapi*, or final ceremony and feast, were held. All the immediate band together with representatives of the various military societies now gathered near the spirit lodge and if several spirits were to be released they identified the man who had first announced his intention and he was designated as the leader, *itancan*, of the spirit-keepers. A filled pipe was then sent to a respected elderly man, inviting him to be the master of the whole final ceremony and the *Ceremony of Restoring the Mourners* commenced. Weasel Bear, who had lost a little girl, said that on that day they were 'to lay aside all signs of mourning' (ibid.: 81) and so he painted himself gaily, putting on all his finest attire, including a war-honor feather; his wife was also gaily attired. The spirit posts were now prepared. These were made within the spirit lodge, carved from cottonwood with a knife which had first been purified in sweetgrass. They were generally about 3 feet (1m) long and had a piece of buckskin with a face painted on it,

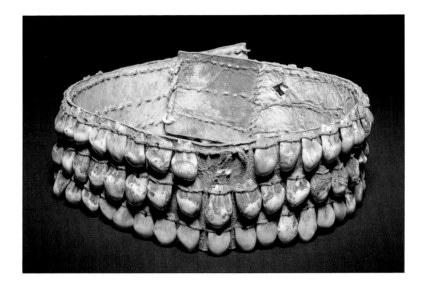

bound at the top; the face represented the one whose spirit was to be released and garments formerly their property were used to dress the post. The 'feeding of the spirits' now commenced.

A woman who was in charge of cooking purified some meat in the smoke of sweetgrass and offered it to the painted mouth on the spirit post. It was at this time that underprivileged community members, orphans and poor people had an opportunity to seek help in the name of the spirits to be released; such a request it is said was never refused.[21] The gifts which had been accumulated by the family of the spirit-keeper and exhibited to the people were now distributed: these consisted of such useful articles as moccasins, belts and leggings, while eagle feathers might be given to the warrior societies who had kept order in the camp for the duration of the ceremonial. This was a time for a great deal of feasting. Opportunity was also taken for prominent families to announce publicly the names which they had bestowed on their children or to have the ears of their children pierced, an honorable ceremonial akin in some ways to the giving of flesh in the Sun-dance.

The final release of the spirits came when the bundles were opened by the master of the entire final ceremony. The action was carried out in four stages, as Weasel Bear reported: 'He did not take all the wrapping from a spirit bundle at once. He removed a portion and then made a brief discourse, doing this in such a manner that there were four acts of unwrapping, the last one occurring about an hour before sunset. Then he unfolded the last wrapping and let the spirit of my child depart' (ibid.:83).

If a white buffalo robe had been used in the ceremonial, a great deal of interest was taken in who would gain the honor of removing it from the spirit lodge. Generally, it was a highly esteemed man who had formerly owned a white buffalo robe and in this task he was sometimes helped by a child who had been through the *Alowanpi* ceremony (see previous page). Together, they laid the white robe over a framework set up outside

TABLE IV.1: PLAINS INDIANS' USE OF THE BUFFALO (after Ewers, 1955; and DeMallie, 1984)

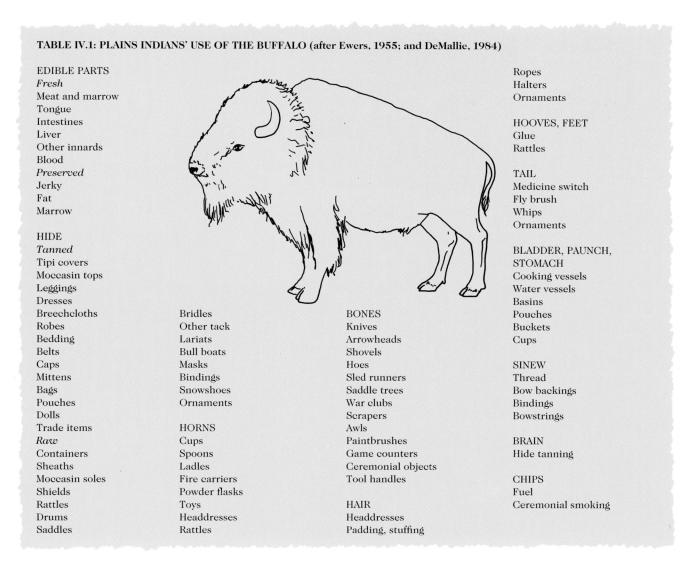

EDIBLE PARTS			Ropes
Fresh			Halters
Meat and marrow			Ornaments
Tongue			
Intestines			HOOVES, FEET
Liver			Glue
Other innards			Rattles
Blood			
Preserved			TAIL
Jerky			Medicine switch
Fat			Fly brush
Marrow			Whips
			Ornaments
HIDE			
Tanned			BLADDER, PAUNCH,
Tipi covers			STOMACH
Moccasin tops			Cooking vessels
Leggings			Water vessels
Dresses			Basins
Breechcloths	Bridles	BONES	Pouches
Robes	Other tack	Knives	Buckets
Bedding	Lariats	Arrowheads	Cups
Belts	Bull boats	Shovels	
Caps	Masks	Hoes	SINEW
Mittens	Bindings	Sled runners	Thread
Bags	Snowshoes	Saddle trees	Bow backings
Pouches	Ornaments	War clubs	Bindings
Dolls		Scrapers	Bowstrings
Trade items	HORNS	Awls	
Raw	Cups	Paintbrushes	BRAIN
Containers	Spoons	Game counters	Hide tanning
Sheaths	Ladles	Ceremonial objects	
Moccasin soles	Fire carriers	Tool handles	CHIPS
Shields	Powder flasks		Fuel
Rattles	Toys	HAIR	Ceremonial smoking
Drums	Headdresses	Headdresses	
Saddles	Rattles	Padding, stuffing	

Above: *The buffalo was essential to the Plains culture and more than eighty products (over seventy shown here) from it were commonly used by the Plains tribes. Little wonder that this animal figured prominently in their ceremonial and religion, it being fundamental to their continuity and existence; in this respect there was considered to be a spiritual link between woman and the buffalo.*

the lodge, the whole resembling a crude effigy of a buffalo. Further valuable gifts such as an elk-teeth dress or eagle feather warbonnet were now placed on the effigy and all this was later given to the society which had given the most support during the spirit-keeping ceremonial.

The lock of hair, the most important and original core of the bundle, was the only thing kept by the family following the distribution of the many gifts associated with the spirit bundle itself. Such was the penance for a lost child that the family gave away virtually all they possessed: 'Nothing was left except the grass on which we stood and the little spirit post. My wife and I had parted with everything. We walked side by side, and I thought with some regret of all I had given away. We went and sat down under a tree in a deep study' (Weasel Bear, ibid.:84).[22]

Buffalo Power

'In the Plains area lived one animal that came nearer to dominating the life and shaping the institutions of a human race

than any other in all the land, if not in the world – the buffalo'
(Webb, 1931:33).

The whole lifestyle of the Plains tribes pivoted firmly around the buffalo and in the early nineteenth century almost everything the Plains people used was, at least in part, derived from the buffalo; it made for a largely meat diet, a roving life, skin dwellings and clothing and crafts and arts, which depended on the flesh, hair, bones, hide, sinew and horns of the animal.

Little wonder that one Indian agent reported in 1858 that the buffalo was the 'staff of life' to the nomadic Plains tribes (U.S.Comm.Indian Affairs, 1858:435). There was also a powerful spiritual link between women and buffalo, both being perceived as having within them the power of the continuity of existence.[23]

Without question, the nomadic Plains tribes exploited their

Below: 'Half breeds hunting buffalo', a painting by Paul Kane, 1846. This illustrates one method of hunting – the chase – which was highly dependent upon the use of well-trained horses. Here, the hunters ride into the herd, single out an animal and despatch it with arrow or bullet. It was a dangerous occupation and accidents were common as shown in this vivid scene which is based upon personal observation by the artist.

rich environment to maximum effect; little thought was given to the actual production of food. They herded no cattle and planted no corn, although this and other farming products were eagerly sought after from the semi-sedentary Missouri River tribes. However, while the nomads returned nothing back to nature, their lifestyle was such that they maximized the rich resources available to them in a highly efficient manner, producing shelter, clothing and artifacts much, but not exclusively, derived from the buffalo.

The buffalo hunt

Although the buffalo was hunted in all seasons, the hides taken in the summer when the hair was short and light were considered the best for tipis and clothing, while the winter coat which was long and heavy was much favored for robes. The movement of the herds depended upon the season; in the spring, they mostly traveled northwards, in autumn south and east, in winter east, returning to the north and west as spring approached. The size of the herds varied from a few hundred to several thousand and some could be of a phenomenal size, one mid-nineteenth century observer recording 'sometimes the whole country for five or six days travel is covered with one moving mass of these animals' (Denig, 1930:530). Buffalo could be hunted by stalking, a technique employed by individuals from time immemorial. It required a careful approach from downwind to avoid being detected by the buffalo, whose sense of smell, unlike its sight, is acute. In summer, a wolf skin might be worn as a disguise since buffalo did allow wolves to approach, while in winter the use of a white blanket hid the hunter as he stalked the herd. During winter, buffalo and other animals became trapped in deep snow and could be easily despatched by hunters wearing snowshoes. All individual hunting, however, was forbidden during the communal hunt for fear of alarming the approaching herds; there was strict regulation of the tribal buffalo hunt by camp police who were derived from the soldier societies (see Chapter II).

The *Piskun*

Prior to the introduction of the horse and firearms, the method of hunting buffalo on a large scale was by use of a specially constructed pound. *Piskun* is the Blackfeet word for these drives or pounds. It translates as 'deep-blood-kettle' (Grinnell, 1893:228). This ancient method was still used in the second half of the nineteenth century by the Cree and Assiniboin who were relatively poor in horses (see Table II.1) and it has been reported that on occasions even the wealthy *Siksika* (Northern Blackfeet) utilized this technique as late as 1872 (Ewers, 1949:358–60).

Perhaps the earliest reference to the use of such drives is by the Hudson's Bay Company trader Mathew Cocking who visited a Gros Ventre 'beast pound' near the Saskatchewan River in

1772. He described the pound as 'a circle fenced round with trees laid one upon another, at the foot of an Hill about 7 feet high & an hundred yards in Circumference; the entrance on the Hill-side where the Animals can easily go over; but when in, cannot return: From this entrance small sticks are laid on each side like a fence, in form of an angle extending from the pound; beyond these to about 1½ mile distant'. While Cocking relates that it was evident that the Gros Ventre had 'great success' the previous spring there being 'Many Skulls & Bones lying in the pound', his own attempts together with those of his Gros Ventre companions were unsuccessful, underlying the seasonal importance of this style of hunting. On 6 December he reported 'no success in pounding'; the season it seems was past (Cocking, Burpee ed., 1908:109–13).

Three types of pound were in vogue depending on the nature of the terrain. Those of the Cree, Assiniboin and *Siksika* who hunted largely on level ground, were built with a timbered causeway leading to the entrance of a corral where there was a drop of 4 to 5 feet (1–1.5m) which maimed many of the animals as they fell in. The Blood and Piegan, on the other hand, who lived farther west nearer the Rocky Mountains, drove the animals over cliffs; such 'buffalo jump' sites were quite rare and so were repeatedly used. It has been estimated that the most famous – referred to as 'Head-Smashed-In' Buffalo Jump near Fort Macleod in present-day southern Alberta – was used for nearly six thousand years. Generally, as with the timbered type, drive lanes were built to direct the herds to the jump; the lanes, made of rock piles and referred to as 'dead men', were arranged like a funnel with a mouth which narrowed toward the jump end. High cliffs required no further additions, the buffalo sustaining serious injury or death on falling but the third variant, where the cliff was low, had a corral at the base which prevented the animals' escape. It was an effective, if at times a wasteful, way of securing a good supply of meat and it did rely upon considerable inter-band organization;[24] additionally, and importantly with the associated ceremonials, it acted as a seasonal unifying factor for the scattered groups.

The value of the buffalo horse

With the acquisition of the horse and the increased wealth and mobility it brought, the surrounding of buffalo and the chase became the most popular hunting methods. In the surround, a large number of horsemen encircled the herd, frightening them so that they milled around in a circle; the confused animals were then shot down. It was a dangerous if expedient method of hunting, a cornered buffalo being exceptionally dangerous at close quarters and by the mid-nineteenth century it had virtually been abandoned in favor of the chase. Here, much could be accomplished by just a few men using strong and well-trained horses – 'the buffalo runners'. Such horses, the Blackfeet said, should have five qualities: (i) enduring speed – the

Below and right: *Tanning buffalo hides, Lakota, Cheyenne River Reservation, circa 1870. The enormous buffalo hides were staked out as shown here and the flesh and hair removed and uniform thickness obtained by a laborious process of scraping and chipping the hide with specially made tools – the 'deflesher' and 'dehairer'. This was time-consuming and exhausting work and was carried out exclusively by women.*

ability to retain speed over a distance of several miles; (ii) intelligence – the ability to respond instantly to commands or to act properly on its own initiative; (iii) agility – ability to move quickly alongside a buffalo, to avoid contact with the larger animal and to keep clear of its horns; (iv) sure-footedness – ability to run swiftly over uneven ground without stumbling; (v) courage – lack of fear of a buffalo (after Ewers, 1955:153)

Such horses were highly valued and if traded fetched the equivalent of several common horses; they were given special care and generally rubbed down after the chase. As Ewers has observed, 'Many Blackfoot men regarded their buffalo horses as priceless possessions' (ibid.).

The chase began with a skirmish line of mounted hunters who slowly approached the herd; when the buffalo became aware of the intruders and started to move away, the hunters charged into the herd each singling out an animal and killing it with lance, arrow or bullet, then sometimes moving on to another. Generally, no more than one or two buffalo were killed by each hunter. It was a dangerous operation and accidents – horse stumbling, guns bursting, hunters being gored by wounded bulls – were common; nevertheless, the chase was always regarded as a great sport by hunters and contemporary descriptions by explorers and others of Plains Indians employing the chase are legion – but whites who attempted to emulate the Plains Indian found it more difficult than it looked. Typical was the observation by the early explorer Anthony Hendry who in 1754 visited the Gros Ventre on the Saskatchewan Plains: 'with the Leader's permission, I rode a hunting with twenty of his young men. They killed 8 Buffalo, excellent sport. They are so expert that with one or two arrows they will drop a Buffalo. As for me I had sufficient employ to manage my horse' (Hendry, 1907:350).

Butchering the buffalo

After the hunt, when the killing of the buffalo was finished, the carcasses were prepared for transportation to the village. Certain individuals were recognized as proficient in this phase of the hunt; they acted as organizers and helped to settle disputes, although ownership could generally be established by the marks on arrows.[25]

If the hide was to be used for a tipi, it was removed whole, the buffalo carcass being turned on its back. Beginning on the under side of a front leg, it was cut to the middle of the breast, then to the lip and behind the nose to between the horns, then a cut down the belly and on the inside of the hind legs together with a split to the tail; this enabled the hide to be removed on either side of the carcass and laid on the ground. The tongue, considered a great delicacy, was then removed. If the hide was to be used as a robe, the animal was first laid on its belly with legs extended and a cut made from the nose along the backbone and to the tip of the tail – this made it easier to handle the two

Above: *Artifacts used in tanning skins and preparing buffalo products, Crow, collected by R. H. Lowie between 1910 and 1913. Top: beaming tool made from the rib of a large animal and used to soften hides. Left: maul with a stone head and wooden handle used to break bones to remove the marrow and also to pound meat to produce pemmican. Middle right: early style of flesher of bone with toothed metal blade. Lower right: adze of elk-horn with metal blade used to dehair the hide and chip to a uniform thickness.*

Left: *Cheyenne women preparing buffalo hides. The woman at the right is using an adze-like tool to work the hide to an even thickness; the same tool could also be used to dehair the hide. The woman on the left is performing the laborious task of softening and drying the hide by it pulling back and forth across an upright post. Preparing skins this way was an activity exclusive to women, the end product being a valuable trade item.*

halves in the tanning process – and on completion, the pieces were sewn back together again, the seam being covered with a quilled or beaded band (see Chapter V). The Lakota informant, *Cetan'ska*, White Hawk, said that it took two horses to take home the meat of one buffalo, the meat being divided into eight portions. Blackfeet informants gave similar information (Densmore, 1918:444; Ewers, 1955:160). A cow buffalo gave some 400 lb (182kg) of meat produce which would be more than the average horse could carry.

Preparation of Pemmican and the Tanning of Hides

After the hunt, an Indian encampment would have presented a scene of intense activity as the meat was cut into long strips to be hung in the open air to dry thoroughly. It was pounded and mixed with wild cherries, other fruits, or animal fat and then packed into parfleches for transporting and keeping for use particularly in the winter months. This high protein food, known as pemmican, was a staple part of the diet of the Plains tribes and kept for an indefinite time.

The green buffalo hides were stretched on the ground or laced on to a vertical wooden frame; since dressed skins everywhere took the place of cloth, the dressing of skins was one of the most important of household industries and, as one observer has recorded, it was not only women's work 'but her worth and virtue were estimated by her output' (Wissler, 1910:63). The tanning process was a time-consuming, tedious and exhausting occupation but the finished item invariably surpasses that of any commercial production, well-dressed Plains hides being exceptionally strong and durable. The process was in several stages. An intermediate process produced *rawhide* which was used for such things as moccasin soles, parfleches, knife sheaths, drum heads and shields. The stretched out hide was first cleaned of tissue, fat and coagulated blood by use of a chisel-like tool in earlier days made entirely of bone but later of iron. Then the hide was reversed and the hair scraped away with an adze-like tool and finally, the hide was worked down to an even thickness by chipping with the adze. Such hides were hard, stiff and very durable and the thickness could be increased by alternately soaking and drying over a slow, smoky fire.

To soft-finish a hide, the rawhide was soaked in water and restretched; the surface was then rubbed with a mixture of mashed brain, cooked liver and fat – possibly also spleen and egg or even vegetable products. The hide was then placed in warm water, working the water through as one would with a permeable membrane, and afterwards wrung out and restretched on the frame and beamed with the chisel-like tool until dry. On removing the hide from the frame, the surface was vigorously worked with a rough-edge stone and dried and whitened by sawing it back and forth through a loop of buckskin, the friction developing heat and both drying and softening the texture. There were considerable variants on this basic method and the method was not exclusive to buffalo hides. It is of interest to note that, either because of subtle variations in the hide dressing techniques or because different animal skins were employed, those of River and Mountain Crow costumes are characterized by a thickness and softness and are generally left the natural white; those from the southern Plains and mountain regions – Comanche, Kiowa, Ute, Southern Arapaho, for example – are also generally soft and thick but are often colored with green or yellow earth paints and sometimes lightly smoked, whereas Sioux and Blackfeet hides are sometimes thin and lack softness and suppleness.

At the height of their powers, the Mandan were apparently recognized as exceptional hide dressers. When La Verendrye visited the Mandan in 1738, he observed 'of all tribes they are the most skillful in dressing leather . . . the Assiniboine cannot do work of the same kind' (La Verendrye, Burpee ed., 1927:332). Sixty years later, however, their position seems to have changed somewhat, as Lewis and Clark imply that leather goods were then predominantly obtained from the nomadic Crow (Lewis and Clark, Thwaites ed., 1904–5:vol.VI:81). Probably the smallpox epidemic of 1780–90, which dramatically reduced the Mandan tribe, also weakened their effectiveness as hunters. The Crow, however, continued to excel in hide dressing. In 1851, the Swiss artist and explorer, Rudolph Kurz – then staying at Fort Union – commented 'the Absaroka are famous for their robes; in no other nation are the dressed skins so soft and pliable' (Kurz, Hewitt ed., 1937:250).

The white buffalo
The buffalo was honored by all Plains Indians as the wisest and most powerful of all creatures. It was considered to be closest to

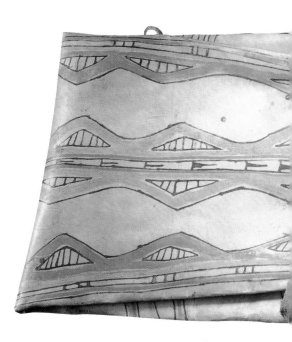

Above: *Parfleche, Blackfeet, collected by A.F. d'Otrante at Fort McKenzie in 1843–4. This particular container was described as being made of buffalo hide and used for storing and transporting dried meat. They are, however, the equivalent of the white man's 'suitcase' and were used for the storage and transport of clothing and other household items. Such articles were generally made and painted by women, the mode of decoration reflecting a definite tribal style.*

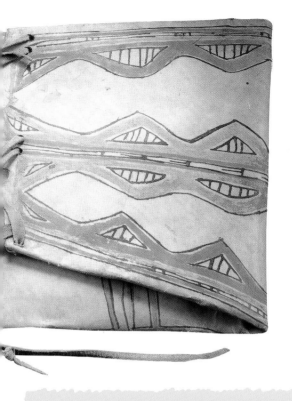

the higher powers and figured prominently in religion and mythology as a symbol of leadership, long life and plenty. The white or albino buffalo was the most revered, particularly by the Mandan who had a women's *White Buffalo Cow Society* which figures in buffalo-calling ceremonials and whose leader wore a white buffalo robe. The Lakota held the same view and one of their most revered supernatural figures was the White Buffalo Maiden, who was credited with bringing important ceremonies and customs to the Teton Sioux.[26]

When such animals were slain, steps were generally taken so as not to offend the spirits. Thus, among the Lakota, the fatal arrow was purified in burning sweetgrass smoke, the skinning knife was purified and the hide carefully removed so that no blood was shed on it; only men who had dreamed of animals were allowed to eat the flesh and the *woman* who ultimately tanned the hide had to be distinguished by the purity of her lifestyle (Densmore, 1918:446).[27]

FOOTNOTES: CHAPTER FOUR

1   In the case of the Kiowa, out of a list of twenty-one Kiowa women, thirteen were most famous for their proficiency in women's crafts, five for their good looks, and three for their abilities in women's sports (Mishkin, 940:56).

2   Among the Cheyenne, Arapaho and to some extent the Cree, a type of chastity belt was worn by unmarried girls. Even among the Sioux and Crow, frequently cited by nineteenth-century observers as having few chaste women, virginity was honored and publicly rewarded (see Weist,1980:258).

3   While women were released from the exhausting task of transporting camp equipment and children with dogs, this was offset by the increase in labor in the production of not only tanned hides for the fur trade but production of larger tipis (Jablow,1950:21).

4   Tanning of buffalo robes was exhausting work. The lengthy process was observed at Porcupine on the Pine Ridge Reservation in the summer of 1988. It took several days of back-breaking toil to soften the gigantic hides.

5   Plains women could obtain visions, although these were often not sought; they could also become shamans and have powers for curing, especially after menopause.

6   Menstruating women, however, were not allowed to participate in religious rituals or enter the same lodge in which an important medicine bundle was kept.

7   In the ceremony of the buffalo tongues which are used as a feast during the Sun-dance, the slicing of the tongues is conducted by a man, usually the father of the holy woman. Throughout the Blackfeet Sun-dance, the *supportive* role of men is emphasized.

8   Kroeber (1902) observes that among the Lakota these amulets sometimes have the shape of the horned toad which the Arapaho described as a 'good animal' which they avoid killing.

9   Cattail down was gathered by men for insulating and diapering babies on journeys during cold weather (Gilman and Schneider,1987:124).

10 As Gilmore observes, however, Kroeber's extensive study of Arapaho symbolism led him to the conclusion that symbolic interpretations were often personal and much depended upon what he called the 'symbolic context' (Gilmore,1990:70).

11 A detailed discussion of Pawnee cradleboards is in Feder (1978:40-50). His studies emphasize the symbolic meaning of the embellishments and the elaborate ceremonial associated with birth and care of the Pawnee infant.

12 It is reported the songs were those as used by the Crow and the Arapaho (Hilger,1952:39).

13 The Lakota said that piercing of the ear was originally done with a bone awl; after the puncture, a piece of copper was inserted 'so that the wound would heal rapidly' (Densmore,1918:137).

14 'Shinny' as it was called, was not confined to the Plains region but was common throughout North America.

15 Buffalo Bird Woman was a Hidatsa woman born in the middle of the

nineteenth century who, together with her brother, Wolf Chief and son Goodbird, worked with the anthropologist Gilbert L. Wilson to record Hidatsa history and culture. They left a priceless legacy of enthographic data (see Gilman and Schneider,1987).

16 When the hair was taken, three motions were made as if to do so and it was cut with the fourth motion (see footnote 18).

17 Beads were seldom used on any of the wrappings of a Spirit Bundle, as 'beads were unknown among the Sioux when the White Buffalo Maiden came to them' (Densmore,1918:79).

18 The number four has special force in many Plains Indian symbolic concepts, actions and groupings often being in fours or multiples of that number, e.g. for the Blackfeet see Wissler (1912(a):126, 247; for the Cheyenne see Michelson (1932:11); for the Osage see La Flesche (1925:245).

19 Earth altars were referred to by the Sioux as *U-ma-ne* and were widely used throughout the Plains region. The mellowed earth space was said to represent the unappropriated life or power of the earth (see Fletcher,1887:284). The Blackfeet used special altars for various types of medicine bundles (Wissler,1912(a):256).

20 The keynote or central idea of this ceremony as held by the Lakota was the affection of a father for his child and his desire that only good should come to it.

21 Any others in need of help might make an appeal at this time, four opportunities being given during the feeding of the spirits (Densmore,1918:82).

22 Not all was lost; that evening, relatives visited with Weasel Bear and his wife, they set up a tipi, brought provisions, kettles, blankets and clothing. 'Our relatives did all this for us, in order that we might begin our lives again' (Densmore,1918:84).

23 This power was expressed for the Lakota by their culture heroine, the White Buffalo Maiden, 'who gave them the bison and their unique way of life' (Weist,1980:260).

24 Denig, Hewitt ed., (1930:532) describes in detail this mode of hunting and the elaborate associated ceremonials, including sacrifices to the Wind and Buffalo Spirits to ensure success.

25 Bear Face told Frances Densmore that he always used a pelican feather on his arrows; others painted sections of the shaft red or blue or small indentations were made in the wood. Each man had his own unique device so his arrows could be easily identified (see Densmore,1918:439).

26 The White Buffalo Society among the Mandan was the highest and last society to which a woman could belong. Women could not be members while they still had menstruation periods, as it 'was believed that the blood would drive the buffaloes away' (Bowers,1950:325).

27 Even a small piece of the robe was said to be worth a horse. The informant, Jaw, said that he obtained two horses, a buffalo hide tipi and 'many other articles' for the skin of a white buffalo which he had killed when living in Canada (Densmore,1918:446-7).

DECORATIVE
ARTS

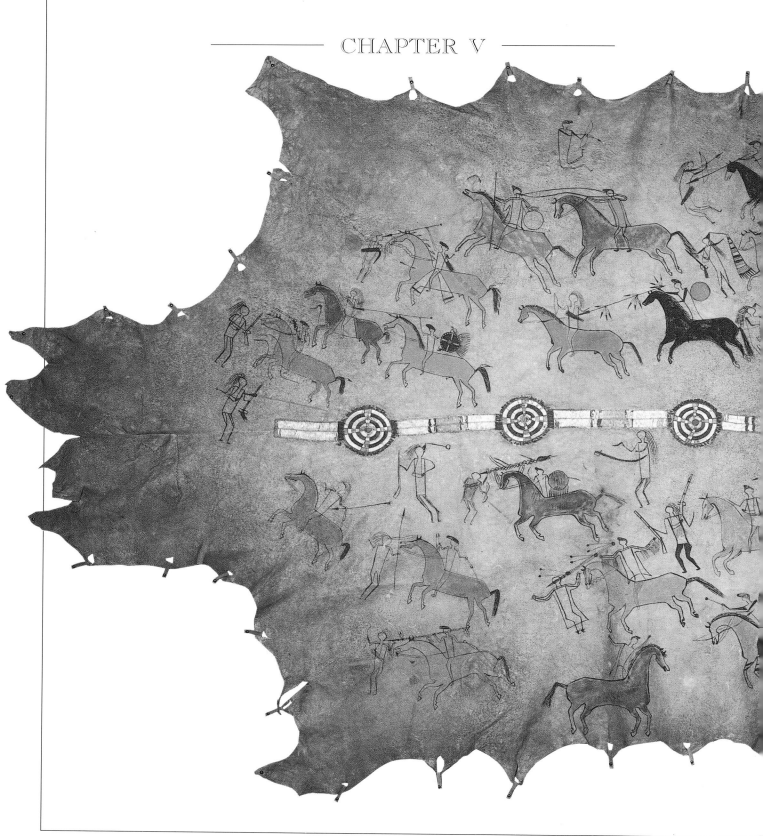

Left: *A painted buffalo robe, Sioux (?), circa 1840. Vividly displayed in pictographs are the exploits of several war expeditions. The hero is identified by his top-knot. Note the fine detail of weapons, costume and shield designs.*

Traditional Clothing – the Buffalo Robe

The traditional clothing of the Plains Indians was made of dressed skins of the buffalo and smaller hoofed animals such as the antelope and bighorn. While cloth was obtained from white traders at an early period and used for everyday wear, garments made for ceremonial purposes emphasized the use of earlier materials. Undoubtedly the most ancient style of garment was the buffalo robe used by both men and women and widely used throughout the Plains region and beyond. Tanned almost entirely – some of the finest being produced by the Crow – this simple garment, while affording good protection against the elements, also had considerable social and religious significance among most of the Plains tribes.

The sentiments relating to ancient clothing may be traced; for example, informants who referred to the Omaha Sacred Legend identified a 'desire for covering . . . with the motive of . . . differentiating himself [from others], a simple act of self-consciousness expressive of the idea fundamental to costume, decoration and regalia' (Fletcher and La Flesche, 1911:357). Recognition was given that man's physical existence is sustained by other forms of life, so the wearing of the simple, complete and unfashioned hide to protect the body was seen as retaining the semblance of the animal and thus increased the Omaha's confidence in the close relationship he considered existed between all other visible forms and himself. Thus, when shamans and chiefs sat with the buffalo robe wrapped around them, they were said to present an appearance of a group of buffalo and it was conceived as a symbolic transfer of power from the buffalo to man. The ideas were extended to other animals by the Omaha and other Plains tribes; for example, leaders of war parties might wear a wolf skin or carry the skin of a swift bird of prey, thus evoking the animal's known powers so that they might be transmitted to the wearer in time of need. This was part of an ethos that was obviously prevalent in North America for thousands of years where success in hunting, war and ceremonial depended on interaction with animal spirits. (For a further discussion on this see Brasser, 1987:99, and, for the circumboreal forests, see Webber, 1983: 60–69.)

The tanning of the hide (see Chapter IV) so as to retain the leg, neck and head sections is technically no easy matter and yet it was a widely practiced custom in North America, seemingly with its roots in the symbolic transfer of animal powers in the retention of the animal form.

Not only did the unfashioned robe make these fundamental symbolic statements but the *way* it was worn could convey in a simple but very definite manner the feelings or the intentions of the wearer. Thus hesitation, the intent to walk or run, the burden of years, courtship, the readiness for speech or action, the actual address or speech stance, anger or change of mental attitude, all could be identified by the way a person wore the uncut robe (Fletcher and La Flesche, 1911: Plates 52 and 53).

119

Superimposed on the background of structural and stance symbolism were the painted and other embellishments which also communicated ideas. The technique was not confined solely to the buffalo robe but also included deer and other skins which might well be utilized for purposes other than clothing. Such customs obviously had ancient roots; traders and explorers to the Mandan villages as early as 1738 referred to the trading of painted buffalo robes to the Assiniboin (La Verendrye, Burpee ed., 1927:19) and in 1755 Alexander Mackenzie described fine painting of beaver and moose hides (1927:xciii), while Wedel (1961:106) located bone paint applicators dating from circa 1700 'to decorate leather articles' in archeological sites in Nebraska.

Unfortunately the earliest extant and well documented robe from the Plains regions dates only from about 1804;[1] almost certainly the *roots* of the designs found on historic Plains painted robes are displayed on some of the earliest skins, such as the painted frame enclosing a central field in which are geometrical figures, similar to those found on nineteenth century Lakota women's robes as well as depictions of buffalo, horses, calumets and human figures found on later Plains men's robes.[2]

The Woman's and Child's Decorated Robe

As has already been indicated, there were basically *two* distinct types of painting done by Plains Indians – those largely using abstract geometrical designs and those showing pictographic

Above: A buffalo robe with feathered-circle pattern and geometrical border, possibly Sioux, circa 1870. Geometric patterns on buffalo robes tended to be associated with women. However, this particular design is generally found on men's robes and was referred to as the black bonnet, sunburst or concentric circle design. Although worn by men, all accounts suggest that the design was painted by women.

figures such as men, horses, buffalo and other animals. Frequently cleverly stylized, the figures are nonetheless usually fully recognizable.

In general, geometrical designs were used on the robes worn by women and girls while the pictographic style was largely the male province; there is one notable exception to this observation in that some men's robes exhibit a conventionalized war-bonnet symbol in the form of a large feathered circle which dominated the middle of the robe.[3] The aspect of *conventionalization* of sacred objects and phenomena to give virtually *unrecognizable* geometric designs has been reported for the Omaha, whose keepers of sacred tribal bundles were tattooed with representations of lightning, ancient stone knives and calumets (Fletcher and La Flesche, 1911:219). Their likeness could really only be appreciated when explained by the initiated; of interest is that the geometrical tattoo pattern has some resemblance to those paintings on an Illinois robes in the Musée de l'Homme which, as Brasser has observed, 'may be interpreted as "cosmograms", plans of a native world view' (Brasser, 1988:6). Thus what was important to the culture often became conventionalized, producing an attractive geometrical pattern but apparently replete in symbolic statements to the initiated.

This was well illustrated by the symbolism associated with the geometrical patterns on a woman's robe (a basic rendering-

Above: Sih-Chida, *or Yellow Feather, Mandan, painted by Karl Bodmer, 1833. Much artwork, highly decorative but replete in symbolic statement, is shown in this portrait. Yellow Feather was a member of the Dog Society and the cluster of feathers on the back of his head are almost certainly the insignia of that society. His robe is embellished with a broad band of pony beadwork.*

Right: *A drawing of an Arapaho buffalo robe from about 1870 displaying a box and border pattern. Traditionally, men's painted robes were replete in symbolic statements, the meaning of which was freely given. In contrast, with the geometrical-type patterns on women's robes, meanings were seldom divulged. This robe is an exception, a detailed interpretation of the patterns being obtained at the time of collection. Whether that interpretation was of a purely personal nature or if it reflected some pattern of established geometrical symbolism used by Arapaho women is conjectural.*

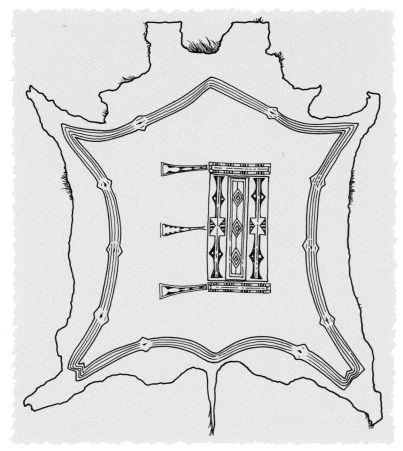

is shown in the drawing on page 121) collected from the Arapaho, the interpretation being obtained at the time of collection. It is so detailed that it suggests genuineness – certainly a great deal is consistent with the known Plains Indian world view such as in the esteem in which they held the buffalo, the power of the earth and sky and the symbolic rendering of the heart, mythical buffalo lodge and the use of white clay symbolizing purity and cleanliness.

The Symbolism of an Arapaho Woman's Robe

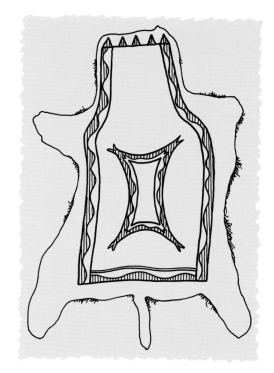

The border as a whole represents a buffalo. Although not shown in color, in the original piece the dark lines along its edges symbolize the skin and hair of the buffalo, the red lines, its veins; the diamond shaped figures represent the pulsation of its heart. In these figures the red central spot symbolizes the heart; the seven yellow or green lines are seven periods of creation. The border as a whole symbolizes a river on which floats pemmican (the diamond shaped figure), this being a reference to an Arapaho legend. The large oblong figure in the center of the robe symbolizes the earth, the red and yellow line surrounding it being the horizon. In this line the red symbolizes the sun, and the yellow, the day. The red, green and yellow strip in the center of this design symbolizes the Path of Life. The three diamonds represent the eyes of the One Above who watches human lives. They also symbolize a man, a woman and animals. The red field surrounding the green triangles represents the Indian race. The designs above and below this central band symbolize the division between night and day. The long yellow line through the center of each represents the Milky Way. The black triangles containing four white squares symbolize the buffalo lodge, where the buffalo were once kept in prison by a white crow. The white squares symbolize the buffalo, but they also symbolize life or abundance and the Four Old Men of Arapaho myth. The triangles with a red spot in the center represent another legendary lodge in which six sisters, who had been sent away from home because they refused to marry, lived for a long time. The long triangular figure below the central design represents a buffalo's tail; the triangles along the edges symbolize hills. The red below it represents the Indian's way of life.

In the perpendicular figures at either end of the large central design, the light central strip represents a road. The triangles at either end of this strip represent tipis; the small red spots in it, people and the green and yellow lines connecting them are paths. The figures along either edge represent day (yellow), and night (black), water and vegetation (green), and the Indian race (red). The long triangular figures below these bands represent the limbs of animals, the color symbolism being the same. The unpainted portions of the robe were whitened with clay, symbolizing purity and cleanliness (from Ewers 1939:63–4).

This robe must be considered as an important specimen which gives insights into the geometrical symbolism in painted

Left: *The design of a spider's web on a Lakota child's robe (after Wissler, 1907: 49). The meaning varied, depending upon the context in which this design was used. On a child's robe it offered protection against thunder and brought good fortune, but if it was used by men it indicated ownership of a medicine-bow which was carried as a standard and considered to have magical power over the enemy.*

Below: *An elkskin, probably Lakota, circa 1850, decorated with ten parallel bands of quillwork broken at intervals with horseshoe-like motifs. This is probably a caparison for a woman's horse rather than a robe for wearing. A very similar piece was sketched by the Swiss artist Rudolph Kurz during his sojourn on the Plains in the early summer of 1851 (Kurz, Hewitt ed., 1937: Plate 36).*

designs of the Plains woman's world;[4] possibly too the ideas embodied here can be extrapolated to other robes which have comparable designs that are not necessarily Arapaho, since many symbolic concepts overlapped among the different tribes.

Geometrical designs also occur on children's robes (see below) such as that painted for a child by a Lakota medicine woman who only explained that the motif evoked powers for the future good of the wearer (Wissler, 1904:248). Further research, however, demonstrated that this is the Lakota symbol for the spider web and such designs were said to have great power, embodying the observed fact that a spider's web is not destroyed by arrows or bullets – they simply pass through it, leaving only a hole; thus to the Lakota, Wissler observed, a rendering of the web symbolically represented a power which protected 'people from harm' (Wissler, 1907:48).[5]

Additionally the corners of the design on this robe were said to represent the heavens and earth and the homes of the Four Winds, while the projections evoke thunder powers. Such symbols were also worked in porcupine quills on a Lakota bag which was used as a receptacle for various mementoes from the funeral rites of a favorite child. When Wissler reported on this

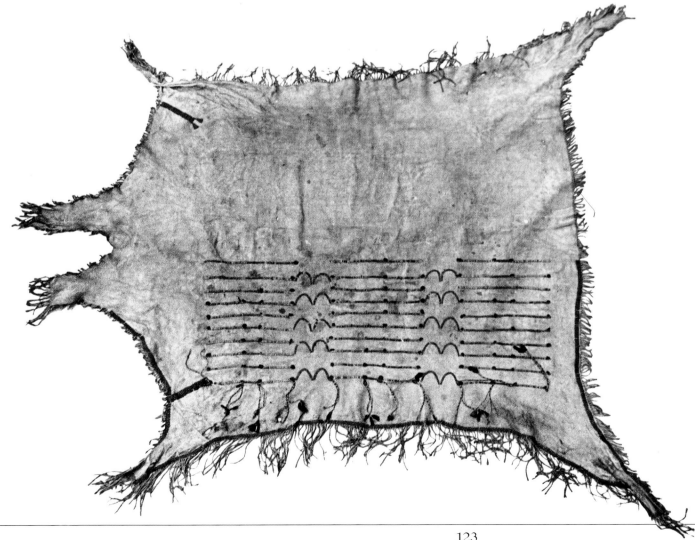

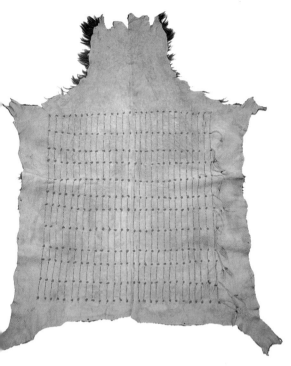

Above: A girl's robe, Lakota, circa 1850, picked up by Lieutenant Warren at Ash Hollow in 1855. Robes of this sort were used in the puberty ceremonial of the Lakota which gave recognitiion to the sexual maturity of a girl, together with elaborate prayers for her future welfare.

Left: Elkskin robe, Blackfeet, circa 1840. This fine and rare robe was worn by the Holy Woman in Sun-dance ceremonials. It is painted with symbols representing the Morning Star (in red), a source of power and protection, and the moth (in green), which acted as a messenger between the sky powers and earthbound man.

design he observed that he had never seen it used 'purely as decoration' and that there can be no doubt 'as to its absolute symbolic [and sacred] value' (Wissler 1904:249).[6]

A robe beautifully embellished with parallel bands of quill-work with interspersed tufts of red wool is shown (left). This was collected by Lieutenant Warren after the massacre of the Brulé Lakota under Little Thunder at Ash Hollow in September 1855 (see Chapter VIII). Objects decorated in this way – saddle bags, saddle blankets, moccasins, robes and parfleches – were generally associated with women. In particular, the lines were said by the Lakota to represent 'the trail on which woman travels' (ibid.:242) and were associated with puberty ceremonials which gave recognition to the sexual maturity of a girl, in which there were elaborate prayers for the 'proper function of her new physiological activities' (ibid.:244). Once the formal ceremonial was complete, the girl adopted the decorations of a woman and she would then paint red lines on her face as a 'public statement of the fact that she has reached sexual maturity and taken the necessary steps recognizing the religious aspect of the case' (ibid.)[7] While no interpretation came with this robe, it is interesting to note that there are twenty-eight parallel lines and twelve tufts of red wool across each line of the Brulé robe, suggestive of both a monthly and yearly cycle.

Another highly symbolic robe associated with children was the *Unnistakhsi*, or Calf Robe, of the Blackfeet. Thus, a *mini-poka*, or favored child, would receive this robe and 'all its spiritual blessings while still very young' (Raczka, 1992:72). The robe of a trimmed rare yellow buffalo calf skin was associated with a legend relating to the Pleiades which were represented by a series of brass buttons sewn across the outer surface of the skin. A large brass disc represented the sun and this was flanked by stuffed weasel skins in both summer and winter coats. Tadpole designs represented underwater powers referring to the ability of that creature to exhibit metamorphosis, which figures prominently in Blackfeet mythology; black dots representing stars on a yellow background were painted on the flesh side of the robe. A child receiving such apparel was given the name of *Calf Robe*. The robe itself was said to represent a sacrifice, having been prepared in a sacred manner as an offering to the sun, while the child was considered now to be under the protection of the sun and all the powers it evoked in Blackfeet religion (ibid.).

A fine robe of elkskin which is part of the d'Otrante Collection in Stockholm (shown left) (Taylor, 1986:271) and collected at Fort McKenzie in 1843–4 illustrates another sacred robe of the Blackfeet which was worn by the Holy Woman or Sun-dance sponsor. It exhibits two motifs which at a glance may seem to be identical but which represent a moth (colored green) and the Morning Star (in red). This strange combination may be explained by a consideration of Blackfeet mythology which is replete in references to flying insects – in particular *apunni*, or the moth – as being messengers from the powers of the skies to earthbound man. Morning Star on the other hand was considered to be the son of the Sun and Moon and a great source of protective power. Thus one figure is a source of power and the other the way its power is transmitted; the robe was important, traditional regalia to be worn in the performance of the duties of the Holy Woman in the Blackfeet Sun-dance (Taylor, 1993:55; Brasser, 1987:124).

Interpreting the Meanings

One of the difficulties in fully interpreting meanings, particularly those associated with women's painted geometrical designs, stems at least in part from the fact that many of the young anthropologists – Clark Wissler, Robert Lowie, James Dorsey, Alfred Kroeber et al. – who traveled to the Plains tribes to collect data as part of a 'salvage anthropology program'[8] were men and that they invariably interviewed male members of the tribes, 'using male language about a [seemingly] male-dominated world' (Weist, 1980:256). Additionally, when women *were* interviewed they were bound not only by the constraints of communication between women and men from an alien society but also by the fact that many of the women belonged to a craft guild where both the work they did and the designs they used were considered sacred; the women were also obliged not to divulge the full meaning of such designs to the uninitiated.[9]

Attitudes of Plains women toward such sacred matters are well summed up by a comment from a Southern Cheyenne woman who told the ethnologist Truman Michelson, 'I became a member of the "Tipi Decorators", which is composed of women only. I was very carefully instructed never to disclose [its secrets] . . . in the presence of males, so I shall be obliged to discontinue the subject' (Michelson, 1932:9).

Women's Dresses

There is some evidence to suggest that the idea for an early style of side-fold dress worn by Lakota women even as late as Maximilian's time (1833) was actually derived from the folded buffalo robe for, as one researcher of such garments has observed (Lessard, 1980), if one folded down the top quarter of a tanned and decorated robe, wrapped it around the wearer and then laced or sewed up the open side, the resulting garment closely resembled the side-fold dress (see right). Thus, the concept of using the entire hide with the idea of stating a close relationship between the woman and the power of the buffalo, or other quadruped, seems almost certainly evident here, for, as Weist has observed of women in Plains society, 'there were continuous symbolic links between women and bison' (Weist, 1980:260).[10]

Bodmer's portrait executed at Fort Pierre in June 1833 of the Lakota woman *Chan-Cha-Uia-Teuin*, Crow Woman, almost certainly shows this style of dress in use. It is very close to one

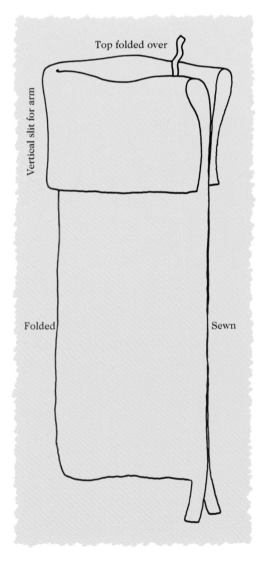

Below: *Pattern for the side-fold dress. This early style of dress was used by women on both the central and northern Plains. While there were variations in style, the basic garment was made of one or more pieces of tanned skin which was wrapped around the body, the top folded over and then sewn or laced on one side. An armhole was cut in the right side and straps across the shoulder kept it in place. There were considerable variations on the basic pattern and detachable sleeves might also be used. The style was gradually replaced by the skin dress, almost certainly due to the influence from the Plateau tribes to the west (drawing after Hail, 1980: 88).*

Top folded over

Vertical slit for arm

Folded

Sewn

which his traveling companion Maximilian collected at the time, bearing pony beaded decoration and cone jingles at the bottom (which would make a musical sound as the woman walked), together with the flaps which are almost certainly the trimmed forelegs of the original hide, since as with the two-skin dress of elkskin, the tail part of the hide was at the top (see Feder, 1984:49).

An ancient and widespread style of dress used by the Woodland tribes and also found on the northeastern Plains was made from two large rectangular pieces of tanned hide and sewn at the sides, the top was folded down and the dress supported by two shoulder straps. Additionally, it had separate cape-like sleeves, which, as with the man's shirt, was sewn only from the elbows to the wrist. The sleeves were laced together at the back and also attached to the body of the dress with tie thongs. In warm weather the sleeves could be disposed with, as illustrated by the artist Rudolph Kurz in a portrait of a Cree (?) woman (see below) in 1851 (Kurz, Hewitt ed., 1937, Plate 23).

Above: *Cree woman, portrait by Karl Bodmer, Fort Union, 1833. This woman is wearing a two-skin dress which displaced the older style of side-fold garment. The skins were folded so that the hind legs were at the shoulders and the tail of the animal hung on the breast, as can be seen here.*

Right: *Cree woman, sketch by Rudolph Kurz, 1851. This woman wears a strap dress which was made of two pieces of hide folded down at the top with straps over each shoulder. A popular style of the northeastern Plains and adjacent Woodlands, the style continued even with the advent of trade cloth.*

It is probable that dresses of this type were worn traditionally by Blackfeet women but styles had mainly changed to the *two-skin* type by the 1830s. This type of dress seems to have originated among tribes on the Plateau – west of the Plains in the Rocky Mountains – being traditional garments of the Nez Perce, Kutenai, Okanagon, Yakima and other tribes of that region (Teit, Boas ed., 1930:233; Spinden, 1908:219–20). This dress was generally made from deer, pronghorn or bighorn sheep hides, having been carefully removed so that the legs and neck remained. The hide was then soft-tanned and most of the hair removed. One skin produced the front and the other the back of the dress, generally with the hair side out. In forming the upper portion of the dress, the tail part of the hide was folded over on the outside, thus making a straight line across the shoulders. This extra fold was then sewn down to give the appearance of a yoke, the triangular tail piece, with the hair still attached, was retained as an ornament at the center of the breast. The sides of the garment were sewn or laced, and sometimes slightly tailored with inserts at the lower part of the dress to give a flare to the skirt; otherwise the shape of the original hide was retained. While there are some variations on the basic design, such as the yoke being sewn on, the overall presentation was similar.

Everyday dresses and those worn for ceremonial occasions were generally made in the same way but the latter were often more elaborately embellished: as Maximilian observed, 'both on the hem and sleeves, with dyed porcupine quills and thin leather strips, with broad diversified stripes of sky-blue and white glass beads' (Maximilian, Thwaites ed. 1906:vol. 23:103) (see Peterson-Swagerty, 1992–3:128).

The majority of these features are exhibited on a fine Nez Perce specimen (above) collected by the agent John Monteith

Above, left: *A woman's dress, Nez Perce, collected by J.B. Monteith and dating from at least 1870. This typical early style of dress used by the Plateau people was later copied by the Plains people.*

Above: *A fine woman's dress, Lakota, from about 1880. The upper beaded part follows the contours of the cape. The deer-tail embellishment has been conventionalized to a U-shaped design in beadwork.*

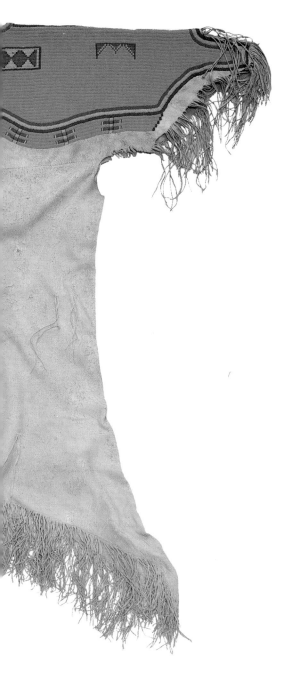

in the 1870s, a typical nineteenth-century woman's decorated skin dress both for the northern Plains and the Plateau. The decoration consists of beaded bands following the contours of the cape and heavily fringed at the sides and bottom. The tail of the deer, a characteristic feature of this style of dress, is at the neck. Other popular decorative features might consist of red and blue flannel inserts to the lower part of the skirt while a particular sign of wealth was the addition of one or two rows of the milk teeth of an elk below the beadwork on the cape, as shown in the fine Blackfeet girl's dress collected in the 1840s at Fort McKenzie (above). In later years such precious embellishments were replaced with small cowrie shells which looked like elk teeth but were easier to come by and thus less expensive.

The Lakota Beaded Dress

Magnificent dresses with the cape completely covered in beadwork were a marked feature of Lakota dresses from the 1870s onward, a fine example of which is shown (left). The lower lines of the beadwork follow the contours of the cape with a blue background in the lazy stitch technique – parallel rows of beads 10mm or so wide, sewn with sinew, the work so neatly executed that little of the stitching could be seen on the back side of the buckskin. The Lakota traditionally referred to such decoration as the 'blue breast beading' (Wissler, 1904:239). Particularly interesting is the fact that the deer tail has now been replaced with a U-shaped design worked in beads which the Lakota women said represented a turtle, further explaining that this had power 'over the functional diseases peculiar to women, and likewise conception, birth, and the period of infancy' (ibid.:242). Clearly there is an association here with fertility, underlined by the fact that pieces of the heart of a turtle were

Above, right: *Girl's dress, Blackfeet, collected at Fort McKenzie by Count d'Otrante in 1843–4. This is fabricated from bighorn skins and decorated with elk teeth and blue pony beads which follow the contours of the cape. The sides and bottom are heavily fringed. Children's dress clothing from this period is very rare and this finely made piece indicates that the two-skin dress was well established among the Blackfeet at this time.*

eaten as a cure for both menstrual disorders and barrenness. It is not improbable that, in keeping with ancient symbolism of the relationship of buffalo to women as giving 'continuity of existence', the beaded diamond flanked by triangles appearing on the upper center part of the cape refer to that creature, since Wissler describes a similar design as representing the 'head, hump, and hind quarters' of a buffalo (ibid.:250).

While appearing to be of the two-skin variety, these dresses actually used part of a third skin so that the cape was further extended. The use of a complete third skin becomes a reality in the attractive dresses so characteristic of the southern Plains (see right). Such dresses were made by sewing together the sides of two deer or antelope skins which had the upper portion cut straight just below the forelegs of the animal. A third skin which had been folded lengthwise was then stitched to the first two, effectively becoming the bodice and skirt, while the third skin was the yoke or cape. Unlike those dresses from the central and northern Plains, the cape was not fully beaded. Instead there was heavy fringing, painting and metal cone attachments and the addition of single lines of beadwork, generally in the very small seed beads so coveted by southern Plains people.

Trade cloth dresses

Cloth dresses became increasingly popular from about 1860 onward, although such tribes as the Lakota 'had cloth early in their history and were using it before they became Plains people' (Lessard, 1980:72). It was, however, an expensive item and as with other Plains tribes was, in early days, often used decoratively rather than for clothing. Maximizing material use, typically such dresses were made from rectangular pieces of cloth folded at the shoulder and with attached shaped sleeves, a slit being cut at the top for the head, the edges often being bound with a contrasting ribbon. Dark blue cloth was popular with the Lakota and ornamentation with sewn beadwork sparely employed, if at all. Instead the dress was heavily embellished with dentalium shells, coveted trade items which were brought in from the Pacific Coast.[11] The shells, which have the shape of a miniature elephant's tusk and varied between 40mm and 50mm in length, were sewn in parallel curved rows, generally across the upper part of the dress, but occasionally covering the entire surface, making a very costly garment. In 1850 such shells were valued at ten for a buffalo robe (Denig, Hewitt ed., 1930:591). Additional ornamentation might be silk ribbon appliquéd at the sleeve ends and hem, or pendant from the dress itself. Metal sequins, sometimes brass buttons or even coins, were attached to give a pleasing contrast to the white/yellow dentalium shells.

Crow women's dresses

The everyday dress of the Crow women in the mid-nineteenth century was made of an undecorated buffalo cowskin which

Above: A Southern Cheyenne dress collected by James Mooney, dating from circa 1890. This is a traditional southern Plains three-skin dress where two deerskins are cut straight at the head end and the third skin, retaining the front and back legs, has been folded lengthwise and sewn to the first two across the top. The upper part of the dress is decorated with more than two hundred elk teeth with bead bands across the body and at the bottom.

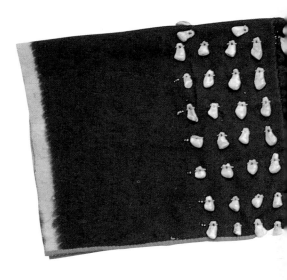

Above: *Crow woman, sketch by Rudolph Kurz, Fort Berthold, summer 1851. This woman is wearing a fine dress of trade cloth embellished with elk teeth.*

Below: *Woman's elk-teeth dress, formerly the property of Rosa Winter Thunder, a Brulé (Lakota). It is a variant of the Crow elk-teeth style dress with tailoring on the body and arms which would fall cape-like when worn.*

Edwin Denig, writing in 1854, described as a 'dressed cowskin cotillion' (ibid.:588) with a value of one tanned buffalo robe (then worth about three dollars). These garments were obviously simply constructed and were probably of the side-fold style described earlier. However, costume for dress occasions was more elaborate, such as a 'Big Horn cotillion trimmed with scarlet [cloth] and ornamented with porcupine quills' or a 'fine white bighorn skin cotillion adorned with 300 elk teeth'. The latter was valued by Denig at '25 robes' (then almost seventy-five dollars) (ibid.:587–8).

It was not, however, the basic fabric which made these dresses so expensive but rather the large number of elk teeth which were used in their decoration. Strictly speaking, only the two lower incisor milk teeth of the animal were considered suitable. As Denig observed, because elk were not killed in great numbers by any one hunter, 'much time and bargaining are required for an individual to collect 300, the number usually wrought on a Crow woman's dress' (ibid.:589). In the 1850s such adornment was expensive, a hundred teeth being equal in value to one horse – perhaps twenty to thirty dollars. Rudolph Kurz – who made several sketches of Crow and Hidatsa women wearing dresses embellished with elk teeth (see left) – reported that this style of ornamentation originated among the Crow (Kurz, Hewitt ed.: 1937:251). This is highly probable since the Yellowstone Valley – the heartland of traditional Crow territory – abounded with wild life, elk being especially numerous.

Dresses of this type, but now made of red or blue trade cloth, were worn by the wives of Crow headmen, who visited Washington in the 1870s and onward. The dress shown (below) illustrates several of the features of this style of dress although it is a

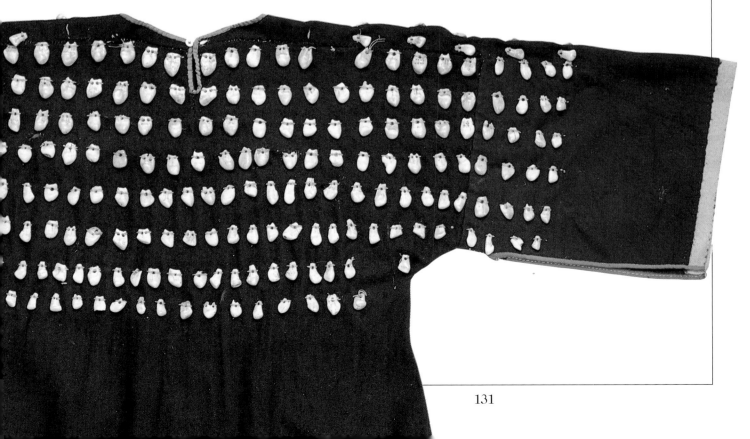

variation of the Crow dress. It is of blue flannel, the arms are edged with red ribbon and the lower part of the dress exhibits the white selvedge edge which was often left as a decorative feature.

There are some four hundred elk teeth attached to this specimen; each tooth has been drilled near the top and a buckskin thong passed through the hole to attach it to the dress. However, not all of the teeth are genuine, as the difficulties encountered in obtaining such items in the Reservation period often led to the use of imitation teeth carved from bone.

The Effects of Trade on Costume Style

Dresses, heavily adorned with elk teeth, were not exclusive to the Crow. Early photographs show their use by Lakota and Cheyenne women and a number have been collected from these tribes. Several of these were undoubtedly gifts or items obtained in trade. As Ewers has observed, after the intertribal wars among the Upper Missouri Indians came to an end in the mid-1880s, 'once friendly relations were established between . . . former enemies, repeated visits and exchanges of gifts followed' (Wildschut, Ewers ed.: 1959:51). Thus, objects of Crow making passed into the ownership of such tribes as the Lakota, Cheyenne and Blackfeet, while there was considerable movement – although the Crow had more horses to offer – of decorated articles to the Crow. For example, the pipe-bag shown (right), which was *collected* from the Crow, is almost certainly of Sioux manufacture. These trade activities were nothing more than an extension of a network which had existed for hundreds of years across the Plains and beyond[12] (see Chapter II).

This exchange of goods has, however, left a legacy of problems associated with the identification of objects relating to the Plains Indians,[13] since at the time of acquisition it was natural to assume that an object acquired from a particular tribe was actually made by them; many objects are subsequently misidentified in the ethnographical collections.

Quill and Beadwork

Porcupine quillwork which preceded beadwork was a widespread and ancient art in North America. The earliest extant examples of this work, although from the Woodlands rather than the Plains area, indicate that sophisticated techniques of application had already been developed by the sixteenth century and unquestionably many of these ideas were taken to the Plains by those people who ultimately became the historic Plains Indians from the eighteenth century onward.

The origins of quillwork are buried in history; the anthropologist Ling Roth has suggested that quillwork possibly originated in Asia, citing examples of woven mats and baskets found there which show basically the same weaving and sewing techniques as those employed in quillwork in North America (Roth, 1923:

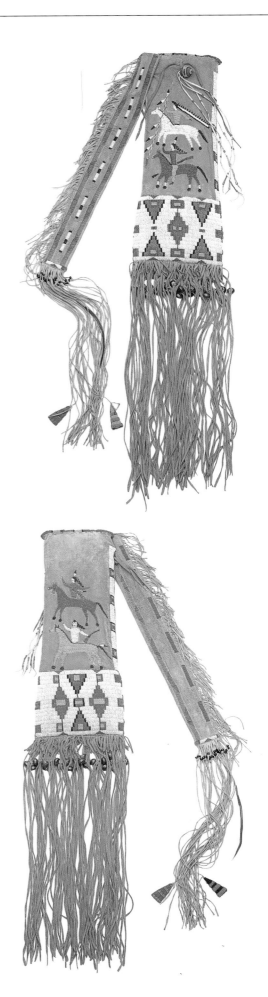

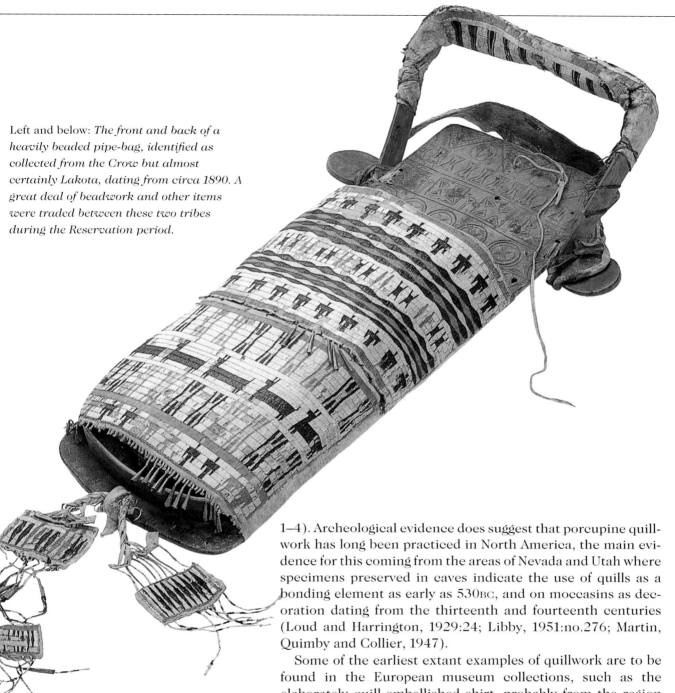

Left and below: *The front and back of a heavily beaded pipe-bag, identified as collected from the Crow but almost certainly Lakota, dating from circa 1890. A great deal of beadwork and other items were traded between these two tribes during the Reservation period.*

Above: *Cradle, eastern Sioux, collected by George Catlin circa 1835. The skill in porcupine quillwork decorative art is exemplified by the lavish embellishment of this cradle, the central part being completely covered with quillwork with conventionalized motifs of deer (?) and Thunderbirds, the latter in particular probably making reference to protective powers. This is an early type of cradle with a wooden 'bow' at the top and a wide backboard and is of a type which was abandoned by the Lakota when they became equestrian nomads.*

1–4). Archeological evidence does suggest that porcupine quill-work has long been practiced in North America, the main evidence for this coming from the areas of Nevada and Utah where specimens preserved in caves indicate the use of quills as a bonding element as early as 530BC, and on moccasins as decoration dating from the thirteenth and fourteenth centuries (Loud and Harrington, 1929:24; Libby, 1951:no.276; Martin, Quimby and Collier, 1947).

Some of the earliest extant examples of quillwork are to be found in the European museum collections, such as the elaborately quill-embellished shirt, probably from the region just north of Lake Huron and collected prior to 1683, now in the Ashmolean Museum, Oxford (Turner, MacGregor ed., 1983:123–30); the Sloane and Christy material in the Museum of Mankind, London (Braunholtz, Fagg ed.:1970:25; King 1982:51 and 65); and the collection of early moccasins and headdresses in the Musée de l'Homme, Paris (Fardoulis, 1979). Porcupine quilled decorated bags, pouches and robes, dating from before 1800 and now in the collection of the Museum of the American Indian, New York, have been described by Orchard (1926:59–68). While most of these specimens are from a region east of the Great Plains, they exhibit wrapped, woven and sewn techniques virtually identical to those found on later Plains specimens. Thus, a fine cradle, made by the eastern Sioux and collected by George Catlin in 1835 (above), exhibits several quill techniques – both sewn and wrapped – with conventionalized animal and Thunderbird motifs.

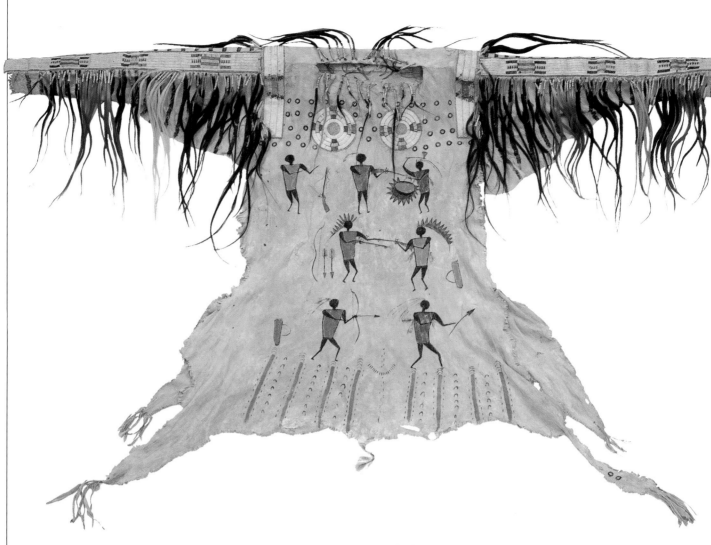

The porcupine (*Erethizon dorsatum*) mainly inhabited the extensive coniferous and deciduous forests which stretch from Alaska to Mexico and from the Atlantic to the Pacific oceans and was to be found on the western and northern Great Plains, particularly during the summer months. Large quantities of quillwork were actually produced in the nineteenth century by those Plains tribes, such as the Lakota and Cheyenne, who lived in regions where at that time the porcupine was not generally found, the quills being a 'significant trade item' (Best and McClelland, 1977:4).

The skin of this animal consists of a dense woolly undercoat, white-tipped guard hairs and quills on the head, back and tail, which function as a defence against predators. The quills are white, stiff, hollow tubes with brown to black barbed tips and those which were used in quillwork varied in size from about 2 to 5 inches (3–14cm) in length and about 1–2mm in diameter. In addition to porcupine quills, bird quills were also sometimes used particularly by those tribes on the Missouri River such as the Hidatsa, Mandan and Arikara. Recently, Feder (1987) has also identified a 'visually distinctive' form of bird quillwork from the region of the Upper Mississippi River, the main producers being the Santee Sioux, although there is some evidence to suggest that the Yankton Sioux, Ojibwa and other tribes in the region also produced such work.

Above: A fine quilled shirt from the Upper Missouri region dating from circa 1840. There are two quilled rosettes on both the front and back of this shirt and the bands on the shoulders and arms are edged with human and horsehair fringes. There are extensive pictographic motifs and, at the bottom, a probable reference to the capturing of horses. The distinctive style of the pictographs suggests that it may be of Gros Ventre origin.

Below: *Buffalo or deer bladder containers for porcupine quills, collected by Lieutenant G.K. Warren in 1855. These were an essential part of a quillworker's kit. The quills were sorted according to size, four categories being recognized, and each quill was placed in the appropriate container.*

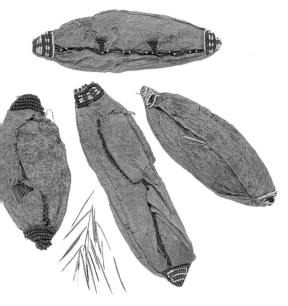

Right: *An Arapaho quilled and beaded rosette made into a bag, circa 1870. The pattern is distinctly Arapaho but the bag is possibly fabricated from pieces which were originally on a child's cradle, which often had a quilled disc of this type with bands of quill-wrapped rawhide strips and dew-claw rattles – all exhibited on this bag.*

Preparation of Quills

Porcupine quills were softened by wetting them, usually by placing in the mouth and then flattening them by drawing them between the teeth or finger nails. While some elaborately carved bone or antler flatteners are to be found in the collections (Orchard, 1916:14; Bebbington, 1982:15), it is probable that most were, in reality, ceremonial in function. The quills were generally dyed either by boiling them with a suitable dye or (later) with colored trade cloth, the color boiling out of the cloth and penetrating the quills. Red, yellow and purple were the commonest colors used, these being combined with the natural white and brown/black. In early days, dyes were obtained from various mosses, roots or berries (Orchard, 1916:9–14), but aniline dyes were introduced in about 1870. After dyeing, the quills were kept in buffalo or deer bladders ready for use (as shown left). Highly formalized quillworkers guilds have been identified among such tribes as the Cheyenne and Arapaho (Grinnell 1923, vol.1:163) and Kroeber, 1902–7). Here, certain designs were considered sacred and could only be produced by initiated women.

Symbolism

An example of the type of work which was produced by these guilds is shown in the illustration (below). Fortunately some anthropological data exist at least to give us a glimpse of the complexity of meaning associated with some of these early

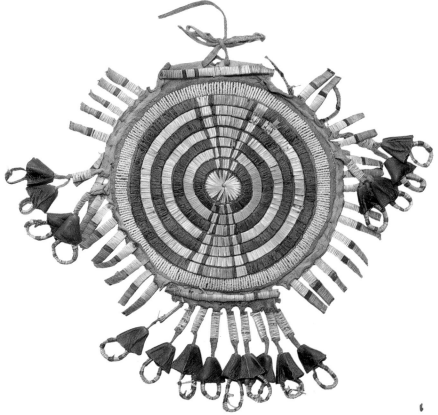

quillwork designs. The pattern in the illustration refers to a mythical figure, Whirlwind-Woman (in Arapaho, *Nayaa Xatisei*), and the course of her path across the then small earth. Confused, she did not known where to rest, moving from place to place, 'as she circled, the earth grew until it reached its present extent. When she stopped, she had gone over the whole earth. It was she who first made this [style of] tent-ornament, which represents what she did' (Kroeber, 1902:60–61). Illustated on page 48 is a quillwork decoration which was collected from the Arapaho before 1893. Although described as a 'tipi ornament' it is almost certainly a symbolic item used to decorate buffalo robe blankets, which were traditionally associated with those men whose 'primary function was to organize and regulate the tribal buffalo hunt' (Brasser, 1984:60). The eyes, ears and the brain of the buffalo were nearly always represented on these backrests; the custom was widespread across the Plains and it has been demonstrated that there was a similarity in the use of such symbolism between the Cree and Ojibwa on the northern Plains and the Arapaho, many hundreds of miles to their south. Kroeber referred to this custom, the ears being particularly distinctive and described as having a design part way across with the middle portion red, bordered by white strips and edges with black lines. Kroeber explained that, as with cradles (see Chapter IV) and tipi embellishments, such items with the *tribal* ornamentations were produced under the direction of the keepers of the seven sacred work bags (Kroeber, 1902:66). Clearly this is good evidence for the ancient origins of such sacred embellishments and patterns predating 'the departure of the Arapaho from the northeastern Plains' (Brasser, 1984:62).

While quillworkers' guilds appear to have been less formalized among the Souian groups such as the Lakota, Mandan, Hidatsa and Crow, several of these tribes, in common with the Plains Algonquians, explain the origin of quillwork in mythological terms (Wissler, 1912(b):92; Simms, 1903; Wissler and Duvall, 1908:131; Lyford, 1940:55) and the Blackfeet traditionally put emphasis on the religious significance of quillwork, an initiation ceremonial being a requirement for women who wished to pursue the craft (see Ewers, 1945:29; Dempsey, 1963:52).

Quillworking Techniques

Some sixteen techniques were used on the Plains. Eight were very common although in combination they can frequently be utilized to determine tribal origin and date of a particular specimen. Tools were simple; in addition to the possible use of the quill flattener referred to earlier, a woman quillworker utilized a bone marker, awl, knife and sinew threads. The marker either simply impressed the surface or was dipped into a colored liquid and then used as a pen. The sinew thread was used to secure the quills to the hide. Great patience was needed in pro-

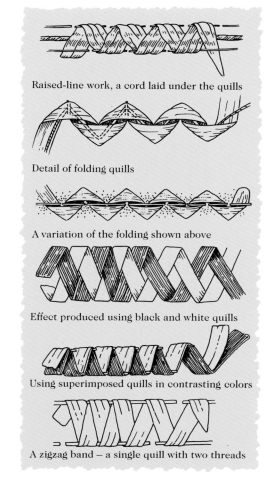

Raised-line work, a cord laid under the quills

Detail of folding quills

A variation of the folding shown above

Effect produced using black and white quills

Using superimposed quills in contrasting colors

A zigzag band – a single quill with two threads

Above: *Porcupine quill techniques. Some sixteen different methods were used by Plains tribes, including not only sewing to the surface as shown here but also wrapping, plaiting and weaving. The quills were first washed and then dyed; when embroidery commenced a few were moistened in the mouth to soften them. They were then flattened by drawing them between the finger nails or teeth.*

Right: *Loom for producing woven quillwork, probably Cree, circa 1860. To keep the warp threads apart at the desired width, birch bark or rawhide pieces were perforated with a row of small holes matching the number of strands used. The flattened quills passed over and under the weft thread were driven up tight against the previous row. This would give a cylindrical bead-like appearance to the finished work.*

Above: *An Arapaho hair ornament, circa 1890. In this fine piece the shafts of the feathers have been decorated with strips of rawhide wrapped with porcupine quills of natural white and dyed yellow, mauve and brown. In this style of headdress, which was worn by dancers to honor a pledge, the middle part of the quillwork was invariably of a different color from the rest of the quillwork.*

ducing this work as the quills had frequently to be spliced together. The numerous techniques employed in this process have been described by Orchard (1916:18–19), but some of the more widely used are shown in the drawing (opposite).

Wrapping techniques on rawhide strips were common and widely used in the decoration of pipe-bags and hair ornaments (see left), which were particularly favored by the Lakota (Lyford, 1940:43; Best and McClelland, 1977:12). More specialized was quill-wrapping on horsehair and the so-called 'plaited technique', both of which were particularly well developed by the Crow for the decoration of shirts, leggings and moccasins but which were also found on similar items collected from the Hidatsa, Mandan, Arikara and Nez Perce, who very probably acquired most of them in trade from the Crow. Very good examples of this style of work, much of it dating prior to 1850, are to be found in European and North American museums (Taylor, 1962, 1981, 1987).

Quillwork on bark, which was very common among such tribes as the Micmac and Ojibwa (Whitehead, 1982), was not found on the Plains; however, the use of moosehair, while firmly associated with the Huron and other Woodland tribes was, on occasions, also used by the Plains Cree (Turner, 1955: Plate VII).

The Cree in particular produced some exquisite quillwork which was woven on a loom (below). Here the warp strands, generally of vegetal fiber, although even at an early period trade thread was employed, were stretched the entire length on a bow. In order to keep the threads spread apart, birch bark or a piece of heavy folded buckskin perforated with a straight row of small holes and corresponding in width to the flattened porcupine quill was used at each end, the threads running through each perforation. Porcupine quills which had first been flattened were then woven over and under a weft thread and between the warp strands. A piece of bark or stiff material such as rawhide or perforated bone which could slide freely along the warp strands was often used to drive the quills up tight 'and insure a straight line across the weave' (Orchard, 1916:57). The finely finished work, always with geometrical designs, has the appearance of being made from fine cylindrical beads.

Several men's shirts, trousers and leggings which exhibit this technique and which were collected from the northeastern Plains region – almost certainly of Cree/Ojibwa origin – are to be found in ethnographical collections and most date from at least 1830.[14]

Although such work was not made by the western nomadic tribes in the historic period, Ewers' Blackfeet informants told him that the tribe 'did woven quillwork long ago' (personal correspondence, July 1959). Possibly then the few extant early forms of 'straight up' headdresses (right), having an exquisite strip of woven quillwork on the front of the headband which are generally identified as Cree and from the northeastern Plains regions, could be an ancient style of Blackfeet headdress from the northern Plains.

In the first half of the nineteenth century, woven quillwork was used to decorate coats, leggings, trousers and horse equipment. This much coveted regalia was almost exclusively made by Cree and Metis people on the Red River (who had settlements at Pembina in present-day North Dakota and at Selkirk in present-day Manitoba). It was an important source of income to the producers and was widely distributed both east and west through extensive trade networks (Washburn ed., 1975:57; Swagerty, Washburn ed., 1988:351–74). The headstall shown (below) is a superb example of such work from this period and is similar to one sketched by Rudolph Kurz while he was residing at Fort Union on the Upper Missouri in 1851.

Above: *A northern Plains double tail headdress, probably Cree, circa 1830. This consists of a long double band with feathers set securely in place, each decorated with quillwork on the shaft.*

Left: *A magnificent headstall, probably Cree, circa 1830. Most of this piece is made of woven quillwork, the bands being sewn on to a buckskin base with quilled discs at the corners.*

Above, right: *Moccasins, probably Crow, circa 1850, with porcupine quills and blue beads. Quillwork is in a 'checker-weave' technique which limits the range of pattern which can be produced to small squares of different colors.*

Right: *Hunting pouch and bullet bag collected by Lieutenant G.K. Warren from Little Thunder's (Brulé) camp after the battle of Ash Hollow. The bag is embellished with blue pony beads with red cloth.*

With the introduction of beads to the Plains tribes in the early nineteenth century, quillwork was progressively displaced as a decorative medium; however, fine traditional costumes decorated with quillwork were still produced in limited amounts as late as the turn of the century on both the northern and central Plains, the Hidatsa in particular excelling in its production, and in 1953 J. C. Ewers of the Smithsonian Institution, Washington, found several Gros Ventre and Assiniboin women on the Fort Belknap Reservation, Montana, well informed on quill techniques of their tribes.[15]

Beadwork

The ancient techniques of painting and porcupine quillwork as decorative embellishments on various accouterments used by the Plains tribes was considerably enhanced with the introduction of beads by white traders, which occurred in the last decade of the eighteenth century.

The history of Plains Indian beadwork falls into two main periods. The first extended from the beginning of the craft which occurred around 1800 and lasted until about 1850. At this time, small, somewhat irregular, opaque china and colored glass beads, 3–4mm in diameter, were brought in by traders and explorers who were progressively introducing European goods to the Plains tribes. The use of beads, however, was not dependent on direct contact with traders. Thus, when the trader Larocque met the Crow in the Yellowstone region in 1805, he reported that they were already in possession of 'small blue glass beads' that they get from the Spaniards but by the second and third man' (Larocque, 1910:22–36), the trade being through the Shoshone who had links with the Spanish settlements to the south (see Chapter II).

Beads of European manufacture were highly prized at this time, comparable in value to the coveted elk teeth mentioned earlier, and the Crow were prepared to give a horse for a hundred of them. Blue was always (and continued to be) the preferred color (ibid.). While most of the beads subsequently traded in increasing quantity to the Plains tribes in the next half century were made in Venice,[16] some of the earlier ones may well have been produced in the Orient; thus Lewis and Clark writing in 1804 observed that the blue beads were 'a coarse, cheap bead imported from China and costing in England 15d the lbs in strands' (Woodward, 1965:14).

Initially these valuable pony beads[17] were used sparingly, often in tasteful combination with small pieces of trade cloth to give contrasting colors such as on the hunting pouch dating from circa 1850 (left). While blue was a preferred color, black, light and dark red and white were also used in various combinations.

Two methods of attaching the beads to the surface of a dressed hide were employed. In the so-called lazy stitch, the beads strung on sinew thread were fastened to the surface at each end of parallel rows, 10–20mm wide, giving a ridge-like effect. This was a technique commonly used on the central Plains (see the drawing, right). Beadwork produced this way closely resembles a number of techniques used in porcupine quillwork, both exhibit narrow bands, are set close together and made up for short parallel rows which run at right angles to the line of the bead. It is thus highly probable that this method of sewing the beads to the surface was suggested by the appearance of the earlier quillwork.

The second method of attachment is the so-called overlaid or spot stitch. Here, strings of beads are tightly attached to the surface with another thread which, in contrast to the lazy stitch, produced a smooth mosaic-like finish. The overlaid method tends to be associated with the more northern tribes such as the Blackfeet and Assiniboin, particularly during the *seed bead* period (circa 1860 onward), but earlier it was also used by the central Plains tribes as, for example, the pair of Lakota leggings dating from the 1850s shown (below).

About 1850, a smaller Venetian bead, generally referred to as a seed bead, was introduced; it became increasingly popular, displacing the pony beadwork as well as much porcupine quillwork. Varying between 1.5 and 2mm in diameter, the beads were sold in a variety of colors, generally in bundles of several strings. Because, in the mid-nineteenth century, these beads were made partly by hand, they tended to be somewhat irregular in shape. Later, around the turn of the century, due to improved methods of manufacture, this irregularity hardly existed and the presence or absence of this unevenness is one factor in determining the age of a particular specimen.

Beadwork Styles and Women's Crafts

Increasingly, from about 1860 onward, several styles of beadwork emerged which were, broadly, typical of a particular region of the Plains.

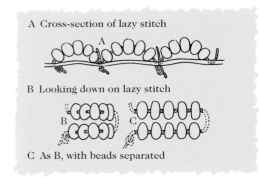

A Cross-section of lazy stitch

B Looking down on lazy stitch

C As B, with beads separated

Above: The lazy stitch (after Lyford, 1940:62). This was a common method of sewing beads onto a skin surface on the central and southern Plains. The finished work gave a banded appearance reminiscent of much sewn porcupine quillwork which may have inspired this technique. The early work was mainly in blue and white pony beads; later (circa 1860) these were replaced by the seed bead in a variety of colors.

Left: Pair of leggings, Brulé (?), collected by Lieutenant G.K. Warren, September 1855. The limited colors available to early beadworkers often resulted in the combination of beads with a colored cloth, as shown at the bottom of these leggings. The broad bands are, however, in a single color and edged with a fringe of dyed horsehair.

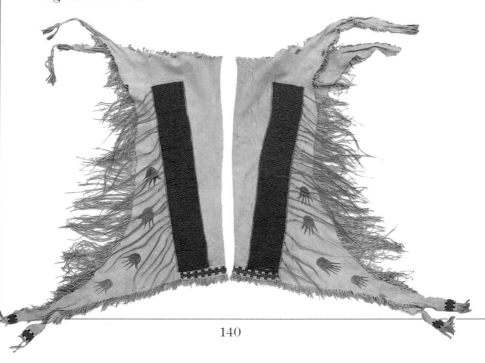

Right: *The overlaid or spot stitch. Here, two threads are used, the bead thread and the sewing thread. The end of the bead thread is attached to the buckskin and the beads strung on. The sewing thread is then stitched at right angles over the bead thread between every two or three beads for fine work and curved patterns.*

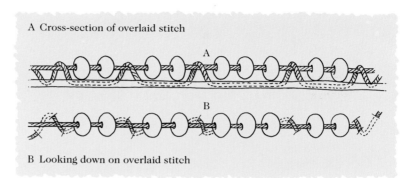

A Cross-section of overlaid stitch

A

B

B Looking down on overlaid stitch

Below: *A fine beaded shirt collected from the Piegan in 1903. This is a typical shirt for the Blackfeet from 1880 onwards. The decoration consists of beaded bands across the shoulders and down the arms, sewn in overlaid stitch. On the chest and back are two large beaded discs. The patterns in both the bands and discs are similar to those found in earlier quillwork. Fringing is in ermine and hair. (This is a back view of the shirt which shows the full decorative features.)*

Thus in the north, among such tribes as the Blackfeet, Plains Cree, Sarcee and, to some extent, the Assiniboin, the overlay stitch was used with a square or oblong as the basic element for patterns. Scores of these small elements were massed into larger units producing squares, triangles, diamonds and crosses. These large figures were generally of a single color and had edges of varicolored squares; the background was usually white although light blue was not infrequently used. A good example of this type of beadwork appears on a buckskin war-shirt, collected at the turn of the century from the Piegan (below). Here the relatively large decorative fields on the arm and shoulder bands have stepped triangles built up of multi-

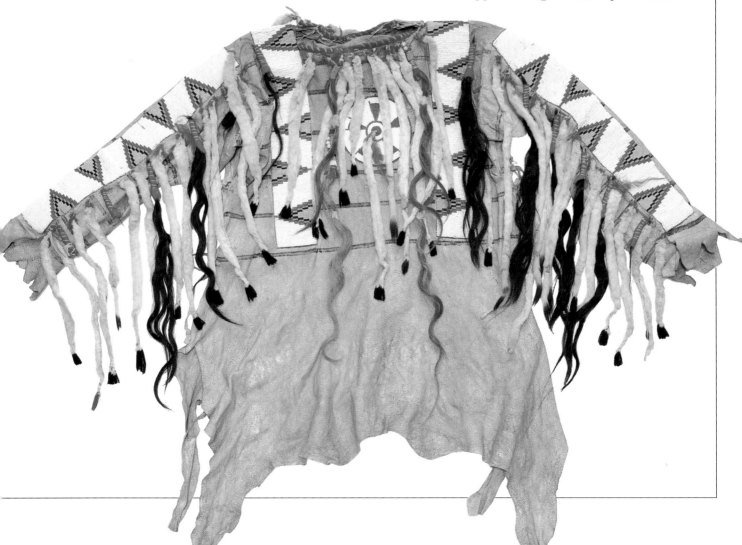

colored squares of beads on a white background: triangles are reversed sequentially along the bands, giving a further variation in the overall design. There is little relationship between the patterns in Blackfeet pony beadwork to those in the later seed beadwork, but the style does have considerable affinity with designs which were used in early porcupine quillwork. A good example of this is the quilled pattern on a shirt worn by the North Blackfeet chief Crowfoot (Ewers, 1945:30), which is almost identical to that worked in beads shown on page 141, while the checkerboard-type patterns so common in the seed beadwork from this tribe resemble those found in the woven

Above: *Fine buckskin dress made by Mrs Minnie Sky Arrow from the Fort Peck Reservation and dating from between 1890 and 1900. This is a very unusual dress and breaks with traditional styles where the cape only was fully beaded; both overlaid and lazy stitch have been used in the decoration of this spectacular piece, which is firmly associated with the Reservation period, having been used as a recital gown.*

Top: *Cheyenne woman's leggings. These are of a traditional style for the Cheyenne and were collected by James Mooney in about 1880. The beadwork is in lazy stitch, the whole finished neatly.*

Above: *A Nez Perce bandolier bag collected by Monteith in 1876. It displays the typical beadwork used by both the Nez Perce and Crow in the last quarter of the nineteenth century.*

quillwork produced by the tribes adjoining the Blackfeet to the east. Further, as has been noted, since the Blackfeet claimed to have done this type of quillwork in earlier days, there is a possibility that when seed beads were introduced this initiated a revival of patterns from the past.

In contrast, the patterns used on the central Plains were often rather light and spread out on a monochrome – generally white – background. Right-angled and isosceles triangles, either alone or combined into diamonds, two-pronged forks and hourglasses, were among the most common of the design elements. The lazy stitch was almost exclusively used in producing such work and while many of the units in a whole design may be somewhat massive in appearance the overall impression is often one of openness and lightness. Although a white background was common, medium to light blue was not unusual, particularly on women's dresses (as on pages 128–9), and around the turn of the century when plenty of beads were available, and 'there just wasn't anything else to do' (Conn, 1986:57), spectacular effects were produced using this technique (see opposite).

The Lakota were the main producers of this style of beadwork but other tribes such as the Arapaho, Cheyenne, Gros Ventre and, to a lesser extent, the Assiniboin, also decorated various items in a very similar way. Nevertheless, not infrequently the combination of elements, patterns and bead type enable a differentiation to be made between one tribe and another. For example, some Cheyenne beadwork exhibits distinctive combinations of stripes within the pattern, worked in very small beads, as shown on a pair of Cheyenne woman's leggings, collected by James Mooney in the late nineteenth century (above, left).

A number of the elements which occur in this style of beadwork, such as the triangle and rectangular units, are obviously derived from the earlier pony bead and quillwork period, several being retained as they belonged to a sacred class, being used by the women's sewing guilds discussed earlier. Years ago, Frederic Douglas observed that settlers moving west carried oriental carpets with them which bore designs very similar to those which started to appear in Lakota beadwork at about the same time. He thus suggested that, because the geometrical designs were not so different from their own, they were subsequently adopted as new beadwork patterns for the tribe.[18]

On the western central Plains the Crow, and to a lesser extent the Shoshone, Nez Perce (see left) and other Plateau tribes developed a style of beadwork, the designs in which strongly resembled those painted on parfleches. The style seems to have emerged some time after about 1860 and flowered from 1880 to 1900. Patterns from earlier styles of quillwork, such as the distinctive quill-wrapped horsehair used by the Crow (Taylor, 1981), were also transferred to beadwork at this period, in particular men's shirts (Wildschut, Ewers ed., 1959:7) and mocca-

Left: *Crow woman's moccasins, collected by W.J. Hoffman at the Crow Agency, Montana, in 1892. These are hard soled and beaded in a variant of the overlaid stitch.*

Right: *An otterskin bow-case-quiver, circa 1880–90, collected by Fred Kober and identified in museum records simply as 'Rocky Mountain Indians'.*

Below: *Typical geometrical Crow-style beadwork is displayed on this partial bow-case-quiver which was collected by Captain Charles E. Bendire sometime before 1892.*

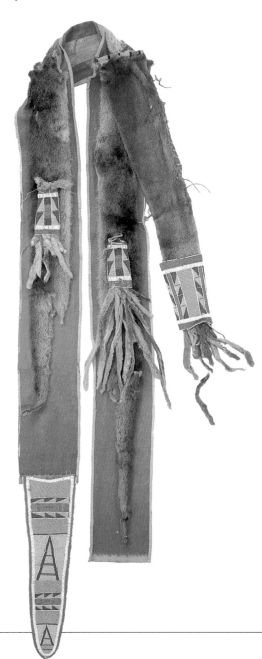

sins (above). Characteristic of such work were massive triangular patterns often with a background of red cloth: sometimes the triangles were very tall, at other times flattened, and may have within them smaller triangles, oblongs, squares or bars, as shown in the Crow bow and quiver case (right and above, right). They were also put in combination, forming diamonds and hour-glasses, or stacked apex against base in a repeated vertical row, while a band of another color often covered the junction of the triangles. Light blue and lavender were favored colors, although old bead sample cards which were used by the traders before 1900 show more than eighty colors of seed beads from which Indian women could choose. Crow women 'generally employed only seven colors in their work and showed little disposition to experiment with different color combinations' (ibid.:45). Unlike the Lakota and Blackfeet, who predominately used white backgrounds, Crow beadworkers showed a very marked preference for light blue and generally only used white beads either in the narrow borders of large design areas or to delineate their larger design elements in a single line of white beads, setting them off from their light blue or lavender backgrounds.

A limited amount of floral beadwork was also done by Crow women during this period, particularly on moccasins (above, far right), but floral patterns were also used on leggings, gauntlets, waistcoats and belt pouches. The patterns were 'conventionalized representation of leaves and stems as well as flowers' (ibid.:44) and, although the work cannot always be differentiated with certainty from the floral beadwork of other tribes, a marked characteristic was the outlining of the patterns with a single line of white beads, as shown (above, far right).

Horse equipment – bridles, cruppers, women's saddles, headstalls and stirrups (below, right) – together with accouterments which were traditionally carried mainly by women in parades, such as lance and sword cases (see illustration on page 22), were also heavily embellished with beadwork.

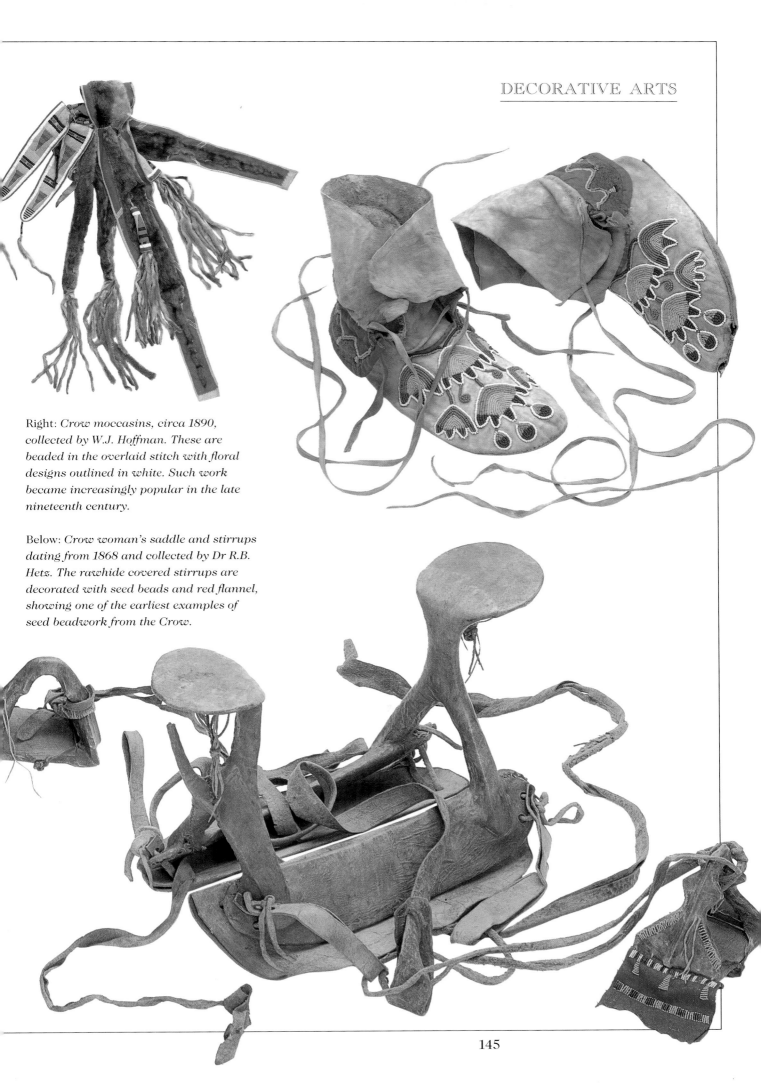

Right: *Crow moccasins, circa 1890, collected by W.J. Hoffman. These are beaded in the overlaid stitch with floral designs outlined in white. Such work became increasingly popular in the late nineteenth century.*

Below: *Crow woman's saddle and stirrups dating from 1868 and collected by Dr R.B. Hetz. The rawhide covered stirrups are decorated with seed beads and red flannel, showing one of the earliest examples of seed beadwork from the Crow.*

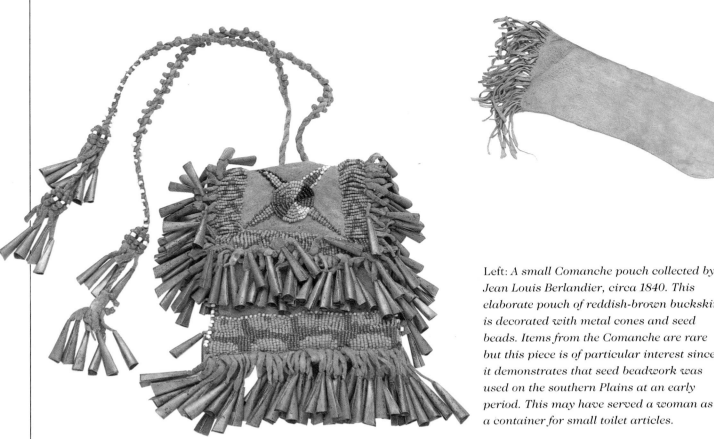

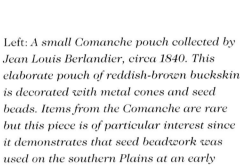

Left: *A small Comanche pouch collected by Jean Louis Berlandier, circa 1840. This elaborate pouch of reddish-brown buckskin is decorated with metal cones and seed beads. Items from the Comanche are rare but this piece is of particular interest since it demonstrates that seed beadwork was used on the southern Plains at an early period. This may have served a woman as a container for small toilet articles.*

Right: *A Nez Perce/Crow gun case collected by J.B. Monteith in 1876. This article underlines the Crow/Nez Perce trade interaction since virtually identical items are found among the two tribes. It is thus exceedingly difficult to distinguish between Crow and Nez Perce beadwork although it is probable that the Crow were the main producers.*

Right: *Comanche woman's upper garment, collected by Jean Louis Berlandier, circa 1840. This is fashioned from a single deerskin with the leg sections preserved; it is folded lengthwise and a transverse slit cut in the skin for the wearer's head and neck. The main decoration is the reddish painted area which extends over the shoulders and down the central front and back of the garment, but additional decoration is in the form of brass beads around the neck and heavy fringes. There is a possibility that this upper cape was worn with a skirt of some sort – a combination which would be the precursor to the three-skin southern Plains woman's dress.*

Although work of this type does occur among the Plateau tribes (above right), much of this can be put down to the extensive trading and exchange of ideas which we know took place between the Crow and Plateau people[19] (Taylor, 1981:46–8).

The large amount of beadwork produced on the central and northern Plains, particularly in the last quarter of the nineteenth century, contrasts markedly with the southern Plains and, while specimens collected as early as the 1840s from the Comanche show that at this time they did embellish bags with quantities of both pony and seed beads (Berlandier, Ewers ed., 1969: Plate 19) (above), a marked characteristic of the southern Plains region is the somewhat limited use of beadwork. This was mainly confined to edging on such items as women's leggings, dresses and high-topped moccasins: beadwork then was but part of the decorative media employed to enhance the overall beauty of the object decorated. Thus, buckskin colored red, but more often yellow and green, the use of silver and brass buttons or studs and elaborate fringes (as shown on the right), together with beadwork, was a decided characteristic of the southern Plains people.

There were some notable exceptions, however. Possibly because of the increasing influence of the Cheyenne and Arapaho in the late nineteenth century, such items as cradles and pouches appeared which were beautifully embellished in a solid mass of beadwork generally using the lazy stitch. (This technique is described on pages 139–40.)

Although, as has been mentioned on page 144, a wide range of bead colors was available from the trading posts,[20] in addition to the popular red background, light and dark blue, pink, a deep 'greasy' yellow and white were almost exclusively favored although black was occasionally used for highlighting.

Quality – that is consistent regularity or faceting of the bead – was also another important factor which governed the selection of beads by the southern Plains craftswoman.[21]

Moccasins and Pipe-Bags

Some of the earliest descriptions we have of Plains Indian moccasins come from François Larocque who observed in 1805 that Crow moccasins were 'made in the manner of mittens having a seam round the outside of the foot only without pleat' (Larocque, 1910:67). This is the one-piece, soft-soled moccasin, which was most common on the Great Plains well into the second half of the nineteenth century. The Blackfeet called this type of moccasin the 'real moccasin' and according to one authority it survived among the Blackfeet until 'the end of buffalo days as the typical, hair lined, winter moccasin' (Ewers, 1945:39). Later moccasins – those produced after about 1860 – tended to be of a two-piece type, having a hard rawhide sole and a soft skin upper, although some moccasins produced at this time continued to be of the soft soled type with an extra piece of heavy hide sewn on the sole.

Many patterns in quillwork, which were applied to the older moccasins, were carried through in beadwork. A common form, widely distributed across the Plains, was a combination of a rosette with a band, the general appearance being an inverted key hole. Such designs were applied to the vamp of the moccasin, covering the central portion of the surface; both the Blackfeet and Crow referred to this design as 'round quillwork' or 'round beadwork'. The Crow not infrequently employed the so-

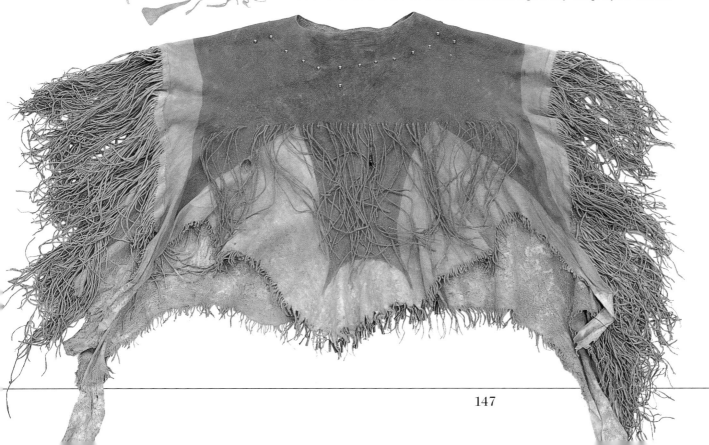

called quill-wrapped horsehair technique in combination with beads to produce patterns of this type, particularly before about 1850 (Taylor, 1981:44–5). Among the Lakota the design is reported to have considerable symbolic meaning, one in particular having an association with buffalo hunting, the pattern referring to a buffalo pound with V-shaped wings leading to it, into which the buffalo were driven and then slaughtered (see Chapter IV).

Moccasins were also embellished by women, under the direction of their husbands (Wissler, 1902:344) to depict military achievements – the capturing of horses or coups counted. Thus, white beaded bands might represent the warpath in winter, triangular represented tipis and small squares in red implied that the wearer was wounded on the warpath. A red square worked between two blue ones conveyed the idea that an enemy was killed by the wearer when he received the wound, and so on. Moccasins so decorated tell the world 'that the wearer went on the war-path in winter, killed an enemy and received a wound' (Wissler, 1902:344). Designs on Crow moccasins were also given military associations; thus the four feather design signified that the wearer had counted the four major coups recognized by the Crow and the horse tracks (below) indicated that the wearer 'had captured horses from the enemy' (Wildschut, Ewers ed., 1959:47).

Below: Boy's moccasins, Crow, collected by W.J. Hoffman in 1892. These fully beaded, hard sole moccasins have, as the predominant decorative element, U-shaped designs on the vamp which the Crow referred to as horse tracks. Some Crow informants stated that when such elements were beaded on moccasins they were indicative of horses captured from the enemy . . . possibly then a reference here to the father's achievements since decoration of this type tended to be subjective.

Another article of dress often bearing military symbols is the pipe-bag. Here the geometrical patterns were built up from a series of elements commonly found in beadwork and given names in order to identify them; they were, however, not necessarily given that meaning when worked on apparel. Thus the design unit had a name so it could be used in giving instructions to beginners or in communication with other artists but when used in combination they could be used to express relatively complex ideas which, as Wissler observed for the Lakota, 'follows a certain sequence common to the tribe, and that any one acquainted with the mode can read the designs with fair accuracy' (Wissler, 1904:263).

So there was much meaning in not only religious and sacred art as described earlier, but also in military art, the interpretation of which gives significant insights into the ethos of the Plains people. It is important, however, to point out that a great deal of beadwork produced by the Plains craftswoman was purely decorative, especially for those items which were made for trading to alien tribes or white collectors and even with the religious and military symbolism of the type discussed, it is exceedingly difficult for the uninitiated to understand and it requires much analysis to use the artifacts as both cultural and historical documents.

FOOTNOTES: CHAPTER V

1 This robe is in the Peabody Museum of Archaeology and Ethnology, Harvard University, Cambridge, Mass., and was collected by Lewis and Clark in 1804 (catalogue number 53121). Some paintings depicting Spanish expeditions to the Plains and dating from circa 1720 have been described by Hotz (1970). They are now in the Museum of New Mexico, Santa Fe.

2 Now in the Musée de l'Homme, Paris. Two skins of particular interest are catalogue numbers 34.33.4 and 34.33.9.

3 Karl Bodmer painted an Assiniboin chief, *Pteh-Skah*, wearing a robe with geometric patterns, so these may be exceptions to this generalization (see Hunt, Gallagher and Orr, 1984:Plate 204).

4 In later years, such designs were done in beadwork. A particularly good specimen is in the Museum of the American Indian, Heye Foundation, New York (catalogue number 29/300).

5 The silken thread which spiders produce is tougher than steel and highly elastic. In recent years scientists at the University of Wyoming have been investigating the remarkable properties of this material. Plains Indians were obviously acutely aware of the uniqueness of the webb and adopted it into their mythology.

6 It was said that women who had certain powers took a favored child to a secluded place where a hammock-like structure was made in the form of a spider web design. The child was placed in this; the ceremony was one of blessing and to bring good fortune.

7 These lines are also said to be the symbols of the 'Four-pipe dance' in which honor is shown to favorite children (Wissler, 1904:246).

8 This was initiated by Franz Boas, Head of Anthropology in the American Museum of Natural History, New York.

9 Sets of forms and a set of symbolic concepts were often conventions with beadworkers. In one context they were highly symbolic, in another purely decorative (see Kroeber, 1902:139).

10 One early form of woman's dress consisted of two pieces of skin sewn together along the sides which was supported by straps over the shoulders. This *strap dress* was used by the Woodlands and northeastern Plains tribes. It seems to have less symbolic association with buffalo power than the *side-fold* dress, suggesting that buffalo power concepts (in apparel) came from the southeast.

11 Olivella as well as dentalium shells have been found in the early (circa 1500) Mandan sites which infer trade contacts, via pedestrian nomads to the west, to the Northwest Coast, some two thousand miles away (see Wood, 1967:2 and 19).

12 A recent analysis of the early Indian trade networks across North America, is in Swagerty, Washburn ed., 1988:figs 1 and 2).

13 Brasser has attempted to overcome this problem by making 'use of large samples of comparable artifacts, and . . . "overlapping"' their meager documentation (1975:45).

14 A shirt from the eastern Sioux and now in the Jarvis collection at the Brooklyn Museum, New York (catalogue number 50.67.4), also exhibits this technique (see Feder, 1964:4 and Taylor, Horse Capture and Ball eds., 1984:34; fig 6).

15 In 1974, the Sioux Museum in Rapid City, South Dakota, assembled an exhibition of contemporary Sioux quillwork. Since that time, a number of Sioux quillworkers have found a 'ready market for their wares' (Bebbington, 1982:30).

16 The manufacture and export of beads 'formed the very backbone of the Venetian glass industry' (Orchard, 1975:95).

17 Said to be called pony beads because they were brought in by the pony pack trains (Lyford, 1940:56). They were referred to as 'real' beads by the Blackfeet (Ewers, 1945:34).

18 See Lyford (1940:67,70,71) and Conn (1986:58) for a further discussion.

19 In recent years, considerable interest has been taken in the history and development of this distinctive beadwork. The studies include its relationship to both earlier quillwork and parfleche designs, the Crow–Plateau interaction, and the various artifacts on which this work occurs. (See Wildschut, Ewers ed., 1959: The 'Special Crow Issue' of *American Indian Art*, Vol.6.No.1, Winter 1980 : Taylor 1981(a) and 1987 : Lessard ed.,1984 :and Conn, 1986.) The interested reader is referred to these more specialized studies.

20 Such as at Bent's Fort and Fort Sill in present-day Colorado and Oklahoma respectively.

21 For some excellent articles relating to the beadwork styles on the southern Plains and adjacent regions, the reader is referred to the journal *Moccasin Tracks*, published at La Palma, California. In particular, papers by Bates, Cooley, Hays, Smith and Fenner.

THE WAY TO STATUS:
LIFE OF THE
PLAINS WARRIOR

--- CHAPTER VI ---

Below: *Crow shield, circa 1840. This belonged to Rotten Belly, a highly respected and successful chief of the River Crow. The cover is painted with a design which is said to represent the moon and which appeared in a vision to Rotten Belly. One so favored was expected to have a long life and high status within the tribe.*

The Way to Status: Life of the Plains Warrior

While there were some notable exceptions, such as the 'Manly-hearted' woman[1] and the Blackfeet Holy Woman who initiated the tribal Sun-dance (see Chapter IV), the status of a Plains Indian family pivoted firmly on the achievements of the man. Chastity in women was highly rated and chastity belts were commonly worn after first menstruation. And yet, as in most human societies, young men sought to dishonor females in a sort of game which was a youthful symbol of prestige.

As one young Cheyenne lady reported: 'I would always ask my mother to accompany me before I would go out. My Mother furnished me rawhide twine and a piece of hide to use as a diaper which was securely tied around my hips – this was done to preserve my virtue against the attacks of an overanxious young man' (Michelson, 1932:4). If men's relationships with women were symbols of prestige, the opposite was certainly not true, and ambivalence toward sex would result in severe penalties, even death, for adulterous women.

Prestige, however, was really only fully gained socially in religion, in acts of generosity such as helping the poor or giving horses and other goods to visitors in 'give-aways', and in tribally sanctioned war. Thus, individuals who had little interest in following the warpath were not excluded from high status – they could gain standing by owning certain medicine bundles or taking on the role of a Holy Man.

Inter-Tribal Warfare

Nearly two centuries ago, when Alexander Henry of the North West Company built a trading post in Cree country near the Red River in present-day North Dakota, he recorded on 18 September 1800 that the Plains were covered with buffalo as far as the eye could see, adding: 'This is a delightful country, and were it not for perpetual wars, the natives might be the happiest people on earth' (Henry and Thompson, Coues ed. 1897, vol.I:99). Henry expanded on this point when he observed of the Piegan: 'War seems to be the Piegan's sole delight; their discourse always turns upon that subject; one war-party no sooner arrives than another sets off. Horses are the principal plunder to be obtained from these enemies on the way ... They take great delight in relating their adventures in war, and are so vivid in rehearsing every detail of the fray that they seem to be fighting the battle over again,' (ibid., vol.II:726).

There is little doubt that such sentiments could also be applied to the rest of the Indians of the Great Plains at that time. Henry was simply reporting on an inter-tribal war complex which had been enacted since time immemorial. Thus, early pictographic renderings between 500 and 1600, suggesting inter-tribal warfare, are to be found at various sites across the Great Plains; at Pictographic Cave, for example, near Billings in Montana, pedestrian warriors are depicted carrying large circular shields – perhaps 3ft or so in diameter – they are painted with designs probably representative of supernatural helpers. They also carry weapons such as clubs and lances.

The rectangular bodies, with peculiar V-shapes at the neck suggest that some may be wearing multi-layered hide armor; this we know from later descriptions was worn by pedestrian warriors such as these.

Later, French explorers who traveled to the region of the western Great Lakes in the 1650s reported on aggressive tribes to the west, who the Algonquians referred to as *Nadoessis*,[2] or 'enemies', while the missionary Father Allouez, who met some of the *Nadoessis* at the head of Lake Superior, described them as 'warlike', and said that they 'have conducted hostilities against all their enemies, by whom they are held in extreme fear' (Kellogg ed., 1917:132).

The roots of inter-tribal warfare were undoubtedly embedded in the nature of *tribalism* itself where there was a common disposition of each tribe 'to regard *their* tribe as "the people", and to look upon outsiders with suspicion' (Ewers, 1975: 398). Thus, Plains Indians were highly patriotic – toward their own tribe; a gesture, described for the Crow (Kurz, 1937: 252) but expressing sentiments typical of the Plains Indians, was the placing of the right hand on the chest and making the utterance: 'Absaroka.' As one ethnologist has put it: 'This is not to deny that other and more specific causes for intertribal conflict existed – competition for choice hunting grounds, capture of women, or horses, or inanimate property, and *individual desire for recognition and status through the winning of war honours*' (Ewers, 1975: 398) (author's emphasis).

Thus, the winning of status and war honors in inter-tribal warfare were high on the list; the gaining of territory was often of marginal interest in a vast land where the population density at that time was not large, probably no more than one person per square mile.

Coup Counting

One of the distinguishing features of the Plains war complex was the counting of coup, which depended markedly on a system of graded war honors, several specific acts of bravery being identified by various tribes and arranged on a fixed scale so that the warrior performing the deed which held first place gained the most honor, and so on down the line. It was war honors of this type – which displayed military virtues – that were given the coup ranking, while protection of women and children, even at great personal risk, was simply taken as a matter of course.

The coup counting system had a marked impact on war motivation where the striking of an enemy with a harmless stick – even just the hand – demanded exceptional bravery. The actual number of times it was acceptable to count coup upon a single enemy varied considerably: among the Cheyenne it was three, while among the Arapaho it was four. On occasions, that differ-

Above: Hotokaueh-Hoh, *or Head of the Buffalo Skin, Piegan, painting by Karl Bodmer, Fort McKenzie, August 1833. While the warpath was one route to high status, another was via ownership of powerful medicine bundles such as the Thunder Pipe. Blackfeet tradition states that the stems were copied after one given to them by the thunder as a token of friendship.*

Right: Kee-akee-ka-saa-ka-wow, *or The Man that gives the War Whoop, Cree Medicine-Pipe owner painted by Paul Kane at Fort Pitt, 1847. This man had been elected the tribe's pipe bearer for four years and he revealed several sacred pipe-stems to Kane.*

ence needed to be resolved; thus, when a mixed party of Cheyenne and Arapaho fought against a common enemy, a single foe could be struck *seven* times. Needless to say, solutions of this sort could cause complications, as Grinnell observed in reporting on a clash between combined forces of Cheyenne, Arapaho, Comanche, Kiowa and Apache against a common Ute enemy: there was 'tremendous confusion' when the coups were counted (Grinnell 1910: 299).

The Plains tribes distinguished between two types of intertribal warfare: that for killing enemies and taking scalps, and that for capturing horses. These were generally referred to as the scalp raid and the horse raid.

The Scalp Raid

It is clear that scalping was practiced early on in North America; associated with it was much symbolism, prestige and ritual. Paramount was a recognition that scalps taken symbolically represented the souls of the enemy who would be slaves to the victor in the next world. Thus, in the early 1700s it was reported that among the 'Nations of Louisiana' the war chiefs bestowed names upon the warriors depending on their conduct in battle such that 'when a person understands their language, the

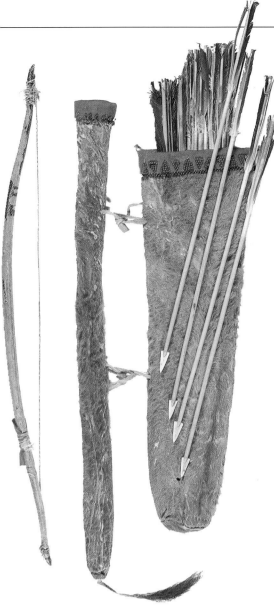

Above, left: *Wolf on the Hill, also known as High Backed Wolf, Cheyenne, painted by George Catlin in 1832. He died in 1833; a star shower in that year fixed the date of his death in the minds of his descendants and emphasized his importance.*

Left: *A stone-headed club, unidentified at the time of collection but probably central Plains, circa 1870. The wooden handle is covered with buckskin and the heavy head is of stone worked to an oval shape. These clubs had ancient origins and were carried by pedestrian warriors.*

Above: *Bow-case and quiver with arrows and bow, probably Dakota and collected by Friedrich Köhler and dated circa 1830. Plains' bows were seldom more than 3ft (1m) in length, arrows some 20in (50cm) with long feathering and flint tips, as shown here. Later they were of steel.*

name itself of a warrior enables him to learn all his exploits' (Kenton ed., 1956: 417).

Many obligations went with the act of scalping. For example, warriors might not sleep 'at their return with their wives', and could not eat meat. This abstinence lasted for six months and failure to observe it was said to bring dire consequences – 'the soul of him whom they have killed will cause them to die through sorcery – they will never again obtain any advantage over their enemies, and that the slightest wounds . . . will prove fatal' (ibid.)

A generation later, a Piegan chief echoed similar sentiments for his tribe, *Saukamappee*, The Boy, telling of a battle in pre-horse days (circa 1730). The successful war party, against the Shoshone to the west, returned with more than fifty scalps. There was much subsequent discussion as to the significance of those taken from the enemy who were found dead under their shields – killed by the gun-armed Piegan – 'as not one could say he had actually slain the enemy whose scalps he held'. There was, however, no doubt about the others; those who had taken the trophy from the head of an enemy they had killed said 'the Souls of the enemy that each of us has slain belong to us and we have given them to our relations in the other world to be their slaves and we are contented' (Henry and Thompson, Coues ed., 1897: 332–3).

In these large inter-tribal battles, the shield was of paramount importance although, as *Saukamappee*'s tale records, it gave little protection against antagonists armed with guns. Additionally, multi-layered hide body-armor was commonly worn by pedestrian warriors, the custom being widely distributed across the Plains, although it is probable that the main users of this form of protective clothing were the Apache and Shoshone. It was copied by the Blackfeet as they took up permanent residence on the Plains.

Armor was not entirely abandoned with the coming of the horse, but it was somewhat modified. Thus, in 1775 the explorer Peter Pond described such protective clothing as used by some Yankton Sioux warriors who wore 'a garment like an outsize vest with sleeves that cum down to thare elboes made of soft skins and several thicknesses that will turn an arrow at a distans' (Innis, 1930: 58). Nevertheless, because of the progressive introduction of the gun, within a decade or so such body armor fell into disuse but it was retained as a single layered soft buckskin garment – the 'war shirt' – which in historic times could only be worn by men of military distinction[3] (see Chapter VII).

The prelude to the large scale scalp raids not only enabled distinguished war chiefs to maintain their high status by sending out invitations to other bands or tribes, but it was an excuse for extensive ceremonial. Generally, there was full public involvement, a great deal of debate, feasting and, most importantly, 'sacrifices by the chiefs and soldiers, and also by many of

the warriors to the several supernatural powers' (Denig, Hewitt ed., 1930: 548). They were all part of the social organization, a vital component in strengthening tribal and alliance ties. 'Sacrifices' could come in various forms, thus *Tokala-lu'ta*, Red Fox, a Lakota warrior, related his experiences prior to his first war expedition when the leaders urged those who wanted to be successful to 'come and join the Sun-dance'. 'There were a hundred men standing abreast in the circle. We were asked "What offer will you make to the great sun shining over your head? Will you give him tobacco? Will you give him your flesh and blood?" When the Intercessor came to me and asked these questions, I said in reply, "I will give my flesh and blood that I may conquer my enemies"' (Densmore, 1918: 376). On returning victorious from war, Red Fox performed the Sundance, his arms were cut seven times below the elbow and two times above the elbow, making eighteen wounds in all.

The main parade prior to the scalp raid was the 'horseback dance, or big dance' (Wissler, 1913: 456), a widespread and popular prelude to such raids. Thus, on the northern Plains, the Blackfeet members of the expedition rode out of camp for some distance where they changed into their war clothes, put warpaint on themselves and their horses, which they also decorated with masks, martingales, feathers and bells, they then mounted and 'converged upon the camp from the four cardinal directions, carrying their weapons' (Ewers, 1955: 196).

There was some variation. The Lakota, for example, referred to these prelude ceremonials as *uci tapi*, the 'charge-around-

Left: *A ceremonial 'no retreat' sash, Northern Arapaho and collected in Sharp Nose's camp, no date given but probably circa 1880. The sash is of buckskin embellished with five quilled discs and eagle feathers. It went over the wearer's head and on the battlefield the end was pinned to the ground beyond which custom decreed he must not retreat.*

Below, left: *Sharp Nose, a Northern Arapaho chief and successor to Black Coal. Photograph taken circa 1876. Captain John Bourke described Sharp Nose as an inspiration on the battlefield who handled men with rare judgement and coolness, and that he was as modest as he was brave.*

Below: *Comanche horned headdress, possibly collected by Jean Louis Berlandier and thus dating from the period 1828–51. Consisting of buffalo horns attached to a heavy buckskin cap embellished with blue and white beads, a similar headdress was depicted on a Comanche in war-dress by the artist Lino Sanchez y Tapia, circa 1830.*

camp', when warriors of distinction stood out on account of the splendor (and value) of their costumes. Prior to the Comanche scalp raid 'the captain and the warriors . . . [were] bedecked with feathers and covered with their war ornaments . . . [they] form two lines in which formation they make a tour of the camps . . . They promise to distinguish themselves in the coming war and to supply all possible succor to those who are exposed to too great danger' (Berlandier, Ewers ed., 1969: 72–3).

In such parades, members of warrior societies could also be distinguished by their distinctive regalia, particularly that costume which would obligate them to do battle in some spectacular way. Thus, the Comanche *Pukutsi*, Cheyenne 'Country Ones', Crow 'Crazy Dogs Wishing To Die', and the Lakota 'Strong Hearts', to name a few, wore a broad 'no retreat' sash, which was slit near the end and was long enough to pass over the head and then trail behind the wearer on the ground (see left). On the battlefield, the wearer was expected to pin the free end to the ground and there take a stand. Even more spectacular, and not without a hint of humor in this grim game of war and death, was that of the Pawnee Crazy Dog who, dispensing with the split sash, tied a cord to his penis, the other end to a stake planted in the ground beyond which he would not retreat – hence the 'Tied Penis Society' (Murie, 1916: 580).

Buffalo horn headdresses were also worn by distinguished members of the warrior societies, such as those of the *Cante Tinza*, 'Strong Hearts', of the Lakota. Each member of the society had one of these headdresses which he wore into battle.

Obligations were strict: if a man had been uniformly successful and had never shown any sign of cowardice he would be buried with the bonnet on his head, 'but if he showed cowardice on the warpath he was punished on his return by being severely reprimanded in the presence of all the members, his headdress was taken away, and he was expelled from the society' (Densmore, 1918: 321).

In this ancient style of warfare the quest was for scalps, war honors and revenge – and it could be brutal. Thus, in 1866, shortly after the Gros Ventre had killed the distinguished Piegan chief Many Horses, members of his tribe raised a war expedition against a village of Crow and Gros Ventre, killing more than three hundred. The ferocity of their charge caused their enemies to panic '*and the killing is said to have ended only when the victors had decided they had killed enough*'. The Piegan remembered this as 'a most decisive victory', but the Gros Ventre recalled it as their 'most disastrous defeat' (Ewers, 1958: 43). Human parts other than scalps were sometimes taken as trophies; thus the necklace shown on page 159 displays the fingers of tribal enemies and within the pouches, it has been reliably stated, are the testicles of several fallen enemy – perhaps one was even an ill-fated Pawnee Crazy Dog![4]

The history of Plains Indians warfare is one of dynamic change. By the 1860s scalp raiding was not pursued with the same intensity, fury or frequency as in earlier years. As the horse increasingly dominated the culture, the horse raid became progressively popular.

Above: *Horned headdress, Sioux, collected at Fort Randall, Dakota Territory, by Dr G.P. Hardenburg in 1877. This consists of a buckskin cap covered with red cloth and with a pair of large buffalo horns attached. Black crow feathers cascade over the cap and tail. This is probably part of the regalia of the military Crow-Owners Society, the crow being associated with success in war.*

Right: *Necklace of human fingers. Cheyenne, 1870s. This was picked up by Captain John Bourke after the attack on Dull Knife's village, 26 November 1876. It consists of a beaded collar to which are attached some eight human fingers, small pouches and stone arrowheads. John Bourke described the piece as a 'ghastly specimen of aboriginal religious art, the especial "medicine" decoration of High Wolf, the chief "medicine man"' (Bourke, 1890:31). The flint arrowheads relate to thunder-power in Cheyenne mythology.*

The Horse Raid

'Watch Your Horses'

Kangi angi Wicasa ....Crow Indian
kim sunk awan ǵlaka po ....You must watch your horses
sunk wama'non ....A horse thief
sa ....Often
miye yelo ....Am I

(Densmore, 1918: 337)

A certain threshold of horse ownership was vital for both the survival and economic security of a typical nomadic Plains Indian family. Thus, Mishkin's studies of the Kiowa indicated that the average family 'owned approximately ten pack animals, five riding animals and two to five buffalo horses. With such a herd a family possessed the pre-requisites for economic security and could easily satisfy all its needs' (Mishkin, 1940: 20). Nevertheless, there were wide variations in horse wealth and a few rich Kiowa families counted their horses in hundreds, while well-to-do families owned up to fifty and 'not a few' owned no horses at all (ibid.: 19). Obviously, with relative wealth in horses as a measure of social status, the possibility of the capture of this animal from enemy tribes became a prime ambition of aspiring young warriors,[5] so that 'running off the enemy's horses was both legitimate and honorable. As a measure of aggression or reprisal, it was doubly effective; it enriched the plunderer while it deprived the plundered of property indispensable to his safety and well-being. A robust, manly pastime, it was also splendid training in the Spartan virtues – patience, cunning, courage – and the young man who excelled in it became a popular hero' (Smith, 1949: 93).

It was, however, a dangerous war-game and even though the objective was capture and not killing, the horse raid party sometimes found more action than it anticipated. As Ewers' Blackfeet informants told him, on occasions whole parties were wiped out and, although some men survived forty or more of these expeditions, others lost their lives in their first effort (Ewers, 1955).

The key figure in any raiding party was unquestionably the leader, a man of high standing whose proven abilities inspired confidence that he could lead his men to the enemy camp, successfully capture horses, and return without loss of party members. In addition to the experienced leader, two most important roles were those of scout and kettle bearer. This latter individual not only took care of the cooking arrangements but also ensured that certain eating and drinking customs, which were a common feature of war party ritual, were adhered to. Several of these customs were dictated by medicine bundles which were owned by different members of the war party; thus, the Cheyenne leader Roman Nose possessed certain medicine

Below: A beaded horse headstall picked up after the attack on Little Thunder's Brulé village at Ash Hollow in September 1865. This is not typical of Lakota work for the period and is undoubtedly a trade item, possibly from the Red River region and thus made by Metis people. It is fabricated from red trade cloth edged with yellow ribbon and embellished with white, pink, green and yellow seed beads. Such luxurious horse regalia would preclude its use by any other than a highly successful individual whose prestige demanded a positive display of wealth and status.

powers which excluded the eating of food that had been cooked in an iron vessel and only elaborate purification ceremonials rectified a violation of the taboo.

Use of the Shield

Surprisingly, considering their importance in pre-horse days, shields were seldom taken on the warpath, even though they were always associated with war medicine bundles. Crow informants explained that they were too cumbersome and heavy and hampered the movements of the warriors in close combat. Two Leggings, the Crow Chief, explained that on one occasion he *did* take a shield on the warpath, but when he returned home the skin of his left arm and shoulder were chafed raw by the continual rubbing of the heavy shield, caused by the jogging of the trotting horse. The problem was resolved by most men either taking the shield cover only (see page 25), by making miniature reproductions (somewhat smaller than the model shown below), or carrying some lightweight embellishment

Below: *Models of shields collected by James Mooney as part of a project relating to Kiowa heraldry, 1891–1904. Left is a shield made by* Padalti, *or Fur Man, grandson of* Dohasan, *head chief of the Kiowa until his death in 1866. Right, shield made to the specification of* Tsonkiada, *the original owner of the design. Note the similarity in the overall appearance of these shields. Mooney found that all warriors carrying shields of the same pattern constituted a close brotherhood with similar body paint, war cries and ceremonial taboos and regulations.*

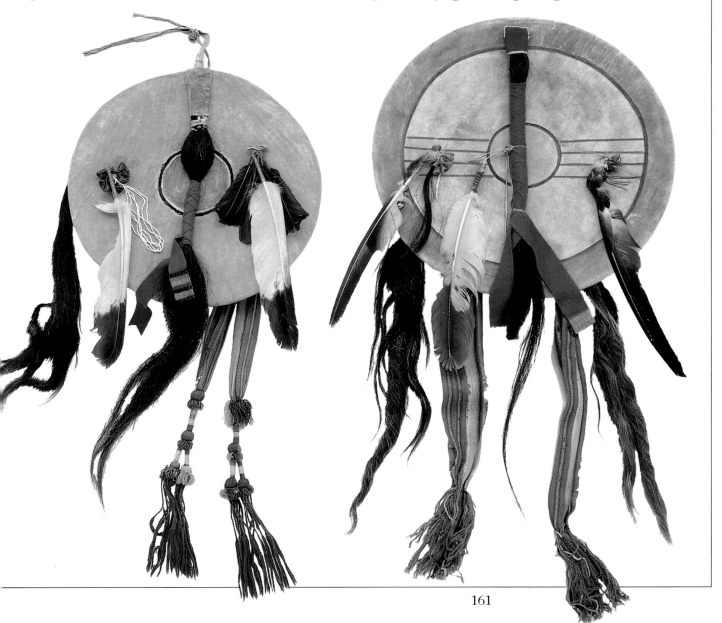

from the shield. These were believed to impart the same protection as the shield itself since it was not the physical protection given against the arrows and bullets of the enemy, but rather the supernatural powers which were represented in various forms on the shield and had been received in a vision (see Wildschut, Ewers ed.:1960: 65–73). A fine shield, which was believed to have been the former property of the Oglala chief, Crazy Horse, is shown (above). On it are embellished symbols that seem mainly to refer to sky powers – the sun, moon, thunder and lightning – but the dragon-fly, so hard to hit in flight, a desirable attribute to any warrior, is also represented.

The Warpath

The Plains warpath could be likened to a piece of string which is doubled so that its ends meet again: the setting out from the

Above: *Shield identified as Oglala and said formerly to have been the property of Crazy Horse. This consists of a disc of rawhide 22in (60cm) in diameter with a painted buckskin cover. The designs of stars, Thunderbird and lightning symbols, together with those of the dragon-fly and bear, are typical of Lakota symbols used to evoke protection and power. In the case of the living creatures, for example, both bear and dragon-fly were difficult to kill or hit – an attribute desired by any warrior.*

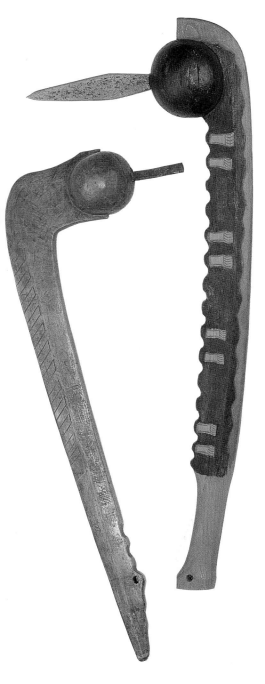

Above, right: *A Yankton Sioux war-club with spear point projecting. Collected by Dr A.B. Campbell, circa 1870. This is an elaborately carved club painted black and red, which, according to the collection history available, took the maker some two months to complete.*

Above, left: *War-club, probably Omaha or Oto, dating from circa 1840. An image of a weasel is carved across the back of the head of this club, undoubtedly symbolic of the desired qualities of any warrior – the ability to strike the enemy swiftly and with deadly effect.*

home camp, the first halt, the journey, the halt before fighting, the battle, the halt after the battle, the halt before entering the home camp, and then the triumphant entrance itself. The battle, or raid, marks the point at which the string is bent back upon itself and, as Smith has observed, there are no records of 'a war party which did not return after its first fight' (Smith, 1938: 444). This meandering path to and from the enemy took much planning. War songs were sung and the powers of the war medicines evoked. Clothing, spare moccasins in particular, and food were made ready for the long and hazardous journey. The leader was also prepared to consecrate the war pipe, which was traditionally carried on such occasions, hence the term 'Pipe holder' used to describe the senior officer of the expedition.[6]

The horse raid offered young men the best opportunity for economic security and social advancement, but not all had their own war bundles. It was common for older men who had powerful war medicine to be consulted; such requests were traditionally preceded by the offering of a pipe and gifts, the men most frequently called upon being known for their 'success in war and/or because younger men who had obtained their help had achieved remarkable success' (Ewers, 1955: 178).

Thus, holders of powerful war medicine held high rank, were much esteemed and consulted and clearly, to them, the war path represented *profit*; such individuals prospered. The bundles were not solely held by men – Root Digger, a Crow woman who had acquired the skull of her brother White Child received visions in which the spirit of White Child, through the medium of the skull, foretold future events. It was said that even in daytime and while she was awake, Root Digger sometimes heard her brother's voice prophesying what was going to happen. Soon the Crow came to regard the skull as a powerful medicine, and Root Digger was frequently approached by Crow warriors to consult the skull on their behalf, for which she received many gifts[7] (Wildschut, Ewers ed.: 1960: 79). These customs underline the great trust which was put in tried and proven war medicines that had been offered from successful people. Clearly, they were traditionally resorted to in preference to originating new medicines. These bundles became invaluable property and could, under certain circumstances, be transferred to new owners, often at considerable cost. Even then, the original owner rarely parted with or duplicated every article which was in the bundle: thus, the Crow considered the original owner and all the supernaturals represented in the bundle as one clan, and that by returning one object from the bundle in his possession, the owner retained his identity with the supernaturals of that clan. The whole system was one of sound regulation, so that by refusing to transfer their power to another, by refusing to interpret certain visions of other men as belonging to the class of Pipe holder or camp chief, they could prevent undesirable individuals from obtaining a status which those in power did not wish them to possess.[8]

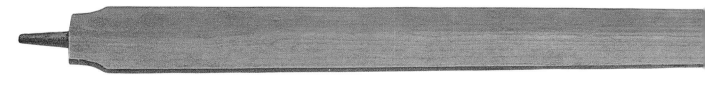

War Pipes

The practice of carrying war pipes derives from the ancient symbolism associated with smoking, which prevailed throughout North America, the act of smoking being a communication with the higher powers. Pipes were utilized for both peace and war interactions and traditionally the stems of those pipes for the former were painted blue by the Sioux 'to signifie [sic] a clear sky or peace and tranquillity' (Carver, Parker ed.: 1976: 111). Those pipes which were to be used for war were painted red on both the shaft and feathers. Of interest is the fact that pipes so embellished were not infrequently painted on Plains warshirts, which was indicative of the number of war expeditions led by the wearer. The name given to the Pipe holder by the Crow clearly defined his status – *Akdoochia-Aketchkan* – 'The-one-who-Manages-the War-Party' (Wildschut, Ewers ed.: 1960: 34).

The use of the pipe tended to follow a formalized ritual; among the Oglala, the aspirant called upon a shaman to consecrate the pipe. He then organized a feast to which he invited men with warpath experience. Having thus formed the core of the war party, it was then open to volunteers (see earlier). The leader, carrying pipe in hand, rode toward camp ahead of the war party, supported by the so-called *blotaunka*, who acted as 'both councilors and lieutenants' (Wissler, 1912 (b): 55). Such a

Above: An Iowa pipe-stem given to President Monroe in 1824 by the Iowa chief White Cloud as a symbol of peace and friendship – an ancient and widespread custom in North America. The stem is beautifully decorated with porcupine quills and a red horsehair fringe.

Right: There were considerable variations in pipe styles across the Plains. This one is less typical, having a bowl of carved catlinite with a round wooden stem, and although collected from the Sioux it may have been made by the Chippewa and then obtained in trade.

Below: A magnificent human effigy pipe-bowl collected from the Santee Sioux prior to 1841. This exceptional piece is made of red catlinite inlaid with lead. These pipes were produced by a limited number of craftsmen mainly for trade, the carved figures making a social comment – in this case the effects of alcohol.

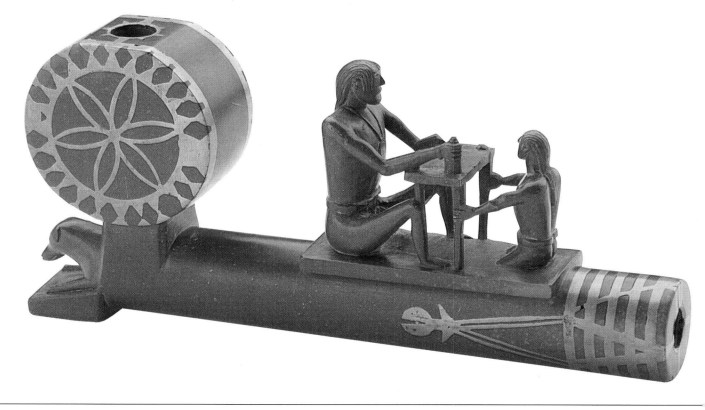

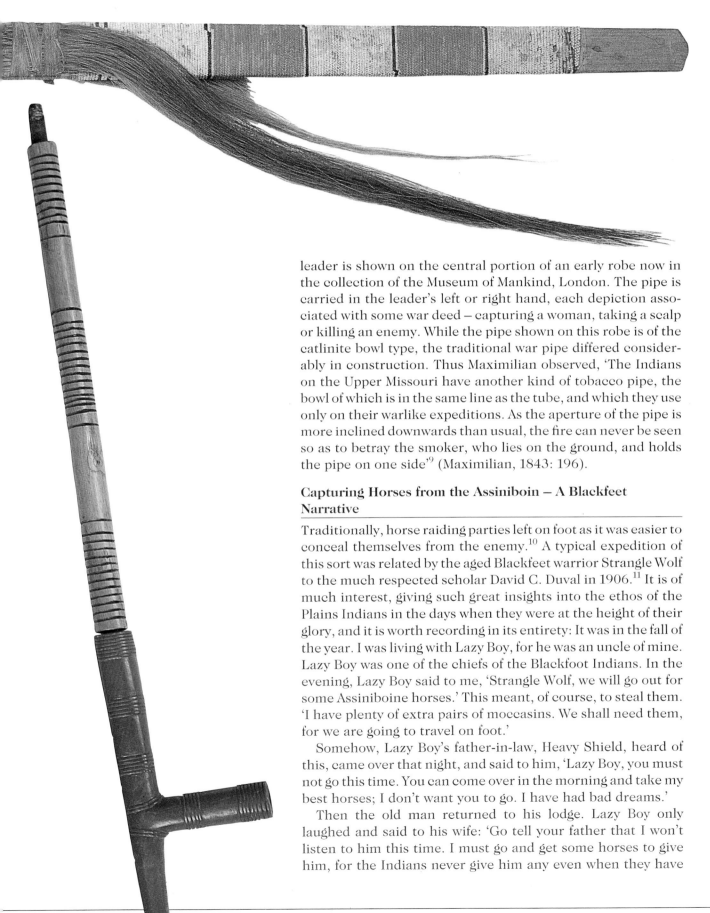

leader is shown on the central portion of an early robe now in the collection of the Museum of Mankind, London. The pipe is carried in the leader's left or right hand, each depiction associated with some war deed – capturing a woman, taking a scalp or killing an enemy. While the pipe shown on this robe is of the catlinite bowl type, the traditional war pipe differed considerably in construction. Thus Maximilian observed, 'The Indians on the Upper Missouri have another kind of tobacco pipe, the bowl of which is in the same line as the tube, and which they use only on their warlike expeditions. As the aperture of the pipe is more inclined downwards than usual, the fire can never be seen so as to betray the smoker, who lies on the ground, and holds the pipe on one side'[9] (Maximilian, 1843: 196).

Capturing Horses from the Assiniboin – A Blackfeet Narrative

Traditionally, horse raiding parties left on foot as it was easier to conceal themselves from the enemy.[10] A typical expedition of this sort was related by the aged Blackfeet warrior Strangle Wolf to the much respected scholar David C. Duval in 1906.[11] It is of much interest, giving such great insights into the ethos of the Plains Indians in the days when they were at the height of their glory, and it is worth recording in its entirety: It was in the fall of the year. I was living with Lazy Boy, for he was an uncle of mine. Lazy Boy was one of the chiefs of the Blackfoot Indians. In the evening, Lazy Boy said to me, 'Strangle Wolf, we will go out for some Assiniboine horses.' This meant, of course, to steal them. 'I have plenty of extra pairs of moccasins. We shall need them, for we are going to travel on foot.'

Somehow, Lazy Boy's father-in-law, Heavy Shield, heard of this, came over that night, and said to him, 'Lazy Boy, you must not go this time. You can come over in the morning and take my best horses; I don't want you to go. I have had bad dreams.'

Then the old man returned to his lodge. Lazy Boy only laughed and said to his wife: 'Go tell your father that I won't listen to him this time. I must go and get some horses to give him, for the Indians never give him any even when they have many. Another thing is that I have my party ready and will start in the morning.'

In the morning, we all started. There were thirty of us in the party. Lazy Boy was the leader. He was noted as a fast walker, and asked me to take the lead with him. Lazy Boy fell to telling me about things he said I ought to know. He said, 'Whenever you are out with a war party, as we are now, and all are on foot, you should keep close to the leader, for if you hang back at the tail end you will always be in a trot to keep up with the others; but if you are in the lead you can keep the gait and not become tired so soon.' Another thing he said to me was, 'When we get to the Assiniboine camps, you must try to get the horses tied close to the lodges for they are the best horses. The Assiniboine always keep up their best horses at night while they drive the others out to the hills.'

We went down the Missouri River. The game was plentiful. Buffalo and elk we saw on our way, so we did not go hungry. Everyone had a little pack of meat on his back and his extra pairs of moccasins. When the sun went down we camped for the night. We made three lodges with sticks and bark. After we had cooked and eaten some meat, the chief said we must sing the wolf songs. These songs are supposed to give us good luck, on a trip, i.e., if we truthfully tell what our sweethearts said when we left them. Each man is supposed to sing a song in which are a few words his sweetheart said to him.

After we got through singing, all went to sleep. In the morning, we all started out again. When the sun was high, we saw something a long way off resembling a person. The Chief said, 'It must be an Assiniboine. We must go after him and kill him.' So we all ran toward him, and as we approached he seemed to be making signs to us. When we got up to it, we found out that it was a black stump with its black branches sticking out like arms. As we all went on, I heard some of the men say that it was a bad sign.

We travelled many days and nights, until we came to a lot of timber along the river. It was snowing and very cold. The Chief always kept two men ahead to look over the tops of the high hills, so that we would not run into some of the Assiniboine that might be waiting for us. At this place we all stopped and the chief called out to two men, 'You go across the river to see if you can find out just where the Assiniboine camps are. We must be close to them now. We will wait for you here.' The two men took off their clothes, tied their leggings and shirts around their heads so as to be able to put them on dry when they got across. The river was wide and deep and the two men swam across. We all waited. When the sun was getting down close to the mountains, Chief Lazy Boy said to one of the men, 'Why can we not cross and wait for them there? It is too cold for the two men to swim back again.'

So we all got a few poles, tied them together and put a rawhide on top of them. Then we put our clothes and guns on top of that.

Then four men tied ropes to the raft and taking the ends of the ropes in their mouths swam across. When we all got across the chief said, 'Athough we are very cold we must not make a fire, for we are close to the camps. They would see the smoke.'

The sun had just gone down when the two scouts came back, saying to the chief, 'We saw two men leading their horses down to the river. Their horses were loaded with meat, so the camps cannot be far off.' We waited here a long time until it stopped snowing. The moon was shining brightly. A little later on we heard dogs barking. It was nearly morning when the Chief said, 'Come, let us go, it is nearly daylight.' All went on until the Chief stopped, when we all stopped beside him. He took a stick and, beating time with it on the barrel of his gun, sang his war song, looking up at the moon. Once he used the following words: 'Elk woman, try your best.' When the Chief had finished, the others in turn sang their war songs. Then we all started again. After we got close to the camps the Chief told me to go back and tell two of the men to come with him, but for me to stay back with the others. He said, 'We shall go through the camp to find out where the best horses are. Then we shall come back to inform you, and then we can all go together.' I told the two men and they went off with him, while the rest of us stayed in the brush. About day-break, we heard a sound as if someone were riding alone. Some of the men said it was a loose horse. One of the men went out to look for signs of our party. At the time the chief left us, four men from our party followed him. Thus there were seven. It is believed to be unlucky when there are only seven in a war party.

Any way, it proved to be at this time. It was just daybreak when we heard three shots, and at the same time the men who went out came back to us saying, 'You said that was a loose horse we heard, here is what its rider lost.' He carried a gun-sack, ramrod, and a saddle blanket. We all got up and ran up the river as fast as we could. We had not gone far when we heard more shooting, war whoops, and galloping horses. We kept on until we got to a place where there was thick timber. We stayed there all day. We heard no more noise for we were now too far away. When night came we all crossed the river and travelled part of the night until we came to one of our old camping places. Our brush lodges were still there. We had planned to meet there after we got our horses. We saw a light in one of them and when we went in we saw one of the men who was with our Chief. He got up, shook hands with us all, and then began to tell about it. He said, 'When we all got near the camps, we met an Assiniboine who ran back into the camp. Then we started back to where we had left you. We had not gone far before we heard three shots. We did not go fast, but when we got to where we had left you we saw that you were gone. Then the chief said that you must have crossed the river. So we began to cross too. We were just about in the middle, when the Assiniboine came upon us, and began to fire. When we got across a number of the enemy were there for their horses could swim faster than we and of course they

Above: Pasesick-Kaskutau, *or Nothing But Gunpowder, an Assiniboin painted at Fort Union by Karl Bodmer, October 1833. Heavy clothing was essential to survive the winters of the northern Plains if excursions on the hunt or warpath were attempted. This man wears a badger skin cap, a coat probably made from buffalo hide and thick mittens.*

headed us off. Then we had a fight. There were only three guns for us to fight with for while we were crossing four of our men lost their guns in the water. Two of our men were killed at the beginning of the fight. Our Chief kept encouraging us saying that we must fight and die bravely for some day our people would hear of our sad end. All this time dirt was flying around us where the bullets struck. The smoke of the guns was like a fog a little above our heads. The Chief was shooting and talking to the Assiniboine, telling them that many of them would fall before the last of us. We kept them away as much as we could, but sometimes they would try to run us down with their horses. After we wounded several of them, they kept at a distance. When the sun was getting close to the mountains, our Chief was killed. Our ammunition was nearly all gone. There was a loose horse near by. I jumped on him and rode away. Then the Assiniboine took after me. When I got to some thick brush, I jumped off the horse and ran into the brush. They took the horse and went back. Then I came on afoot. That is how I come to be here with you now.'

We all lay down to rest for the night and about daybreak started home. Just then the other three men came along. They got away from the Assiniboine after dark. We travelled on for many nights and days until we reached home.

When we got home we stopped on a hill near the camp, but did not sing the song of victory. We gave the sad sign that three warriors had been killed. One of our men stood out alone, took three robes and, while the people in the camp were watching, threw them away one by one. Then the Indians all knew that three of our party had been lost and came running out to meet us (Wissler, 1911:33–4).

Maps and Messages

Expeditions of this type could last up to two months, involve a round trip of over one thousand miles, and a complex, meandering route to take account of natural barriers. Maps and a means of communication between split parties were essential and in this respect great ingenuity was shown by the Plains Indian.

The trader Edwin Denig, who spent some twenty-three years (1833–56) working for the American Fur Company at forts Pierre and Union on the Upper Missouri, reported in some detail on the use of maps produced by Indians and how they were employed in communication of ideas. He recorded that, when in conversation with most elderly Indians regarding locations, travels, or to explain battles and other events, 'resort is had by them to drawing maps on the ground, on bark with charcoal, or on paper if they can get it, to illustrate more clearly the affair in question'.

In his journal published in 1930, Denig reproduced a detailed map drawn by an Assiniboin warrior at Fort Union in December 1853, commenting that it embraced 'a circumference of 1,500

Below: *Map drawn by an Assiniboin Indian for the trader Edwin Denig at Fort Union in December 1853. Maps were frequently drawn by Plains Indians which were accurate and could be understood by whites. This particular one is of the north bank of the Missouri leading from Fort Union to beyond Fort Benton some two hundred miles away. Because maps were often rendered in a non-permanent medium, such as sand or earth, they are a rarity in the ethnographical collections.*

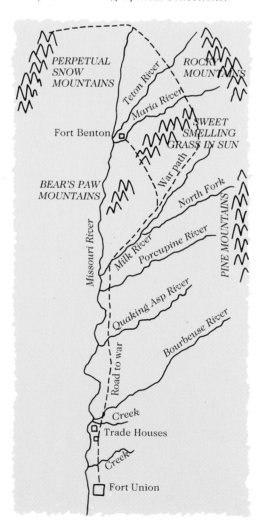

miles', with the different encampments which would be made during the travels, and adding, 'so correct was the drawing that we had no difficulty in finding their camp the following winter in deep snow, one month's travel from this place' (Denig, 1930:605). Denig was obviously used to reading maps produced by Plains Indians. However, to a white observer unfamiliar with their methods of delineation, some maps would appear very confusing. Thus, they were seldom drawn to a linear scale, distances generally being expressed in terms of intervals of time such as the number of days, camps, pauses and smokes. Clark Wissler obtained two maps from Blackfeet informants which illustrate several of these features, and refer to explicit directions which were left by one war party for another 'by a kind of map marked in the sand or in bare earth' (Wissler, 1911:43). He asked his informant to sketch the map and copied it afterwards. This map, redrawn for our purposes, is shown on page 169.

Like Denig, Wissler reported that the geographic features were 'easily recognized by one having a knowledge of the country', and that the V-shaped marks in this case were said to give the direction of movement. Wissler said that in this type of map, pebbles or pieces or charcoal represented the proposed camping places, the number in each case indicating the length of stop. Thus, it is indicated here that the next camp would be one day's journey from the nearest river and that after a stay of two nights, they camped one night on the nearest fork and two nights on the second. Additional details, indicating that the war party was joined by another, are shown by the V-shapes converging on a camp site at 'a' where they camped two nights; they then moved on to camp 'b' where they fought members of an enemy tribe (shown by two sticks painted red). It will be seen that between the sticks are shown two shoulder blade bones 'c' upon which the result of the engagement was pictured; they then moved on to 'd', camping two nights (Wissler, 1911:43–4).

Here, then, in these two simple maps, we can see elements of the spatial and time concepts of Plains Indians well illustrated. The map is not apparently scaled, Wissler pointing out that the angle of the V-figure – which might well be in the form of a bent willow stick – also indicated the distance to the next camp site and time indicated by the number of actual camp stops, a further sophistication in this being the use of yellow pebbles to indicate that the stops were then by day and travel was by night. Maps of this type have been described for the Omaha, Fletcher and La Flesche emphasizing that the topography of the country through which the tribe was accustomed to hunt was well known to the Omaha, and that in giving directions this was not infrequently supplemented by a 'rude map' of the country traced on the ground with the finger or stick, on which were indicated trails, streams and possibly additional details of suitable places to make camps. A further consideration regarding direction was that 'these maps were always oriented, so that one could follow the course laid down, by the sun during the day

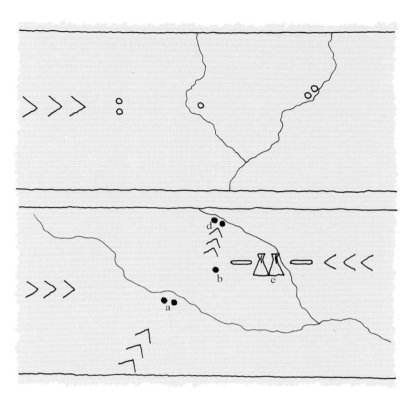

Right: *Two maps drawn by Blackfeet Indians and collected by Clark Wissler in the late nineteenth century. The first map indicates the course of a war party and the stops they made, the second a battle and subsequent movements. Ingenious techniques were used to convey direction, distance and time. Thus a bent stick pointed the direction of travel but the magnitude of the angle of the bend indicated the distance, while colored pebbles referred to night or day stops and the number of pebbles the planned time of stay. (See text for additional details.)*

or at night by the north star' (Fletcher and La Flesche, 1911:88).

Similar methods of map-making seem widespread in the Plains region; for example, Comanche informants interviewed at the Office of Anthropology, Santa Fe, in the 1930s and 1940s described mapping styles close to those used by the Omaha and Blackfeet. They gave, however, additional data on time scales: 'a map was plotted on the ground showing rivers, hills, valleys . . . then a line was drawn to represent the route planned for the first day. From a bundle of sticks, marked consecutively beginning with "one", a stick with a single notch was stuck at the point where the party was to camp at the end of the first day's journey . . . the second day's journey was illustrated in the same manner' – and so on (Wallace and Hoebel, 1952:254).

During the course of research among the Nez Perce of Idaho some twenty years ago, the author was told by one reliable informant (Mylie Lawyer) that in buffalo hunting days maps of the Plains region were drawn 'on rawhide' (Taylor, 1975:63); this may be an exception.

One obvious reason for the rarity of maps from Plains Indians in collections is that they were invariably drawn – as attested by several sources referred to – in a non-permanent medium with charcoal, in sand or earth – and unless they were recorded some other way at the time, as did Wissler with his Blackfeet informants, they were lost.

One map, drawn by a Cheyenne chief, Little Robe, and now preserved in the Blackmore collection in the Museum of Mankind, London was recently examined by the author. It had been sent to Colonel Dodge by Little Robe in September 1872 and

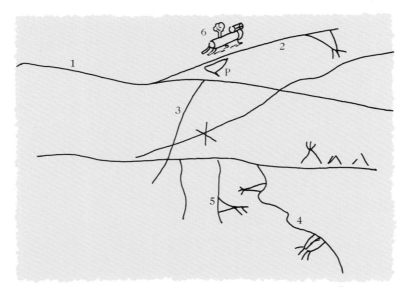

Above: *Little Robe, the Cheyenne chief, traveled to Washington in 1871 to meet the President of the United States and negotiate on behalf of his people.*

was subsequently given to William Blackmore late in the same year. It is a very simple map, originally drawn with pencil on blue paper and shows additional details of a locomotive together with a 1–6 key. It refers to terrain near the Arkansas River in what is now southern Kansas (Dodge was at that time stationed at Fort Dodge). He reported that buffalo were relatively plentiful in the area at the time; however, the railroad was now penetrating the region much to the alarm of the Cheyenne and Arapaho because this was bringing in white buffalo hunters who slaughtered the animals only for their hides. Dodge subsequently reported for the following year that 'where there were myriads of buffalo the year before, there were now myriads of carcasses' (Dodge, 1882:295). Thus, Little Robe's map (see above) and the accompanying diagram of the train probably refer to these potential problems, as it can be seen that the railroad had then reached just north of the Arkansas River (shown as '1' on the map), to the south of which were the three camps of Cheyenne (shown by the tipi symbols); the railroad ('2') had already run adjacent to another Cheyenne camp, north of the Arkansas.

As with the map produced by the Assiniboin referred to earlier, this one also shows some white influence and they have all been subsequently annotated. However, several features, such as the straight lines, the emphasis on what is there rather than how it appears to the observer (the inverted tipis, for example) and limited perspective, strongly indicate native roots. It is first and foremost a map, but is additionally a type of pictographic message of great importance to the Cheyenne chief.

Pictographic Messages

In addition to maps used to convey vital information, pictographic messages were used to communicate between separated groups of the war party; the techniques were ingenious and obviously were used from a very early period. Thus, in 1820,

Governor Lewis Cass referred to complex and meaningful pictographic communication between two tribes linguistically unrelated, and generally hostile to one another, namely the eastern Sioux (probably Santee) and Ojibwa. The message was concerned with the establishment of a permanent peace between the two tribes. Approaching Sioux territory in the vicinity of the mouth of the St Peter's River (not far from present-day St Paul), the Ojibwa found a message left by the Sioux on 'a piece of birch bark, made flat by fastening between two sticks at each end and about 18 inches long by 2 broad'. A similar message had been sent earlier by the Ojibwa, found by the Sioux, and this was their reply.

Cass reports that the Ojibwa could readily understand the message from the Sioux and that 'the effect of the discovery of the bark upon the minds of the Ojibwas was visible and immediate'. Cass also remarks upon the spatial concepts of American Indians in their map delineation. 'No proportion was preserved in their attempt at delineation. One mile of the Mississippi, including the mouth of the St Peter's, occupied as much space as the whole distance to Sandy Lake, nor was there anything to show that one part was nearer to the spectator than another' (Cass, in Mallery, 1893:359–60).

Early evidence of the use of pictographs by Plains Indians to convey comparatively complex messages to another party was touched on by Maximilian (Lloyd trans. 1843:352) during his sojourn at Fort Clark on the Missouri from November 1833 to April 1834; three hundred yards upstream was the main Mandan village, *Mih-Tutta-Hang-Kusch*. Maximilian reproduced a 'letter' from a Mandan to a fur trader and gave details of its meaning (see below).

The cross means 'I will barter or trade'. The three animals which are drawn to the right of the cross represent a buffalo, weasel and otter and the writer offers in exchange for the skins of these animals the articles which he has sketched on the left side of the cross – a beaver and a gun. To the left of the beaver, the thirty lines – each set of ten separated by a longer line – convey the idea of an exchange of thirty beaver skins (local value

Right: *A pictographic message drawn by a Mandan Indian at Fort Clark during the winter of 1833–4 and collected by the German explorer Maximilian. This was directed to a fur trader and refers to a proposed exchange of the skins of otter, weasel and buffalo in return for a gun and beaver skins. The parallel lines are grouped in sets of ten – the number of beaver skins required for a successful transaction.*

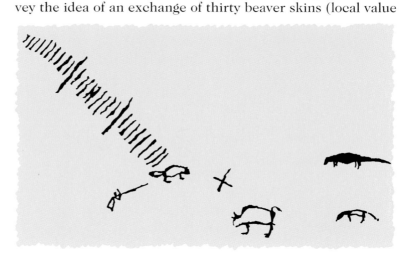

Left: *The Six, chief of the Plains Ojibwa, painted by George Catlin, 1832. Originally a Woodland people, the Plains Ojibwa took many traditions with them when they moved west to adopt the buffalo hunting, nomadic way of Plains life-style. This man had the reputation of being a great warrior, as confirmed by his magnificently embellished warshirt – quillwork, hair, and pictographic paintings. He was a man of huge proportions but great dignity of manner, and Catlin further commented that his shirt was 'painted in curious hieroglyphics, the history of his battles and charts of his life' (Catlin,1841:58).*

approximately fifteen dollars each) and 'a gun for the skins for the three animals on the right side of the cross' (ibid.).

The universal aspect of the recording of messages to other parties, together with the associated symbolic representation, seems to have been widespread and apparently well understood in the Plains region. Thus, Grinnell refers to an encounter between the Cheyenne and Pawnee where the latter completely annihilated the opposition. The Pawnee commemorated this event by drawing with charcoal a pictographic record of the battle on a large white log. Later, when a party of Sioux found the log, neither the Sioux nor friends of the dead Cheyenne had difficulty in understanding the message (Grinnell, 1926: 33–4). Likewise, Wissler's earlier reference to the Blackfeet use of the shoulder blade bones on which the messages were recorded was a technique used by the Comanche at least one thousand miles south of the Blackfeet. Schoolcraft refers to a bone found in Texas depicting 'the strife for the buffalo existing between the Indian and white races' (Schoolcraft, 1851–7, vol.III:73), and the Hidatsa employed a technique of tallying which was similar to that used and described earlier for their southern neighbors the Mandan. It would appear that a good deal of pictographic work was strongly influenced by the sign language which was universally employed and early used on the Plains. Mallery suggests that those pictographs which 'in the absence of positive knowledge, are the most difficult of interpretation were those to which the study of sign-language might be applied with advantage' (Mallery, 1893:637). Therefore, the cross in the Mandan pictograph which Maximilian suggested gave the message 'I will barter or trade' can be related to the gesture-sign for 'trade', where the arms are interchanged in position, the objects to be exchanged then occupying the previous position of the other (ibid.:603).

Petersen has also given several other examples of the practical use of pictography in composing everyday messages, with the observation that 'knowing how to read and write the pictographic language was, for an Indian, a tool for survival (Petersen, 1971:28).

Not only was the pictographic language a 'tool for survival', but there is some evidence to suggest that it was also employed in the documentation of ceremonials and ownership. Although the data available is scattered and fragmentary for the Plains, it has been well described by Hoffman for the Ojibwa and other Algonquian-speaking groups of the Woodlands, particularly in the context of *Midewiwin*, or Grand Medicine Society. While Hoffman makes the point that the pictographic delineation of ideas is not necessarily 'fully intelligible to another', he quotes from a paper read by Garrick Mallery that for the 'initiated Ojibwa' the illustrations supply 'the order of the stanzas and also the general subject-matter of each particular stanza and the latter would be a reminder of the words' (Hoffman, 1891:287).

Return of the War Party

'There were many brave and successful warriors of the Cheyennes . . . who on their war journeys tried to avoid coming into close contact with enemies, and had no wish to kill enemies. Such men went to war for the sole purpose of increasing their possessions by capturing horses; that is, they carried on war as a business – for profit' (Grinnell, 1923, vol.II:2).

The return of a successful war party was an occasion for much celebration. Generally, the expedition made camp before entering the home village. They prepared for a grand entrance, donned war and society regalia, rehearsed songs and victory dances. As they approached the village, they rode in, singing their war songs; victory dances and the recounting of war honors and generous gifts of horses[12] followed, all reinforcing and further elevating the status of the successful Pipe holder, while those who had particularly distinguished themselves viewed such actions as serving 'as a steppingstone to leadership'[13] (Ewers, 1955: 189).

If 'scalps' had been taken, some of the returning warriors rode into camp with their faces painted black. Thus, Lakota war parties who had defeated the enemy without loss to themselves designated four warriors who had killed the enemy and taken scalps, to use the black face paint.

ite'isa'bye ....Black face paint
aö'pazan ....(and a) feather
owa'le ....I seek

Right: *A dance mirror board, probably Eastern Sioux, dating from circa 1830. This consists of a small rectangular glass mirror set in a long triangular-shaped wooden frame which is decorated with incised and curving lines filled with black, red and blue-green paint. Such mirrors were used by war-dancers as an aid to making up, one observer of the Sioux commenting that the young men 'spent much time in painting their faces with various kinds of paints' (Feder,1964:32).*

Below: *'Bringing home the spoils', painting by Charles Russell, 1909. This is obviously the return of a victorious horse-raiding party, the leader proudly out ahead, the captured horses in the background. The return was one of celebration; as the warriors rode in with their spoils, they sung their victory songs. Once safely home, celebrations in the form of dances, recounting of war deeds and the gift of horses followed.*

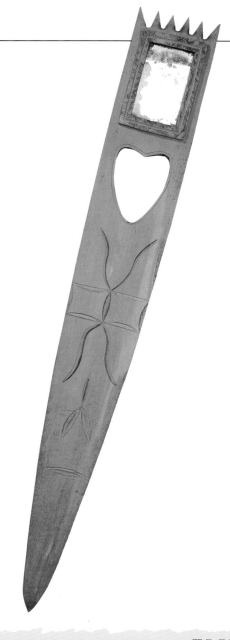

ća ....So
he'camon ye ....I have done this

(Lakota war song. Densmore, 1918:405).

'Each pole [with a scalp attached] is borne by a squaw, usually a relative of the warrior who took it, who leads in the dance, the warriors and squaws all arrayed in their best attire following her in single file in a circle of a size proportioned to the number of dancers. The step of the dance is little more than a march in quick time, to the music of a song peculiar to the dance. Where the number of dancers is considerable, several rings are formed in different parts of the tent and the dance is frequently kept up with intervals of rest, for twelve or fourteen days' (Bradley, 1923:269–70).

As the anthropologist Ruth Benedict observed, there was emphasis on a display of uninhibited triumph, the recognition that prayers had been answered. The complete lack of concern with any danger or dread associated with the dead enemy not only exemplified the Dionysian[14] characters of the Plains Indians but contrasted in a marked way, and distinctively set them apart from most of the other cultural areas in North America. Elsewhere, there was emphasis on rituals at removing from the slayer the curse and 'dangerous supernatural potency of the scalp'[15] (Benedict, 1932:16).

When the celebrations were over, the war exploits and the whole status and standing of the man were recorded in a complex system of heraldry – for all to see (see Chapter VII).

FOOTNOTES: CHAPTER SIX

1 These women broke away from many restrictions. They were ambitious, often handsome; they owned property and held high positions.
2 This name now survives in the abbreviated form of Sioux.
3 This style of hide body armor was found so useful that members of the Coronado expedition adapted it in preference to their own. More than two centuries later, Spanish soldiers of Sonora still wore knee-length sleeveless jackets of six or eight layers of well-cured deerskin as armor against their Apache enemies (see Pfefferkorn, Treutlein ed., 1949: 155).
4 The term Dog Soldier was commonly employed by whites to describe these Societies which concerned themselves with warlike activities. Possibly 'Wolf' would be more appropriate since wolves were not infrequently considered as war fetishes among the Plains tribes (see Densmore, 1918: 333).
5 It was reported by Mishkin that some individuals developed an insatiable desire to acquire more and more horses. Thus, an aged and respected Kiowa warrior became so obsessed with horses that it developed into 'kelptomania [sic]'. He was, however, 'tolerated by his amused tribesmen'! (Mishkin, 1940:52).
6 From an early period, the French trappers and traders used the term 'partizan' to describe the leader of a war party (James, 1823, vol.II: 14).
7 The augury properties of war-medicines seems to be an ancient widespread custom. The Omaha, for example, used a wolf skin from the sacred War Pack not only to learn of future success, but also to ascertain conditions in hostile territory (Fletcher and La Flesche, 1911: 415).
8 See Wildschut, Ewers ed., 1960 for a detailed discussion of the medicine bundle compiled not only among the Crow but also the comparative survey (pp.147-73).
9 It is clear that the use of ritual pipe smoking was widely practiced on the Plains. The Comanche – the dominant military force on the Southern Plains – formally smoked a sacred pipe after the evening meal, passing it to each warrior in turn. There were prayers to guardian spirits for help and wisdom (see Wallace and Hoebel, 1952: 255-6).
10 In the 1870s, mounted parties gained in popularity among the Blackfeet since they could travel much faster and could more easily evade white authorities who were attempting to prevent inter-tribal horse raiding (see Ewers, 1955: 185).
11 David C. Duvall died at his home in Browning, Montana, in July 1911 at the age of thirty-three. His mother was a Piegan, his father a Canadian-French fur trade employee at Fort Benton. He acted as an interpreter for the anthropologist Clark Wissler (from the American Museum of Natural History in New York), his contributions to an understanding of Blackfeet ethnology were immense and, as Wissler said in his memorial, 'his untimely death is a distinct loss (see Wissler, 1911: 2).
12 It was not unusual for the raiding parties to return with one hundred or more horses depending on the size of the expedition. Too many raised the practical difficulties of containing them.
13 Discussions and customs relating to the honesty of a warrior in claiming a particular deed were ritualized. Thus, the Omaha had a special ceremonial, the Wat'gictu (the gathering together of acts accomplished) where war deeds were solemnized. Here the keepers of the four Packs Sacred to war reminded the men to state the truth, for the bird messengers contained in the packs would report their deeds to Thunder, the god of war (Fletcher and La Flesche, 1911: 434).
14 Benedict characterized the Plains personality as Dionysian – given to extreme indulgence in violence, grief, trance and other emotional states (Benedict, 1932: 1-27).
15 Note the reference to the Indians of Louisiana mentioned earlier. The Papago engaged in almost three weeks' purification ritual after the taking of a scalp.

MEN'S CEREMONIAL REGALIA

CHAPTER VII

Men's Clothing on the Plains

Up until the middle of the nineteenth century, men's clothing was almost exclusively made of soft-tanned skins of deer, antelope, elk and buffalo. The smaller, largely untrimmed, hides were used to fabricate shirts and leggings which were laced or tied together with thongs or sewn with sinew, while the larger hides were tanned virtually in their entirety and used as robes. Footwear consisted of moccasins which at this time, as has been discussed earlier, on both the central and northern Plains were generally made from a single piece of hide having an outer side seam and soft sole.

While there were some variations on this basic costume style, in general ceremonial regalia was an elaboration of everyday wear, although the undecorated shirt had only limited distribution (Taylor, 1984(a):19). Regional, frequently tribal, styles can be identified, however, due to the several complex trade networks across the Plains, which recognized specialized skills and resources (Taylor, Lessard eds, 1984(b); Swagerty, Washburn ed., 1988:352). Several styles of dress, ornaments and weapons were often used by tribes who did not actually make them. As was discussed in earlier chapters, some particularly innovative centers for elaborate regalia were the Crow villages in the Yellowstone River region, who traded both east and west. Grizzly bear claw necklaces (as shown below) were sometimes worn by distinguished warriors and, as was discussed earlier, both sexes wore ornaments of shell, which were obtained in trade – dentalium and discs of conch being particularly popular. Tattooing was fairly common and indicated rank or status; it tended to be limited to the chests and arms of men and the faces of women and was particularly favored by the Missouri River tribes. Hair styles varied considerably: roaching, single and double braiding, pompadour and artificial lengthening were some of the more popular styles.

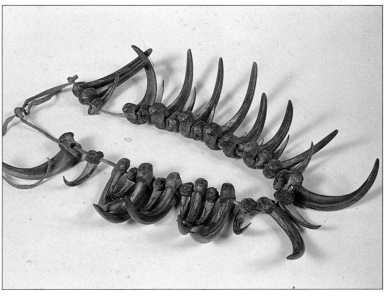

Variation of Styles

Men's costumes varied considerably, from north to south, in the degree of ornamental embellishment. Southern men's costume is marked by a smaller amount of beadwork, compared with the central and northern tribes and quillwork was virtually non-existent. The use of fringes was, however, highly developed, reaching its peak in the twisted variety, which is among the finest and most attractive of all fringe types, being used on shirts, leggings and, occasionally, moccasins. One characteristic of the southern Plains man's was a limited but definite degree of tailoring of both leggings and shirts, possibly due to influences from the Pueblo people to the south, with whom tribes such as the Comanche and Kiowa were in constant contact.

In contrast, on the northern Plains, among such tribes as the Blackfeet, Cree, Assiniboin and Gros Ventre, many types of very elaborate clothing were common, and these often highly ornamental with quillwork, beadwork, paint and various embellishments, such as buckskin and hair fringing. Central Plains tribes tended to occupy a middle ground and used elaborate or plain clothing styles in some degree, according to their relation to the north and south and the established trade links.

Paint – mainly yellow, green, red and blue – was used throughout the whole area, solid colors predominating in the

Above, left: Mixkenoteskina, *or Iron Horn, a prominent Blackfeet headman, portrait by George Catlin at Fort Union in the summer of 1832. The quilled rectangular chest panel is an ancient form of embellishment.*

Above: *An early style of combined bow-case and quiver in the collections of Opocno Castle Museum, Czech Republic, possibly Crow in origin and circa 1850.*

Right: *A magnificent man's shirt, identified as Cheyenne and dating from circa 1870. Much of the fringe is horsehair and may refer to horses captured or wounded in battle.*

south, where the entire surface of shirts or leggings might be covered by rubbing dry, finely powdered green or yellow paint into the buckskin. Unlike tribes on the central and northern Plains, who often embellished ceremonial shirts and leggings with pictographic motifs, this custom was seldom in evidence on the southern Plains. An ancient garment, the buffalo robe was, however, commonly used by tribes throughout the entire Great Plains, although, as with other apparel, the type of embellishment, quill, beadwork, painting and fringing varied from region to region.

Typically, in the 1850s, a successful warrior on the central and northern Plains would own a painted buffalo robe, a quilled shirt, leggings and moccasins, a decorated bag and possibly a headdress. In addition, he might own a combined bow-case and quiver. Within the various regional style of costume across the Plains it was the Crow who produced some of the finest dress costume. Thus, in 1833, Maximilian recorded: 'Crow women are very skillful in various kinds of work, and their shirts and dresses of bighorn leather, embroidered and ornamented with dyed porcupine quills, are particularly handsome' (Maximilian, Thwaites ed., 1906, vol.22:359–60).

Pictographic Exploit Robes, Central and Northern Plains

Buffalo robes – those worn by successful warriors often being decorated with paintings of the wearer's exploits and quill and beadwork – were first described by the Canadian trader François Larocque when he visited the Crow in 1805 (Laroc-

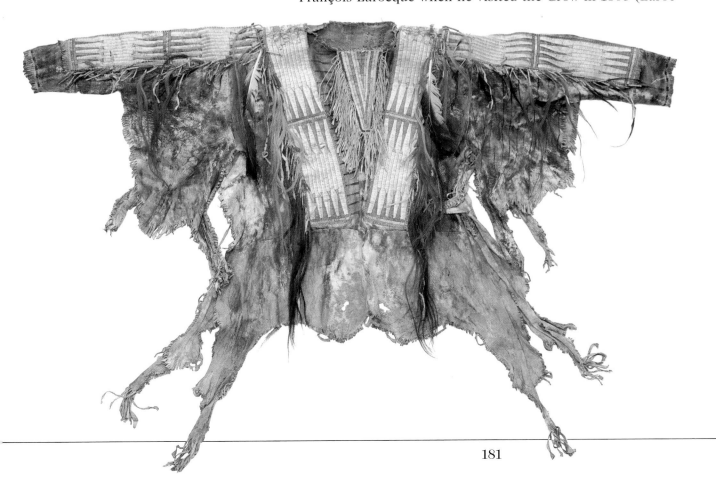

que, Burpee ed., 1910:67–8). However, it was not until some twenty-five years later that we find pictorial records of such robes, when George Catlin and Karl Bodmer traveled to the Missouri region in 1832 and 1833. Such fine robes impressed many white observers, not least Rudolph Kurz who observed in December 1851 that a band of River Crow under the leadership of Rotten Tail who visited Fort Union to trade, wore 'robes of extraordinary beauty; the skins were entire, including both the head and tail; they were not cut at all, the hair was long and silky, the skin as soft and pliable as a woollen blanket' (Kurz, Hewitt ed., 1937:251). The Crow were widely recognized for the high quality of their hide dressing. Kurz further recorded that the 'Absaroka [Crow] are famous for their robes; in no other nation are the dressed skins so soft and pliable' (ibid.:250). Such robes were generally painted with the owner's exploits and, especially if we include the closely related Hidatsa, robe and shirt pictographs were virtually interchangeable, a characteristic also of Sioux and Blackfeet regalia but generally less emphasized. The structural, quill and other types of embellishment of several early Crow robes have already been considered in some detail (Taylor, Lessard eds, 1984(b):42; Taylor, Krusche ed., 1987:305–8) but here we will consider the pictographic features which illustrate much of the scalp and horse raids, as discussed in Chapter VI.

One marked feature of early Crow pictographic work is the emphasis on enumeration of separate encounters, together with associated exploits; while virtually nothing has been reported on this by contemporary observers, it does seem possible to reconstruct a plausible interpretation of the various pictographic motifs. The robe shown (right) was collected by L. A. Schoch before 1838 and is now in the Bern Historische Museum, Switzerland. At right angles to the broad quilled band (worked in the so-called plaited technique and edged mainly with dark blue and yellow pony beads) are twelve brown

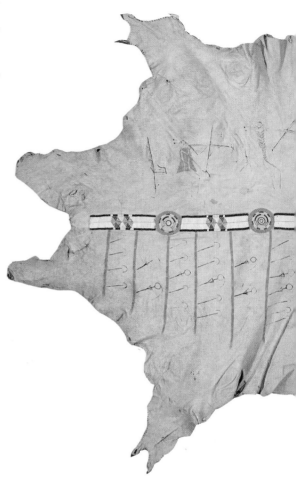

Left: *A Crow warrior on horseback. Sketch by the Swiss artist Rudolph Kurz at Fort Union, 1851. This is probably the River Crow chief Rotten Tail, dressed in war ceremonial regalia and carrying lance and shield. His leggings appear to be embellished with porcupine quillwork in the so-called plaited technique. Rotten Tail may also be claiming bear power – note the realistic rendering of a bear on his moccasins.*

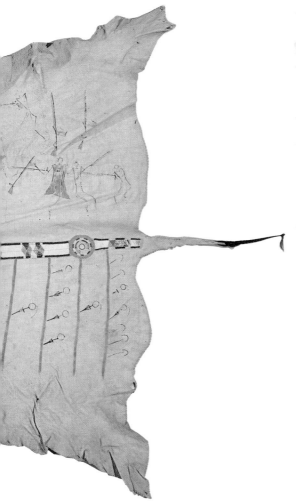

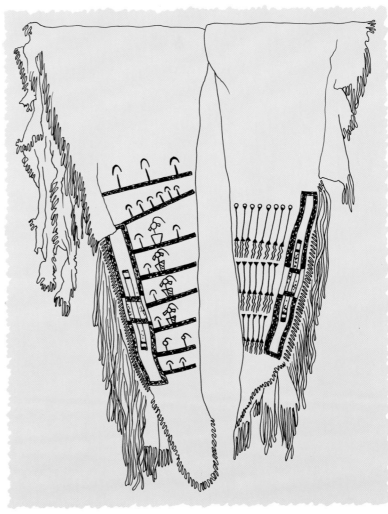

Above: *A fine buffalo robe, almost certainly Crow and now in the Historical Museum in Bern. This was collected by L.A. Schoch prior to 1838 and is embellished with the war exploits of its owner.*

Above, right: *A pair of ceremonial leggings, probably Crow and dating from circa 1840. The leggings are decorated with bands of quill-wrapped horsehair edged with beads and embellished with numerous pictographs relating to horses captured and scalps taken. Sketch after Imre Nagy.*

painted, thick lines; on five of these are horseshoe-like motifs with a short straight line running from the center (↑). These probably represent horses captured and cut from the picket pin within the heart of the enemy encampment.[1]

While this type of convention was used by the Crow and Hidatsa, it was also employed in a slightly different form by the Blackfeet, an even more highly conventionalized symbol being used to record the picket pin exploit; then the pin *alone* was used to represent the horses captured (Wissler, 1911:41).[2] The killing of enemy on all but one of these expeditions is indicated by the pointed triangular shaped figures, their legless appearance conveying permanent immobility, a widely used technique often employed to show the slain. The warrior opposition is indicated by the emphasized scalp-lock on all of these figures. This contrasts with the disc- and rod-type motifs which are shown on the Hidatsa robe collected by Maximilian, and which are symbols of scalps removed and fastened to poles for use in a victory dance.[3] Both of these symbols occur on a pair of Crow leggings (above) and additionally the tribal identification of the enemy is suggested by details of hair style. They are probably a Missouri River tribe (most likely Arikara or Mandan), several of whom not only wore a scalp-lock but cut their hair, which produced the bobbed effect; also, the half-shaded bodies of three of these figures almost certainly refer to the tattooing which was practiced by these tribes, while the tally of eight, apparently separate expeditions[4] is similar to that on the robe.

The circular quilled discs on the Crow robe are devices which are almost certainly representative of time; both Corbusier (Mallery, 1893, vol.1:265) and Walker (1917:85) make reference to the circle as a symbol of a time cycle. In particular, a symbol which was broken at regular intervals (–O–O–O–) – just as with the quilled band – conveyed the idea of a time sequence.

When the robe was worn, it was wrapped around the body so that the quilled band ran horizontal and overlapped; thus, if the discs do represent time intervals, a plausible interpretation would be five separate episodes of warfare activity in which some twenty-two prize horses were captured and thirty enemy killed. It should be stressed that exploits displayed this way did not necessarily relate to those of the individual, but reflected the *privilege of a leader to document the successes* of the *whole war party* which he had led.[5]

The upper part of the Crow hide shows at least five separate encounters; of particular interest here is the great emphasis put on the capturing of guns and, although the paintings are mainly realistic, there is an interesting symbolic motif (extreme left) of a conventionalized right hand with long pointed fingers and the thumb bending upward conveying a grasping action.[6] The same feature occurs on another robe, now in the National Museum, Copenhagen (right) and also on a shirt in the Museum of the American Indian, New York, both almost certainly Crow and from about the same period, that is about 1850. This motif has not been found elsewhere and may thus be a conventionalization exclusive to the Crow. In virtually all the scenes, weapons are being captured; generally these are guns but sometimes also bows. This underlines the coup counting system of the Crow as documented by Lowie (1935:216–18) because, although four men might count coup on the same enemy,[7] only one man ranked as the striker of the first coup and the first striking of other adversaries *in the same engagement* was not so rated; in consequence, the snatching away of a bow or gun in a close encounter, as so vividly shown on these artifacts, was among the most common of war exploits. With the danger which accompanied this exploit, however, even the best of Crow warriors achieved but few of these feats. Bell-rock, for example, considered to be among the most successful of Crow warriors, had captured five guns and Gray-bull, who was esteemed for his bravery, only three (ibid.:216). Thus, the large number of stylized guns painted adjacent to the quilled shoulder bands on the Museum of the American Indian shirt referred to above, almost certainly document the deeds of the war

Above: *The Crow 'capture hand' on a painted shirt now in the National Museum of the American Indian, New York. Note that the hand, shown as a rake-like motif, appears to be snatching a gun from an antagonist at the left and is shown detached from the figure at the right.*

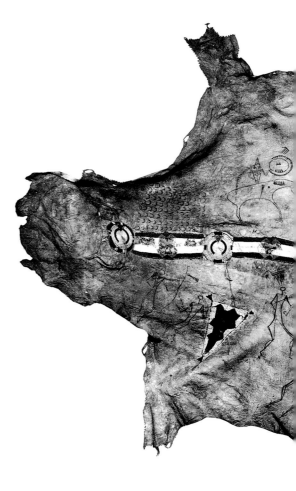

Below: *The robe shown below, almost certainly Crow, is now in the National Museum, Copenhagen, and probably dates from circa 1850. It is heavily embellished with the war exploits of its owner. Much fine detail is displayed on this robe, some of which is documented in the table (right). The central band is the so-called plaited technique, the rosettes in quill-wrapped horsehair edged with blue and pink beads.*

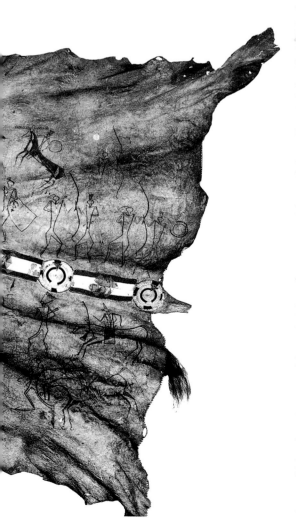

TABLE VII.1: PICTOGRAPHIC CONTENT OF CROW ROBES AND THEIR PROBABLE MEANING (Continued over)

Pictographic Feature			*Comment*
Men	Hair styles/head ornament		Scalp-lock
			Pompadour hair-style. This 'was sufficiently common to be used as a tribal mark in Dakota pictographs' (Lowie, 1954:53)
			Cone headdress
			Metal (trade) discs (top left)
	Chevron on bodies		Associated with at least three figures on horseback and two on foot. All these figures wear a cone-like headdress[8]
	Elongated bodies, exaggerated calves, thin arms, no hands		Seems typical of Crow military pictographic work of this period[9]
	Snatched weapons/ directed coup		The 'Crow hand' is shown adjacent to the shield, gun and two long bows
Horses	Elongated style/ equipment		Tails tied on two, loose on four. Spanish chelino on three (?). Buttonhook hooves.[10] One wood saddle
	Action		One killed (open mouth, single legs front and back). (Top left) Three moves – bow, spear and coup (central lower)
	Stolen		Almost one hundred horses run off (hooves on left hand side)
	Color embellishments		Bays, piebald and chestnut. Saddle cover on two. Clipped ears on one (top right)

party which the owner of the shirt had led.

Crow symbols of both protective and destructive power appear to be displayed on the mantle worn by the upper central figure on the Copenhagen robe, which shows unusually realistic painting of the eagle, generally symbolic of the Thunderbird – lightning strike and the quick ability of the eagle to pounce upon its enemy being intertwined in Crow mythology. Thus a war medicine bundle which belonged to Two Leggings, a River Crow chief, contains eagle parts – head, feathers and claws – which were said to evoke both lightning and eagle power

PICTOGRAPHIC CONTENT OF CROW ROBES AND THEIR PROBABLE MEANING

Pictographic Feature		*Comment*
Weapons/ coup sticks	Guns 	Four guns carried, each of which is embellished with triangular flaps. Great details shown of flint and hammer[11]
	The Crow *ictaxia ha'tskite* or long bow (possibly the only illustrations extant of this type of accouterment)	These were slender sticks tied together and used to count coup. They seem to be a variant of the ceremonial bow spear[12]
	Spears/arrows	At least two are shown in use by the warriors on horseback – and in both cases they have the wood saddle to offset shock impact. Spear and arrow heads are shown in flight or embedded – for example on the slaughtered horse (top left)
	Shields	Four small shields shown (typically 0.5m or so in diameter). It is probable that the surrounding sawtooth pattern refers to the protective power of the shield against spears and arrows. The six dots and triangular patterns (top right and left respectively) probably refer to impacting bullets and arrows/spears[13]
	Society staff 	In addition to the long bow-type, one horseback warrior (top right) carries a short staff with feathering at one end. This may well be an illustration of the straight staff carried by both the Fox and Lumpwood Society members. These were wrapped with otter skin; owners of such staffs were not supposed to retreat on the battlefield (see Chapter VI and Lowie, 1935: Fig. 12D)

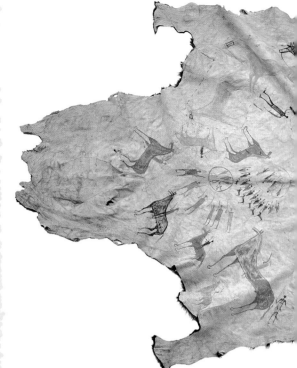

Left: *Pictographic symbols on a Crow robe dating from the middle of the nineteenth century and now in the National Museum, Copenhagen (shown previous page).*

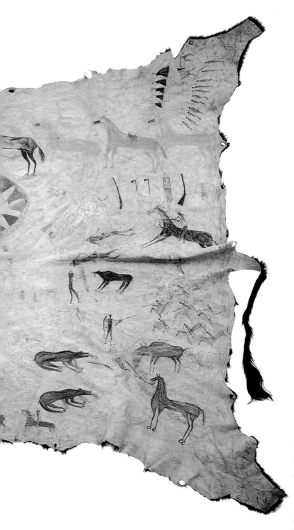

Above: *Blackfeet hide painted by the young Piegan artist Sharp in the spring of 1892. This documents the war exploits of White Grass, a Piegan chief. The somewhat static aspect of the pictographs is a typical Blackfeet style for this period.*

(Wildschut, Ewers ed., 1960:52–3).[14] The star motif, on the other hand, is almost certainly a symbolic reference to the Morning Star which was associated with one of the most sacred war medicine bundles, the so-called hoop medicine. This medicine was first introduced to the Crow by the warrior Blows Down and it was said to have originated with the Morning Star who told Blows Down that it would warn him of approaching enemy and also enable him to see the enemy's location together with the strength of their attacking force. In recognition of Morning Star's help, the bundle was embellished with a four-pointed star virtually identical to that so carefully depicted on the mantle (ibid.:47).[15] An analysis of the pictographic features on these robes gives some fascinating insights into the culture that produced them and shows the remarkable detail used by the artist to convey information (Table VII.1).

The Blackfeet referred to pictographic motifs as *sinaksin*, meaning 'made marks'. Much concerned with communicating information relating to the owner's war record, Blackfeet artists, as with the Crow, employed ingenious techniques to convey their ideas with an eye to fine detail, a point which caught Maximilian's attention when he recorded in August 1833, 'Today I received the hide of a buffalo calf or cow from the Blackfoot Indians with painted hieroglyphics . . . on the red horse on the top one can see the way the Indians let the ropes of their horses slide on the ground . . . the deeds of an outstanding warrior are represented here who wears the long feather head-dress by which one can recognise him by all the individual deeds represented here.' Further descriptions refer to the flight of the bullets, the blood from the wounds and the number of rifles, bows, scalps and horses captured (Maximilian Diary, Joslyn Art Museum, vol.2:155). Although produced more than half a century later, the tanned hide shown on this spread exhibits many of the typical Blackfeet pictographs that Maximilian referred to in 1833. Of particular interest is that when it was painted by a young Piegan artist called Sharp, in the spring of 1892. Dr Z. T. Daniel, a physician on the Blackfeet Reservation in Montana, obtained a very detailed explanation of all the action pictures and these were sent with the robe to the Smithsonian Institution. While these pictorial war histories cannot be 'easily read' as Dr Daniel suggested, they are replete in symbolic statements enumerating 'the number of contenders on each side in small-scale actions, indicate the casualties inflicted and the kinds of war trophies brought back by the victors' (Ewers, 1983:56). The robe mainly documents the war exploits of White Grass, a chief of the Buffalo Chip Band of the Piegan, who earned the reputation as a very successful warrior through his involvement in many actions against enemy tribes and the counting of numerous coup. One of White Grass' most outstanding exploits was that of entering a Flathead campsite – across the Back-bone-of-the-World (the Rocky Mountains) – freeing two picketed horses and then capturing the chief's bow, arrows and quiver. This outstanding deed is given prominence on the painted robe as the central circular figure in blue in which are drawn a bow, quiver, two horses and sixteen tipis, all representing the night camp of the Flathead and Pend d'Oreilles. The man at the left of the circle with knife in hand and an otter skin tied to his hair has laid down his gun and is moving into the circle of tipis; this is White Grass, who seizes the bow and quiver, cuts the horses loose (the best were always picketed close to the tipi) and escapes with them. The exploit was considered so daring and outstanding that it was rendered at the central place of honor on the robe.

An Early Exploit Robe from the Central Plains

A magnificent robe, shown on this spread, is now in the collection of the Museum of Mankind, London. It is a large buffalo hide (approximately 6.5 × 5 feet (2 × 1.5m)) which has been dehaired and soft-tanned and has been cut lengthwise for ease of tanning and resewn with sinew; there are several holes on the outer extremities where the hide has been stretched for tanning. It has received little attention in the literature but its cultural and historical content has been briefly touched on by Taylor (1971) and Brotherston (1979). The former put emphasis on the use of this robe in the context of headgear styles of Plains tribes and referred to the fact that such pictographs could be 'good sources of information for costume and ethnographical detail' (Taylor,1971:13), while Brotherston has considered the war exploits depicted on the robe with the enemy in disarray and the victors forming 'strong fourfold ranks across the field' (Brotherston,1979:219).

The acquisition history and tribal identification of this robe have been lost but it may well be Lakota, dating from the first half of the nineteenth century. Possibly it is one of the robes which were collected by the Duke Paul of Württemberg because some twenty of his artifacts were transferred to the British Museum in 1869 (these had been collected on two trips up the Missouri, one in 1823 and the other in 1829) (Gibbs,1982:52–61).[16] Whatever its actual history and tribal identity, it is a rich source of information for the central Plains which gives insights into perspectives, values and material culture as perceived by the native American who produced this outstanding cultural document. The robe displays some eight separate war encounters, every one of which involved the victor wearing a distinctive straight-up style of eagle feather headdress and a necklace which appears to be of claw or horn. There are thirty-two human figures (definitely including one woman and perhaps five children) and five horses together with details of spears, quivers, costume styles, bows, guns and a dew claw rattle. Analysis shows more than a score of different accouterments carried or worn by the lively and dramatic figures depicted on this robe, together with details of some unusual deeds of valor (Table VII:2).

Below: *Painted exploit robe, possibly Lakota, circa 1830. Some eight separate war episodes are depicted on this robe; the leader is shown wearing an eagle feather headdress and carrying the war pipe. His outstanding bravery is symbolized by the wearing of a no retreat sash in some of the exploits (top left). Note the exaggerated scalps carried by two of the lower figures.*

TABLE VII.2: ANALYSIS OF EARLY EXPLOIT ROBE FROM CENTRAL PLAINS

Associated with the warriors	*Other features*
Pipes	*Deeds recorded*
Bows and arrows	Counting coup/capturing a woman
Warbonnets	Deflected missiles
Necklace	Scalps taken
Bow case and quiver	Eight separate encounters
No retreat sash	
Scalps	*Clothing/featherwork/hair styles*
Mirror	Leggings
Guns	Breechcloth
Bow lance	Straight-up bonnet with tipped
Shield	feathers
Sword	Breath plumes
Wrapped lance	Braided scalp-lock
	Woman's dress
Trade items	Men's shirt styles
Red and blue (?) trade cloth with	Hide shirt acting as protective cover
selvedge edge	Woman's hair style
Mirror	
Steel knife	*Horse regalia and features*
	Spanish bridle
	Quirt
	Reins – probably loop type
	Clipped ears
	Tied tails

Right: *The pictographic content of the Lakota (?) robe now in the collections of the Museum of Mankind in London and dating from prior to 1850.*

The central figure shows the distinguished warrior whose war exploits are documented on the robe. Adjacent to his left hand is a pipe drawn in an elevated position; as discussed earlier, this indicates that he was the leader of a war party, often referred to as a 'partizan', a term which, according to James, was used by the French to describe the influential warrior who became a leader (James, 1823:14). The pipe is very realistically drawn, clearly showing the heavy and separate red catlinite pipe-head, the dimensions of which indicate a hand-carved piece with a flaring bowl; this shape distinguishes it from those turned out in their thousands in later years when the white man made them on a lathe, while the thin black line suggests the typical flat wooden stem associated with such pipes. One feature which is of particular interest, and unusual, is the red band adjacent to this stem. Pipes were used in both peace and war; traditionally, the stems of such pipes for *peace* were painted blue by the Sioux and red if war was contemplated, thus the pipe shown here is so decorated to emphasize that it was to be used in war. Such motifs were also painted on ceremonial shirts, symbolic of the number of war expeditions which the owner had led. On this robe great emphasis is put on scalp-taking exploits to the extent that the scalp is exaggerated in comparison to the size of the shield – indeed it could be confused with one, but the blood and braided scalp-lock tell us otherwise.

Some five episodes of scalp taking are documented and in each case a dotted line runs from the slain warrior to the victor; the head of the former is bloody and his scalp with the braided lock is now held by his killer. In one episode, the hero of these exploits has apparently taken a woman from an opposing party, all of whom have been immobilized, and it is probable that their lack of breechcloths represents the insignificance of the corpse, with its life force withdrawn.

A large claw or horn is hung around the neck of the 'partizan' – possibly identifying him. This is the most unusual detail, as is the fact that both a buffalo horn and bear claw are attached to a Lakota shirt, collected by Duke Paul of Württemberg and stated by him to signify the owner's name – most probably Bull Bear, a famous Oglala chieftain. Of great interest is that the spotted effect shown in the garment of the victorious warrior is similar to the extensive spotting on the Lakota shirt: the features are so unusual that it is not improbable that this belonged to the same person, namely the Oglala chief Bull Bear.

In one dramatic episode, the ball from an enemy gun has struck the 'partizan' but failed to penetrate, and a later action suggests that the spent ball was then thrown back at the enemy. In contrast to the 'Crow hand' discussed earlier, the hand is shown in a more realistic three-dimensional manner as is the quirt which is adjacent to the right hand.[17] While the apparent ineffectiveness of the gun could be due to the use of a multi-layered leather shirt which it is known the Sioux used in the early 'post-gun' period (Secoy,1953:74), it was probably abandoned by about 1820; a more plausible explanation would thus be that most of the guns used by the Plains tribes in the first half of the nineteenth century were, as one contemporary observer reported, 'of the most nondescript character, old Tower muskets, and smooth-bores of every antique pattern . . . after firing he reloaded in full career . . . pouring into his gun an unknown quantity of powder' (Dodge,1882:450).

Above: Mato-Tatanka, *or Bull Bear, a famous chieftain of the Oglala, portrait by Alfred Jacob Miller in 1837. This ceremonial shirt (below) may have belonged to Bull Bear. It is embellished with red and black paint, white beads and horsehair locks. Its collector, Duke Paul, noted that the buffalo horn and bear claw on the left sleeve were 'synonyms of the owner's name'.*

Above: *A Sioux robe(?), which may date as early as 1820, displays an unusual depiction of a bear, such renderings rarely being shown on war history robes. It has been suggested that the meandering dotted line (showing the trail of the bear) leading to the figure of a pipe-carrying leader is meant to convey that this man had acquired bear power (see Ewers, 1982:42)*

The grizzly bear which from time immemorial – and for good reason[18] – was held in awe by the Plains tribes is given some prominence on a robe now in the collection of the Smithsonian Institution (above). Recognizing it as a symbol of immense strength and courage, ambitious warriors sought to acquire some of the grizzly's power for themselves in visions or dreams of the animal or by purchasing bear power from others who had obtained it earlier in their own vision quests. The prominence given to the bear, whose movements are shown by a meandering, dotted path across the robe, suggests that the artist intended to convey that the man whose exploits are depicted on the robe had obtained bear power, and that the power enabled him, or the members of his party, to kill four of their enemies – note the four immobilized figures between the pipe-carrying partisan. Bear cults, which were composed of those few men who had obtained supernatural power through dreams of a bear, were relatively common and widespread among the Plains groups, although there are only scattered references in the literature (Ewers, 1968:131–45). One custom referred to for the Santee Sioux which is particularly relevant here was the performance of a ceremonial bear hunt as a prelude to the departure of a war party. The first person to lay his hands on a man dressed up as a bear was said then to acquire the power to kill an enemy (Lowie, 1913:121–22).

The shield shown on page 25 clearly shows the idea of protection which was also associated with bear power; although only identified as from the 'Upper Missouri River' it may well be of Crow origin since this tribe often embellished their shields with bear designs (Hoxie, 1989:73–6).

The Ceremonial Shirt

While the painted buffalo robe was an important way of signifying an individual's position within the social and political order of the Plains tribes, the custom was extended to certain styles of body covering; thus special forms of leggings were worn by Omaha chiefs which, cut and embellished a certain way, not only referred to the sacred and responsible character of their office, but also stated the connections of power with the 'Upper World' (Fletcher and La Flesche,1911:354–5). Likewise, the Lakota designated 'executives of the nation' by use of hair-fringed leggings as a badge 'of their exalted position' (Hassrick,1964:28–9). Without question, the most forceful of the visual statements is to be found in the use of the ceremonial shirt as shown (above right), which was used by certain individuals on the northern and central Plains.

The ceremonial shirt: basic symbolism

Among the Pawnee, for example, the wearing of the skin shirt was 'one of the outstanding symbols of high status. Very few men were privileged to wear them', and even 'able chiefs' might be excluded (Weltfish,1977:375) and the sacred character of a special style of hair-fringed shirt among the Lakota – as mentioned in Chapter II – was emphasized by the elaborate rituals of conferment.[19]

Most of the ceremonial shirts have quilled or beaded bands over the shoulders[20] and bands down the arms as shown (below right). These invariably, although not exclusively, were worked separately on a leather base and then sewn on to the shirt. Although Wissler (1916:103) suggested that these bands were used to cover the seams of the garment and hence the embellishment was determined by the structural make-up of the garment, it is probable that their origin and meaning were based on the early shamanistic traditions in North America where the limbs and joints of a man were tattooed or painted. Such tattooing and Inuit parka embellishment has been reported on by Driscoll (1987:198) and in the case of the Plains ceremonial shirt the same idea is sometimes strongly suggested with the appearance of designs within the band as if to emphasize the shoulder or elbow joint.[21] For example, an analysis of early Crow shirts embellished with quillwork revealed the design elements within the bands coincided with the joints of the wearer in sixteen out of twenty-one specimens (Taylor,1981(a):Figs 13 and 14 : Lessard,1984:Fig. 2A).

These quilled or beaded bands varied considerably in size and use, which undoubtedly reflects a change in their importance as a visual statement from region to region. On the northwest and central Plains they were often large, while on the northeast Plains and among the eastern Sioux – such as the Santee – the shoulder band might be small or non-existent.

Although the patterns *within* these bands could be highly symbolic, at least one tribe – the Crow – are reported as asso-

Above: *The Miniconjou leader Kicking Bear, photographed in Washington in 1896. He wears a magnificent beaded shirt embellished with human hair-locks and eagle feathers. This specimen is now in the collections of the Smithsonian Institution, Washington, D.C., and is shown here at top right. The blue and yellow paint on the upper and lower parts of this garment refers to sky and earth powers.*

Right: *A hair-fringed shirt identified as Crow and now in the Smithsonian Institution. This is an unusual piece for Crow craftwork, and since it dates from circa 1880 it is highly probable that it was obtained from an alien tribe such as the Lakota who traded or gave many items of their distinctive beadwork to the Crow during the early Reservation period. The view here is taken from the rear.*

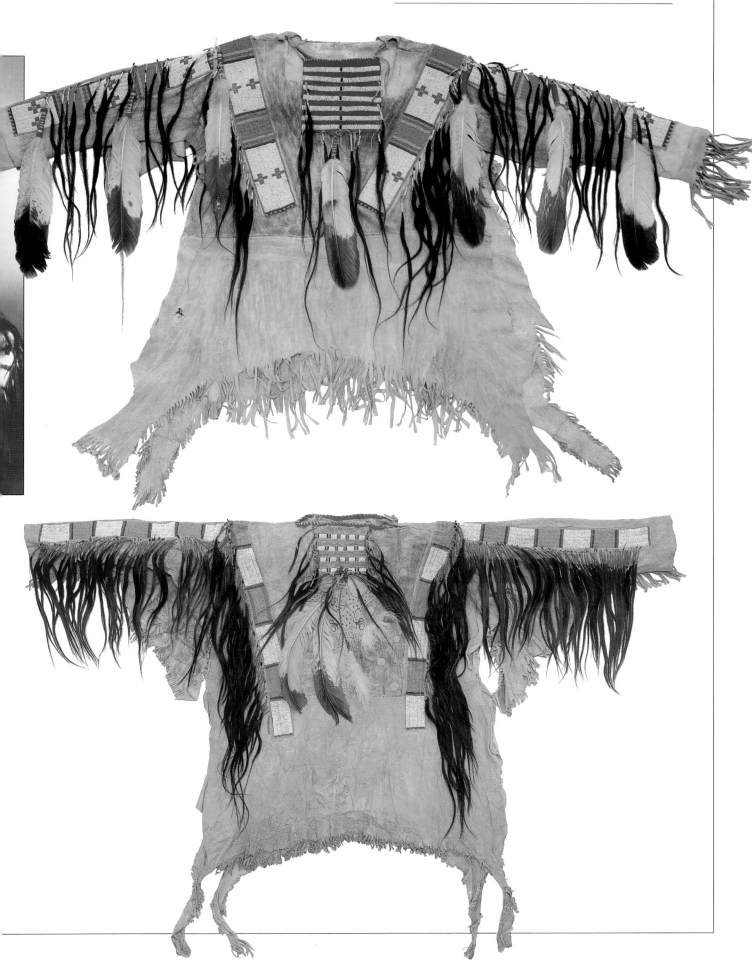

ciating the use of the four bands across the shoulders and down the arms with the achievement of striking an enemy, one of 'the most important of the four major coups' (Wildschut, Ewers ed.,1960:38). A typical Crow-style shirt showing these bands embellished in the so-called plaited quillwork technique is shown on page 195.

In addition to the bands, there are some further significant embellishments in the form of quilled discs – later beaded – or rectangular quilled panels (see below), worked separately and then sewn on the chest and the back of the shirt. Discs might also be used within the arm bands and, on occasions, within the shoulder bands and, although not an exclusive northern characteristic, it becomes increasingly rare west and south of the north-central eastern Plains region. The quilled discs seem to have their origin in the uses of circular pieces of shell or mosaic medallions which were used in a symbolic context by the Woodland tribes at an early period. The white and iridescent discs were viewed as powerful sun symbols by the tribes of the eastern and central Great Lakes region (Phillips,1987:58) and seemed to combine the power of the underwater spirits with the life-bestowing powers of the sun (Hamell,1981:13). At the same time the reflectiveness of the

Below: *A buckskin fringed ceremonial shirt, probably Blackfeet, circa 1840. The decoration consists of bands of pony beadwork over the shoulders and down the arms with a porcupine quill panel on the chest and back – an ancient form of decoration which was progressively replaced by the quilled disc.*

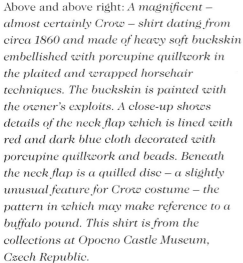

Above and above right: *A magnificent – almost certainly Crow – shirt dating from circa 1860 and made of heavy soft buckskin embellished with porcupine quillwork in the plaited and wrapped horsehair techniques. The buckskin is painted with the owner's exploits. A close-up shows details of the neck flap which is lined with red and dark blue cloth decorated with porcupine quillwork and beads. Beneath the neck flap is a quilled disc – a slightly unusual feature for Crow costume – the pattern in which may make reference to a buffalo pound. This shirt is from the collections at Opocno Castle Museum, Czech Republic.*

shells was considered by the Omaha to be symbolic of the cosmic forces 'which brought the universe into being and maintained its life' (Fletcher and La Flesche,1911:494).[22]

Superimposed on these ancient and basic concepts, and indeed emerging in most cases with the early nineteenth-century Plains horse culture as the most dominant, was the meaning of the patterns worked within these discs. For example, there were representations of the Morning Star, the whirlwind, four quarters and conventionalized versions of the thunder powers (Taylor,1993:46–7).

Color symbolism: the use of red and blue

Ceremonial objects from the northern Plains, such as medicine bundles, headdresses, leggings and, not least, shirts, were frequently covered with red paint. Such paint was used in ancient days and archeologists have documented its very widespread use in North America (Hamell,1981:6).[23] In historic times the Blackfeet referred to it as *Nitsisaan*, or 'real paint': this was quarried only in certain areas, and was reported on as early as 1797 by the explorer Alexander Henry as being 'profusely' daubed on garments by the Blackfeet and allied tribes (Henry and Thompson, Coues ed.:1897,vol.II:525).[24] The paint was said by both the Blackfeet and the Lakota to symbolize blood (Wissler,1912(a):134; Densmore,1918:77), evoking the concept of a type of *life metaphor* symbolism which Hamell suggests this color had for mankind in general (Hamell,1981:5).[25]

Blue paint was greatly coveted by a number of tribes on the central Plains and was extensively used on ceremonial shirts.

The choice of these colors undoubtedly reflected the natural world – certainly the red of the sunrise as well as the sunset caught the attention of at least one white observer who lived with the Blackfeet on the northern Plains in the late nineteenth century (McClintock,1923:111, 296), while the 'frequent redness of the soil in the Arapaho habitat' was commented on by Kroeber (1907:418). As *Siksikaí-koan*, a Blackfeet guide,

Above: The Lakota warrior Little Big Man. There is much display of ceremonial regalia in this photograph, such as the hair-fringed shirt, elaborate pipe-bags and catlinite pipe. At Little Big Man's right is a magnificent eagle feather headdress, each feather tip embellished.

explained, the Sun was considered to be the Great Power: 'He is in the birds and wild animals . . . prairies and mountains . . . he makes the grass and berries grow; and upon them the birds and animals depend for life' (McClintock,1923:16). Red paint represented, and clearly evoked, this energy which the Blackfeet said permeated through all things essential to life.[26] Little wonder that the medicine woman of the Blackfeet Sun-dance had 'her face, hands, and clothing . . . covered with the sacred red paint' (Grinnell,1893:265). This was considered a directive from the sun itself, such as 'This woman/man I am making her/his body *holy, powerful*,' the shaman would say during the course of applying the sacred red paint (Wissler,1918:244).[27]

The 'immensity of the heavens' perceived by one white observer in the traditional territory of the Lakota hints at the basis of the *wakan* ethos deeply embodied in Siouan religion, which, for the Lakota *wicasa wakan*, 'holy man', at least, while perceiving the close relation between *Wi*, the 'sun', and *Skan*, the 'sky', viewed the latter as *the* energy source which gave 'life and motion to all things' (Walker,1917:155).[28] This is a belief remarkably close to that of the Blackfeet. Thus, although a different color was used on northern and central Plains ceremonial shirts, both seem to have been a fundamental symbolic recognition of an all-pervading power of the universe; it bestowed an aura on the wearer who was thus recognized as being not only sanctified but also endowed with powers not possessed by the common man.[29]

The hair-fringed shirt of the Lakota

As discussed in Chapter II, four councillors of the Oglala were referred to as 'shirt wearers', since upon investment of office they were given a special form of hair-fringed shirt. Such garments and elaborated versions of them represent an immense amount of Lakota heraldry relating to the obligations of both war and leadership.

The shirt shown (above) was collected just over a century ago by the army officer Captain John Bourke from the Lakota warrior Little Big Man who had told Bourke that it had once belonged to 'the great chief of the Sioux, Crazy Horse, or had at least been worn by him' (Bourke,1892:476).[30] At the time of acquisition, Bourke was unable to obtain details regarding its symbolism but speculated that the colors of yellow and blue represented the earth and water or sky, the attached feathers were a reference to birds and the painted circle on the breast was an image of the sun. He was particularly interested in the significance of a cocoon attached to one shoulder of the shirt, but was unable to determine its meaning. In the traditional Plains style the shirt is made from two complete deerskins, the upper part of each forming the arms, the lower the body, and, as Bourke described it, the upper is painted blue, the lower yellow. Other features are truncated triangular neck flaps, hair-fringing and red zigzag lines, some of which are forked at the end,

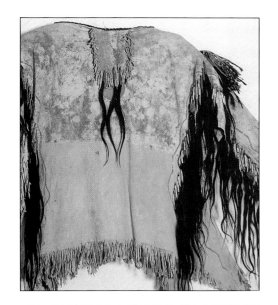

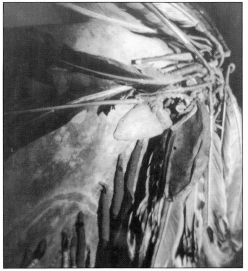

Above: *Details of an Oglala hair-fringed shirt which is said to have been used by Crazy Horse, circa 1870. The blue paint on the upper part of this garment is symbolic of the energy or moving force of the Lakota universe, while the arrowhead and cocoon (lower) makes reference to lightning and whirlwind powers.*

painted on the body and the arms. Attached adjacent to the cocoon, are woodpecker feathers and a flint arrowhead.

The shirt is one of two now extant in the world's ethnographical collections and they were spoken of by the Lakota as 'owned by the tribe' (Wissler,1912(b):7), being bestowed on those who acted on behalf of the tribal leaders.

Leaders of Men

An earlier discussion briefly outlined the Lakota political system where authority for various divisions was through the *Nacas Ominicia*, or 'Chiefs Societies', who in turn elected the *wicasa itacan*, 'leaders of men'. Men of extremely high caliber, it is highly probable that many of them were themselves young, virile, *ongloge un* or, 'shirt wearers' in earlier days, who could combine in their later years high warrior status with the role of an influential diplomat.

Such outstanding leaders, now active in the political realm rather than that of warfare, wore a more complex form of ceremonial shirt. These garments were still fringed with hair and painted blue and yellow but had many additional embellishments: a magnificent example now resides in the Plains Indian Museum, Cody, Wyoming (page 199, top). It was worn by Red Cloud on two occasions when he led delegations to Washington in the 1870s: research has shown that the heraldic embellishments not only state allegiance but evoke most of the awesome powers of the Lakota universe to support the negotiations on behalf of his people (Taylor,1987:247–53).

The custom of wearing ceremonial shirts to designate high ranking individuals became particularly apparent when various delegations traveled east to negotiate for the allocation of their lands, particularly in the last quarter of the nineteenth century. Thus when the Blood leader, Red Crow, visited Ottawa in the fall of 1886 (Dempsey,1972:204), he wore a beaded shirt (opposite, below), bearing conventionalized symbols of the Thunderbird, a mythical creature to both Blackfeet and Cree, and used as a symbol of protection and courage (McClintock,1968:52; Cadzow,1926:24–5). Similar motifs appear on a magnificent quilled and beaded shirt from the northern Plains and dating prior to 1840 (above), indicating the early use of the Thunderbird symbol, which, in this form, is virtually diagnostic of Cree, Blackfeet or Assiniboin origin.

Headgear of Warriors

While for more than four hundred years the allegorical symbol of the North American Indian, in European as well as American art, has been that of a warrior figure wearing a crown of feathers (Sturtevant, Doggett, Hulvey and Ainsworth eds,1992:28), nowhere has this been more emphasized than in the portrayal of the Plains Indian warrior, where several very distinctive styles of headdress were worn. The horned bonnet, the feathered band with the feathers standing straight up and the bonnet

Above: *Cree (?) pony beaded shirt with quill disc on the chest displaying a Thunderbird motif. This contrasts with the Lakota and Blackfeet shirts (right).*

Right: *An Oglala ceremonial shirt worn by Red Cloud and others in the delegation to Washington, D.C., in the 1870s. Research suggests that the embellishments evoke much of the Lakota cosmos and ethos.*

Below: *Crowfoot (left) and Red Crow (right), Blackfeet chiefs.*

Right: *The shirt worn by Red Crow (in the photograph) is now in the collections of the Museum of Mankind, London.*

where the feathers flared out like a fan are the most notable examples. The origins, generally in a simple form, can often be traced back to the Eastern Woodlands: thus, a number of early headdresses have almost identical characteristics to those found a century later on the Great Plains.

The Blackfeet Straight-Up Headdress

The simplest type, whose early history is embedded in a style which had virtually intercontinental distribution, was the so-called 'straight-up' headdress, which reached its fullest development among the Blackfeet and other northern Plains

Above: *A Blackfeet delegation displays much traditional regalia of the tribe, although the flaring style headdress worn by Wolf Plume (left) was of a type copied from the Lakota in the late nineteenth century. The straight-up headdresses worn by Curly Bear and Bird Rattler (center and right respectively) represent a style anciently used on the northern Plains.*

Above: *The Blackfeet warrior Mountain Chief wears a classic style of straight-up headdress constructed of eagle feathers and embellished with weasel skins and horsehair. The front plume may make reference to membership of the Blackfeet Horns Society.*

Above, right: *Headdress collected by George Catlin in 1832, probably Crow Indian, and now in the collections of the Smithsonian Institution, Washington, D.C. Although resembling a straight-up headdress, this is actually a flaring style where the feathers have freedom of movement. An unusual feature is that the feathers have been dyed orange. Although in poor condition, this is a valuable specimen for its structural and decorative content.*

tribes. Because of its ancient origins, the Blackfeet considered it to be a very sacred type of headdress, explaining that only very few people had the right to wear it (Ewers,1945:61). Traditionally, such headdresses were said to have originated with the Bull Society and various myths relate that it was a gift from the buffalo. Straight-up headdresses were made by folding a piece of rawhide or heavy leather lengthwise as a base for the headband; holes were then cut at evenly spaced intervals along the fold into which the feathers were inserted and laced in place. Then the band was tied together at the back so as to fit the wearer's head. Decoration was in the form of ermine skins, red cloth and brass tacks. As with all Plains feathered headdresses, the tail feathers from the immature golden eagle – which were white with dark brown or black tips – were the most preferred and were considered extremely valuable: in 1850 twelve such feathers could be exchanged for a good horse (Denig, Hewitt ed.,1930:589).

By the Reservation period the Blackfeet had adopted the flaring style bonnet of the Lakota. This style had no religious meaning to the Blackfeet – as, for example, had those which were associated with the straight-up headdress and which was firmly reserved for ceremonials, reflecting Blackfeet mythology and ritual. For this reason, a headdress of a straight-up style was retained by Blackfeet women for use in the Sun-dance; this was replete in symbolic statements, parts making up the headdress referring to the blessings which had been received from the Sky and Earth powers (Brasser,1987:122).

The Flaring Headdress

In contrast to the straight-up style of headdress, the flaring headdress was so constructed – with loops at the bottom of the feathers for lacing to a buckskin skull cap – so that there was easy freedom of movement. The feathers were spaced out by means of another lace running through the quill about half-way up the feather (right, and detail opposite). The credit for the invention of this ingenious, lightweight form of headgear was, by some tribes at least, given to the Crow (Clark,1885:398). Certainly one of the best early illustrations which shows such a bonnet is that of the Crow chief 'He-who-jumps-over-everyone' by George Catlin, who also collected two such bonnets which are thought to be of Crow make (see page 201).

Whether or not it was the Crow who invented this form of headdress, it is nevertheless fairly well established (Taylor, 1962, 1994(b)) that it flourished predominantly in the Upper Missouri region, being associated with tribes such as the Crow, Arikara, Hidatsa, Mandan and Dakota who put emphasis on coup feather designation by the use of eagle feathers. Such featherwork was described by Maximilian for the Mandan: 'they put a variety of feathers in their hair, frequently a semicircle of feathers of birds of prey, like radii, or sunbeams . . . or small rosettes made of broad raven's feathers, cut short, in the centre of which is the tail of a bird of prey spread out like a fan' (Maximilian, Thwaites ed.,1906:vol.XXIII:260).

Symbolism

With regard to the symbolism of the feathers, the Ponca informant Buffalo Chief said that, 'eagle feathers alone should be used' and that feathers set upright on the crown indicated the number of captures made in battle, one feather being worn for

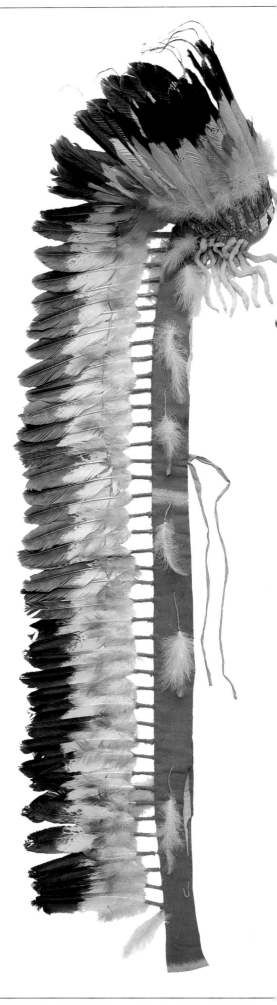

202

Below left: The Crow warrior He-who-jumps-over-everyone, painted by George Catlin in 1832. Both horse and rider are dressed in ceremonial regalia and wear feathered headdresses of the flaring style. It is possible that the one worn by the warrior is the same as that shown on page 202.

Left: A Cheyenne feather bonnet with a long tail of eagle feathers attached to a strip of trade cloth and said formerly to have been the property of Stone Calf. Traditionally, the feathers in a headdress represented deeds of valor not only of the wearer but also those who supported him. Such regalia could only be worn by those who had the esteem of the people.

Right: The Lakota leader American Horse wearing highly decorated ceremonial regalia so typical of his tribe. The shirt is the same as that worn by Red Cloud (see pages 198–9); his leggings and moccasins are heavily beaded and he holds a fine pipe with the stem embellished with porcupine quills and fitted with a head of red catlinite stone.

Below: Detail of Cheyenne headdress shown opposite. The headband of three lanes of beadwork shows a typical 'mountain' design worked in blue beads. The feathers have been attached by rawhide loops covered with red trade cloth and ermine skins embellish each side of the headdress.

each capture. Feathers inclined toward the right indicated the number of scalps taken; feathers set low on the head and inclined toward the left indicated war leaders who had achieved power and control through prowess in battle; feathers stripped nearly to the top, leaving the black tip which would flutter in the breeze when worn, indicated a successful scout who had succeeded in discovering many dwellings – the black tip symbolizing the smoke-blackened tipi or earth lodge tops. Such feathers, Buffalo Chief said, were commonly worn upright in the crown, 'but the meaning is the same when attached to the clothing or to the mane or tail of the horse' (Mcgee,1898(a):157). While soft downy eagle feathers were symbolic of mysterious forces, the continuous movement of the fine filaments of the feather suggested communications with higher powers, ideas which prevailed among the Crow and Lakota also.

The fullest data on the symbolic meaning of the eagle feather headdress come from Fletcher and La Flesche's studies of the Omaha (1911) which, on consideration, can undoubtedly be extended to other tribes.

Referring to the flaring-type bonnet, the Omaha said that it could, traditionally at least, only be possessed and worn with the consent of a man's fellow warriors, and then strictly by an individual who had gained 'war honours' and the 'respect' of the leading men in the community. It 'established a social relation and underlined the interdependence of men' (Fletcher and La Flesche,1911:447).

The manufacture depended on the assistance of many people. Each feather in the bonnet stood for a man; the tip of the hair fastened to the feathers and dyed red represented the man's scalp-lock and, before the feather could be fastened on the bonnet, a man had to count the war honor which actually entitled him to wear the feather and so enable him to prepare the feather for use in decorating the warbonnet. Since many individuals were required ceremonially to prepare the feathers (and it took some time), a feast was organized to which warrior friends were invited; they then counted their honors on the eagle feathers and so made them ready for use. Traditionally, only the man who had taken a scalp could put the tip of red hair on the eagle feathers and so every feather actually stood for two honors – the feather itself for one of the first three war honors, the tip for taking the scalp.

When the warrior counted his honors, he held up the feathers which were to represent them, saying, 'In such a battle I did thus', and so on. At the conclusion of the recital, the feather was handed to the man making the bonnet, who then put the feather in the proper place. Strips of ermine were fastened to the sides of the bonnet, which, according to informants, represented the desired characteristics of the ermine itself – alertness and skill in evading pursuit (ibid.).

Buffalo horn headdresses were used early on to distinguish men of high rank (below left and right). Maximilian gives a particularly good description of such headgear in his discussion of Mandan costume, reporting, 'They likewise wear the large horned feather cap; this is a cap consisting of strips of white ermine, with pieces of red cloth hanging down behind as far as the calves of the legs, to which is attached an upright row of black and white eagle's feathers, beginning at the head and reaching to the whole length. Only distinguished warriors, who have performed many exploits, may wear this head-dress. If they give away one or more of these head-dresses, which they estimate very highly, they are immediately considered men of great importance; the regular price of such a cap is a good horse; for a single eagle's feather is always valued at one or two dollars. On their buffalo robes they often represent this feather cap, under the image of a sun' (Maximilian,Thwaites ed.,-1906:vol.XXIII:260–61).

Right: *Man-On-A-Cloud, a Southern Cheyenne, photographed in 1892 wearing a magnificent single tail eagle feather bonnet. Each feather is tipped with dyed horsehair stuck on with gypsum.*

Far right: *Horned headdress, Cheyenne, decorated with long split horns with beaded browband and tail of eagle feathers. The use of horns for headdresses is an ancient custom evoking, traditionally at least, buffalo power.*

Below, right: *A Sioux horned headdress surmounted with buffalo horns, attached to the top of which are horsehair locks. Eagle feathers hang pendant at the back with the cap covered with strips of ermine. Such headdresses were often military society regalia.*

Below: *A Sioux horned headdress with head and back drop decorated with fur. The white brown-tipped split horns have been decorated with brass studs.*

The Cheyenne also put great emphasis on the use of buffalo horns on sacred or distinguishing regalia. A single horn-like fossil became a highly potent medicine bundle (Grinnell,1926:24). Perhaps the most ancient Cheyenne horned headdress is the *Issiwun*, or sacred buffalo hat, which almost certainly had its origins in the east.

An interesting custom of the Northern Cheyenne in the 1870s was actually to attach horns to a flaring-style bonnet (above). Cheyenne men said that they were supplied by tribal medicine men and were believed to give protection in battle, making the wearer bullet-proof. At the time of the Battle of the Rosebud in June 1876, only fifty-nine pairs were available, so only fifty-nine warriors took part in the fight, even though the Cheyenne village was camped on the Tongue River nearby. It was considered

extremely unlucky to ride into battle without wearing the horns; however, by the time of the Custer Battle a week or so later, all the Northern Cheyenne warriors who fought wore the symbolic protective horns.

Changing Meaning: Perpetual Image

With the closing of the frontier and the formation of Reservations, the sacred and military symbolism of the various style of headdress progressively decreased. However, the most attractive and portable of them, namely the flaring bonnet, took on a new meaning. It became a sign of 'Indianness', so that by the 1890s tribes as widely separated as the Pueblo of New Mexico to the Penobscot of Maine adopted this style of Plains bonnet; it simply became expected of them (Ewers,1965:541).

Above: *The Oglala Cinte Muzza, or Iron Tail, who for many years worked with Buffalo Bill. In all his acts Iron Tail invariably wore a fine eagle feather warbonnet which reinforced and perpetuated the Plains Indian as a symbol of the North American Indian.*

This image of 'Indianness' was given great exposure with the formation of Buffalo Bill's Wild West in the 1880s when often to be seen leading the Indian cavalcade was *Cinte Muzza*, or Iron Tail, an Oglala from Pine Ridge, South Dakota. Always dressed in beaded outfit, Iron Tail invariably wore a magnificent feathered headdress and he, together with others like him, was seen by countless audiences both in America and Europe. If the message conveyed was different, it at least perpetuated an image of the North American Indian.

FOOTNOTES: CHAPTER SEVEN

1   This feature is also exhibited on a Hidatsa robe collected by Maximilian (Hartmann,1973:Plate 4), where the village enclosure is emphasized by conventionalized pictographs showing the tripod bases of enemy tipis; adjacent to each is the picket pin and horse symbol.

2   Wissler did, however, caution at this time that the crossed lines could be symbolic of other deeds when used by the Hidatsa and Lakota; for example, in the case of the latter, it was employed as a rescue symbol (Wissler,1911:41).

3   (a) A particularly good sketch by an Assiniboin warrior, drawn in 1853, of scalps attached to poles for use in the scalp dance, is reproduced in Denig, (Hewitt ed., 1930:Plate 71);(b) In his description of Crow war honors and insignia, Wildschut relates that 'the taking of a scalp was indicated by tying it to the end of a coup stick' (Wildschut, Ewers ed.,1960:37).

4   Denig said that tattooing was 'a mark of rank in the men, distinguishing the warrior when elaborately executed' (Denig, Hewitt ed.,1930:592).

5   Perhaps the clearest statement on this comes from Bowers for the Hidatsa who stated that in addition to the personal coups he counted, such leaders were credited with all 'enemies killed and struck, with the right to show this accomplishment on his clothing': further, such men could 'wear as many scalp segments on his shirt or leggings as enemies scalped by warriors under his leadership' (Bowers, 1965:258 and 279-80). (See also Maximilian, Thwaites ed., 1906,vol.XXIII:352.)

6   Bill Holm first suggested to the writer that this feature 'looks like a very stylized hand' (Holm,April 1986).

7   As Lowie's informants conveyed it 'the honor diminished with each successive blow' (Lowie,1935:216).

8   Rotten Belly's shield displays a human-like figure with eleven chevrons painted on the body. This was said to represent the man who appeared to Rotten Belly in a vision; it was said to have great augury powers. The moon was a much favored vision by the Crow because those adopted by it were frequently given long life and, although their mythology related that it was a great gambler, it was 'invariably the winner' (Wildschut,Ewers ed.,1960:10).

9   This is an extension of the custom of using the track of an animal or bird to identify it; thus, the hook-like foot identifies the horse almost beyond question.

10   A woven blanket of the Mexican type is shown in both pictographs. These typically had broad stripes running across them. They were traded from the Southwest via Shoshone intermediaries. (See also Mallery,1893,vol.II:569.)

11   This detail is not unique to Crow pictographs; the Blackfeet also tended to give much attention to the firing mechanism of the guns.

12   The Plains bow was usually no more than 3¾ feet long (1.2 m); such extensive bows as shown in these pictographs suggest something different. Lowie's brief description of the Crow long bow – a ceremonial accouterment – which was used to count coup, seems the most convincing interpretation to date (Lowie,1935:85).

13   The Lakota used a complete surround to indicate 'fear' (Mallery,1893,vol.II:591). Closely related are the glancing-type pictographs (Wildschut, Ewers ed.,1960:70-71) and the protective bear power symbols on Crow shields (Ewers,1982(a):37).

14   Note that Rotten Tail, chief of the River Crow, carried a shield painted with a stylized eagle (Kurz, Hewitt ed.,1937:Plate 48).

15   Such stars were later worked in seed beads on the headstalls of Crow horses, probably to evoke Morning Star's help (Wildschut, Ewers ed.,1959:fig.28; Lowie,1922:fig.12).

16   (a) John Ewers was of the opinion that this was 'fairly early 19th century in terms of style' (Ewers to Taylor, February 1989); (b) Duke Paul describes four 'worked robes' of bison bull and cow; they were 'beautifully embroidered and decorated and wonderfully drawn and

seem to represent warpath and peace-councils in allegoric paintings'. They were collected from the Pawnee, Arikara, Sahone (Northern Lakota) and Mandan. (Museum of Mankind, London. Ethno-Coll.P.P.W.,nd,.items 65 and 185.)

17   John Ewers suggested that the artist who executed the pictograph may have intended to represent the rider shooting a gun or pistol with his left hand (Ewers to Taylor, 1989). If Dr Ewers is correct in this interpretation, we thus have a series of episodes sequential in time.

18   This creature would weigh nearly 1000 pounds (453 kg) and when fully standing was 8 feet (2.4 m) or more. It could become a vicious killer when aroused.

19   Even in the Reservation period when such garments were being made for collectors, special rituals were still performed during its fabrication and transferral (Wissler,1912(b):40).

20   The use of the band across the shoulder as an embellishment was undoubtedly developed at a very early period: the shirt of about 1650 at the Ashmolean Museum, referred to earlier, exhibits a small but definite band across the left shoulder. Examination of this piece indicates that the right shoulder was also similarly decorated. Earlier this century, Wissler considered the possibility of aboriginal origin of such bands as against influence by white military costumes (Wissler,1916:100-103).

21   (a) Even today, some Blackfeet and other northern Plains artists will depict an animal not only with the heart line or other internal organs, but also with the joints marked, although when asked the reasons for actually doing this, it 'could not be explained' (Dempsey,Hastings, September 1988); (b) Early illustrations, c.1585, which show the use of body paint or tattooing to emphasize the bones and joints by the Virginian and Florida Indians, are by White and Le Moyne. See particularly Hulton (1984:Plates 48 & 61).

22   The Pawnee associated with shell the emergence of life from 'a primordial pond' (Weltfish,1977:261).

23   See also Fletcher (1887(b):285) who reports that the wearing of paint was regarded as 'an offering of prayer'.

24   It is reported for the Arapaho, red 'is the paint *par excellence* and that it was used extensively for 'religious motives' (Kroeber,1907:418).

25   So valuable were the sources of red earth to the Blackfeet that when their Reserve was being laid out in the nineteenth centry, Crow Eagle, a prominent Piegan negotiator, asked for an extra portion of land 'closer to the mountains where they obtained their red ochre' (Dempsey, December 1988).

26   *Siksikaí-koan* or 'Blackfeet Man', was a guide to McClintock in the summer of 1896. *Siksikaí-koan*'s mother was Blackfeet, 'my tribe', but he had spent much of his youth with the Cree whose language he spoke fluently (McClintock,1923:3, 10).

27   Dr Hugh Dempsey also informs me that the paint was not considered to have power 'until it was blessed with sweetgrass incense' (Dempsey, September 1988). Wissler (1907) refers to similar customs for the Lakota. Fletcher observed that, for the Sioux, red was considered to be symbolic of the sun and 'the procreative force' (Fletcher,1887(a):285).

28   Blue does seem to be firmly associated with the Lakota. The term 'Sioux blue' is commonly used to describe the light blue beads found on seed beaded items made by these people from circa 1860 onwards. Fletcher refers to the crushing into powder of a blue ornament made from blue beads and then scattering it on the buffalo skull during the White Buffalo Festival of the Hunkpapa (Fletcher,1887(b):274).

29   This recognition of all pervading power of the universe, DeMallie suggests, is the 'very basis of religion' (DeMallie and Lavenda,1977:164).

30   'Indian Notes' (MAI,:1928). Crazy Horse was one of the last shirt-wearers of the Oglala Sioux – he was killed at Fort Robinson, Nebraska, in 1877.

THE WINDS
OF CHANGE

— CHAPTER VIII —

Below: *Close-up of a Sioux dance bustle showing eagle head and wings. To the Plains tribes the eagle was a symbol of power and liberty, but even as far back as the early 1800s this was progressively eroded as the white man moved west.*

The Louisiana Purchase and its Repercussions

When the seventeen United States signed the Louisiana Purchase with the French in 1803 – and at the stroke of a pen more than doubled the land area of the young nation – they were faced with a complex set of problems. Two powerful colonial powers, Spain and Great Britain, possessed colonies to both the south and north of the new territory, and in this vast tract of land were numerous, little known Indian tribes. For almost a century and a half, Spain and Great Britain had traded with a number of tribes but now, with much of the territory belonging to the United States, officials planned to reduce the encroachments and tap the region's rich fur resources.

The problems were confronted by the formation of the Corps of Volunteers for North-Western Discovery in 1803. The brainchild of the President, Thomas Jefferson, the Corps was jointly led by Captains Meriwether Lewis and William Clark. While their brief was to assess the potential and map the newly acquired lands, an added obligation – a specific directive from the President – was to treat the Indians they encountered 'in the most friendly and conciliatory manner' and 'if a few of their influential chiefs, within practicable distance, wish to visit us, arrange such a visit with them, and furnish them with the authority to call on our officers, on their entering the United States, to have them conveyed to this place at public expense' (Lewis and Clark, Thwaites ed.,1904–5:247).

Diplomatic Contacts

The expedition was highly successful and, in their travels from St Louis on the Mississippi to the shores of the Pacific Ocean, they logged more than nine thousand miles, spent some eighteen months in the Upper Missouri and Yellowstone regions, met eleven of the fourteen or so tribes who inhabited that vast area and, while staying in the Mandan villages in August 1806, arranged for one of their chiefs – *Shahaka*, or Big White – to visit Washington. (*Shahaka* is shown in the illustration on page 211.)

Jefferson had chosen his men well, for William Clark was a born diplomat and in reply to the Mandan chief, Black Cat, who said he wished to visit the Great Father in Washington but was afraid of being killed by the Sioux on the way down river, Clark reported: 'I informed them that I still spoke the same words which we had spoken to them when we first arrived in their country in the fall of 1804. We then invited them to visit their great father the President of the United States and to hear his own councils and receive his gifts from his own hands and also see the population of a government which can at their pleasure protect and secure you from all your enemies, and chastize all those who will shut their ears to his councils. We now offer to take you at the expense of our government and send you back to your country again with a considerable present in merchandise which you will receive of your great Father' (ibid.:339).

It was all part of an important political game: returning chiefs – generally much fêted – would report on what they had seen of the white man's world, impressed by the marvels and power of civilization. It was a pattern which would be repeated many times over the next three quarters of a century.[1]

Big White had agreed to make the journey on the condition that one of his wives and his only son went along with him, while René Jessaume, a Frenchman married to a Mandan woman, was to accompany the party as an interpreter. The parting was one of deep concern and sorrow; Big White smoked a last pipe with his friends then put his arm 'round all the head men's necks of his nation', men as well as women were weeping aloud (Turner,1951:31).

Arriving at the Arikara village a few days later, Clark, together with Big White, attempted to get some of the chiefs to join them on the trip to Washington, but despite a feast and much parleying on the peace pipe, none could be persuaded to attempt the journey, telling Clark that their chief who had left eighteen months before to see the Great White Father had still not returned.[2] On 22 September they reached a trading post located on the site of Bellefontaine, an old Spanish fort about a half-day's journey above St Louis; here, the bearded travelers were all given free haircuts while *Shahaka* received a smart suit of tailor-made clothes. Although in 1806 St Louis was a rough frontier town of hardly a thousand inhabitants, to the weary travelers, and to *Shahaka* in particular, it was the acme of civilization. The party was toasted at a 'splendid dinner' held in the Christy's Inn, followed by a Grand Ball. An enthusiastic Meriwether Lewis then despatched a letter to President Jefferson reporting that he had 'prevailed on the principal chief of the Mandans to accompany me to Washington; he is now with my worthy friend and colleague Capt. C . . . [we are] in good health and spirits (Lewis and Clark, Thwaites ed.,1905,vol.VII:337). Jefferson's reply reached Lewis at Charlottesville: 'Tell my friend of Mandane . . . that I have already opened my arms to receive him. Perhaps, while in our neighborhood, it may be gratifying to him, and not otherwise to yourself to take a ride to Monticello and see in what manner I have arranged the tokens of friendship I have received from his country particularly, as well as from other Indian friends' (ibid.:345). Clearly, Jefferson, a man of science, was deeply interested in the indigenous people of his country and many of the ethnographical specimens which Lewis and Clark had sent back the previous year, together with other curios, were on display at Monticello in a 'kind of Indian Hall' (ibid.). These included a fine painted buffalo robe showing a battle between Mandan and enemy tribesmen which had taken place in about 1797[3] – an item which would be of particular interest to *Shahaka*.

Late in December 1806, *Shahaka*, his wife and son, accompanied by Meriwether Lewis, arrived in Washington. It was now nearly five months since they had left the Mandan village after a

Top and above: *Captains Meriwether Lewis and William Clark, joint leaders of the expedition west to explore land acquired from the French in the Louisiana Purchase of 1803. At Thomas Jefferson's request they encouraged prominent Indians to visit Washington.*

Right, above: *'Floyd's grave', painting by George Catlin, 1832. Sergeant Charles Floyd was the only casualty on the Lewis and Clark expedition, dying of* Biliose Chorlick *in August 1804, not far from present-day Sioux City, Iowa.*

Right: *The Mandan chief* Shahaka, *or Big White, one of the earliest representatives of the Plains tribes to visit Washington. His round trip took him more than three years; few of his fellow tribesmen believed his seemingly fantastic stories of the white man's world.*

journey of almost two thousand miles, and on 30 December Jefferson warmly welcomed the visiting Mandans, acknowledging the long and hazardous journey which they had undertaken, which was 'proof that you desired to become acquainted with us. I thank the Great Spirit that he has protected you through the journey and brought you safely to the residence of your friends, and I hope He will have you constantly in His safe keeping, and restore you in good health to your nations and families' (Jefferson,Bergh ed.,1903,vol.XVI:412). The Mandans now became honored guests of the government. On New Year's Day, they attended a levee hosted by the President in the White House and the celebrations continued with a special gala dinner for the safe return of the Corps of Discovery, when a toast was drunk honoring the people *Shahaka* represented; it was to:

'The Red People of America – Under an enlightened policy, gaining by steady steps the comforts of the civilized, without losing the virtues of the savage state' (Turner,1951:39).

As with members of other Indian delegations, *Shahaka*'s silhouette was made by the aid of a physionotrace, showing him in

profile. This portrait showing a chubby faced man with black
hair, heavy silver ear pendants and with a robe over his
shoulders would ultimately join others in the American Philosophical Society's collections where they would be available for
study by those who believed that there was a relationship between 'physiognomy and intellect' (Sellers,1947:158).

His diplomatic role and sightseeing in the east completed,
Shahaka, together with his wife, son and the interpreter Jessaume, left Washington in early summer of 1807. By now,
William Clark had been made Superintendent of the Indian
tribes of the West and it was his responsibility to get the party to
St Louis in time to join the first trading expedition headed
upriver. Attempts, however, were foiled. When the party arrived
at the Arikara villages on 9 September, the tribe was openly hostile, threatening to kill *Shahaka* if he proceeded further
upriver;[4] with only a small fighting force, the party decided to
turn back. Jefferson heard of *Shahaka*'s plight, recording 'I am

Above: Ah-jon-jon, *or The Light, an Assiniboin warrior, portrait by George Catlin, circa 1837. This man, a highly respected hunter and warrior, traveled to Washington in 1831 but on his return he was ridiculed by fellow tribesmen who considered his tales outlandish.*

uneasy . . . about the Mandan chief . . . [we must find] measures for restoring him to his country. That is an object which presses on our justice and our honor, . . . I suppose a severe punishment of the Ricaras [would be] indispensable . . .' (Jefferson, Bergh ed.,1903,vol.XII:99).

In spring 1809, a company of militia consisting of one hundred and twenty-five men under the command of Pierre Chouteau Jr, and costing the United States government $7,000, acted as an escort to *Shahaka*'s party; not only was the Mandans' journey a lengthy one but it was also proving to be expensive!

Shahaka and his family reached home in September 1809. The total journey had taken more than three years, but the obligations of 'justice and honor' which so concerned Jefferson, had been met. As to *Shahaka* and his family, the home-coming proved to be an unhappy one. Nobody believed his stories of the wonders he had seen in the white man's world, that their numbers were infinitely more numerous than those of the Mandan tribe, of the enormous cities, great armories with their roaring cannons, the vast house in which the Great Father lived, roads as straight as a 'gun barrel' and where the waters constantly rose and fell every day (the Atlantic). They were, said the powerful Mandan chief, One Eye, the product of the fertile imagination of a man who was nothing more than a 'bag of lies' (Brackenridge,1816:184). To the Plains Indians, tales of such a land were just too incredible to be true; and nearly a quarter of a century later, when an Assiniboin leader, *Ah-jon-jon*, or The Light, returned from journeys east with similar tales, his too were considered so incredible that they led to his assassination by an unbelieving Hidatsa (Ewers,1968:78).[5]

Garrisoning the Plains

'I would have more confidence in the Grandfather at Washington if there were not so many bald-headed thieves working for him' (Sitting Bull, about 1855).

One of the most important trading posts on the central Plains was Fort Laramie, which stands at the junction of the Laramie and North Platte Rivers in present-day southeastern Wyoming.[6] Founded in 1834 by two enterprising fur traders, William Sublette and Robert Campbell, it was located in a long recognized trappers' paradise, in an area abundant in prized beaver whose pelt was used to make the elegant beaver hat so fashionable both in the eastern States and in Europe where it became a status symbol. The fort was purchased by the American Fur Company in 1836 and up until the early 1840s it was largely dominated by fur traders, explorers, missionaries, and trappers, while bands of Cheyenne, Arapaho and Lakota, seeking trade with the white man, generally camped near the post in large numbers.

The situation changed dramatically, however, in the summer of 1843, which saw the first sizeable Oregon migrations of more

than a thousand people. The emigrants obtained vital help at
the fort which offered protection and refreshments to the weary
travelers. From then on and over the next two decades, some
two hundred thousand emigrants including the Mormons and
gold seekers en route to California stopped at Fort Laramie and
covered wagons became a familiar sight in the early summer of
each year.

For a decade, Fort Laramie thrived, but by 1846 the fur trade
in the region was on the decline and, realizing a need for continued protection and support of the emigrants, the government arranged to purchase the fort from the American Fur
Company for $4000 (Hieb,1954:7). By 1849, Fort Laramie was a
military post, garrisoned with nearly two hundred men and
officers, consisting of mounted riflemen and infantry. Almost
immediately, the army began erecting further buildings and in
less than a decade the fort was to become a sprawling military
post which, although too large to be walled in, was strong
enough to deter Indian attack.

Fort Laramie was not unique in its changing role; progressively,
within the next two decades, the fur trading forts along the
Missouri were purchased by the government and turned into military posts; augmented by purpose-built establishments, they
would become essential to the westward expansion.[7]

These developments increasingly alarmed the Plains tribes;
not only was the game destroyed or frightened away, but
diseases —Asiatic cholera, measles, whooping cough and smallpox — took their toll. Recognizing the potential dangers of increasing hostilities, early in 1851 Congress authorized holding a
great Treaty Council with the Plains Indians, choosing Fort
Laramie as the meeting place. By late summer, representatives
of all the principal tribes who lived between the Yellowstone
and Arkansas rivers, between the Rocky Mountains and Missouri River were gathering near the fort. The fort stood in the
middle of the hunting grounds of the allied Sioux, Cheyenne
and Arapaho who were present in great numbers but there were
also large bands of Crow, Assiniboin, Mandan, Hidatsa, Arikara
and Shoshone. Because of the countless ponies accompanying
the gathering of an estimated ten thousand Indians – probably
'the largest assemblage of Indians in the history of the Plains'
(Vestal,1948:3) – the entire encampment moved to the lush
meadowlands at the mouth of Horse Creek, some thirty miles
east of the fort. Here traditional enemies mixed and at times
tension mounted; the chiefs, however, had pledged a truce for
the duration of the Treaty, and the Army was there in numbers,
with a force of just under three hundred dragoons and mounted
rifles.

By 17 September, after much speech-making and distribution of twenty-seven wagon loads of presents,[8] the Council
broke up. The government pledged to make an annual payment
to the Lakota in goods valued at $50,000 for fifty years. In
return, there was to be unmolested emigrant travel along the

214

Left: *Fort Laramie, one of the principal fur trading posts founded in 1834. Painting by Alfred Jacob Miller, 1834. The fort stood at the confluence of the Laramie and North Platte rivers and was acquired by the American Fur Company in 1836. It became a haven for emigrants traveling the Oregon Trail. By 1849, however, it had become a military garrison post which would stand witness to much of the red–white conflict to come.*

Below: *Arapaho ceremonial dance kilt, part of the distinctive regalia of the tribe's age-graded societies. The type of embellishment varied depending on the degree, but most were painted yellow with green stripes and had a red cloth edge as shown here. Earth and sky powers were also evoked with these colors, while the attached feathers were said to make the wearer's horse run more swiftly.*

Oregon Trail following the Platte River and west to the mountains. The principal tribes also agreed to a Treaty of Peace between themselves and – which at the time was perhaps the most contentious issue – a Brulé headman, Conquering Bear, was nominally appointed as a single chief over the Lakota bands, an arrangement which went against the established political structure of the tribe; indeed, the Oglala refused to sign even though in subsequent years they regularly accepted their share of the Treaty goods.

Conquering Bear, who emerges as a man of unquestioned courage and ability, was decidedly reluctant to accept the appointment, declaring that there were older and wiser men than himself, men who knew the whites better; he was just a buffalo hunter . . . if he had known they had intended to make *him* chief, he would never have come to the Treaty Council. Conquering Bear clearly foresaw what would happen to an individual who assumed such sway over his people, declaring: 'Father, I am not afraid to die, but to be chief of *all* the nation, I must be a *big chief*, or in a few moons I shall be sleeping [dead] on the prairie. I have a wife and children I do not wish to leave. If I am not a *powerful chief*, my enemies will be on my trail all the time' (ibid.:17).

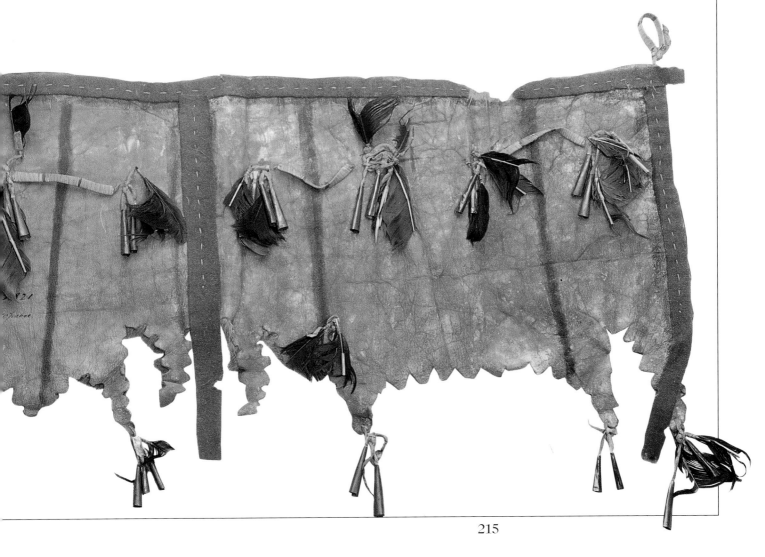

Ash Hollow : Destruction of a Brulé Village

In August 1854 the Grattan Massacre occurred. This unfortunate and avoidable incident convinced the army that the Indians must be punished and a force of some six hundred men under General W. S. Harney marched westward from Fort Leavenworth, in present-day Kansas. Unable to locate the slayers of Grattan, he attacked Little Thunder's band at Ash Hollow on 2 September 1855.[10] These Indians were Brulé Lakota and Harney subsequently admitted in his report on the battle, that they were in fact largely blameless of the Grattan affair.[11]

The encounter was a brutal one, the village being attacked from both sides, 'the infantry . . . poured a murderous volley into the [Indians] then the cavalry plunged down the opposite slope. Dropping their baggage, the Brules scattered in wild retreat. The cavalry followed, cutting down fleeing fugitives . . . "There was much slaughter in the pursuit", observed [one officer]' (Utley,1967:117).

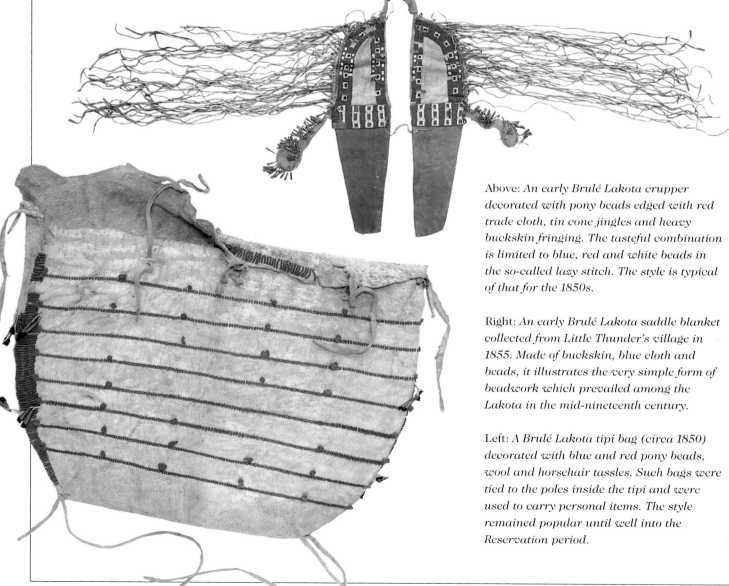

Above: *An early Brulé Lakota crupper decorated with pony beads edged with red trade cloth, tin cone jingles and heavy buckskin fringing. The tasteful combination is limited to blue, red and white beads in the so-called lazy stitch. The style is typical of that for the 1850s.*

Right: *An early Brulé Lakota saddle blanket collected from Little Thunder's village in 1855. Made of buckskin, blue cloth and beads, it illustrates the very simple form of beadwork which prevailed among the Lakota in the mid-nineteenth century.*

Left: *A Brulé Lakota tipi bag (circa 1850) decorated with blue and red pony beads, wool and horsehair tassles. Such bags were tied to the poles inside the tipi and were used to carry personal items. The style remained popular until well into the Reservation period.*

*Left: Sacred Bull, a Brulé Lakota,
photographed circa 1865. It was in
September 1855, after the so-called Grattan
Massacre in August 1854, that a small
Brulé village under Little Thunder was
attacked by General Harney and more than
eighty people killed. Several of Sacred
Bull's relatives were among those killed in
the massacre.*

The topographical engineer, Lieutenant Gouverneur K. Warren, who went through the village after the battle was over, was horrified by the scene. Many women and children had been slaughtered and he found two dead mothers with their dead babies in their arms. He arranged the transport of the wounded and brought in a 'piteous load' of two women and children grievously wounded. He carried in his arms, 'a little boy shot thro' the calves of his legs and thro' his hams' (Hanson,1986:9). Fewer than half of the two hundred and fifty people in the village escaped; there were at least eighty-five dead and seventy women and children were made prisoners. Warren was greatly disillusioned by the callous attitude of the soldiers whose tales of valor he countered with the comment that there were but 'few who killed anything but a flying foe' (ibid.).[12]

Harney's brutality at Ash Hollow earned him the Lakota appellation of 'The Butcher' and for the way he invaded their territory, 'Hornet'; others referred to him as 'Squaw Killer'.

*Right: A fine Brulé Lakota woman's dress of
deerskin and decorated with blue, white,
orange and black pony beads. This piece
was collected by Lieutenant G.K. Warren
after the attack on Little Thunder's camp at
Ash Hollow in September 1855. This is the
forerunner of the fully beaded cape dresses
of the 1880s onward which were so popular
with the Lakota during the Reservation
period.*

The Great Peace: Rise of the Indian Barrier on the Southern Plains

Even as early as 1832, any white man moving westward from Arkansas into Kiowa and Comanche territory experienced increasing hostility as these powerful Plains tribes began to realize the consequences of emigration from the east, which included thousands of eastern Amerindians who were shifted west of the Mississippi as part of the Indian Removal Act passed by President Andrew Jackson's government in 1830. As one historian put it, 'intruding Indians from the east were going into the prairies and antagonizing the native Indians by killing their game, and the Great Plains country was anything but safe for the few whites who dared to enter it.' (Richardson,1933:79).[13]

In 1832, with a view to laying the foundation for a peace treaty, a Dragoon Expedition under Colonel Henry Dodge traveled into Kiowa and Comanche territory. George Catlin accompanied the force and gives vivid accounts of his first contact with the Comanche at their great village, pronouncing them 'the most extraordinary horsemen that I have seen yet in all my travels, and I doubt very much whether any people in the

Above: A Comanche camp on the southern Plains, probably Para-coom's, *or Bull Bear's, photographed by William Soule in February 1875. In the foreground is a fine buffalo hide tipi. As the buffalo herds declined in number, tipis of government issued canvas gradually replaced hide ones.*

Right: A feathered warbonnet collected by James Mooney from the Kiowa in 1892. This is an unusual and distinctive headdress suggesting that it had particular symbolic meaning to the owner, although this was, unfortunately, not recorded. The front brow band is in blue floral type beadwork and the long tail is of dark eagle feathers attached to a broad band of red trade cloth.

Above: *A Comanche powder horn collected by Jean Louis Berlandier, probably before 1850. The horn appears to be from a domesticated animal rather than buffalo. It is heavily decorated with brass tacks, including two crosses along its length.*

Right: *Smoked Shield, Comanche, painting by George Catlin, 1834–5. This highly distinguished warrior was almost seven feet tall and the fastest runner in the tribe, being able to run down a buffalo and despatch it with a knife. The large shield is of the type carried in pre-horse days.*

world can surpass them' (Catlin,1841.vol.II:66).[14] Dodge explained to the Comanche that it was hoped to establish a 'system of trade that would be beneficial to both' (ibid.:56). While a number of the expedition died from drinking stagnant water, and Catlin himself was very ill, the purpose of the expedition – to establish a peace treaty – was successfully concluded at Camp Holmes the following year.[15]

The continued influx of Amerindians and whites from the east and also from Texas to the south was further aggravated by a move of the southern bands of the Cheyenne to trade at Bent's Fort – possibly due to the marriage of Owl Woman, daughter of White Thunder (and keeper of the sacred Medicine Arrows) to William Bent, which took place in the early 1830s. The newly located Cheyenne allied themselves with the Southern Arapaho and in 1838, at the Battle of Wolf Creek, they defeated the Comanche alliance (Kiowa, Plains Apache and Comanche), who were then forced to accept the Arkansas River as the northern boundary of their territory.

Above, left: *Little Raven photographed with his two sons, daughter and William Bent at Fort Dodge, circa 1868. Both Bent and Little Raven were much involved in Arapaho and Cheyenne politics.*

Above: Teh-toot-sah (Dohasan), *or Little Bluff, painting by George Catlin, 1834. He protested unsuccessfully to the U.S. Commissioners' proposal in 1865 to restrict Kiowa and Comanche territory.*

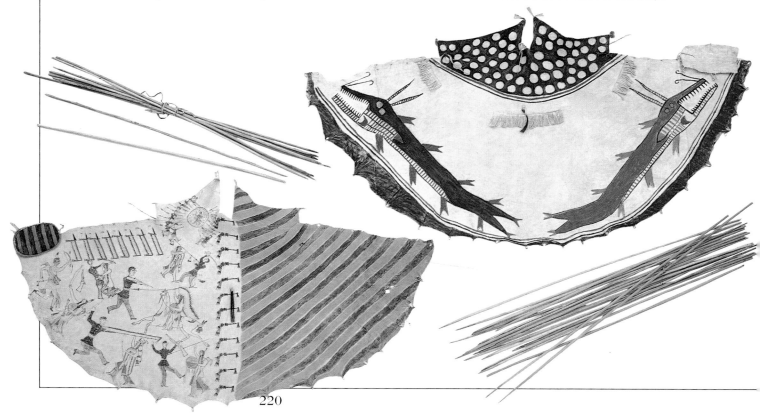

Above: *Chief Yellow Bear, a Southern Arapaho who, along with five others, John Bourke noted, were 'able men to whom the Arapahoes looked up'. He is carrying a pipe inlaid with lead or pewter and wears a medal awarded for having cooperated with the agent in peace efforts.*

Left: *Models of Kiowa painted tipis collected by James Mooney in the period 1891–1904. The designs are based on actual decorations painted on buffalo hide tipis prior to the Reservation period. These were used by prominent Kiowa families and could be handed down through successive generations. While no more than twenty per cent of Kiowa tipis were painted, those that were vividly declared the status of the owner. Far left is Little Bluff's famous Tipi with Battle Pictures, the original being a gift from the Cheyenne chief Sleeping Bear. The other seems to refer to* zemoguani, *or 'horned fish', of Kiowa mythology (Ewers, 1978:32).*

Pressed now on three sides and unwilling to accept any terms for surrendering their lands to the whites, the Comanche alliance combined with the Cheyenne and Arapaho, the intermediaries at a critical point in this initiative being the Plains Apache. The new Alliance was referred to as The Great Peace and it combined the strength of all the tribes in the region and, by putting a stop to intertribal warfare, it enabled the warriors' best efforts to be directed against the whites and other intruders. The outcome was a formidable barrier to any development of the southern Plains for almost a quarter of a century.[18]

For years , the members of the Alliance considered themselves superior to any American force which might be sent against them and, as the buffalo herds began to decrease in the mid-1850s, in an effort to reduce competition for precious resources near their borders, organized war parties moved against Amerindian tribes in Kansas and there were increased raids into Texas. The attitude of the Alliance was reflected in the response of *Dohasan*, or Little Bluff, the Kiowa head chief who, cautioned by Indian agent Miller that if they did not cease their warring, the government would send troops to punish them, sprang to his feet and said: 'The white chief is a fool. He is a coward. His heart is small – not larger than a pebble stone. His men are not strong – too few to contend against my warriors. They are women. There are three chiefs – the white chief, the Spanish chief, and myself. The Spanish chief and myself are men. We do bad toward each other sometimes, stealing horses and taking scalps, but we do not get mad and act the fool. The white chief is a child, and like a child gets mad quick. When my young men, to keep their women and children from starving, take from the white men passing through our country, killing and driving away our buffalo, a cup of sugar or coffee, the white chief is angry and threatens to send his soldiers. I have looked for them a long time, but they have not come. His heart is a woman's. I have spoken. Tell the great white chief what I have said' (Mayhall,1962:189).

Sand Creek

'Nothing lives long, Except the earth and the mountains' (White Antelope death song. Cheyenne. Sand Creek, November 1864). Up until 1863, the Alliance remained both masters and arbiters of the southern Plains. The Civil War had resulted in the withdrawal of most of the soldiers from the region and the Alliance feared no military action. The discovery of gold in Colorado in 1858 led to increasing numbers of emigrants crossing the Plains and the Alliance sought to exert both its superiority and authority: war was brewing on the southern Plains.

The strongest and bravest of the Cheyenne soldier bands were the *Hotam itau iu*, or 'Dog Men'; a legend relating to their formation led to them being designated as the watchdogs of the tribe and territory once gained was not easily relinquished. It was these Dog Soldiers, combined with some Brulé Lakota, who in June 1864 attacked a family of emigrants almost within sight of Denver and killed all the men, women and children. The attack created a panic; ranches in the neighborhood were abandoned, everyone fleeing to Denver, and rumor spread that the Indians were advancing on the town. Although the danger was exaggerated, mutilated bodies displayed in Denver convinced most people in Colorado that the only solution to the Indian problem would be to exterminate them (Grinnell,1956:151).

The depredations continued and on 28 June a train of thirty wagons was attacked and all the mules run off. The same day a coach was attacked en route to Fort Lyon; on 17 July several attacks on emigrant trains near the South Platte resulted in the deaths of seven men and on 7 August five men were killed at the Cimarron Crossing.

The outburst had long been coming and pent up emotions ran high. As the trader George Bent observed when he visited the Alliance encampments: 'As I rode from one camp to another . . . I saw scalp dances constantly going on; the camps were filled with plunder taken from the captured wagon-trains; warriors were strutting about with ladies' silk cloaks and bonnets on and the Indian women were making shirts for the young men out of the finest silk' (ibid.:156).

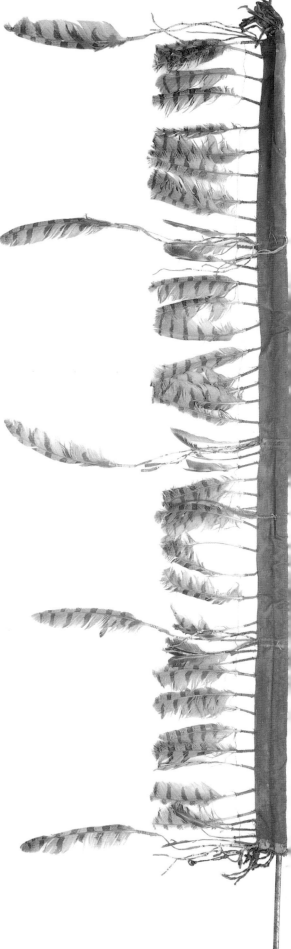

Left: *An Arapaho banner lance, probably circa 1870. Over seven feet in length, the handle is covered with red trade cloth to which are attached striped hawk wing and tail feathers. The long steel head appears to have been made from a cavalry sword.*

Below, left: *Photograph taken circa 1868 of George Bent and his wife* Mo-ho-by-vah, *or Magpie, a Cheyenne and niece of Black Kettle. The Bent family had extensive connections with the Cheyenne. William Bent, George's father, had first traded with the tribe in 1820 and married the Cheyenne, Owl Woman.*

Below: *Camp Weld, Colorado, September 1864. Here the Cheyenne and Arapaho under Black Kettle and White Antelope met with Colonel J.M. Chivington to establish peaceful relations. Two months later the Sand Creek Massacre occurred.*

In August, the road west to Denver was closed and mail had to be sent to Panama, up the Pacific coast and then from San Francisco, east by overland stage to Denver; the city was virtually isolated, provisions ran short and trade was badly disrupted. That month, Governor Evans of Colorado issued a proclamation advising parties of citizens to hunt down the Indians and to kill any hostiles they might meet. 'The result of this proclamation was to put the friendly Indians at the mercy of any revengeful emigrant who had been attacked by hostiles, and any man who coveted an Indian's pony or other property could shoot him as a hostile and seize the property as his lawful prize' (ibid.:154).

In the autumn of 1864, Black Kettle, White Antelope, Left Hand, together with other chiefs, were camped on the south bend of Sand Creek, which was about one hundred miles southeast of Denver and some thirty miles northeast of Fort Lyon and where earlier that summer some of the chiefs, together with Black Kettle, had met Governor Evans and Colonel J. M. Chivington, an officer of the Colorado Volunteers. This encampment of some one hundred tipis, of Cheyenne and Arapaho were, in the main, 'friendly', while the more hostile bands, including the Cheyenne Dog Soldiers, were more than one

hundred and fifty miles farther north near the headwaters of the Republican River. On the morning of 29 November 1864, the egotistic Chivington, who had been a Methodist minister always convinced of his own righteousness, led his regiment of Colorado Volunteers in an attack on Black Kettle's and White Antelope's settlement and in the ensuing onslaught White Antelope was mown down under a hail of bullets. Black Kettle, who had endeavored to convey their peaceful intentions, miraculously escaped along with some of the other survivors to a cottonwood grove, 'Big Timbers', about fifty miles to the northeast. Eventually, destitute and exhausted, they joined up with other Cheyenne bands, having lost at least sixty-nine of their group including many women and children. They had been victims of a frenzied attack, scalped and mutilated in the most brutal manner, rivaling 'if it did not surpass, in barbarity and savagery, any outrage committed by the Indians' (Nye,1968:20).

Above: *Cheyenne delegation to Washington in the early 1850s. From left to right are White Antelope, Man-On-A-Cloud and Little Chief. Little Chief wears an elaborate eagle feather headdress with beaded leggings, but the ceremonial shirts worn by all three men appear to be decorated with porcupine quillwork.*

Above: *Cheyenne and Kiowa delegation photographed in the White House conservatory, March 1863. The four Indians in the front row have been identified as (from left to right) War Bonnet, Standing In The Water, Lean Bear and Yellow Wolf. The first two were to die in the Sand Creek Massacre the following year. Note the pipe-bag carried by War Bonnet, the decoration being a very typical Cheyenne style for the period, as are the beaded shirt and leggings worn by Lean Bear.*

Wishing to avoid any further trouble after the Sand Creek Massacre, Black Kettle made his slow way south down into Comanche territory, but the Cheyenne Dog Soldiers stayed put and the leaders, White Horse and Tall Bull, determined to try and keep the whites away from their lands, extended invitations to some of the northern tribes to join them in their intent. The Northern Cheyenne, Roman Nose, and Pawnee Killer of the Lakota, both accepted the invitation and between them they developed a 'continuous harassment' policy. 'The hostiles raided nearly every stage station, ranch and settlement between the forks of the Platte and Denver, killing and burning and tearing down the telegraph line . . . It was the beginning of a long and bitter war' (Vestal,1948:75).

One Englishman, Dr William A. Bell, gives us a vivid glimpse of the brutal encounters between red and white men in that region at that time. In the spring of 1867, Bell – a charter mem-

ber of the Ethnological Society of Great Britain – joined a government expedition to survey routes for a trans-continental railway across the southern Plains. In June 1867, near Fort Wallace on the Smokey Hill Trail, a large war party of some four hundred Indians was observed signalling to one another by the use of mirrors. A detachment of fifty cavalry sent in pursuit were suddenly confronted by the war party: '. . . They halted a few minutes; a powerful-looking warrior fancifully dressed, galloped along their front shouting suggestions; and then, like a whirlwind, with lances poised and arrows on the string, they rushed on the little band of fifty soldiers. The skirmishers fired and fell back on the line, and in an instant the Indians were amongst them. Now the tide was turned. Saddles were emptied, and the soldiers forced back over the ground towards the fort. The bugler fell, pierced by five arrows, and was instantly siezed (sic) by a powerful warrior, who, stooping down from his horse, hauled him up before him, coolly stripped the body, and then, smashing the head of his naked victim with his tomahawk, threw him on the ground under his horse's feet. On the left of our line the Indians pressed heavily cutting off five men, among them Seargeant Frederick Wylyams. With his little force, this poor fellow held out nobly until his horse was killed, and one by one the soldiers fell, selling their lives dearly . . . By this time it was more than evident that on horseback the soldiers were no match for the redskins. Most of them had never been opposed to Indians before; many were raw recruits; and their horses became so dreadfully frightened at the yells and the smell of the savages as to be quite unmanageable so Captain Barnitz gave

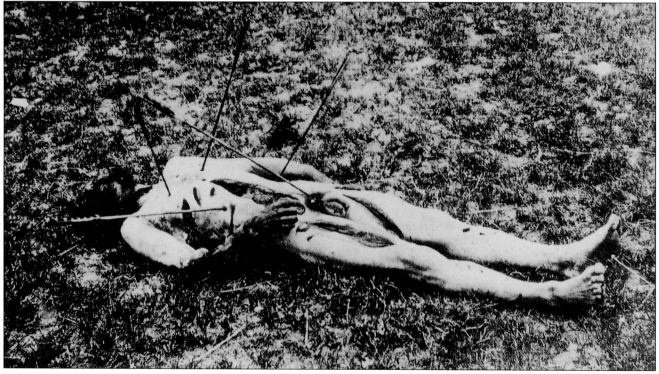

Left: *A Crow(?) bow-case and quiver of mountain lion skin embellished with white pony beads and red cloth, probably dating from circa 1850. Plains bows seldom exceeded 3ft (1m) in length while arrows were some 20in (60cm) long; the bow was a deadly weapon in skilled hands.*

Left, below: *Sergeant Frederick Wylyams. Massacres such as Sand Creek caused brutal retaliation; this Old Etonian was unfortunate enough to be ambushed by a combined force of Cheyenne, Sioux and Apache near Fort Wallace, Kansas, on 26 June 1867. Photograph by Dr William Bell, a fellow Englishman.*

Below: *The brutality of the Indian–white confrontation is vividly illustrated by this photograph of a hunter, Ralph Morrison, who was killed and scalped by Cheyenne near Fort Dodge, Kansas, on 7 December, 1868. The two military men are Lieutenant Philip Reade, of the Third Infantry, and John O. Austin, Chief of Scouts. Incidents like these led to the establishment of Fort Sill and to the appointment of George A. Custer.*

the order to dismount. When the dismounted cavalry commenced to pour a well-directed volley from their Spencers, the Indians for the first time wavered, and began to retire. For two hours Capt. Barnitz waited with his thinned ranks for another advance of the Indians, but they prudently held back; and, after a prolonged consultation, retired slowly with their dead and wounded beyond the hills, to paint their faces black and lament the death of one of the bravest leaders of their inhuman race.[17] I have seen in days gone by sights horrible and gory – death in all its forms of agony and distortion – but never did I feel the sickening sensation, the giddy, fainting feeling that came over me when I saw our dead, dying and wounded after this Indian fight. A handful of men, to be sure, but with enough wounds upon them to have slain a company, if evenly distributed. The bugler was stripped naked, and five arrows driven through him while his skull was literally smashed to atoms. Another soldier was shot with four bullets and three arrows, his scalp was torn off and his brains knocked out. A third was riddled with balls and arrows but they did not succeed in getting his scalp, although, like the other two he was stripped naked. James Douglas, a Scotchman, was shot through the body with arrows, and his left arm was hacked to pieces. He was a brave fellow, and breathed out his life in the arms of his comrades. Sergeant Wylyams lay dead beside his horse and as the fearful picture first met my gaze, I was horror stricken. Horse and rider were stripped bare of trapping and clothes, while around them the trampled, blood-stained ground showed the desperation of the struggle' (Bell,1869:vol.I:61–4).

Medicine Lodge Treaty

With so much unrest among the southern Plains tribes, particularly after Sand Creek, in July 1867 Congress implemented a general Peace Policy whose aims were to abolish Indian wars forever by 'removing their causes', persuading the tribes to 'abandon their nomadic life and take up farming', to keep the Indians from 'interfering with the construction of railroads' and finally to stop them from 'attacking frontier settlements' (Vestal,1948:114). The Peace Commission proceeded first to North Platte, Nebraska, to confer with the Oglala, Brulé and Northern Cheyenne. While waiting for several weeks, the Commission heard of the Wagon Box and Hayfield clashes and the wrecking of a train at Plum Creek; their mission desperately needed to succeed. They finally met with the Alliance – Comanche, Kiowa, Cheyenne, Arapaho and Plains Apache – at Medicine Lodge Creek in southern Kansas some seventy miles south of Fort Larned. Although all the chiefs of these tribes signed the Treaty during the week of 21–27 October 1867, 'in order to get their presents' (ibid.:128), nobody on the frontier really believed 'that those wild Indians would even try to abandon their wandering habits and become farmers overnight' (ibid.).

As predicted, the Treaty met with little success and in particular the continued building of the Kansas and Pacific railroad incensed the tribes who knew that it would bring more white hunters in who slaughtered the buffalo simply for their hides. There was much unrest and further demands by the settlers in Colorado, Nebraska, Kansas and Texas for better military protection – and action.

On the morning of the 26 November 1868, dividing his regiment into three detachments, Lieutenant-Colonel George A. Custer struck the Cheyenne under Black Kettle, on the Washita, in present-day Oklahoma. As with Lieutenant Warren at Ash Hollow more than a decade earlier, at least one officer was sickened by the carnage. Captain F. W. Benteen – who in later years emerged as one of the most respected officers in the Seventh Cavalry – wrote to a friend: 'A great deal remains to be done. That which cannot be taken away must be destroyed. Eight hundred ponies are to be put to death. Our chief [George A. Custer] exhibits his close sharp-shooting and terrifies the crowd of frightened, captured squaws and papooses by dropping the straggling ponies in death near them. Ah! He is a clever marksman. Not even do the poor dogs of the Indians escape his eye and aim as they drop dead or limp howling away . . . Now commences the slaughter of the ponies. Volley on volley is poured into them by too hasty men, and they, limping, get away only to meet death from a surer hand. The work progresses! The plunder having been culled over, is hastily piled; the wigwams are pulled down and thrown on it, and soon the whole is one blazing mass. Occasionally a startling report is heard and a steamlike volume of smoke ascends as the fire reaches a powder bag, and thus the glorious deeds of valor done in the

Left: *Wolf Robe, a Southern Cheyenne. This fine looking man epitomizes the image of the Plains Indian. He is wearing a peace medal and holding a long stemmed pipe with a large bowl made of catlinite. The beautifully beaded bag which is attached to the pipe-stem is typical Cheyenne work of the period, as are the moccasins with patterns of striped beadwork.*

Right: *George A. Custer with his wife Elizabeth ('Libbie') and favorite brother, Tom, at Fort Riley, Kansas, in 1867. In the summer of 1866 a new cavalry regiment was organized for service on the Plains. This was the Seventh U.S. Cavalry with its headquarters at Fort Riley and Custer as its commanding officer. Its first duty was to guard the building of the Kansas Pacific Railroad.*

Below: *Big Mouth, a Southern Arapaho war chief. Photograph by Alexander Gardner, 1872. The unrest among the southern Plains tribes was increased by the Sand Creek Massacre of November 1864. The following year, on 14 October 1865, Cheyenne and Arapaho chiefs signed the Treaty of the Little Arkansas to establish peace between the United States and the two tribes. Then came Washita . . .*

morning are celebrated by the flaming bonfire of the afternoon. The last pony is killed. The huge fire dies out; our wounded and dead comrades – heroes of a bloody day – are carefully laid on ready ambulances, and as the brave hand (sic) of the Seventh Cavalry strikes up the air, "Ain't I glad to get out of the Wilderness", we slowly pick our way across the creek over which we charged so gallantly in the early morn. Take care! do not trample on the dead bodies of that woman and child lying there! In a short time we shall be far from the scene of our daring dash, and night will have thrown her dark mantle over the scene . . .' (Graham,1953:213).

Of course, the Cheyenne were not entirely blameless; there was evidence in the village that some of the occupants had recently been on raiding parties – unopened mail, daguerreotypes and paper money being found in the smoking rubble of the destroyed village. Much could be put down to the activities of the younger warriors, although considering the fierce independence of the Plains Indians, the majority probably supported them – in spirit at least. Weighing the evidence, however, history tends to judge Washita as 'Custer's Massacre', for as the historian Elmo Scott Watson observed, 'in an engagement in which the number of women and children exceeds the number of fighting men two to one, that engagement is more properly called a massacre than a battle' (Watson and Russell,1972:6).

Washita broke the spirit of the southern Plains Indian and spelt the beginning of the end of their independent and free life. Councils followed raids and raids followed councils and the army took on a role of policing, attempting to arrest the trouble-makers rather than the policy of an all-out confrontation of attacking village communities. Both *Satanta* and *Satank*, Kiowa chiefs, chose death rather than confinement but many young men, Cheyenne in particular, were sent to Florida to be confined in the forbidding St Augustine prison.[18] Adding to the troubles were the professional buffalo hunters who, with easy access along the completed railroad, slaughtered the animals in vast numbers solely for their hides and left the rest to rot. Thus, when the Englishman William Blackmore traveled through Kansas in October 1873, he reported that 'there was a con-tinuous line of putrescent carcasses, so that the air was rendered pestilential and offensive to the last degree' (Black-more,1877:2).[19]

Below: *In the early 1870s the white outcry against raiding on the southern Plains led to a policy of arrest and confinement of many young warriors who were sent to Fort Marion in St Augustine, Florida. This photograph, taken in May or June of 1875, shows Kiowa, Cheyenne and Arapaho internees shortly after their arrival at the prison. Later, a number of them would distinguish themselves as artists depicting, in vivid pictographs, their former life on the Plains.*

Visits to New York and Washington

Delegations of chiefs and leading warriors now began the long trek to the east to plead their cause – and to be duly impressed – as had *Shahaka* two generations earlier. Typical was the Cheyenne, Arapaho and Wichita delegation in the early summer of 1871 led by the head chief of the Arapaho, *Ohnastie*, or Little Raven. On the evening of 1 June a grand reception was held for the Indian chiefs at the Cooper Institute, New York. Little Raven accompanied by Powder Face and Bird Chief of the same tribe, Little Robe and Stone Calf of the Cheyenne and the Wichita Buffalo Good, were guests of honor and some of their speeches, including that of Little Raven were reported in detail in the following day's press. Later in the same month, William Blackmore, founder of the Blackmore Museum in Salisbury, England, and who was in New York at that time, arranged for J. Gurney & Sons, respected photographers of Fifth Avenue, to photograph all the visiting Indians 'for the Trustees of the Blackmore Museum'.

The Oglala chief, Red Cloud made four visits to Washington between 1870 and 1877 and in 1872 he led an impressive delegation of Oglala and Brulé. The seventeen-year-old nephew of William Blackmore, Sidford Hamp, described meeting the

Below right: Arapaho, Cheyenne and Wichita delegation to Washington, June 1871. This was just one of the many delegations of chiefs and leading warriors which went to Washington to plead their cause to the Great White Father. Left to right, seated, are: Little Raven, head chief of the Arapaho; Bird Chief, second war chief of the Arapaho; Little Robe, head chief of the Cheyenne; and Buffalo Good, chief of the Wichita.

Below: Powder Face, a distinguished Arapaho chief, circa 1870. He wears a hair-fringed shirt and carries a lance indicative of membership of the Arapaho Spear Society and of a warrior who was expected never to retreat in battle. By the early 1870s, however, this man, and others, had cooperated so effectively to bring peace to the southern Plains that he was recommended for a medal.

Indian group on 25 May: '. . . the first we saw was a chief named "Red Cloud" to whom Uncle gave a knife, and the chief shook hands, and said how! how! which is the utmost extent of their English. We next saw two squaws to whom Aunt gave each a shawl, and some sham jewelry, they were very pl[e]ased and chatted in their own tongue . . . Then we saw 8 or 9 Indians of the Sioux in a room sitting on their beds, and we all shook hands with them, . . . After dinner we went to the 'Smithsonian Museum' and so did the Indians. Lots of people were there to see them, . . . they were dressed in plain clothes, which did not look at all well. They were mostly big fellows, but they did not seem able to stand much fatigue' (Hamp,1942:261).

Later in the month, on the 29th, a steamer ride was arranged down the Potomac for the visiting Indians together with some of William Blackmore's friends. Lunch was served on the *Lady of the Lake*, which must have been a most amusing occasion. Again Hamp recalls, ' . . . one mixed strawberries and olives together, another plumb cake and pickled oisters. Some ate holding the things in their hands, and some ate ice cream, pineapple, and fowl all at once, with a knife and fork. Altogether they managed very well' (ibid.:262). Again, William Blackmore made personal arrangements for the group to be photographed, this time by the Scotsman, Alexander Gardner (formerly an employee of Mathew Brady, the photographer of American Civil War fame) and whose studio was in Washington. Blackmore himself was photographed at this time with Red Cloud (see right) and this series of photographs was the first taken of the Sioux delegation.

Red Cloud and Powder River Country

The 1865 Harney–Sanborn Treaty had guaranteed to the Lakota, Arapaho and Cheyenne exclusive use of the Powder

Above, left: *Crow Indian delegation to Washington in 1873. Seated in the middle is Blackfoot, or He-who-sits-in-the-middle-of-the-land, head chief of the Mountain Crow. At his left is Iron Bull, chief of the River Crow. Their wives stand behind with the agent and interpreter.*

Right: *Red Cloud and the Englishman William Blackmore, photographed by Alexander Gardner in Washington, 1872. Blackmore, who had a deep interest in American Indians, met Red Cloud on several occasions and he personally arranged for photographs to be made of a number of delegations to Washington in the 1870s.*

Above: *A Sioux delegation to Washington led by Spotted Tail and Red Cloud photographed at the Corcoran Gallery of Art in October 1877. From the lone visits of the Mandan Big White and the Assiniboin The Light in the early 1800s, delegations became increasingly larger.*

River region, a vast area lying between the Black Hills, the Yellowstone River and the Rocky Mountains, consisting of luxuriant valleys watered by clear streams and teeming with game; it was probably the best buffalo country on the central Plains.

The discovery of gold deposits in Montana, however, led to the development and increasing use of the Bozeman Trail which was the shortest route from the Oregon Trail to the gold fields in Montana and passed directly through the Powder River country. The demands that this shorter route be made safe for travel led to the establishment of Fort Phil Kearney by Colonel Henry B. Carrington in July 1866. Situated on Little Piney Creek in the very heart of Powder River country and capable of garrisoning more than one thousand men, its construction was bitterly opposed by Red Cloud and in its short two year history it saw more bloody action against hostile Lakota and Cheyenne than virtually any other military post in frontier history.[20]

On the 21 December 1866, in pursuit of Indians who were attacking the wood train, eighty-one officers and men under Brevet Lieutenant-Colonel Fetterman were decoyed into an ambush and completely annihilated. Fetterman had been cautioned not to venture beyond Lodge Trail Ridge 'as per map in your possession' but the 'ambition . . . to win honour' proved too much and they took their stand against overwhelming odds almost one mile beyond the ridge (Brininstool,1955:41–2). 'In the grave,' wrote Carrington, 'I bury disobedience' (ibid.:51).[21]

The continued harassment throughout the rest of the winter and into the spring demanded strong protection of the vital wood supply trains and in August 1867 there was another major clash when a wood train was attacked. The accompanying troopers, who had been recently issued with new Springfield breech-loading rifles, held off a massive force of Lakota and Cheyenne for more than four hours: 'So sure was Red Cloud of

victory that he allowed the women and children to witness the battle from the surrounding hills. The rapidity with which the soldiers could reload, however, confounded the Sioux tactics previously so effective against the old muzzle-loader, when they rode the enemy down before there was time to reload' (Taylor,1975:102). Red Cloud, it has been estimated, lost sixty-seven of his best warriors and one hundred and twenty were wounded – some crippled for life.[22]

In April 1868, another Treaty was convened at Fort Laramie; this time the Peace Commissioners were prepared to listen to Red Cloud's grievances and the outcome was the complete abandonment of all the forts along the Bozeman Trail; by

Above: A fine Brulé Lakota quilled and hair-fringed shirt obtained from Chief Spotted Tail at Fort Laramie in 1855 by Second Lieutenant Charles G. Sawtelle (Sixth Infantry).

Below: Lakota chiefs at Fort Laramie in 1868, photographed by Alexander Gardner. From left to right, they are: Spotted Tail, Roman Nose, Old-Man-Afraid-Of-His-Horses, Lone Horn, Whistling Elk, Pipe, and probably the Oglala, Slow Bull.

November 1868, they had all been burned to the ground. It was against this background that Red Cloud – now increasingly engaged in a battle of words, and in an attempt to better the conditions on the Reservations – made his visits to Washington.

The Black Hills and Custer

'Look at me – see if I am poor, or my people either . . . You are fools to make yourselves slaves to a piece of fat bacon, some hard-tack, and a little sugar and coffee' (Sitting Bull to the Agency Indians, about 1874).

The 1868 Laramie Treaty confirmed the Harney–Sanborn Treaty of 1865 in setting aside unceded Indian territory, somewhat vaguely defined as 'that country north of the North Platte River and east of the summits of the Big Horn Mountains' – most of the Powder River country and also the Black Hills.

Here, the last free bands of Lakota and Cheyenne continued to roam, under leaders such as Sitting Bull, Crazy Horse and Dull Knife. Not all was peaceful, however; the Northern Pacific Railroad surveying parties, together with military escorts, invaded the unceded territory in 1872 and 1873 but it was really the Custer expedition to the Black Hills in 1874 which completely swept aside Indian rights, military interests now favoring a penetration of the Black Hills with a view to locating a suitable site for a military post. Further, since rumor had for years endowed the Black Hills with great mineral wealth, the expedition included two 'practical miners'! (Utley,1973:244).

The Seventh Cavalry, numbering more than one thousand men, left Fort Abraham Lincoln on 2 July 1874. The march has been described as a grand picnic amid game-rich forests and lush meadows cut by clear streams full of fish. Custer named the principal peaks after various military figures – Terry, Har-

Above: Makhpiya-luta, or Scarlet Cloud, better known as Red Cloud (1822–1909). A principal chief of the Oglala, he was active in the Indian wars of the 1860s and one of the negotiators at the Fort Laramie Treaty.

Below: Negotiations at the Fort Laramie Treaty in April 1868. Here, the United States government agreed to withdraw the military from the Bozeman Trail forts and that 'all wars between the parties to this agreement shall forever cease'.

ney and himself – and located, near Bear Butte on the north-eastern border of the hills, a suitable location for a military base. It was an audacious position as '*Mato tipi*' was a particularly sacred spot – a landmark in the Lakota domain.

Newspaper despatches reported in glowing terms of the rich farming and lumbering potential of the Black Hills and, although references to the mineral prospects were generally restrained, one report referred to 'gold among the roots of the grass' (ibid.). Alarmed at the consequence of a possible gold rush, the President announced that the army would bar would-be prospectors from the Lakota domain, but as the *New York Tribune* observed, 'If there is gold in the Black Hills, no army on earth can keep the adventurous men of the west out of them' (ibid.). That observation became a reality and although the army under the redoubtable General Custer attempted to expel intruders, some '800 miners worked the streams of the Black Hills during the summer of 1875' (ibid.:245).

The government attempted to solve the problem by offering to purchase the Black Hills from the Lakota and, when Red Cloud and Spotted Tail visited Washington in June 1875, an offer of $6,000,000 was made to purchase it outright or lease it for $400,000 per year. Red Cloud and Spotted Tail – by now experienced negotiators – demanded more than ten times that amount but these and subsequent negotiations at the Red Cloud Agency in September ended in stalemate. Sitting Bull summed up the attitude of the free Lakota: 'We want no white men here. The Black Hills belong to me. If the whites try to take them, I will fight' (Vestal,1957:133).

Below, left: *George Armstrong Custer and his scouts on the Yellowstone Expedition of 1873. The purpose of the expedition was to protect surveyors for the Northern Pacific Railroad. Custer's favorite scout, the Arikara Bloody Knife, is at his right.*

Below: *Ulysses Simpson Grant, general and eighteenth President of the United States (1822–85). Grant hosted both Red Cloud and Spotted Tail at the White House in June 1870; everything possible was done to impress them with the Great Father's power and they were assured that it was the government's desire to do what was right by the Indians.*

On 3 November 1875, a meeting held at the White House, which included President Grant and the Commissioner of Indian Affairs, decided to withdraw troops from the Black Hills and to initiate measures to force the hunting bands out of the unceded territory and on to the Reservations. The unceded territory – which was not only the domain of the hunting bands but acted as a buffer on the borders of the Great Sioux Reservation – was to be opened for settlement and by January 1876 more than fifteen thousand miners had flooded into the Black Hills.

In December 1875, the agents on the Great Sioux Reservation, acting on instructions from the Secretary of the Interior, Zachariah Chandler, sent out runners to notify all Indians in the unceded territory to move on to the Reservation by the end of January 1876.[23]

Predictably, the response to this ultimatum was negligible; one factor was undoubtedly the appalling prevailing weather conditions, but more important was the fierce independence of the hunting bands who wished to continue their old way of life. But their status had changed: they were no longer hunting bands, but 'hostiles'.

Sitting Bull's War

A winter campaign against the hostile Cheyenne and Lakota was now hastily organized under the direct command of General Sheridan. Success was seen as dependent on a rapid move against the Indians while they were immobilized in their winter camps and were without reinforcements from the

Below: *Group of Seventh Cavalry officers and ladies taken at Fort Abraham Lincoln shortly before the regiment embarked on the Little Bighorn campaign. The third officer from the left is General Custer; Mrs Custer is the first lady from the left, lower step.*

Left: Tatan'ka-iyo'take, *better known as Sitting Bull, photographed by D.F. Barry, 1885. A great spiritual leader of the non-treaty Sioux, his refusal to go on a Reservation led General Sheridan to begin the campaign which resulted in the annihilation of Custer's command in 1876.*

Below: *Bowie-type butcher knife with horn handle and said once to have belonged to Sitting Bull. The lower part of the handle has a flat nickel silver plate.*

Agencies.[24] The worst adversary for the campaign turned out to be the weather and, although Colonel Joseph Reynolds did manage to locate and destroy the Cheyenne camp under Two Moons on the Powder River on 17 March, the whole winter campaign was considered a failure. As Reynolds afterward observed to Sherman, 'General, these winter campaigns in these latitudes should be prohibited . . . The month of March has told on me more than any five years of my life' (Utley,1973:251).

A strategy of a summer campaign was now evolved and on 29 May 1876 Lieutenant-General P. H. Sheridan wrote to General W. T. Sherman in Washington, outlining the plan of the three-pronged campaign under Terry and Crook:

'Headquarters, Military Division of the
Missouri, Chicago,Ill.,
29 May, 1876

General: Brigadier-General Terry moved out of his command from Fort Abraham Lincoln in the direction of the mouth of Powder River on the 17th instant. The total strength of his column is about nine hundred men exclusive of a force of three companies in charge of the supply-camp at Glendive Creek, the old supply station on the Yellowstone.

Brigadier-General Crook will move from Fort Fetterman with a column about the same size.

Colonel John Gibbon is now moving down north of the Yellowstone and east of the mouth of the Big Horn with a force of about four hundred, all but four companies of which are infantry.

As no very accurate information can be obtained as to the location of the hostile Indians, and as there would be no telling how long they would stay in one place, if it was known, I have given no instructions to Generals Crook or Terry, preferring that they should do the best they can under the circumstances . . . as I think it would be unwise to make any combinations in such a country as they will have to operate in, as hostile Indians in any great numbers, cannot keep the field as a body for a week, or at the most ten days. I therefore consider — and so do Terry and Crook — that each column should be able to take care of itself, and to chastise the Indians, should it have the opportunity . . .

I presume the following will occur: General Terry will drive the Indians towards the Big Horn valley and General Crook will drive them back towards Terry; Colonel Gibbon moving down on the north side of the Yellowstone, to intercept if possible such as may want to go north of the Missouri to Milk River. The result of the movement of these three columns may force many of the hostile Indians back to the agencies on the Missouri River and to Red Cloud and Spotted Tail agencies.

P. H. Sheridan Lieutenant-General

Bismarck, Dakota Territory, 5 July 1876

Draped in black and with flag at half-mast, the steamer *Far West* nosed into the Bismarck Landing. On board – after a journey of over seven hundred miles from the mouth of the Little Bighorn – were some of the wounded and dead casualties of the '76 summer campaign against the hostiles. Just before midnight, the telegraph key clicked out the tragic message: 'Bismarck D.T. July 5 1876:- General Custer attacked the Indians June 25, and he, with every officer and man in five companies, were killed . . .'

The nation, engrossed in celebrating the centennial of its birth, was stunned and horrified – General George Crook had been defeated, and Custer, with two hundred and twenty-five officers and men, annihilated by a combined force of Lakota and Cheyenne under the leadership of Sitting Bull and Crazy Horse!

House of Representatives, Washington, D.C., 8 July 1876

'One repulse does not give enemies final victory . . . the blood of our soldiers demand that these Indians shall be pursued . . . [they must] submit themselves to the authority of the nation . . .' (Mr C. Maginnis. Territorial Delegate, Montana. Congressional Record, July 1876)

Below: A mounted warrior spearing a soldier during the Custer battle in 1876. Plains Indian pictography was a welding of the aesthetic and the historical into a pleasing art form and it often displayed fine detail of costume and accouterments. Shown here is the tied tail of the war-horse, the magnificent headdress trimmed with ermine, the unusually long braids and a realistic soldier's uniform.

Above: *A Spencer caliber .56-56 military carbine of the U.S. Army carried at the Battle of the Little Bighorn by a Cheyenne warrior.*

Below: *Custer's dead cavalry, drawn by Red Horse, a prominent Lakota warrior. This striking pictograph illustrates the considerable mutilation of the bodies.*

Below right: Wasechun-tashunka, *or American Horse, an Oglala chief and the son or nephew of the American Horse who joined Sitting Bull's force and was killed at Slim Buttes on 29 September 1875.*

Almost immediately, Congress approved the increase of army strength – two thousand five hundred cavalry and, if necessary, five thousand state and territorial volunteers – while the control of the Sioux Agencies was passed over to the military. A cantonment, Fort Keogh, was built at the mouth of the Tongue River and a two-pronged winter campaign against the Lakota and Cheyenne commenced.

Washington, D.C., 15 August 1876

Congress enacts a law providing that 'until the Sioux relinquished all claim to the Powder River country and the Black Hills, no subsistence would be furnished them'. Agency Indians agree. 'We have now agreed' said Bull Ghost at Standing Rock, 'when do we eat?' The Commission reported, 'Our cheeks crimsoned with shame' (Vestal,1948:244–5).

Slim Buttes, 8 September 1876

Captain Anson Mills attacks American Horse's camp. Village captured and destroyed. American Horse mortally wounded. Crazy Horse repulsed.

Red Cloud and other Sioux Agencies, October 1876

Crook subdues Agency Indians by a show of strength. Ranald S. Mackenzie disarms and dismounts the occupants. Red Cloud deposed. Spotted Tail 'a progressive', now recognized as 'chief of all the Sioux'.

Cedar Creek, 20 October 1876

Parley between Colonel Nelson A. Miles and Sitting Bull. Johnny 'Big Leggins' Brughière is interpreter. Sitting Bull denied he was looking for trouble with the white men, and accuses Miles of being the aggressor: 'He spoke like a conqueror and he looked like one' (Miles,1897:176). Miles concludes, 'that something more than talk would be required' (Utley,1973:273). Negotiations broken off and two day running battle commences. Lakota abandon tons of winter meat supplies.

Red Fork of Powder River, 25 November 1876

General Ranald Mackenzie attacks Dull Knife's and Little Wolf's village of two hundred lodges. Frank North leads with his Pawnee scouts. Village destroyed 'wiping off the face of the earth many products of aboriginal taste and industry which would have been gems in the cabinets of museums' (Bourke,1890:29).

242

Left: The Cheyenne chiefs Little Wolf and Dull Knife. Imprisoned at Fort Robinson, Nebraska, in the winter of 1879 and being starved into submission, Dull Knife and his followers made a desperate bid for freedom. More than sixty were killed and fifty wounded in their ensuing flight.

Left, below: These Pawnee men were photographed by W.H. Jackson in his Omaha studio, circa 1868. He also photographed several of the famous Pawnee scouts who, under Major Frank North, saw much service against the Sioux, Cheyenne and Arapaho from 1860 to 1876.

Below: Nelson A. Miles (center). As a colonel in 1874, Miles had distinguished himself in rapidly subduing the hostile southern Plains tribes. Later, he commanded substantial forces against Crazy Horse and Sitting Bull, and was active in the Sioux campaign of 1890–91.

Wolf Mountains, Big Horn Range, 8 January 1877

Colonel Nelson A. Miles attacks Crazy Horse's village containing some three thousand five hundred Cheyenne and Lakota – including refugees from Mackenzie's assault. Artillery bombards concentrations of warriors. Large portion of Indians' supplies lost and ammunitions exhausted. Miles jubilant over his achievements – '*find, follow* and *defeat*' (Utley,1973:277).

Tongue River Village, January 1877

Sitting Bull visits Crazy Horse and announces his intention to retreat to live in the country of the 'Great Mother', Queen Victoria (Canada). They discuss surrender but Sitting bull replies that 'I do not wish to die yet' (Vestal,1957:182).

Muddy Creek, Rosebud River, 7 May 1877

Miles attacks Lame Deer's village of Miniconjou who had vowed 'never to surrender'. Miles almost killed. Lame Deer and Iron Star killed. More than half the captured horses slaughtered. Miles receives further substantial reinforcements.

Red Cloud Agency, Nebraska, May 1877

Crazy Horse surrenders with two hundred lodges: 'the chief felt lonesome . . . after Sitting Bull had struck out for Canada and

his allies, the Cheyenne, had gone to join the whites' (Vestal,1948:267).

Wood Mountain, Saskatchewan, Canada, May 1877

Sitting Bull interviewed by the Mounted Police and promises to observe the laws of the Great Mother. The Lakota flatly refuse to return to the United States: 'The country there is poisoned with blood' . . . . 'Once I was rich, plenty of money, but the Americans stole it all in the Black Hills. What should I return for? To have my horse and my arms taken away? I have come to remain with the White Mother's children' (Sitting Bull. MacBeth,1931:83).

Fort Robinson, Nebraska, 7 September 1877

Crazy Horse 'silent, sullen, lordly and dictatorial' is bayoneted by a guard. The wound is mortal and dying, Crazy Horse utters 'My father, I am bad hurt. Tell the people it is no use to depend on me any more now' (Utley,1973:282; and Vestal,1948:272). Crazy Horse died in the early hours of 8 September 1877.

Fort Robinson, Nebraska, 9 January 1879

Cheyenne, under Dull Knife, burst from the army barracks where they have been imprisoned for a week without food, water and fuel. Of the one hundred and fifty people, sixty-four

Above: *The officer corps of the Seventh U.S. Cavalry at Pine Ridge, January 1891. At this time the corps still included veterans of the Little Bighorn campaign of 1876. Seated, left to right: Capt. W.S. Edgerly, Capt. H.J. Nowlan, unknown, Capt. C.A. Varnum, Col. J.W. Forsyth, Maj. S.M. Whitside, Capt. M. Moylan, Capt. E.S. Godfrey, and unknown.*

Above, right: *Ghost-dance shirt, Arapaho, circa 1889. This shirt of heavy buckskin reflects much of ancient Arapaho religious art. For instance, the image of the turtle was symbolic of the regenerative powers of the spirit world.*

Right: *Ghost-dance staff, Lakota, 1890. At the commencement of the dance a leader waved a staff over the heads of the dancers and said a prayer. He then hung the staff – symbolic of the power to grow – on the sacred tree.*

244

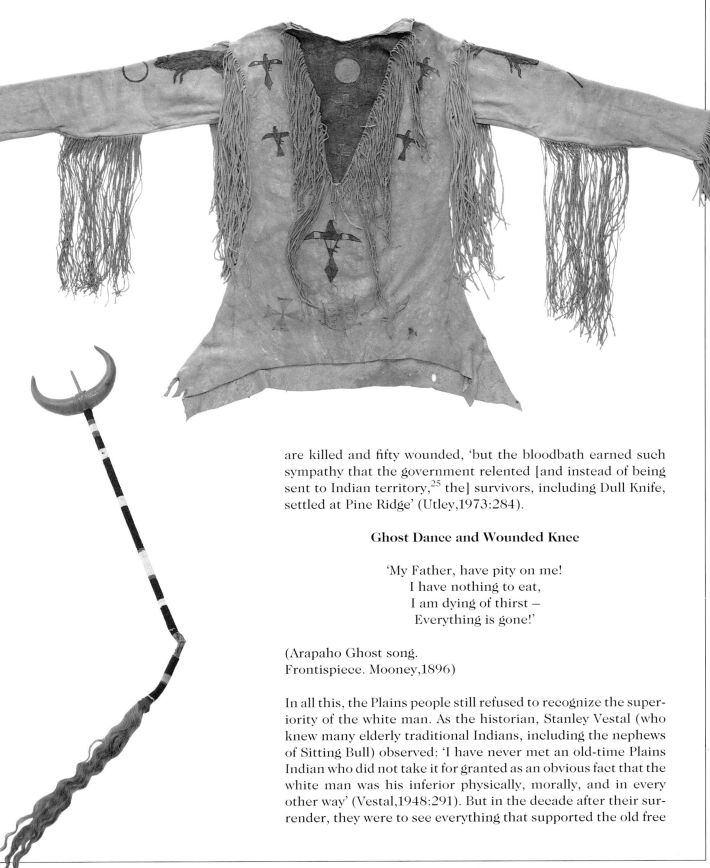

are killed and fifty wounded, 'but the bloodbath earned such sympathy that the government relented [and instead of being sent to Indian territory,[25] the] survivors, including Dull Knife, settled at Pine Ridge' (Utley,1973:284).

Ghost Dance and Wounded Knee

'My Father, have pity on me!
I have nothing to eat,
I am dying of thirst –
Everything is gone!'

(Arapaho Ghost song.
Frontispiece. Mooney,1896)

In all this, the Plains people still refused to recognize the superiority of the white man. As the historian, Stanley Vestal (who knew many elderly traditional Indians, including the nephews of Sitting Bull) observed: 'I have never met an old-time Plains Indian who did not take it for granted as an obvious fact that the white man was his inferior physically, morally, and in every other way' (Vestal,1948:291). But in the decade after their surrender, they were to see everything that supported the old free life completely swept away – virtual extermination of the buffalo and the established patterns of intertribal trade, religion, warfare, ceremonial and social organization, were all but destroyed. The entire system of values by which they interpreted and organized their lives was gone; all the people now had were their memories:

iki cize	a warrior
waon kon	I have been
wana	now
hena la yelo	it is all over
iyo tiye kiya	a hard time
waon	I have

(Sitting Bull, 1889)

Then, suddenly, like a prairie fire under a high wind, a new religion swept across the Plains. A distant Paiute prophet, *Wovoka*, had predicted the end of the white man's domination and the return of the Indians' old free days. The buffalo and

Right: *Ghost-dance bow and gaming wheel. Lakota, 1890. At the start of the dance a woman shot arrows in each of the four directions. They were then gathered up and hung in the sacred tree, together with a gaming wheel representing the universe.*

Below, right: *The carnage in Big Foot's camp at Wounded Knee, January 1891. In the foreground is the Lakota medicine man Yellow Bird, lying in the debris of a burned tent or tipi. The dark bundles in the snow are some of the other slain.*

Below: *Ghost-dance shirt collected at the Cheyenne River Agency in 1890. These shirts of white muslin were almost exclusive to the Lakota and were painted with designs which were believed to protect the wearer from enemy bullets.*

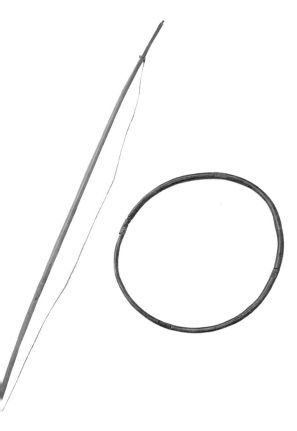

other game, the Indians said, would come back and the dead would be restored to life.

Thus, in the 1890s, came the *Ghost dance*, each tribe putting their own interpretation on *Wovoka*'s message.[26] The unrest led to the attempted arrest and the death of Sitting Bull, shot down by Indian Police on the Grand River on 15 December 1890.[27]

At Wounded Knee Creek on 28 December, *Sitenka*, Big Foot, and his three hundred-odd Miniconjou, virtually surrounded by a force of some four hundred and seventy cavalry and infantry under Colonel Forsyth, hoisted a white flag in the center of the camp, 'as a sign of peace and a guarantee of safety' (Mooney,1896:868).

The next day, Colonel Forsyth requested surrender of their arms, assuring Big Foot 'that they were perfectly safe in the hands of their old friends the soldiers, and that starvation and other troubles were now happily at an end' (Utley,1963:206). But tension mounted as the disarming proceeded and Yellow Bird, a medicine man, harangued the subdued warriors,[28] suddenly scooping a handful of dust from the ground and throwing

it in the air. At that instant, several young warriors sprang from the ground, rifles leveled at K Troop; they hesitated, rifles cocked: 'I thought, "the pity of it! What can they be thinking of?"' (Lieutenant Mann. ibid.:212).

At that instant, the volley crashed into Troop K. 'Fire! Fire on them!' screamed Mann.[29] In those first few seconds, the hundred carbines of Troops K and J mowed down half the able warriors . . . at the sound of the first volley, the Hotchkiss guns opened fire on the tipi village . . . two pound explosive shells at the rate of almost fifty a minute . . . 'mowing down everything alive'. The terrible effect may be judged from the fact that one woman survivor, Blue Whirlwind . . . received fourteen wounds, while each of her two little boys was also wounded by her side . . . (Mooney, 1896:869).

The aged Eagle Elk later recalled one of many personal tragedies. He saw a Lakota woman holding a child under her blanket and she was crying. Not until she looked up did Eagle Elk recognize her as a young girl he had known in the Grandmother's land:

'O, Shonka' kan! Shonka' kan!
They have killed him! They have killed him!'

Below: Pictograph on buckskin of the Cheyenne/Arapaho Ghost-dance drawn by a Ute Indian, Yellow Nose, in 1891 while a captive of the Cheyenne. Here are shown dancers wearing eagle feathers, some holding hands in a circle; others fall unconscious and will tell later of their visit to Wovoka's paradise.

Eagle Elk put her on his horse and led them away, and all the while the girl held the child close under her blanket, crying hard – it was a little boy and he was dead (see Taylor,1975:140).

'Hoo-oo! My children, my children. In days behind, many times I called you to travel the hunting trail or to follow the war trail. Now those trails are choked with sand; they are covered with grass, the young men cannot find them.

'My children, today I call you to travel a new trail, the only trail now open – the White Man's Road.'

(Cheyenne herald. Vestal,1948:309)

FOOTNOTES: CHAPTER EIGHT

1 An Act of Congress passed on 3 March 1871 ceased to recognize the tribes as independent nations, with which the United States was obliged to solemnly enter into Treaty.

2 That chief, Lewis and Clark learned a few days later, had died in Washington, the fate of not a few visiting Indians. It underlined the hazards of the journey east.

3 This robe is now in the Peabody Museum of Archaeology and Ethnology, Harvard University, Cambridge, Mass.

4 The Arikara chief, *Ankedoucharo*, who visited Washington, died there in April 1806, which contributed to the hostility shown by the Arikara to the whites. *Shahaka*'s successful trip clearly concerned the Arikara; they believed that the white trade from the south would be centered at the Mandan villages with whom, at the time, they had an uneasy alliance (see Meyer,1977:40).

5 The year after The Light's death, a group of St Louis doctors requested some Indian skulls. The Light's tree burial was ransacked and his head cut off and 'sent downriver to the civilization that had been the cause of his undoing' (Ewers,1968:88).

6 In earlier days, the fort site was variously referred to as Fort John or Fort William, but was always more commonly called Fort Laramie after the river on whose banks it stood. The name derives from Jacques La Ramée, an unfortunate French trapper, who was killed in the area by Indians in 1821.

7 In 1860, there were just three military establishments in the Dakotas and Wyoming – Fort Abercrombie in North Dakota, Fort Bridger and Fort Laramie in Wyoming. By the end of 1864, there were twenty-eight (Mattison,1954:2).

8 Uniforms and swords for the chiefs, beef and bacon, flour and soda, coffee, thread, cotton cloth, knives, awls, paints, brass buttons, beads, tobacco and blankets to name a few.

9 A fine account of the battle is available, based on research by Dr Lloyd E. McCann of Butler University, Indianapolis, Indiana, using data from House and Senate Executive Documents, an interview with Red Cloud by Judge E. S. Ricker at Pine Ridge, South Dakota, 24 November 1906, and a narrative now in the National Archives, Washington, of Man-Afraid-of-his-Horses, a respected and trusted Oglala chief.

10 Ash Hollow is located some one hundred and fifty miles south of Fort Laramie, near the Platte River, in present-day western Nebraska.

11 (a) Little Thunder was the successor to Conquering Bear, the brave 'paper chief', who had died in the Grattan encounter. Although he had been warned by Agent Thomas S. Twiss of Harney's approach, he obviously considered himself in no danger; (b) There were, however, young men in the village who had been responsible for some depredations on the Platte road in the previous winter. In the village after the battle, the troops discovered papers stolen from the Salt Lake mail, the scalps of two white women and the clothing of some of Grattan's men (see Utley,1967:117).

12 Lieutenant G. K. Warren made an outstanding collection of artifacts which he picked up on the battlefield and subsequently sent to the Smithsonian Institution in Washington. A number of these artifacts have been used to illustrate this volume.

13 These tribes included many eastern remnants, such as Shawnee, Delaware, Kickapoo and Cherokee. They were usually better armed and organized than the western tribes. There were repeated clashes 'most of which occurred beyond the American frontier and so never entered the American consciousness' (Fehrenbach,1974:278).

14 Catlin produced some of the earliest views of the Arkansas River Valley and left priceless written and pictorial records of a number of Southern Plains tribes, such as the Kiowa, Comanche and Wichita.

15 This, however, was later abrogated by the Comanche when they realized that it permitted the border Indians to hunt game in their territory (see Jablow,1950:71).

16 The warriors' path to glory and wealth, however, was *not* blocked by the Peace. Although the Cheyenne could no longer raid the Kiowa and Comanche for horses, they *joined* them in horse raids on the Spanish settlements in the Southwest and Mexico.

17 Bell had described the leader as a tall warrior, riding a white horse and carrying a lance, who was killed in the encounter by Corporal Harris of G Company. Bell erroneously identified the leader as Roman Nose.

18 While in prison, many of these young Cheyenne produced superb pictographs depicting life on the Great Plains. They left a priceless record relating to the hunt, war and religion (see Petersen,1971).

19 Five years earlier in the same area, Blackmore had reported, while standing on the crest of a hill near Monument Station at sunset on a fine day in October, that he had observed in all directions 'of from ten to twenty miles, nothing but herds of buffalo in sight; so far as the eye could see with a powerful opera glass, nothing but Indian cattle were visible, quietly browsing in small groups of from twenty to fifty each' (Taylor,1980:31).

20 Within six months of its establishment, there were more than fifty skirmishes with the Lakota and their allies. Some seventy whites were killed, twenty wounded and nearly seven hundred animals – cattle, mules and horses – were captured (Brady,1905:19).

21 Within weeks, Carrington was relieved of command at Fort Phil Kearney and sent to the small frontier post of Fort Casper. It took him almost twenty years to clear his name.

22 This is often referred to as the Wagon Box Fight, which took place on 2 August 1867. It was so-called because wagon boxes were drawn up for protection. When they returned to the fort, the men were suffering from complete nervous exhaustion from which some never fully recovered.

23 Realizing the implications of this move, the Commissioner of Indian Affairs, E. P. Smith, resigned in protest.

24 The hunting band numbers were swelled in the spring and summer by young men leaving the Agencies.

25 Down south in the barren and windswept climate of what is now Oklahoma, from which the Cheyenne were desperate to escape.

26 When the Kiowa, Wooden Lance, visited *Wovoka* in Nevada, he was told that some tribes, 'especially the Sioux, had twisted things and made trouble, and now *Apiatan* [Wooden Lance] had better go home and tell his people to quit the whole business' (Mooney,1896:913).

27 The police, led by Lieutenants Bullhead and Red Tomahawk, had been given orders by Agent James McLaughlin, 'You must not let him escape under any circumstances' (Vestal,1957:opp.282).

28 A young man 'of very bad influence and in fact a nobody', aggravated the situation by protesting that he had paid much money for his gun and he was not going to give it to anyone unless he received pay in return (Utley,1963:212).

29 Mann wrote an extended account of the battle in a letter to his brother just after Wounded Knee. He died of wounds a month later, received in a skirmish at the Drexel Mission the next day.

BIBLIOGRAPHY

Abley, Mark 1987. Tales from the foothill country. Book Review in *The Times Literary Supplement*. 1 May 1987, p.460. London.

Agent, Dan 1992. La Flesche Papers Reveal Osage Intellect and Logic, in *Smithsonian Runner*, No. 92-4. Smithsonian Institution, Washington, D.C.

Antrei, Albert 1963. Father Pierre Jean DeSmet, in *Montana*, Vol.XIII, No. 2. Helena, Montana.

Bebbington, Julia M. 1982. *Quillwork of the Plains*. Glenbow-Alberta Institute, Calgary.

Bell, W. 1869. *New Tracks in North America*. 2 Vols. London.

Benedict, Ruth Fulton 1924. The Concept of the Guardian Spirit in North America. *American Anthropological Association. Memoir 29*. Menasha, Wisconsin.
1932. Configurations of Culture in North America. *American Anthropologist*, Vol. XXXIV.

Berlandier, J. Louis 1969. *The Indians of Texas in 1830*. Edited by John C. Ewers. Smithsonian Institution Press, Washington, D.C.

Best, Alexander and McClelland, Alan 1977. *Quillwork by Native Peoples in Canada*. Royal Ontario Museum, Toronto, Ontario.

Blackmore, William 1877. *The North American Indian*. Introduction, Dodge, 1877. Chatto & Windus, London.

Blair, Emma Helen ed. 1912. *The Indian Tribes of the Upper Mississippi Valley and Region of the Great Lakes*. 2 Vols. Cleveland, Ohio.

Blish, Helen H. 1967. *A Pictographic History of the Oglala Sioux*. University of Nebraska Press, Lincoln, Nebraska.

Bolton, Herbert Eugene ed. 1916. *Spanish Explorations in the Southeast*. New York.

Bourke, Captain John G. 1890. *Mackenzie's Last Fight With the Cheyennes*. (Reprint.) The Old Army Press, Bellevue, Nebraska.
1892. The Medicine-men of the Apache. *9th Annual Report of the Bureau of American Ethnology 1887-8*:443-595. Smithsonian Institution, Washington, D.C.

Bowers, Alfred W. 1950. *Mandan Social and Ceremonial Organization*. University of Chicago Press, Chicago, Illinois.
1965. Hidatsa Social and Ceremonial Organization. *Bureau of American Ethnology, Bulletin 194*, Smithsonian Institution, Washington, D.C.

Brackenridge, Henry M. 1816. Journal of a Voyage up the Missouri River Performed in Eighteen Hundred and Eleven, in *Early Western Travels, 1748-1846*, Vol.6. Edited by Reuben Gold Thwaites. Cleveland, Ohio.

Bradley, James J. 1923. Characteristics, Habits and Customs of the Blackfeet Indians. *Montana Historical Society Contrib.*, Vol. 9.

Brady, Cyrus Townsend 1905. *Indian Fights and Fighters*. McClure, Phillips & Co., New York.

Brasser, Ted J. 1975. A Basketful of Indian Culture Change. *Mercury Series*, No. 22, National Museum of Man, Ottawa.
1982. The Tipi as an Element in the Emergence of Historic Plains Indian Nomadism. *Plains Anthropologist*, 27-98, Pt 1.
1984. Backrest Banners Among the Plains Cree and Plains Ojibwa, in *American Indian Art*, Vol.10, No.1, pp.56-63. Scottsdale, Arizona.
1987. By the Power of their Dreams, in *The Spirit Sings*. McClelland and Stewart, Toronto.
1988. Skin Painting Along the Eastern Edge, Plains Indian Seminar, Cody, Wyoming.

Braunholtz, H. J., Fagg ed. 1970. *Sir Hans Sloane and Ethnography*. Edited by William Fagg. Trustees of the British Museum, London.

Bray, K. M. 1982. *Making the Oglala Hoop: Oglala Sioux Political History (1804-1872). Part I 1804-1825*. English Westerners' Society, American Indian Studies Series: No.2. London.

Brininstool, E. A. 1955. *Fighting Indian Warriors*. Transworld Publishers, London. (Reprint.)

Brotherston, Gordon. 1979. *Image of the New World: The American Continent Portrayed in Native Texts*. Thames and Hudson, London.
1989. The Time Remembered in the Winter Counts and the Walam Olum, in *Festschrift*, edited by Bruna Illius, University of Freiburg, Germany.

Brown, Joseph Epes ed. 1971. *The Sacred Pipe: Black Elk's Account of the Seven Rites of the Oglala Sioux*. Penguin Books, Harmondsworth, Middlesex.

Buechel, Rev. Eugene 1983. *Lakota-English Dictionary*. Red Cloud Indian School Inc., Pine Ridge, South Dakota.

Bullchild, Percy 1985. *The Sun Came Down: The History of the World as My Blackfeet Elders Told It*. Harper & Row, San Francisco.

Bushotter Texts 1887-8. George Bushotter, Teton. National Anthropological Archives 4800, Washington, D.C.

Carver, Jonathan Parker ed. 1976 *The Journals of Jonathan Carver: and Related Documents 1766-1770*. Edited by John Parker. Minnesota Historical Society Press, St Paul, Minnesota.

Cadzow, D. A. 1926. The Prairie Cree Tipi, *Indian Notes*, Vol.III, No.1. Museum of the American Indian, Heye Foundation, New York.

Catlin, George 1841. *Letters and Notes on the Manners, Customs, and Condition of the North American Indians*. Published by the author at the Egyptian Hall, Piccadilly, London.

Chamberlain, Von Del 1982. *When Stars Came Down to Earth: Cosmology of the Skidi Pawnee Indians of North America*. Ballena Press/Center for Archaeoastronomy Cooperative Publication, University of Maryland, College Park, Maryland.

Clark, Captain W. P. 1885. *The Indian Sign Language*. L. R. Hamersly & Co., Philadelphia.

Cocking, Mathew 1908. An Adventurer from Hudson Bay. Journal of Mathew Cocking from York factory to the Blackfeet country, 1772-1773. Edited by Lawrence J. Burpee. *Trans. Royal Soc. Canada. Ser. 3* (2 vols).

Conn, Richard 1986. *A Persistent Vision: Art of the Reservation Days*. Denver Art Museum, Denver, Colorado.

Conner, Stuart W. 1982. Archaeology of the Crow Indian Vision Quest, in *Archaeology in Montana*, Vol.23, No.3. Butte, Montana.

Conner, Stuart and Conner, Betty Lu 1971. *Rock Art of the Montana High Plains. The Art Galleries*. University of California, Santa Barbara.

Culbertson, Thaddens A. 1952. Journal of an Expedition to the Mauvaises Terres and the Upper Missouri in 1850. Edited by John Francis McDermott. Smithsonian Institution, *Bureau of American Ethnology, Bulletin 147*, Washington, D.C.

Curtis, Edward S. 1907-30. *The North American Indian*. 20 Vols. Norwood, Mass.

De Smet, Pierre Jean 1905. *Life, Letters and Travels of Father Pierre-Jean de Smet, S.J., 1801-1873; Missionary Labors and Adventures Among the Wild Tribes of the North American Indians*. 4 Vols. New York. Edited by Hiram Martin Chittenden & Alfred Talbot Richardson.

DeMallie, Raymond J. 1984. The Buffalo, in The First Voices, *NEBRASKAland Magazine*, Vol.62,No.1. Nebraska Game and Parks Commission, Lincoln, Nebraska.

DeMallie, Raymond J. and Lavenda, Robert H. 1977. *Wakan:* Plains Siouan Concepts of Power, in *The Anthropology of Power*, edited by Raymond D. Fogelson and Richard Adams. Academic Press, New York.

DeMallie, Raymond J. and Parks, Douglas R. eds 1987. *Sioux Indian Religion*. University of Oklahoma Press, Norman, Oklahoma.

DeVoto, Bernard 1948. *Across the Wide Missouri*. Eyre and Spottiswoode, London.

Denig, Edwin Thompson 1930. Indian Tribes of the Upper Missouri. Edited by J. N. B. Hewitt. *Extract from the Forty-Sixth Annual Report*. Smithsonian Institution, *Bureau of American Ethnology*, Washington, D.C. (pp.375-628).
1953. Of the Crow Nation. Smithsonian Institution, *Bureau of American Ethnology, Anthro. Papers No. 33, Bulletin 151*, Washington, D.C.

Densmore, Frances 1923. Mandan and Hidatsa Music. *Bureau of American Ethnology, Bulletin 80*. Smithsonian Institution, Govt. Printing Office, Washington, D.C.

Dempsey, Hugh A. 1963. Religious Significance of Blackfoot Quillwork, in *Plains Anthropologist*, Vol. 8. University of Nebraska Press, Lincoln, Nebraska.
1972. *Crowfoot, Chief of the Blackfeet*. University of Oklahoma Press, Norman.

Devereux, George 1969. *Reality and Dream, Psychotherapy of a Plains Indian*. Doubleday & Company, New York.

Diessner, Don 1993. *There Are No Indians Left But Me! Sitting Bull's Story*. Great Native American Leaders Series. Vol.1. Upton and Sons, Publishers, El Segundo, California.

Dodge, Colonel Richard Irving 1882. *33 Years Among our Wild Indians*. Archer House, Inc., New York.
1877. *The Hunting Grounds of the Great West*. Chatto & Windus, London.

Dorsey, James Owen 1894. A Study of Siouan Cults. Smithsonian Institution, *Bureau of American Ethnology, Eleventh Annual Report*, Washington, D.C.
1904. Traditions of the Skidi Pawnee. *Memoirs of the American Folk-Lore Society, 8*. Boston and New York.
1905. The Cheyenne: I. Ceremonial Organization. Field Columbian Museum, *Publication 99, Anthropological Series*, Vol.IX, No. 1. Chicago.

Driscoll, Bernadette 1987. Pretending to be Caribou, in *The Spirit Sings*. McClelland and Stewart, Toronto.

Ewers, John C. 1939. *Plains Indian Painting*. Stanford University Press, California.
1945. *Blackfeet Crafts*. Department of the Interior, United States Indian Service, Haskell Institute, Lawrence, Kansas.
1949. The Last Bison Drives of the Blackfoot Indians. *Washington Acad.Sci.*, Vol.39, No.11.
1955. The Horse in Blackfoot Indian Culture. Smithsonian Institution, *Bureau of American Ethnology. Bulletin 159*. Washington, D.C.
1958. *The Blackfeet: Raiders on the Northwestern Plains*. University of Oklahoma Press, Norman, Oklahoma.
1965. The Emergence of the Plains Indians as the Symbol of the North American Indian. Publication 4636. From the Smithsonian Report for 1964:531-44. Smithsonian Institution, Washington, D.C.
1968. *Indian Life on the Upper Missouri*. University of Oklahoma Press, Norman, Oklahoma.
1971. When Red and White Men Met. Reprint from *The Western Historical Quarterly*, Vol.II, No. 2.
1975. Intertribal Warfare as the Precursor of Indian-White Warfare on the Northern Great Plains. *The Western Historical Quarterly* (Reprint), Vol.VI, No.4.
1976. Artifacts and Pictures as Documents in the History of Indian-White Relations, in *Indian-White Relations: A Persistent Paradox*. Edited by Jane F. Smith and Robert M. Krasnicka. Howard University Press, Washington, D.C.
1979. Introduction, in Mooney (1898).
1982. The Awesome Bear in Plains Indian Art, in *American Indian Art*, Vol.7,No.3. Scottsdale, Arizona.
1983. A Century and a Half of Blackfeet Picture-Writing, in *American Indian Art*, Vol.8, No.3. Scottsdale, Arizona.

Fardoulis, Anne 1979. Le cabinet du Roi et les anciens Cabinets de Curiosités dans les collections du Musée de l'Homme. Musée de l'Homme, Paris.

Feder, Norman 1978. Pawnee Cradleboards, in *American Indian Art*, Vol.3 No.4, pp.40-50. Scottsdale, Arizona.
1984. The Side Fold Dress, in *American Indian Art*, Vol.10 No.1. Scottsdale, Arizona.
1987 Bird Quillwork, in *American Indian Art*, Vol.12 No.3. Scottsdale, Arizona.

Fehrenbach, T. R. 1974. *Comanches: The Destruction of a People*. Book Club Association, London.

Fenega, Franklin 1959. An Early Nineteenth Century Account of Assiniboine Quillwork. *Plains Anthropolist.*

Flannery, Regina 1953. *The Gros Ventres of Montana: Part I: Social Life*. Anthropological Series, No. 15. The Catholic University of America Press, Washington, D.C.

Fletcher, Alice C. 1887(a). The Elk Mystery or Festival. Ogallala Sioux, in *16th Report*. Peabody Museum of American Archaeology and Ethnology, Harvard University, Cambridge, Mass.
1887(b). The White Buffalo Festival of the Uncpapas, in *16th Report* (1882). Peabody Museum of American Archaeology and Ethnology, Harvard University, Vol.III, Cambridge, Mass.
1903. Pawnee Star Lore. *Journal of American Folk-Lore*, 16, pp.10-15.

Forbis, Richard G. 1977. Cluny: An Ancient Fortified Village in Alberta. *Occasional Papers No.4*, Department of Archaeology, The University of Calgary, Alberta.

Gilman, Carolyn and Schneider, Mary Jane 1987. *The Way to Independence*. Minnesota Historical Society Press, St Paul, Minnesota.

Gilmore, Robert 1990. The Northern Arapaho Cradle, in *American Indian Art*, Vol.16, No.1, pp 64-71. Scottsdale, Arizona.

Gibbs, Peter 1982. The Duke Paul Wilhelm Collection in the British Museum, in *American Indian Art*, Vol.7, No.3. Scottsdale, Arizona.

Graham Colonel W. A. 1953. *The Custer Myth*. The Stackpole Company, Harrisburg, Pennsylvania.

Grinnell, George Bird 1893. *Blackfoot Lodge Tales*. David Nutt, London. (Reprint: University of Nebraska Press, Lincoln, 1962.)
1910. Coup and Scalp Among the Plains Indians. N.S.12, *American Anthropologist*.
1923. *The Cheyenne Indians: Their History and Ways of Life*, 2 vols. Yale University Press, New Haven, Conn.
1926. *By Cheyenne Campfires*. Yale University Press, New Haven, Conn.
1956. *The Fighting Cheyennes*. University of Oklahoma Press, Norman, Oklahoma.

Gunnerson, Dolores 1956. The Southern Athabascans: Their Arrival in the Southwest. *El Palacio*, Vol.VI.

Gunnerson, Dolores and Bouc, Ken 1984. A Time of Change, in The First Voices, *NEBRASKAland Magazine*, Vol.62, No.1. Nebraska Game and Parks Commission, Lincoln, Nebraska, pp.52-69.

Innis, Harold A. 1930 *Peter Pond, Fur Trader and Adventurer*. Toronto.

Hail, Barbara A. 1980. *Hau, Kola!* Haffenreffer Museum of Anthropology, Brown University, Bristol, Rhode Island.

Hamell, George R. 1981. The Magic of Glass Beads – Trade Beads as Crystals. 21st Northeastern Anthropological Association Meeting, Skidmore College, Saratoga Springs, New York.

Hamp, Sidford 1942. Exploring the Yellowstone with Hayden, 1872: Diary of Sidford Hamp. Edited by Herbert Oliver Brayer, in *Annals of Wyoming*, Vol.14, No.4, pp.1-47.
Hanks, Lucien M. Jr, and Richardson, Jane 1945. *Observations on Northern Blackfoot Kinship*. American Ethnological Society, Monograph 9.
Hanson, James 1986. Artifacts from the Battlefield, in *NEBRASKAland*, Vol.64, No.5, pp.6-13. Lincoln, Nebraska.
Harrod, Howard L. 1987. *Renewing the World: Plains Indian Religion and Morality*. University of Arizona Press, Tucson, Arizona.
Hartmann, Horst 1973. *Die Plains-und Prärieindianer Nordamerikas*. Museum für Völkerkunde, Berlin.
Hassrick, Royal B. 1964. *The Sioux. Life and Customs of a Warrior Society*. University of Oklahoma Press, Norman, Oklahoma.
Hendry, Anthony 1907. York Factory to the Blackfeet country. The Journal of Anthony Hendry, 1754-55. Edited by Lawrence J. Burpee. *Trans. Royal Soc. Canada, Ser. 3*.
Henry Alexander and Thompson, David 1897. *New Light on the Early History of the Greater Northwest. The Manuscript Journals of Alexander Henry and David Thompson 1799-1814*. 3 Vols. New York. Edited by Elliott Coues.
Hieb, David L. 1954. *Fort Laramie*. National Park Service Historical Handbook Series No.20, U.S. Department of the Interior, Washington, D.C. (Reprint 1961).
Hilger, Sister M. Inez 1952. Arapaho Child Life and its Cultural Background. Smithsonian Institution, *Bureau of American Ethnology, Bulletin 148*, Washington, D.C.
Hinman, Eleanor H. 1976. Oglala Sources on the Life of Crazy Horse. Reprint from Nebraska State Historical Society, Lincoln, Nebraska.
Hodge, Frederick Webb ed. 1907-1910. *Handbook of American Indians North of Mexico*. 2 Vols. Smithsonian Institution, *Bureau of American Ethnology*, Washington, D.C.
Howard, James H. 1962. Report of the Investigation of the Huff Site 32M011 Morton County, North Dakota 1959'. *University of North Dakota, Anthro. Paper No. 2*, Bismarck, North Dakota.
1974. The Arikara Buffalo Society Medicine Bundle, in *Plains Anthropologist*, Vol. 19, No. 66, Part I.
Hornaday, W. T. 1887. The Extermination of the America Bison. *Annual Report of the United States National Museum*, Smithsonian Institution, Washington, D.C.
Hotz, Gottfried 1970. *Indian Skin Paintings from the American Southwest*. University of Oklahoma Press, Norman, Oklahoma.
Hoxie, Frederick E. 1989. *The Crow*. Edited by Frank W. Porter, III. Chelsea House Publishers, New York and Philadelphia.
Hultkrantz, Ake 1968. Shoshoni Indians on the Plains: Appraisal of the Documentary Evidence. *Zeitschrift für Ethnologie*, Band 93, Heft 1 u 2, Braunschweig.
Hulton, Paul 1984. *America 1585. The Complete Drawings of John White*. University of North Carolina Press and British Museum Publications, London.
Hunt, David C., Gallagher, Marsha V. and Orr, William J. 1984. *Karl Bodmer's America*. Joslyn Art Museum and University of Nebraska Press.
Hyde, George E. 1937. *Red Cloud's Folk*. University of Oklahoma Press, Norman, Oklahoma.
1959. *Indians of the High Plains: From the Prehistoric Period to the Coming of Europeans*. University of Oklahoma Press, Norman, Oklahoma.
1974. *The Pawnee Indians*. University of Oklahoma Press, Norman, Oklahoma.
Jablow, Joseph 1950. *The Cheyenne in Plains Indian Trade Relations 1795-1840*. University of Washington Press, Seattle and London.
James, Edwin 1823. *An Expedition from Pittsburgh to the Rocky Mountains*. Compiled from the notes of Major Long (and others). 3 Vols. Longman, Hurst, Rees, Orme, and Brown, Paternoster-Row, London.
Jefferson, Thomas 1903. *The Writings of Thomas Jefferson*. Edited by A. E. Bergh. 20 Vols, Washington, D.C.
Jones, David E. 1972. *Sanapia, Comanche Medicine Woman*. Holt, Rinehart and Winston, New York.
Johnson, Michael G. 1994. *The Native Tribes of North America*. Macmillan, New York, and Maxwell Macmillan Canada, Toronto.
Kehoe, Alice B. 1973. The Metonymic Pole and Social Roles. *Journal of Anthropological Research 27*: 266-74.
Kellogg, Louise Phelps ed. 1917. *Early Narratives of the Northwest, 1634-1699*. New York.
Kenton, Edna ed. 1956. *Black Gown and Redskins*. Longmans, Green and Co., London, New York and Toronto.
Keyser, James D. 1977. Writing-on-Stone: Rock Art on the Northwestern Plains. *Canadian Journal of Archaeology*, No. 1.
1987. A Lexicon for Historic Plains Indian Rock Art: Increasing Interpretative Potential, in *Plains Anthropologist*, Vol.32, No. 1.
King, J. C. H. 1982. *Thunderbird and Lightning*. British Museum Publications Ltd, London.
Kroeber,Alfred L. 1902-1907. The Arapaho. *Bulletin of the American Museum of Natural History*. (Reprint, University of Nebraska Press, Lincoln and London, 1983.)
Kurz, Rudolph 1937. Journal of Rudolph Friederich Kurz. *Bureau of American Ethnology, Bulletin 115*, Smithsonian Institution, Washington, D.C. Translated by Myrtis Jarrell. Edited by J. N. B. Hewitt.
La Flesche, Francis 1921. The Osage Tribe. Rite of the Chiefs: Sayings of the Ancient Men. *36th Annual Report of the Bureau of American Ethnology*, Government Printing Office, Washington, D.C.
1925. The Osage Tribe. Rite of Vigil. *39th Annual Report of the Bureau of American Ethnology* (1917-18). Smithsonian Institution, Washington, D.C.
La Verendrye, P. G. V. 1927. *Journals and Letters of Pierre Gaultier de Varennes de la Verendrye and his Sons*. Edited by Lawrence J. Burpee. Champlain Society Publication 16, Toronto.
Lane, Elizabeth H., Markoe, Matilda. and Schulte, Julia L. 1914. *A Handbook of the Church's Mission to the Indians*. Church Missions Publishing Company, Hartford, Conn.
Larocque, Francois 1910. Journal of Larocque from the Assiniboine to the Yellowstone, 1805, *Canadian Archives*, No.3, Ottawa, edited by Lawrence J. Burpee.
Laubin, Reginald and Gladys 1957. *The Indian Tipi*. University of Oklahoma Press, Norman, Oklahoma.
1977. *Indian Dances of North America: Their Importance to Indian Life*. University of Oklahoma Press, Norman, Oklahoma.
Lessard, F. Dennis ed. 1984. Crow Indian Art. Papers presented at the Crow Indian Art Symposium, Chandler Institute, Mission, South Dakota.
Lessard, Rosemary T. 1980. A Short Historical Survey of Lakota Women's Clothing, in *Plains Indian Design Symbology and Decoration*. Edited by Gene Ball and George P. Horse Capture. Buffalo Bill Historical Center, Cody, Wyoming.
1990. Lakota Cradles, in *American Indian Art*. Scottsdale, Arizona. Winter:44-53.
Lewis, Meriwether and Clark, William 1904-5. *The Original Journals of Lewis and Clark, 1804-1806*. 8 Vols. Edited by Reuben Gold Thwaites.
Lewis, Oscar 1942. The Effects of White Contact upon Blackfoot Culture. *Centennial Anniversary Publication, The American Ethnological Society 1842-1942*, University of Washington Press, Seattle.
Libby, W. F. 1951. Radiocarbon Dates, II, in *Science*, No. 114, pp.291-6. Washington, D.C.
Linderman, Frank B. 1930. *Plenty-Coups Chief of the Crows. The Life Story of a Great Indian*. The John Day Company, New York. (Reprint, Faber & Faber, London.)
Linton, Ralph 1922. *The Thunder Ceremony of the Pawnee*. Field Museum of Natural History, Chicago.
Loud, Llewellyn L. and Harrington, M. R. 1929. *Lovelock Cave*. University of California Publications in American Archaeology and Ethnology, No.25:1. Berkeley, California.
Lyford, Carrie A. 1940. Quill and Beadwork of the Western Sioux. United States Department of the Interior, Bureau of Indian Affairs, Haskell Institute, Lawrence, Kansas.
Lowie, Robert H. 1913. Dance Associations of the Eastern Dakota. *Anthropological Papers, American Museum of Natural History*, Vol.XI, Part 2. New York.
1916. Plains Indian Age Societies: Historical and Comparative Summary. *Anthropological Papers of the American Museum of Natural History*, Vol.11, Part 13. New York.
1922. Crow Indian Art. *Anthropological Papers of the American Museum of Natural History*, Vol.XXI, Part 4. New York.
1935. *The Crow Indians*. Farrar & Rinehart, New York.
1954. Indians of the Plains. *Anthropological Papers of the American Museum of Natural History*, No.1. New York.
MacBeth, R. G. 1931. *Policing the Plains*. The Musson Book Company, Ltd, Toronto.
McCann, Lloyd E. 1956. The Grattan Massacre. Reprint from *Nebraska History*, Vol. XXXVII, No.1.
McClintock, Walter 1923. *Old Indian Trails*.Constable, London.
1968. *The Old North Trail*. University of Nebraska Press, Lincoln and London. (Bison Books Reprint.)
Mcgee, W. J. 1898. Ponka Feather Symbolism. *The American Anthropologist*, Vol.XI.
Mackenzie, A. 1927. *Voyages from Montreal on the River St Lawrence through the Continent of North America 1789 and 1793*. Toronto.
Mackenzie, Charles 1889. The Missouri Indians. A Narrative of Four Trading Expeditions to the Missouri 1804-1805-1806, in Masson, 1889,Vol. I.
Mallery, Garrick 1886. Pictographs of the North American Indians. Smithsonian Institution, *4th Annual Report, Bureau of American Ethnology*, Washington, D.C.
1893. Picture Writing of the American Indians. *10th Annual Report, Bureau of American Ethnology*, Washington, D.C.
Martin, Paul S. Quimby, George I. and Collier, Donald 1947. *Indians Before Columbus*. University of Chicago Press, Chicago.
Masson, L. R. ed. 1889. *Les Bourgeois de la Compagnie du Nord-Ouest*, Vol.I.
Mattison, Ray H. 1954. *The Army Post on the Northern Plains 1865-1885*. Oregon Trail Museum Association, Gering, Nebraska.
Maximilian, Prince of Wied, Lloyd (trans) 1843. *Travels in the Interior of North America*. Translated by H. Evans Lloyd. Ackermann & Co., London.
1906. *Early Western Travels 1748-1846*. Edited by Reuben Gold Thwaites. The Arthur H. Clark Company, Cleveland, Ohio.
Mayhall, Mildred, P. 1962. *The Kiowas*. University of Oklahoma Press, Norman, Oklahoma.
Meyer, Roy W. 1967. *History of the Santee Sioux: United States Indian Policy on Trial*. University of Nebraska Press, Lincoln and London.
1977. *The Village of the Upper Missouri: The Mandans, Hidatsas, and Arikaras*. University of Nebraska Press, Lincoln and London.
M'Gillivray, Duncan 1929. *The Journal of Duncan M'Gillivray of the Northwest Company at Fort George on the Saskatchewan, 1794-1795*. Edited by Arthur S. Morton, Toronto.
Michelson, Truman 1932. The Narrative of a Southern Cheyenne Woman. *Smithsonian Miscellaneous Collections*, Vol.87, No.5, Washington, D.C.
Miles, General Nelson A. 1897. *Personal Recollections of General Nelson A. Miles*. Chicago.
Mishkin, Bernard 1940. *Rank and Warfare Among the Plains Indians*. University of Washington Press, Seattle and London.
Mooney, James 1896. The Ghost Dance Religion and Wounded Knee. *14th Annual Report, Bureau of American Ethnology*, Smithsonian Institution, Washington, D.C. (Reprint. Dover Publications Inc., New York, 1973.)
1898. Calendar History of the Kiowa Indians. *17th Annual Report, Bureau of American Ethnology*, Smithsonian Institution, Washington, D.C.
Moore, John Hartwell 1974. A Study of Religious Symbolism among the Cheyenne Indians, Ph.D. Thesis. New York University.
Morgan, Lewis Henry 1959. *The Indian Journals 1859-62*. Edited by Leslie A. White. University of Michigan Press, Ann Arbor, Michigan.
Mulloy, William 1942. The Hagen Site, a Prehistoric Village on the Lower Yellowstone. University of Montana, *Publication in Social Sciences*, No. 1.
Murie, James R. 1916. Pawnee Indian Societies. *Anthro. Papers of the American Museum of Natural History, New York*, Vol.XI.
Nagy, Imre 1994. A Typology of Cheyenne Shield Designs, *Plains Anthropologist*, 39-147.
Neihardt, John G. 1932 *Black Elk Speaks*. William Morrow & Company, New York.
Newman, Peter C. 1989. *Empire of the Bay: An Illustrated History of the Hudson's Bay Company*. Edited by John Geiger. A Viking Studio/Madison Press Book, Toronto.
Nye, Wilbur Sturtevant 1968. *Plains Indian Raiders*. University of Oklahoma Press, Norman, Oklahoma.
Orchard, William C. 1916. *The Technique of Porcupine-Quill Decoration among the North American Indians*. Contribution from the Museum of the American Indian, Heye Foundation, iv.,I., New York.
1926. *Porcupine-Quill Ornamentation*, Vol.III, No.2. Indian Notes, Museum of the American Indian, Heye Foundation, New York.
1975. *Beads and Beadwork of the American Indians*. Museum of the American Indian, Heye Foundation, New York.
Pakes, Fraser J. 1968. The 'No-Flight' Societies of the Plains Indians. *The English Westerners' Brand Book*, Vol.10, No.4. London.
1989. Making War Attractive. *The English Westerners' Society*, Vol.26, No.2. London.
Paper, Jordan 1988. *Offering Smoke: The Sacred Pipe and Native American Religion*. University of Alberta Press, Edmonton, Alberta.
Perrins and Middleton 1985. *Encyclopaedia of Birds*. Allen & Unwin, London.
Petersen, Karen Daniels 1971. *Plains Indian Art from Fort Marion*. University of Oklahoma Press, Norman, Oklahoma.
Peterson-Swagerty, Jacqueline 1992-3. *Sacred Encounters*. The De Smet Project.

Washington State University, Pullman, Washington.
Pfefferkorn, Ignaz Trentlein ed. 1949. Pfefferkorn's description of the Province of Sonora. Edited by Theodore E. Trentlein. *Coronado Cuarto Centennial Publ.*, Vol.12, Albuquerque.
Phillips, Ruth B. 1987. Like a Star I Shine, in *The Spirit Sings*. McClelland and Stewart, Toronto.
Powell, Father Peter J. 1969. *Sweet Medicine*. 2 vols. University of Oklahoma Press, Norman, Oklahoma.
Raczka, Paul M. 1992. Sacred Robes of the Blackfoot and other Northern Plains Tribes, in *American Indian Art*, Vol.17, No.3. Scottsdale, Arizona.
Ray, Arthur J. 1974. *Indians in the Fur Trade: their role as hunters, trappers and middlemen in the lands southwest of Hudson Bay 1660-1870*. University of Toronto Press, Toronto and Buffalo.
Richardson, Rupert Norval 1933. *The Comanche Barrier to South Plains Settlement*. Glendale, California.
Riggs, Thomas L. 1958. Sunset to Sunset. *Report and Historical Collections of the South Dakota State Historical Society*, XXIX.
Roth, H. Ling 1923. American Quillwork: A Possible Clue to its Origin. *MAN* (August).
Sandoz, Mari 1961. *Crazy Horse: The Strange Man of the Oglalas*. University of Nebraska Press, Lincoln, Nebraska.
Schoolcraft, Henry R. 1851-1857. *Historical and Statistical Information Respecting the History, Condition, and Prospects of the Indian Tribes of the United States*, Vol.III. Bureau of Indian Affairs, Philadelphia.
Schultz, J. Willard 1919. *Running Eagle, the Warrior Girl*. Boston.
Secoy, Frank Raymond 1953. *Changing Military Patterns on the Great Plains*, University of Washington Press, Seattle, Washington.
Sellers, Charles Coleman 1947. *Charles Willson Peale, Later Life: 1790-1827*. Philadelphia.
Sharrock, Susan R. 1976. Crees, Cree-Assiniboines, and Assiniboines: Interethnic Social Organization on the Far Northern Plains, *Ethnohistory*.
Simms, S. C. 1903. Traditions of the Crows. *American Anthropology*, Vol.II. Field Columbian Museum, Chicago.
Smith, DeCost 1943. *Indian Experiences*. The Caxton Printers Ltd, Caldwell, Idaho.
Smith, G. Hubert 1980 *The Explorations of the La Verendryes in the Northern Plains, 1738-43*. Edited by W. Raymond Wood. University of Nebraska Press, Lincoln and London.
Smith, Marian W. 1938. The War Complex of the Plains Indians. *Proceedings of the American Philosophical Society*, Vol.78, No.3.
Spinden, Herbert Joseph 1908. The Nez Percé Indians. *Memoirs of the American Anthropological Association*, Vol.II, Part 3. Kraus Reprint Co., New York, (1974).
Stands In Timber, John and Liberty, Margot 1967. *Cheyenne Memories* (with the assistance of Robert M. Utley). Yale University Press, New Haven and London.
Stanley, George B. 1936. *The Birth of Western Canada: A History of the Riel Rebellions*. London.
Stewart, Frank H. 1974. Mandan and Hidatsa Villages in the Eighteenth and Nineteenth Centuries. *Plains Anthropologists*, Part I, pp.19-66.
Stolzman, R. 1989. The PIpe and Christ.
Sturtevant, William C. and Taylor, Colin F. 1991. *The Native Americans*. Edited by Richard Collins. Salamander Books, London, and Smithmark, New York.
Sturtevant, William C. Doggett, Hulvey and Ainsworth eds 1992. The Sources for European Imagery of Native Americans. Edited by Rachel Doggett, Monique Hulvey, and Julie Ainsworth, in *New World of Wonders: European Images of The Americans 1492-1700*, pp.25-33. The Folger Shakespeare Library, Washington, D.C.
Swagerty, William R. 1988. Indian Trade in the Trans-Mississippi West to 1870. Edited by Wilcomb E. Washburn. Essay in *Handbook of North American Indians: History of Indian-White Relations*. Vol.4. Smithsonian Institution, Washington, D.C. (pp.351-74).
Swanton, John R. 1952. The Indian Tribes of North America. *Bureau of American Ethnology, Bulletin 145*, Smithsonian Institution, Washington, D.C.
Sword et al. 1914. Letter of transmittal to James Mooney. (1897-g Dakota:Teton). National Anthrop. Archives, Washington D.C.
Tabeau, Pierre-Antoine 1939. *Tabeau's Narrative of Loisel's Expedition to the Upper Missouri*. Edited by Annie Heloise Abel. Translated by Rose Abel Wright. University of Oklahoma Press, Norman, Oklahoma.
Taylor, Colin 1962. Plains Indian Headgear. *The English Westerners' Brand Book*, Vol. 4, No.3. London.
1962. Early Plains Indian Quill Techniques in European Museum Collections, in *Plains Anthropologist*, Vol.7. University of Nebraska, Lincoln, Nebraska.
1971. Iron Tail's Warbonnet Part 2, in *American Indian Crafts and Culture*, Vol. 5, No.5. Tulsa, Oklahoma.
1973. The *O-kee-pa* and Four Bears: An Insight Into Mandan Ethnology. *The English Westerners' Society Brand Book*, Vol. 15, No.3. London.
1975. *The Warriors of the Plains*. Hamlyn, London.
1980. Ho, For The Great West! Title Essay in The Silver Jubilee Publication of the English Westerners' Society, London. Edited By Barry C. Johnson.
1981(a). Costume with Quill-Wrapped Hair: Nez Perce or Crow? Vol.6, No.3, in *American Indian Art*. Scottsdale, Arizona.
1981(b). *Crow Rendezvous: The Place of the River & Mountain Crow in the Material Culture Patterns of the Plateau & Central Plains circa 1800-1870*. The English Westerners' Society, American Indians Studies Series No.1, London.
1984(a). Analysis and Classification of Plains Indian Ceremonial Shirt: John C. Ewers' Influence on a Plains Material Culture Project, in Fifth Annual (1981) Plains Indian Seminar in Honor of Dr John C. Ewers. Edited by George P. Horse Capture and Gene Ball. Buffalo Bill Historical Center, Cody, Wyoming.
1984(b). Crow Rendezvous, in *Crow Indian Art*. Edited by D. and R. Lessard. Chandler Institute, Mission, South Dakota.
1986. Catlin's Portrait of Iron Horn: An Early Style of Blackfeet Shirt, in *Plains Anthropologist*, Vol.31, No.114. Lincoln, Nebraska.
1987. Early Nineteenth Century Crow Warrior Costume, in *Jahrbuch des Museums für Völkerkunde zu Leipzig*. Edited By Rolf Krusche. Band XXXVII, Akademie-Verlag, Berlin.
1989. *Wakanyan*: Symbols of Power and Ritual of the Teton Sioux, in *Amerindian Cosmology Cosmos 4*, Yearbook of the Traditional Cosmology Society. Edited by Don McCaskill. The Canadian Journal of Native Studies, Brandon, Manitoba.
1993. Saam. *The Symbolic Content of Early Northern Plains Ceremonial Regalia*. Bilingual Americanistic Books, Dietmar Kuegler, Wyk auf Foehr, Germany.
1994(a) *Taku Skanskan*. Power Symbols of the Universe: Parallels in the Cosmos of Plains Indians and White Missionaries, in PRESS (Paper read at Cody Conference, Plains Indian Museum, Buffalo Bill Historical Center, Cody, Wyoming, 1992).
1994(b) Wapa'ha: *The Plains Feathered Headdress* (Die Plains Federhaube). Verlag für Amerikanistik, Wyk auf Foehr, Germany.
Teit, James A. 1930. The Salishan Tribes of the Western Plateaus. Edited by Franz Boas. *Extract from the 45th Annual Report of the Bureau of American Ethnology*. United States Government Printing Office, Washington, D.C.
Thompson, David 1916. *David Thompson's Narrative of his Explorations in Western America, 1748-1812*. Edited by J. B. Tyrrell, Toronto.
Tixier, Victor. 1940. *Tixier's Travels on the Osage Prairies*. Edited by John Francis McDermott. Norman, Oklahoma.
Trudeau, J. B. 1914. Trudeau's Journal. *South Dakota Historical Collections*, Vol. VII, pp.403-74.
Turner, Geoffrey 1955. Hair Embroidery in Siberia and North America. Edited by T. K. Penniman and B. M. Blackwood. *Occasional Papers on Technology* 7. Pitt Rivers Museum, University of Oxford, Oxford.
1983. *Tradescant's Rarities*. Edited by Arthur MacGregor. Clarendon Press, Oxford.
Turner, Katherine C. 1951. *Red Men Calling on the Great White Father*. University of Oklahoma Press, Norman, Oklahoma.
Utley, Robert M. 1963. *The Last Days of the Sioux Nation*. Yale University Press, New Haven and London.
1967. *Frontiersmen in Blue: The United States Army and the Indian, 1848-1865*. The Macmillan Company, New York. (Collier-Macmillan Ltd, London.)
1973. *Bluecoats and Redskins: The United States Army and the Indian, 1866-1891*. Cassell, London.
Vestal, Stanley 1948. *Warpath and Council Fire*. Random House, New York.
Vestal, Stanley 1957. *Sitting Bull: Champion of the Sioux*. University of Oklahoma Press, Norman, Oklahoma.
Walker, J. R. 1917. The Sun Dance and other Ceremonies of the Oglala Division of the Teton Dakota. *Anthropological Papers of the American Museum of Natural History*, Vol. XVI, Part II. New York.
1980. *Lakota Belief and Ritual*. University of Nebraska Press, Lincoln and London. Edited by Raymond J. DeMallie and Elaine A. Jahner.
1982. *Lakota Society*. University of Nebraska Press, Lincoln and London. Edited by Raymond J. DeMallie.
Wallace, Ernest and Hoebel, E. Adamson 1952. *The Comanches: Lords of the South Plains*. University of Oklahoma Press, Norman, Oklahoma.
Watson, Elmo Scott and Russell, Don 1972. *The Battle of the Washita or Custer's Massacre?* Vol.15, No.1. Publication No. 182. The English Westerners' Society, London.
Waugh, Earle H. 1990. Blackfoot Religion: My Clothes are Medicine, in *The Scriver Blackfoot Collection: Repatriation of Canada's Heritage*. Edited by Philip H. R. Stepney and David J. Goa. Provincial Museum of Alberta, Edmonton.
Webb, Walter Prescott 1931. *The Great Plains*. Grosset & Dunlap, New York.
Webber, Alika Podolinsky 1983. Ceremonial Robes of the Montagnais-Naskapi, in *American Indian Art*, Vol. 9. No.1. Scottsdale, Arizona.
Wedel, W. R. 1959. An Introduction to Kansas Archaeology. Smithsonian Institution, *Bureau of American Ethnology, Bulletin 174*. Washington, D.C.
1961. *Prehistoric Man on the Great Plains*. University of Oklahoma Press, Norman, Oklahoma.
Weist, Katherine M. 1980. Plains Indian Women: An Assessment, in Wood and Liberty eds, 1980:255-271.
Weltfish, Gene 1977. *The Lost Universe: Pawnee Life and Culture*. University of Nebraska Press, Lincoln and London.
West, George A. 1934. Tobacco, Pipes and Smoking Customs of the American Indians. *Bulletin of the Public Museum of the City of Milwaukee, 17*. Wisconsin.
Whitehead, Ruth Holmes 1982. *Micmac Quillwork*. The Nova Scotia Museum, Halifax, Nova Scotia.
Wildschut, William 1959. *Crow Indian Beadwork*. Museum of the American Indian, Heye Foundation, New York. Edited by John C. Ewers.
1960. *Crow Indian Medicine Bundles*. Museum of the American Indian, Heye Foundation, New York. Edited by John C. Ewers.
Williams, Glyndwr 1983. The Hudson's Bay Company and The Fur Trade: 1670-1870. *The Beaver* (special issue), Winnipeg, Manitoba (Autumn).
Wilson, Gilbert L. 1907. *Diary*, Vol.5. Wilson Papers. Minnesota Historical Society, St Paul, Minnesota.
1913. *Field Report*, Vol.13. Wilson Papers. Minnesota Historical Society, St Paul.
1934. The Hidatsa Earthlodge. Edited by Bella Weitzner. *American Museum of Natural History, Anthropological Papers*, Vol. XXXIII, New York.
Wissler, Clark 1902. Symbolism in the Decorative Art of the Sioux. Congres International des Americanistes, New York, pp.339-45.
1902. FN. Field Notes on the Dakota Indians: Collected on Museum Expedition of 1902 (unpublished). Manuscript from Library of the American Museum of Natural History New York (1911).
1904. Decorative Art of the Sioux Indians. *American Museum of Natural History*, Vol. XVIII, New York.
1905. The Whirlwind and the Elk in the Mythology of the Dakota *The Journal of American Folk-Lore*, Vol.XVIII, No. LXXI.
1907. Some Protective Designs of the Dakota. *American Museum of Natural History*, Vol.I Part II. New York.
1910. Material Culture of the Blackfoot Indians. *American Museum of Natural History* Vol.V. New York.
1911. Social Organization and Ritualistic Ceremonies of the Blackfoot Indians. Part I: The Social Life of the Blackfoot Indians. *American Museum of Natural History*, Vol.VII. New York.
1912(a) Social Organization and Ritualistic Ceremonies of the Blackfoot Indians. Part II: Ceremonial Bundles of the Blackfoot Indians. *American Museum of Natural History*, Vol.VII. New York.
1912(b) Societies and Ceremonial Associations in the Oglala Division of the Teton-Dakota. *American Museum of Natural History*, Vol.XI. New York (1916).
1913. Societies and Dance Associations of the Blackfoot Indians. Vol.XI. *Anthro. Papers of the American Museum of Natural History*. New York.
1916. Structural basis to the decoration of costumes among the Plains Indians. *American Museum of Natural History* Vol.XVII. New York.
1918. The Sun Dance of the Blackfoot Indians, in *Anthro. Papers of the American Museum of Natural History*, Vol.XVI. New York (1921).
Wissler, Clark and Duvall, 1908. Mythology of the Blackfoot Indians. Part I *American Museum of Natural History*, Vol.II. New York (1909).
Wissler, Clark and Spinden, Herbert J. 1916. The Pawnee Human Sacrifice to the Morningstar. *American Museum Journal*, 16.
Wood, W. Raymond 1967. An Interpretation of Mandan Culture History. Smithsonian Institution, *Bureau of American Ethnology, Bulletin 198*, Washington, D.C.
Wood, W. Raymond and Liberty, Margot eds 1980. *Anthropology on the Great Plains*. University of Nebraska Press, Lincoln and London.
Woodward, Arthur. 1965. *Indian Trade Goods*. Oregon Archaeological Society, Museum of Science & Industry, Portland, Oregon.

ACKNOWLEDGMENTS

A considerable number of the photographs in *The Plains Indians* were taken at the Museum Support Center in Suitland, Maryland, which is a part of the Department of Anthropology at the National Museum of Natural History, Smithsonian Institution, Washington, D.C. The publishers are grateful to be given the opportunity to photograph some of the outstanding Plains artifacts in the museum's collection and offer thanks to the following: U. Vincent Wilcox, Director, Museum Support Center; Candace Greene, Museum Specialist; Deb Hull-Walski, Collections Manager; Lou Holley; and especially Deborah Wood, Museum Consultant, who so ably and professionally assisted us before, during and after the shoot in February 1994. Her contribution was a notable one.

Unless otherwise indicated in the following list of acknowledgments, indicated by page number, all color artifact photographs were taken at the Museum Support Center.

Front endpaper Smithsonian Institution (hereafter abbreviated to SI); **ii** SI; **iv/v** SI; **vi/vii** Buffalo Bill Historical Center, Cody, Wyoming. Gertrude Vanderbilt Whitney Trust Fund Purchase; **8** Nita Stewart Haley Memorial Library, Midland, Texas; **9** courtesy of the Ethnology Department, Royal Ontario Museum, Toronto; **10** Stark Museum of Art, Orange, Texas; **16** (below) originally photographed at the National Museum of Natural History, SI; **17** both National Museum of American Art, Washington, D.C./Art Resource, New York; **18** (above) Joslyn Art Museum, Omaha, Nebraska. Gift of the Enron Art Foundation, (below) Linden-Museum, Stuttgart (photograph Ursula Didoni); **19** Linden-Museum, Stuttgart (photograph Ursula Didoni); **20** Stark Museum of Art, Orange, Texas; **21** (above) National Museum of American Art, Washington, D.C./Art Resource, New York, (below) Staatliche Museen zu Berlin, Preussischer Kilturbesitz, Museum für Völkerkunde (photograph Dietrich Graf); **22** (below) The National Museum of Ethnography, Stockholm (photograph Bo Gabrielsson); **23** (above) National Museum of American Art, Washington, D.C./Art Resource, New York; **24** Bernisches Historisches Museum, Bern (photograph Stefan Rebsamen); **26** (above) Joslyn Art Museum, Omaha, Nebraska. Gift of the Enron Art Foundation; **26/27** courtesy of the Ethnology Department, Royal Ontario Museum, Toronto; **32** Staatliche Museen zu Berlin, Preussischer Kulturbesitz, Museum für Völkerkunde (photograph Dietrich Graf); **34/35, 36** Joslyn Art Museum, Omaha, Nebraska. Gift of the Enron Art Foundation; **37** Staatliche Museen zu Berlin, Preussischer Kulturbesitz, Museum für Völkerkunde (photograph Dietrich Graf); **39** (above) National Museum of American Art, Washington, D.C./Art Resource, New York (below) and **40** Bernisches Historisches Museum, Bern (photograph Stefan Rebsamen); **41** Stark Museum of Art, Orange, Texas; SI; **42** Staatliche Museen zu Berlin, Preussischer Kilturbesitz, Museum für Völkerkunde (photograph Dietrich Graf); **48** (below) National Museum of Art, Washington, D.C./Art Resource, New York; **49** SI; **50** Staatliche Museen zu Berlin, Preussischer Kilturbesitz, Museum für Völkerkunde (photograph Dietrich Graf); **51** C.F. Taylor; **52** (above) Joslyn Art Museum, Omaha, Nebraska. Gift of the Enron Art Foundation, 52/53 (below) The National Museum of Ethnography, Stockholm (photograph Bo Gabrielsson); **54** (above) courtesy of the Ethnology Department, Royal Ontario Museum, Toronto, (below) Stark Museum of Art, Orange, Texas; **55** (above) Joslyn Art Museum, Omaha, Nebraska. Gift of the Enron Art Foundation, (below) C.F. Taylor; **56** (above) Stark Museum of Art, Orange, Texas; **57** Bernisches Historisches Museum, Bern (photograph Stefan Rebsamen); **58** Stark Museum of Art, Orange, Texas; **60/61** The National Museum of Denmark, Department of Ethnography (photograph Kit Weiss); **63** Bernisches Historiches Museum, Bern (photograph Stefan Rebsamen); **64/65** SI; **66** Walters Art Gallery, Baltimore; **69** National Museum of Art, Washington, D.C./ Art Resource, New York; **71** C.F. Taylor; **72** © The Field Museum, Neg. # A111527C, Chicago. Photographer Diane Alexander White; **73** C.F. Taylor; **74** (above) SI; **74/75** (medals) The American Numismatic Society, New York; **75** (above) SI; **76** C.F. Taylor; **77** SI; **78** SI; **81** C.F. Taylor; **82** Linden-Museum, Stuttgart (photograph Ursula Didoni); **83** SI; **84** C.F. Taylor; **85** SI; **86/87** SI; **88** The National Museum of Denmark, Department of Ethnography (photograph Kit Weiss); **91** SI; **92** (above) National Museum of American Art, Washington, D.C./ Art Resource, New York; **94/95** SI; **99** SI; **100** SI; **101** photograph courtesy of the National Museum of the American Indian, Smithsonian Institution; **102/103** SI; **104/105** SI; **106** (above) SI, (below) Bernisches Historisches Museum (photograph Stefan Rebsamen); **107** SI; **108** The National Museum of Ethnography, Stockholm (photograph Bo Gabrielsson); **110/111** courtesy of the Ethnology Department, Royal Ontario Museum, Toronto; **112/113, 114** SI; **115** American Museum of Natural History, New York; **116/117** The National Museum of Ethnography, Stockholm (photograph Bo Gabrielsson), **118** Deutsches Ledermuseum Offenbach/M; **120** photograph courtesy of the National Museum of the American Indian, Smithsonian Institution; **121** (above) Joslyn Art Museum, Omaha, Nebraska. Gift of the Enron Art Foundation; **123** C. F. Taylor; **124** The National Museum of Ethnography, Stockholm (photograph Bo Gabrielsson); **127** (above) Joslyn Art Museum, Omaha, Nebraska. Gift of the Enron Art Foundation, (below) Bernisches Historisches Museum, Bern (photograph Stefan Rebsamen); **129** (right) The National Museum of Ethnography, Stockholm; **131** Bernisches Historisches Museum, Bern (photograph Stefan Rebsamen); **137** C.F. Taylor/ Royal Scottish Museum, Edinburgh; **138** (above) C.F. Taylor/Pitt Rivers Museum, Oxford, (below) C.F. Taylor; **139** (above) Opočno Castle Museum, Opočno, Czech Republic; **151** photograph courtesy of the National Museum of the American Indian, Smithsonian Institution: **152** Joslyn Art Museum, Omaha, Nebraska. Gift of the Enron Art Foundation; **153** courtesy of the Ethnology Department, Royal Ontario Museum, Toronto; **154** (above) National Museum of American Art, Washington, D.C./Art Resource, New York, (right) Opočno Castle Museum, Opočno, Czech Republic; **155** Staatliche Museen zu Berlin, Preussischer Kulturbesitz, Museum für Völkerkunde (photograph Dietrich Graf); **156** (left) SI; **165** (below) Opočno Castle Museum, Opočno, Czech Republic; **167** National Museum of American Art, Washington, D.C./Art Resource, New York; **168** Joslyn Art Museum, Omaha, Nebraska. Gift of the Enron Art Foundation; **172** C.F. Taylor; **174** National Museum of American Art, Washington, D.C./Art Resource, New York; **176** Buffalo Bill Historical Center, Cody, Wyoming. Gift of William E. Weiss; **177** Bernisches Historisches Museum, Bern (photograph Stefan Rebsamen); **179** C.F. Taylor; **180** (left) National Museum of American Art, Washington, D.C./Art Resource, New York, (right) Opočno Castle Museum, Opočno, Czech Republic; **182/183** Bernisches Historisches Museum, Bern (photographs Stefan Rebsamen); **184/185** C.F. Taylor; **188/189** British Museum; **190** (below) C.F. Taylor/Museum of Mankind, London, (above) Walters Art Gallery, Baltimore; **195** Opočno Castle Museum, Opočno, Czech Republic; **197** (above) C.F. Taylor, (below) courtesy Gary Galante; **198** (above) National Trust of Scotland (photograph Jim Henderson); (below) C.F. Taylor/Glenbow Archives, Calgary; **199** (above) Buffalo Bill Historical Center, Cody, Wyoming. Adolph Spohr, Gift of Mr Larry Sheerin; **200** SI; **201** (left) SI; **202** (below) C.F. Taylor; **203** (above) photograph courtesy of the National Museum of the American Indian, Smithsonian Institution; **205** (above, left) SI; **206** C.F. Taylor; **210** In the Collection of The Corcoran Gallery of Art. Gift of Violet Sargent Ormond and Emily Sargent; **211** (above) National Museum of American Art, Washington, D.C./ Art Resource, New York, (below) C.F. Taylor; **212** (above) Joslyn Art Museum, Omaha, Nebraska. Gift of the Enron Art Foundation, (below) National Museum of American Art, Washington, D.C./Art Resource, New York; **213** C.F. Taylor; **216** (above) SI; **218** SI; **219** (above, right) National Museum of American Art, Washington, D.C./Art Resource, New York; **220** (above, left) SI, (above, right) National Museum of American Art, Washington, D.C./Art Resource, New York; **221** C.F. Taylor; **222** (left) SI; **223** SI; **224/225** SI; **226** (below) SI; **227** SI; **228, 229** (below) photographs courtesy of the National Museum of the American Indian, Smithsonian Institution; **229** (above) Peter Newark's Western Americana; **230, 231** (left) SI; **231** (right) C.F. Taylor; **232/233** SI; **234** (above) photograph courtesy of the National Museum of the American Indian, Smithsonian Institution, (below) SI; **235** (above) SI, (below) photograph courtesy of the National Museum of the American Indian, Smithsonian Institution; **236** (left) Burlington Northern; **237** C.F. Taylor; **238** SI; **240** (below) and **241** (below, left and right) SI; **241** (above) artifact courtesy Buffalo Bill Historical Center, Cody, Wyoming; **242** SI; **243** Denver Public Library, Western History Department; **244** James S. Hutchins/Library of Congress; **247** (below) Nebraska State Historical Society; **back endpaper** photograph courtesy of the National Museum of the American Indian, Smithsonian Institution.

In addition, the editor wishes to thank the following: Mrs Ursula Didoni, Dr Axel Schulze-Thulin of the Linden-Museum, Stuttgart; Dr Pøul Mork, Nationalmuseet, Copenhagen; Dr Thomas Psota, Mrs Heidi Hofstetter of the Bernisches Historisches Museum, Bern; Dr Peter Bolz, Museum für Völkerkunde, Berlin; Dr Staffan Brunius, The National Museum of Ethnography, Stockholm; Ing. Josef Jirák, Opočno Castle Museum, Opočno. Grateful thanks to Sanna Törneman, Curator, Photo Collections, The National Museum of Ethnography, Stockholm, whose calm professionalism, kindness and constant assurance helped immeasurably. Finally, the editor acknowledges the part played by Colin and Betty Taylor, both of whom worked themselves into the ground during the production of the book.